Video Editing Made Easy with DaVinci Resolve 20

Second Edition

Create quick video content for your social media, the web, and business

Lance Phillips

<packt>

Video Editing Made Easy with DaVinci Resolve 20

Second Edition

Portfolio Director: Pavan Ramchandani
Relationship Lead: Larissa Pinto
Content Engineer: Mohd Hammad
Technical Editor: Vidhisha Patidar
Copy Editor: Safis Editing
Indexer: Tejal Soni
Proofreader: Mohd Hammad
Production Designer: Aparna Bhagat
Growth Lead: Priya Bhanushali

First published: May 2023

Second edition: February 2026

Production reference: 1060226

Published by Packt Publishing Ltd.
Grosvenor House
11 St Paul's Square
Birmingham
B3 1RB, UK.

ISBN 978-1-83620-883-9
`www.packtpub.com`

I would like to dedicate this book to my friend Donovan, who, as well as donating some footage for the book, was the first person to pre-order a copy.

I am impressed by his positive can-do attitude in spite of the challenges that 2025 brought to many in the film/TV industry. I hope this year will be a fruitful one.

I would also like to dedicate this book to the many university students around the world who read the first edition and used it to further their knowledge and understanding of Resolve. Without the support of 414 universities, governments, and public libraries worldwide, this book would not have reached such a wide audience.

It is thanks to every reader of the first edition that this second edition now exists.

Finally, I would like to thank my wife for her patience and support as I spent long hours of the day and night writing this book, including this content, putting off all those household renovation projects I need to complete with her.

Now where's that drill?

– Lance Phillips

Foreword

I have known Lance for over seven years as a fellow Avid Editing Trainer, and I am aware of his passion for teaching DaVinci Resolve, just as I am for teaching Avid.

Lance was my trainer on the official Blackmagic Design DaVinci Resolve 19 Beginner's course, which I attended live online. As an Avid editor moving across to learn editing in Resolve, I found that Lance's approach made the learning curve far less steep than I had expected.

As someone who is neurodivergent myself, the pace of the course worked very well with my learning style. Lance always makes sure that the students he is teaching are at the same stage and does not simply keep moving on, unlike some training courses I have attended. Some trainers read through the training material as quickly as possible without checking in with their students. Lance is different. He ensures that students understand the wider context of the techniques they are using.

Editing has changed significantly over the past 20 years, and editors who can use a range of tools within DaVinci Resolve are increasingly sought after in the film and television industries.

Learning Resolve requires a combination of skills, including video editing, color correction, audio work using Fairlight, and visual effects using Fusion. The demands placed on editors have evolved, and we are often expected to use these skills to finish projects independently or attract clients. Lance was able to break these skills down into digestible chunks and clearly explain the meaning of any technical jargon.

Much like Lance's teaching style, the tone of this book is friendly, the instructions are clear, and the layout is designed for quick reference and immediate application.

The inclusion of media to accompany the book is also immensely helpful, as it allows readers to follow the techniques at their own pace.

Video Editing Made Easy with DaVinci Resolve 20 is a must-have for anyone who wants to learn this software.

Nigel G Honey

Certified Avid Trainer, Ability Post Production Academy

Contributors

About the author

Lance Phillips is a qualified teacher, actor, lecturer, and Certified DaVinci Resolve Trainer, with 30 years of experience in providing training and mentoring to media/film professionals, from beginners to established filmmakers.

Lance has delivered a color-grading module at master's level for **London South Bank University (LSBU)**, and has guest lectured at other London universities, including UCA and The Met Film School at Ealing Studios.

As a Blackmagic Design Training Partner for DaVinci Resolve software, Lance's training business, Physical Folk, offers certification courses in DaVinci Resolve. Lance also provides filmmakers with bespoke personal training and consultancy in using DaVinci Resolve on their current projects.

Special thanks to my friends who supplied practice media for this book:

Dr. Awais Ali, dentist and videographer for filmdental.com, for supplying his wedding video for Chapters 7, 8, 9, and 10.

Donovan Parsons, multi-skilled lighting cameraman of ITN and SET-EST LTD, for supplying the greenscreen footage for Chapter 11.

Special thanks also to the fellow trainers and training staff at Blackmagic Design for sharing their knowledge with me and allowing me to share my own educational insights with them.

Also special thanks to Mohd Hammad, Alex Berry, and the rest of the Packt team for their input and support during the course of writing this book.

Of course, finally, I would like to thank my wife for her patience and support as I spent long hours of the night writing this book.

About the reviewer

Alex Berry has been working in postproduction for 25 years, starting at an independent post house, then a national broadcaster, before founding Quality Control TV, a boutique color-grading studio based in London. He has worked for many leading brands at an international level.

As a self-taught editor and then colorist, he's always needed to personally seek out information and resources to improve his craft, which is why he's happy to endorse this book, which will help you to do the same.

Alex presents a course on color grading in DaVinci Resolve, which you can find on the Domestika learning platform. It follows on from the excellent foundation provided by this book.

Table of Contents

Chapter 5: Creating Additional Sound 147

Part II: Fixing Audio and Video 175

Chapter 6: Working with Archive Footage 177

Part III: Advanced Techniques with DaVinci Resolve 20 235

Chapter 9: Split Screens and Picture-in-Picture 237

Preface

DaVinci Resolve is used to enhance the color of Hollywood films, TV shows, and commercials, and does so better than any other video editing software. Version 20 enables you to edit, compose VFX, mix sound, and deliver to different platforms, including social media – all in one piece of software.

This book provides a hands-on approach to using DaVinci Resolve to create and enhance your videos for social media and the web, using a Hollywood-standard video editing suite of tools.

Feel free to post your video creations on social media and use the hashtag `#ResolveEasyEdits` to share them with us.

Who this book is for

This book is for emerging creatives, social media influencers, and content makers; anyone with an idea they want to realize and publish online will benefit from this book.

Not only will the budding content maker who is looking for quick techniques to improve their work benefit from this book, but it will also be useful for experienced content makers who want to begin using DaVinci Resolve for its more advanced features. It is a useful and practical training manual for social media marketers, influencers, small business owners creating their own content, short film and vertical content makers, vloggers, and film/media studies students at schools, colleges, or universities.

What this book covers

Chapter 1, Getting Started with Resolve – Publishing Your First Cut, teaches you how to quickly import, organize, review, assemble, and publish video footage to social media from the Cut page's timeline.

Chapter 2, Adding Titles, Transitions, and Simple Visual Effects, helps you enhance the project you created in Chapter 1 by adding a basic title and motion graphics, using Fusion FX and transitions on the Cut page.

Chapter 3, Polishing the Camera Audio – Getting It in Sync, looks at how recording separate audio can improve your video and how Resolve makes it easy to sync this audio with your video on the Media page.

Chapter 4, Adding Narration, Voice Dubbing, and Subtitles, looks at making a completed video accessible by adding narration, voice dubbing, and subtitles.

Chapter 5, Creating Additional Sound, looks at creating a sound library and importing sound effects into Fairlight to then use on our timeline.

Chapter 6, Working with Archive Footage, looks at using Fusion FX to restore old video footage and changing the timing of our dubbed audio to match the timing of the video.

Chapter 7, Stabilizing Shaky Footage, teaches you how to stabilize shaky video footage on the Cut, Edit, and Color pages.

Chapter 8, Hiding the Cut – Making Our Edits Invisible, looks at continuity editing and how to use cutaways, cut-ins, and split edits on the Cut page to hide bad cuts.

Chapter 9, Split Screens and Picture-in-Picture, looks at creating a split screen using composite footage and video resizing, as well as picture-in-picture effects using the Resolve FX Transform Video Collage filter on the Cut page.

Chapter 10, Enhancing Color for Mood or Style, introduces color theory as used in Hollywood films and how to use color FX tools on the Cut page to fix color.

Chapter 11, Adding Greenscreen Effects, covers how to shoot for a green screen and how to work with it in DaVinci Resolve, using different types of keyers.

Chapter 12, Studio-Only Techniques – Mostly AI, looks at the AI Neural Engine tools, only available in the Studio version of DaVinci Resolve, which can speed up your edit process.

Chapter 13, Glossary, defines some of the common terms used throughout the book and in video editing.

Chapter 14, Answers to Questions, contains answers to the questions that were at the end of each chapter.

To get the most out of this book

For this book, you do not need to have any previous technical knowledge, apart from a basic understanding of how to upload content to social media and how to organize files on your own computer.

You will need at least the latest version of DaVinci Resolve 20.3 installed on your computer. The exercises in this book should also work with future releases of DaVinci Resolve. Some of the exercises will also work with older versions of DaVinci Resolve, from version 18 onwards.

Software/hardware requirements for the book	Operating system requirements
DaVinci Resolve 20.3	Windows, macOS, or Linux

You will need the Studio version of DaVinci Resolve 20.3 for some of the features explained in this book, particularly *Chapters 4*, *6*, and *12*.

Download the color images

We also provide a PDF file that has color images of the screenshots/diagrams used in this book. You can download it here: `https://packt.link/gbp/9781836208839`.

Conventions used

There are a number of text conventions used throughout this book.

`CodeInText`: Indicates code words in text, database table names, folder names, filenames, file extensions, pathnames, dummy URLs, user input, and X/Twitter handles. For example: "Name your bin's `drb` file something useful, such as `Video Bins wo Credits`."

Bold: Indicates a new term, an important word, or words that you see on the screen. For instance, words in menus or dialog boxes appear in the text like this. For example: "Click on the **New Project** button in the bottom-right corner of the **Project Manager** window."

> Warnings or important notes appear like this.

> Tips and tricks appear like this.

Free benefits with your book

This book comes with free benefits to support your learning. Activate them now for instant access (see the "*How to unlock*" section for instructions).

Here's a quick overview of what you can instantly unlock with your purchase:

How to unlock

Scan the QR code (or go to packtpub.com/unlock). Search for this book by name, confirm the edition, and then follow the steps on the page.

UNLOCK NOW

Note: Keep your invoice handy. Purchases made directly from Packt don't require one.

Get in touch

Feedback from our readers is always welcome.

General feedback: If you have questions about any aspect of this book or have any general feedback, please email us at customercare@packt.com and mention the book's title in the subject of your message.

Errata: Although we have taken every care to ensure the accuracy of our content, mistakes do happen. If you have found a mistake in this book, we would be grateful if you reported this to us. Please visit http://www.packt.com/submit-errata, click **Submit Errata**, and fill in the form.

Piracy: If you come across any illegal copies of our works in any form on the internet, we would be grateful if you would provide us with the location address or website name. Please contact us at copyright@packt.com with a link to the material.

If you are interested in becoming an author: If there is a topic that you have expertise in and you are interested in either writing or contributing to a book, please visit http://authors.packt.com/.

Share your thoughts

Once you've read *Video Editing Made Easy with DaVinci Resolve 20*, we'd love to hear your thoughts! Scan the QR code below to go straight to the Amazon review page for this book and share your feedback.

`https://packt.link/r/1836208839`

Your review is important to us and the tech community and will help us make sure we're delivering excellent quality content.

Part 1

Starting with DaVinci Resolve 20

The objective of this part is for you to gain an understanding of how to use the Cut page in DaVinci Resolve as a tool to quickly create a finished video for social media or the web.

This part of the book includes the following chapters:

- *Chapter 1, Getting Started with Resolve – Publishing Your First Cut*
- *Chapter 2, Adding Titles, Transitions, and Simple Visual Effects*
- *Chapter 3, Polishing the Camera Audio – Getting It in Sync*
- *Chapter 4, Adding Narration, Voice Dubbing, and Subtitles*
- *Chapter 5, Creating Additional Sound*

1

Getting Started with Resolve – Publishing Your First Cut

As a video content maker, whether you are creating videos for the web, YouTube, or TikTok, there will come a point where you will need to edit the videos you have made using dedicated video editing software, rather than struggle with the limitations of a phone application. Dedicated video editing software applications can be quite daunting for a beginner, but once mastered, they can provide a whole host of powerful features to take your videos to the next level.

There are many video editing applications to choose from. This book will cover how to use DaVinci Resolve, a powerful video editor that is used by the film and TV industry to edit, color, and add sound and visual effects to films. It is amazing that Resolve, which used to cost thousands of dollars, is now available for free!

Resolve is an incredibly powerful piece of software. It is not just one software program – it is a combination of several very powerful software programs that the film industry has been using separately for decades. Each page in Resolve has the power of each of these software programs. We will cover some of these pages later in this book, but since you are a beginner, we will be mostly focusing on using the **Cut** page to help you create your edited video quickly and simply.

Fun fact – the editing term **cut** is named after the physical cutting process that was used in the early years of editing film, where a razor blade was used to cut out unwanted footage before it was all taped back together for the final edit. Today, it is a lot safer just to use DaVinci Resolve to *cut* your films digitally!

The **Cut** page is an incredible tool for quickly putting together your first video edit or *cut*. Many more tools are available in the rest of DaVinci Resolve, but they have been simplified into one page to make them quicker and easier to use.

In this chapter, you will learn how to quickly import, organize, review, assemble, and publish video footage on the **Cut** page's timeline. Additionally, you will learn how to start a new project and set and save your project settings for future use. You will be shown the interface of Resolve and the **Cut** page, learn how to customize it, and be able to save certain settings so that you can have a user workspace that suits you. Then, you will import media that you want to edit together (that is, audio, video, photos, and computer graphics) and use the unique features of the **Cut** page, such as **Source Tape** and **Smart Insert**, to review and add footage to the timeline to quickly create a basic edited video. Finally, you will export and publish a video directly to YouTube from within the **Cut** page of DaVinci Resolve rather than having to export it first and then upload it later.

All these tools combined will make editing and publishing short-form films and videos much quicker, saving you time and freeing you up to make more content.

In this chapter, we are going to cover the following main topics:

- Creating your first project in DaVinci Resolve
- Customizing your digital workspace
- Getting your media files in and organized
- Reviewing your shots and cutting them all together
- Publishing your video to social media

Your purchase includes a free PDF copy + exclusive extras

Your purchase includes a DRM-free PDF copy of this book, a 7-day trial to the Packt+ library (no credit card required), and additional exclusive extras. See the *Free benefits with your book* section in the *Preface* to unlock them instantly and maximize your learning.

Technical requirements

To complete this chapter, you will need to install a copy of DaVinci Resolve version 20. Some exercises may work in older versions of Resolve after version 16. However, to get the most from this book, it is best to have the latest version of DaVinci Resolve. You can download the latest free version of DaVinci Resolve from the Blackmagic Design website: `https://www.blackmagicdesign.com/uk/products/davinciresolve/`.

Also, ensure you download the **DaVinci Resolve Bins (drb)** file from `https://packt.link/gbz/9781836208839`.

All exercises will also work with the paid Studio version of DaVinci Resolve. The technical requirements for your computer to run DaVinci Resolve can be found on the Blackmagic Design website: `https://www.blackmagicdesign.com/support/readme/d8c4a8297ebb4d94b14a045ba7eda2eb`.

The purpose of this chapter is to get you up and running quickly on editing your own footage. However, if you want to practice on video footage already shot, I have listed, in the *Further reading* section at the end of this chapter, download links to sources of free-to-use video footage that you can use. Later in the book, I will supply you with specific video footage to download to help illustrate the exercises in those chapters.

With these requirements in place, let us start learning!

Creating your first project in DaVinci Resolve

When opening Resolve for the first time, it can be quite confusing knowing where to start. In this section, you will learn how to create a new project and where to set and save project settings in DaVinci Resolve so that you can load them up quickly for future projects.

Opening Resolve for the first time

After installing Resolve, the first time you open it, you will be greeted with the welcome screen (*Figure 1.1*), which gives you an overview of the latest features. This can be found in the **Help** menu. From there, you can choose **Welcome to DaVinci Resolve**:

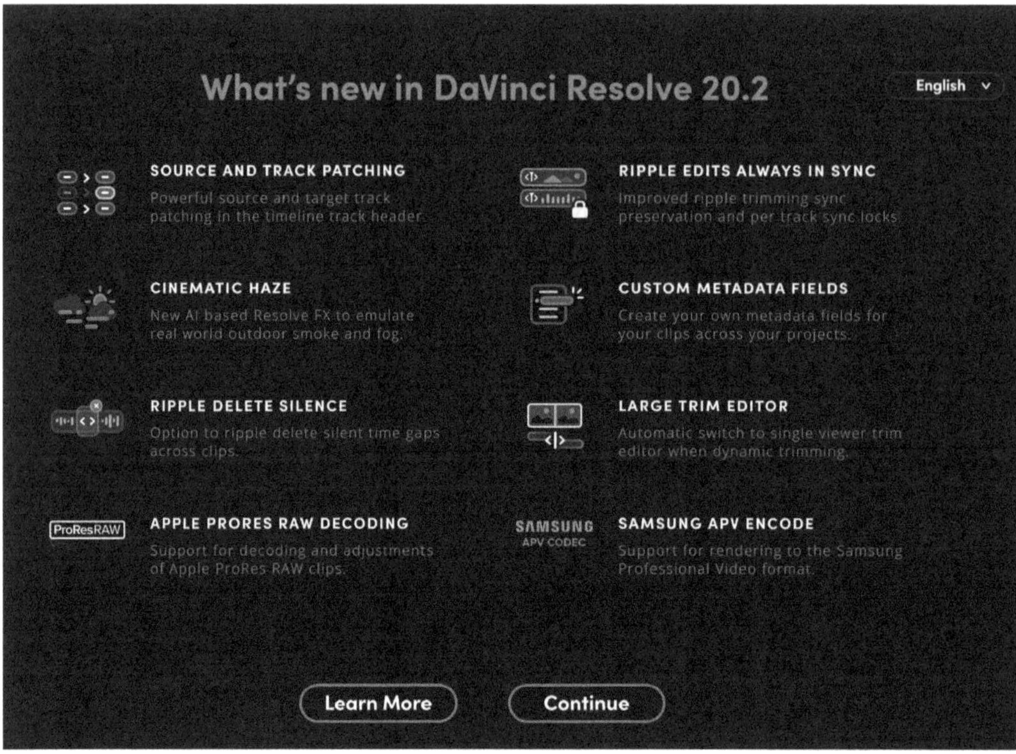

Figure 1.1: Welcome screen

Next, after clicking the **Continue** button *(Figure 1.1)*, Resolve will ask where you want to save the files it needs to be able to work. You can always change these locations later, but first, let us look at what they are so that you can better understand where to tell Resolve to store them.

Cache files

Cache files are media files that Resolve stores temporarily for easy access to help Resolve access them more quickly while you are editing. This also helps with playing media back faster in the timeline. It is best to store these cache files on the internal hard drive on your computer or, if it is faster, an external **Solid State Drive** (**SSD**) connected to your computer. If you are using an external drive for your cache files, remember to plug it in before you start Resolve; otherwise, Resolve will not know where to store your cache files and present the following message (*Figure 1.2*):

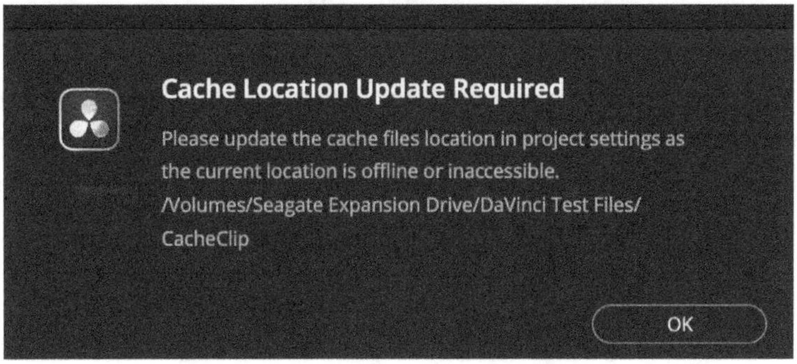

Figure 1.2: Cache files warning message

Stills

Resolve also needs to know where to save your stills. Otherwise, you will get the following message (*Figure 1.3*) if Resolve cannot find the drive your stills folder is linked to:

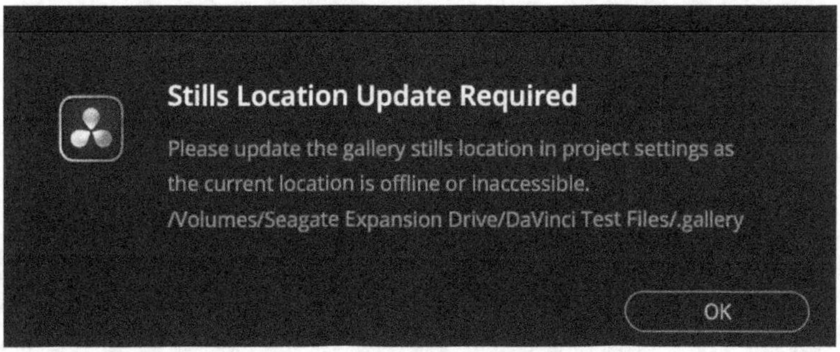

Figure 1.3: Stills warning message

Note that this is not where you store still photos you use in your edit. It is where Resolve stores still images of frames you select from your timeline. It is a bit like a screenshot or photo of a moment in time of your edit.

This can be useful if you want to share an image from your timeline as a thumbnail for your social media posts. You can store these stills on a hard drive anywhere. It does not need to be a fast drive – save that for your cache files.

If you change your mind, you can change the cache and stills locations later. It is good practice to store the cache and stills files directly on your computer, as Resolve will not lose the link to them – unless, of course, you move the folders when tidying up your computer. In this case, you can relink them to the moved folder or create a new folder to link to if you have deleted it.

Creating your first project

Now that we have told Resolve where to store the files it needs to create to work fluidly, you can create your first project. This can be done in the **Project Manager** window (*Figure 1.4*):

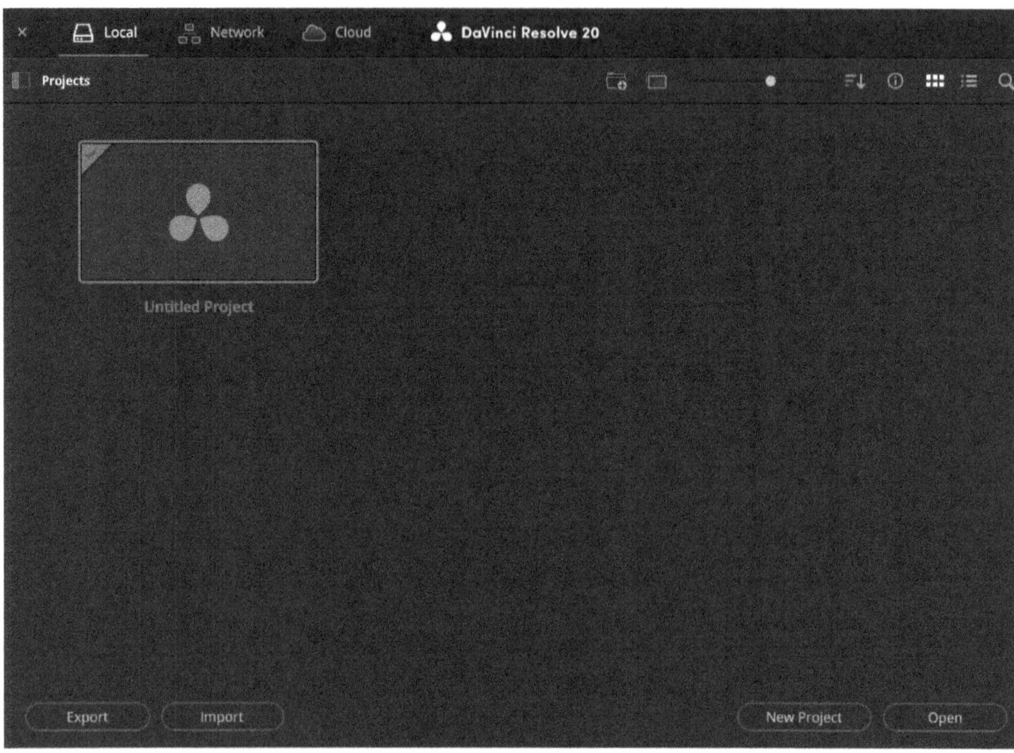

Figure 1.4: Project Manager

There are two ways to create a new project:

- Click on the **New Project** button in the bottom-right corner of the **Project Manager** window
- Alternatively, open the **Untitled Project** template

Which you choose is up to you.

As for DaVinci Resolve 20, there is no difference between using **New Project** or **Untitled Project**; both will ask you to name your project and decide where on your computer you want to save it.

Now that you have created your first project, let us look at the visual layout or **user interface** (**UI**) of Resolve and how you can customize it to suit how you work.

Customizing your digital workspace

When using Resolve for the first time, it can be a little confusing as there are so many pages, all with a myriad of functions, which, to a beginner, can be understandably overwhelming. It is like learning to fly for the first time using a Jumbo Jet! Thankfully, we can simplify the workspace by hiding many of the pages so that our interface is more appropriate for a beginner, so it is much more like learning to fly in a small propeller plane. It is still daunting, but much more achievable!

However, first, let us look at how Resolve is unique in using pages in the first place.

Understanding Resolve's pages

Blackmagic Design, the owner of DaVinci Resolve, has created a separate page for each of these theoretically different software programs, laid out in a row at the bottom of the software interface (*Figure 1.5*). The benefit of this is that you can create advanced sound, color, and visual effects without having to export your film edit into another application. Resolve is the only editing software that has this function. Other editing programs rely on plugins or exporting the edit into another application to do more advanced work and then reimporting it back in to do further edits. Of course, if you prefer to work this way, then Resolve will let you do this too. However, this is a more advanced and time-consuming technique and is beyond the scope of this book.

You might have noticed that the pages are laid out in the order of a traditional filmmaking workflow. Namely, viewing and organizing raw footage, quickly cutting (assembling) footage, making a more precise cut of the footage, adding special effects, color grading, sound mixing, and then exporting. However, the beauty of Resolve is that you can go back and forth between the pages and work in any order that you want.

In this chapter, and for most of this book, we will be using the **Cut** page, which is the default page that Resolve will take you to when you first open a new project.

The **Cut** page is used for creating quick edits and is great for quickly creating and publishing social media content or a **rough cut** for a feature film:

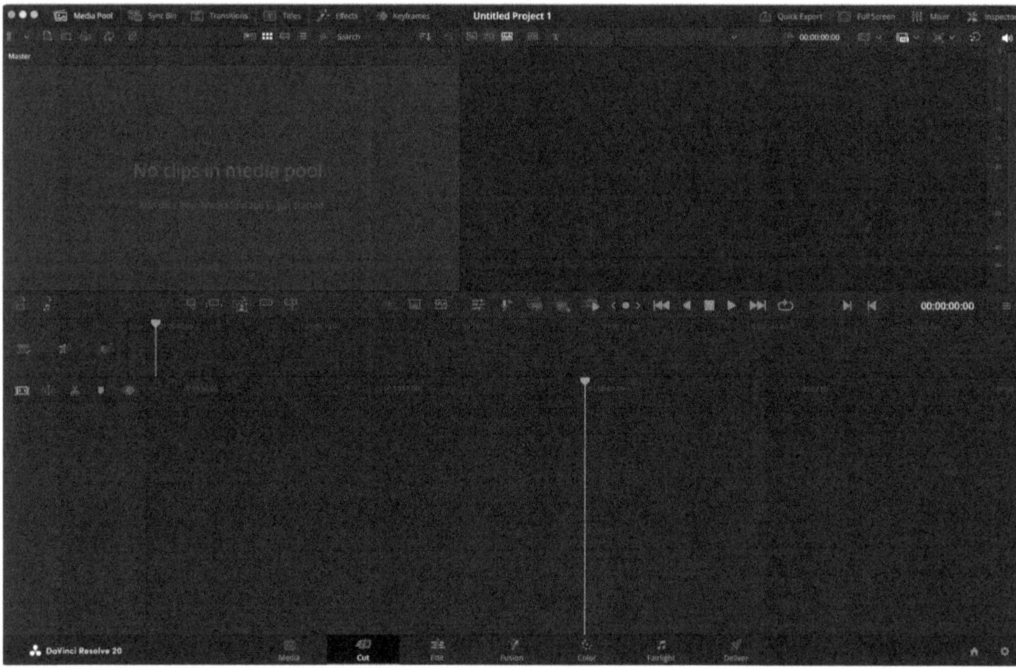

Figure 1.5: The Cut page

Now, let us simplify our workspace so that we can focus mainly on the **Cut** page without the distractions of the other pages.

Simplifying the workspace

Having so much software functionality can be great when you need to use all of the powerful features of Resolve for your feature film. However, if you just want to use one or a few of the pages, Resolve has a handy feature where you can temporarily hide the page you do not want. Let us do that now. For now, we are going to hide the **Media**, **Edit**, **Color**, **Fusion**, **Fairlight**, and **Deliver** pages:

1. Select the **Workspace** menu in the top-right corner of Resolve (the **Menu** bar).
2. Select **Show Page**.

3. Click on the pages you want to hide – in this case, the **Media**, **Edit**, **Color**, **Fusion**, **Fairlight**, and **Deliver** pages.
4. There will now be a check mark next to the pages Resolve will show, and no check mark next to the pages Resolve will hide. By default, all pages are preselected.

Now that your workspace is a lot simpler, you can save this new look as a preset, which you can quickly load again when you want to use it in the future:

1. From the **Menu** bar, select **Workspace**.
2. Select **Layout Presets** > **Save Layout as Preset...**.
3. In the **Enter Preset Name** textbox, name your preset `Basic Workspace`.
4. Click on the **OK** button or press the *Return* key on your keyboard.

Well done! You have now created your first workspace preset that you can quickly recall later.

> You can save your layout presets on a USB stick (or even in cloud storage such as Google Drive or Dropbox) so that when you are working on a version of Resolve on someone else's computer, you can load your workspace without affecting the way *they* like to lay it out.

Now that we have simplified your workspace, let us start importing your media.

Getting your media files in and organized

The **Media** page has some advanced functions for importing media that big-budget feature films use. However, it is quick and easy to import media directly into the **Cut** page. Every page has the space to quickly import media – it is called the **Media Pool**. The **Media Pool** is located in the top-left corner of every page (*Figure 1.6*), which makes it easy to locate.

Import Media

In the top-left corner, underneath the **Media Pool** button of the **Cut** page, two icons allow you to quickly import media into Resolve:

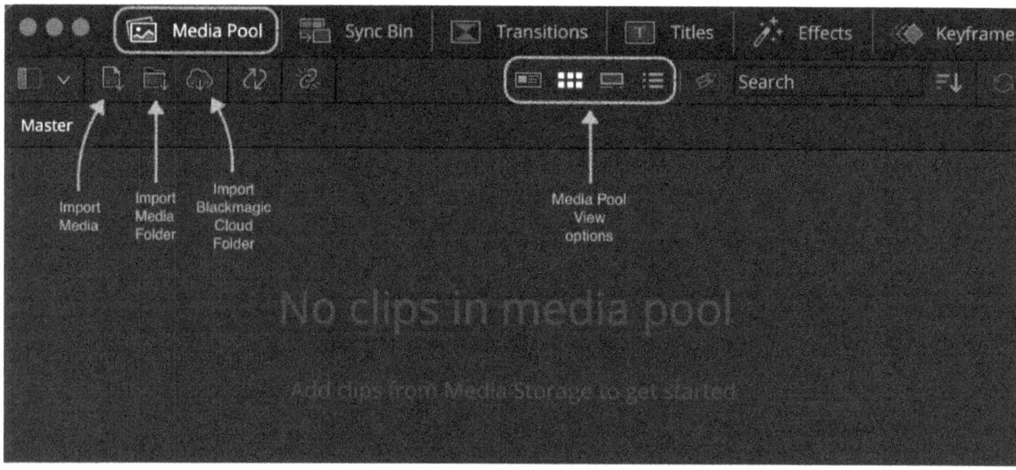

Figure 1.6: Media Pool

The first button, **Import Media** (*Figure 1.6*), imports media files:

1. Left-click on the **Import Media** button.
2. In your computer's **File Manager** window that pops up, navigate to where you want your media files to be stored.
3. Select the files you want to import.
4. Click on the **Open** button.
5. If your imported footage (clip) does not have the same **frame rate** as your project's frame rate, you will get a pop-up message (*Figure 1.7*) asking you to change the project's frame rate so that it matches the footage you are importing:

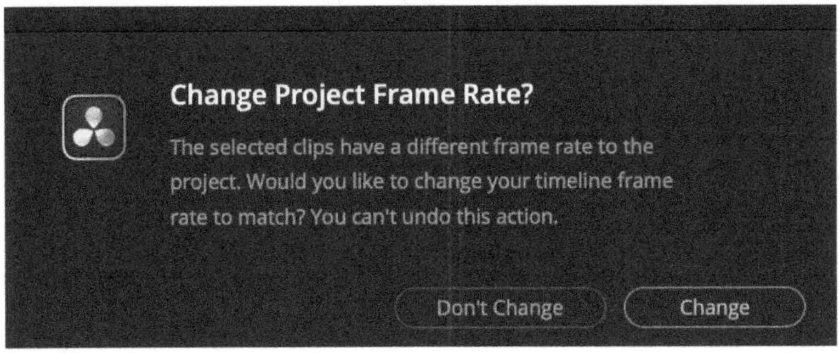

Figure 1.7: The Change Project Frame Rate? pop-up message

6. Go ahead and click on **Change** to change the project's frame rate so that it matches the frame rate of your imported clips. We will cover project frame rates in more detail later.

   You should notice that your **Media Pool** is now filled with the media you just imported.

Now, let us look at the different ways we can view our clips in the **Media Pool** so that we can check we have the right footage before moving it to the timeline.

Media Pool – changing your views

By default, your imported media is shown as thumbnails, but you can change this at any time. Let us do this now:

1. Click on the **Media Pool View** option (*Figure 1.6*) in the top-right corner of the **Media Pool**.
2. Select **List View** (the fourth button from the left).

The thumbnails will disappear, but you will now see a more detailed list of the file properties of the media you imported.

The most common property of a file is the name of the file, also known as its **filename**. The problem with most cameras or audio recorders is that they name the files they create with a semi-random name, such as `SA478937.mov`. This probably means a lot to the camera but means nothing to us.

Of course, the temptation is to change the filenames on our computer to make the file's content easier to understand. The problem with this approach is that each time you change the filename on your computer (after you have imported it into Resolve), Resolve can no longer find it because it looks for the previous filename.

A better approach is to use a feature in Resolve called **Clip Name**, which means you can change the name of the media in your bins as often as you like while retaining the original filename on your computer. To do so, follow these steps:

1. Make sure you are in the **List View**.
2. Select **Clip Name**.
3. Type inside the **Clip Name** field to change the clip name to something memorable.
4. Press the *Return* key on your keyboard or click outside the text field.

You have now changed your clip names so that you can easily identify what they are.

If you want to see a combination of the **Thumbnail** view and the **List** view, with a list of the most common properties of the media file, select the **Metadata** view.

Now, let us preview some of the files that you have imported to see whether they were the ones you wanted to import:

1. Select **Thumbnail View** again (the second button).
2. Select a clip to load it into the **Viewer** window.
3. Hover your mouse over the thumbnail.
4. Move your mouse cursor over the thumbnail.

As you move your mouse cursor over the thumbnail, you will notice that the media will play back in the **Viewer** window.

This is a quick way to review your footage before committing it to the timeline. There is an even quicker way if you have a lot of media to review, something we will show you later.

A few words about bins

By default, Resolve has a **Master bin** in the **Media Pool** that contains all the media (video, audio, and graphics) you have imported into your video project.

You might be wondering why it is called **Master bin** since, like in real life, a bin on a computer is usually where we delete files.

Bin is a word that professional film editors use for a folder. It comes from the early days of **celluloid film editing**, where strips of film would be pegged up over a bin, waiting for the film editor to splice them into the main edit (*Figure 1.8*):

Figure 1.8: An old 1925 photo of film over a bin (source: https://itoldya420.getarchive.net/amp/media/william-seiter-filmmaker-examining-film-strip-ef63e6)

Creating a new bin

You can create extra bins to keep your media organized – for example, you can use one bin for separate audio, such as music and sound effects, and another one for video. Let us do that now:

1. Right-click anywhere on a blank space inside the **Master bin**.
2. Select **New Bin**.
3. A new bin will be created in the **Master bin**.
4. Name the bin `Video`. There are two ways to do this:
    - Right-click on the bin and select **Rename Bin**.
    - Type directly into the **Bin Name** field under the **Bin** icon.

5. Create another bin using the preceding steps and name it `Audio`.

> You can rename any bin apart from the **Master bin** by right-clicking on the bin and selecting **Rename Bin**. Right-clicking on other objects, such as media, the timeline, and viewers, will also reveal a hidden options menu. Try it out and see what hidden options you can discover!

Now that we know what a bin is and we have created our own, let us look at the second button we can use to import media with: **Import Media Folder**.

Import Media Folder

The **Import Media Folder** button imports media, but also imports the folders that are on your computer and converts them into bins:

1. Click on the **Import Media Folder** (*Figure 1.6*) button.
2. In the pop-up window that appears, navigate to where your media files are stored.
3. Select the folder and files you want to import.
4. Click on the **Open** button.

You will notice that nested inside the **Master bin** are other bins with the same name as the folders that held the media on your computer.

It is good practice to put all your media into appropriately named folders on your computer and import them using this second option rather than using the time-consuming approach of creating your bins from scratch every time you edit. The other way to save time is to import the bins that have already been created in another project.

Importing bins

Let us import some of the bins that I have created for you:

1. From the menu bar, select **File > Import > Bin...**.
2. In the pop-up window that appears, choose where on your computer you want to import your bins from.
3. Look for the `Lances_Bins.drb` file you downloaded onto your computer.
4. Click **Open**.

You will now see a series of bins in your **Master bin** called **Video**, **Audio**, **Credits**, and **Graphics**.

Deleting bins

You are likely not going to need the **Credits** bin, so let us delete it:

1. Right-click on the **Credits** bin.
2. Select **Remove Bin...**.
3. The bin should now be removed.
4. If you have more than one **Video** bin, then you can delete this as well.

Selecting the bin with your mouse and pressing the *Delete* key on your keyboard will also delete the bin.

Exporting bins

If you have a favorite layout for your bins, as of version 17, you can now export your bins structure as a `drb` file and store this on your USB with your UI presets. Let us export your new bin structure without the **Credits** bin:

1. Click on the **Bin List** button (or the drop-down arrow next to it) to reveal a list of bins (*Figure 1.9*):

Figure 1.9: Bin List

2. Right-click on the name of the bin you want to export.
3. In the pop-up window that appears, choose where on your computer you want to export your computer.
4. Where it says **Save as**, name your bin's `drb` file something useful, such as `Video Bins wo Credits`.
5. Select **Save**.

With that, you can create, delete, rename, import, and export bins to better organize and keep track of all your project's media. Now, let us start reviewing and editing our media.

Reviewing your shots and cutting them all together

The **Cut** page has some fantastic features that allow you to quickly review and edit video footage together. We will go through each step one at a time, but in reality, once you have mastered these tools, each step will only take seconds to execute, making your edit much speedier.

Reviewing your footage

You might recall how we used the mouse to scrub through each video clip's content quickly. However, this can be time-consuming if we have to do this for every clip. I am glad to say that Resolve has a far more efficient way to review all your video footage at once: **Source Tape** mode.

Source Tape

Source Tape (*Figure 1.10*) is a way to watch all your "source" video footage together at the same time as if you are playing it as one continuous videotape, hence the name **Source Tape**:

Figure 1.10: Source Tape mode

Let us see how it works:

1. Select the **Cut** page.
2. In the top-left corner of the media viewer, select the **Source Tape** button (*Figure 1.10*).

3. The **Viewer** window (*Figure 1.10*) will now populate with all the media in the selected bin.
4. Scrub through the mini transport timeline in the **Viewer** window to review all your footage quickly without having to load each clip into the **Viewer** window:
    - The spacebar will play back footage at normal speed.
    - Pressing the spacebar again will stop the video playback.
    - Pressing the *L* key on your keyboard will also play through the footage at normal speed.
    - Pressing the *L* key twice will fast-forward twice as fast. Three presses will be 4x as fast, four presses will be 8x as fast, five presses will be 16x as fast, and six presses will be 32x as fast.
    - Pressing the *J* key on your keyboard will play the footage backward.
    - Pressing the *J* key twice will reverse twice as fast. Three presses will be 4x as fast, four presses will be 8x as fast, and so on.

> Although I have focused on using keyboard keys to play back our footage (as it is quicker than clicking back and forth with a mouse), you can use a mouse to click on each of the video playback controls (also called transport controls, *Figure 1.10*) underneath the **Viewer** window. These are the same symbols you will find on your CD/MP3 or DVD player, if you have one, and they work in the same way.

You may have noticed that, in **Source Tape** mode, the bin icons disappear and are replaced with dates instead. These are the dates when the video footage was created. You can change this view to show the bin names by selecting the **Sort** button. Let us do this now.

5. Click on the **Sort** button (*Figure 1.11*):

Figure 1.11: The Sort button

6. From the drop-down list, select **Bin**.

You can isolate the playback of the footage to just the contents of one bin rather than everything in the **Master bin**, perhaps to review footage of a bin you have just imported:

1. Select a bin from the **Master bin** using the **Bin List** icon (*Figure 1.9*) in the top-left corner of the **Media Pool**.
2. Select **Source Tape** mode again (if it is not selected already).
3. Play back and review the footage by pressing the spacebar or the *J* and *L* keys.

   You will have noticed several things when playing back footage in **Source Tape** mode:

   - What gets played back in **Source Tape** mode depends on what bin you have selected
   - The vertical lines in the **Viewer Transport Timeline** (*Figure 1.10*) represent the beginning and end of clips
   - As each clip is played back, it is highlighted (with an orange border) in the **Media Pool**

Now, you can see how useful **Source Tape** is at reviewing all the footage in your master or selected bins quickly, rather than having to select each clip individually.

However, there is an even quicker way within **Source Tape** that you can use to review your footage: **Fast Review**.

Fast Review

Fast Review uses simple **artificial intelligence** (**AI**) to adjust the playback speed of the clip based on the clip's length. So, long clips are played back faster, while short clips are played back slower, so that you do not miss them. Let us try it out:

1. Make sure **Source Tape** is selected.
2. Select **Fast Review** (*Figure 1.12*) from the far left of the playback controls under the **Viewer** window:

Figure 1.12: Fast Review mode

Fast Review gives you a quick and easy way to review your video footage so that you can make decisions on what to include in your edit.

Editing your footage together

Before you edit your footage, let us describe what a **timeline** is and how it uniquely works on Resolve's **Cut** page.

The Cut page's timelines

All editing software has what is called a **timeline**. This is a long horizontal strip/line onto which footage (frequently referred to as **clips**) is dropped, with the "time" or duration of the edited video displayed along the top of the **timeline**.

Timecode

The time is displayed in hours, minutes, seconds, and frames and is called a **timecode**. It is displayed as `HH:MM:SS:FF` (*Figure 1.13*):

Figure 1.13: The timeline timecode

Upper Timeline

What is unique about the **Cut** page is that it has two timelines (*Figure 1.14*). The topmost timeline, known as **Upper Timeline**, is the overview of your entire edit, which displays the whole duration of your entire video, regardless of how long it is and how many clips there are. This is great for quickly navigating to any part of your timeline and seeing how all your clips are edited together:

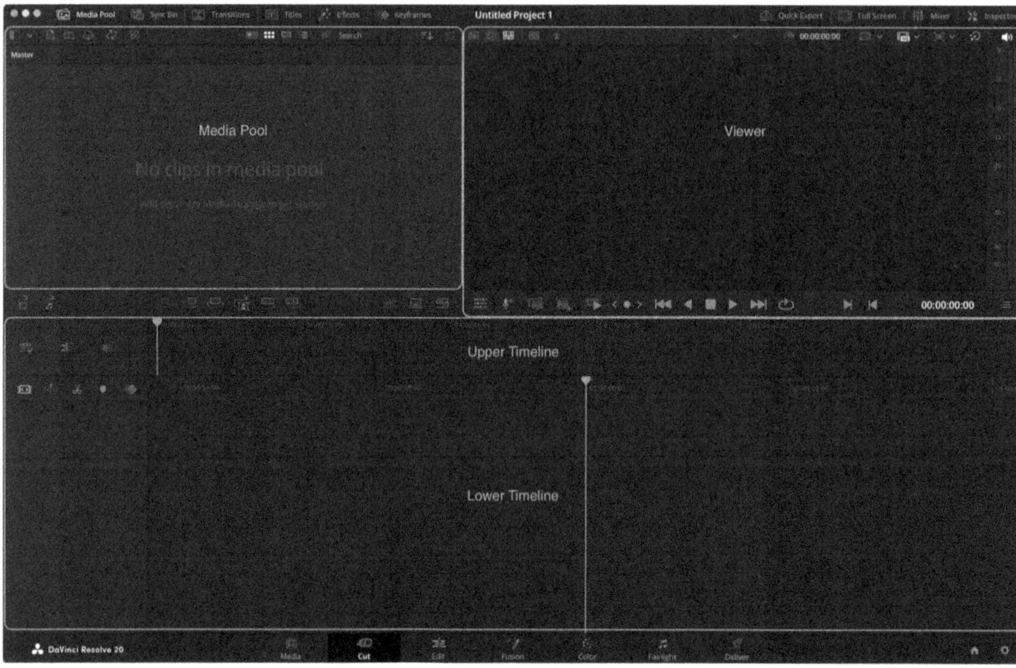

Figure 1.14: Cut page timelines

Lower Timeline

The second timeline (**Lower Timeline**), which can be found just below **Upper Timeline**, is a more traditional editing timeline that shows a zoomed-in view of **Upper Timeline**. This is a lot easier to see and make your edits with.

> **Key concept – timelines, tracks, and shots**
>
> In a timeline, each layer of the video is called a **track**, and each track is made up of a series of **clips** representing different camera shots or angles. So, the hierarchy of content goes like this: **Project** > **Timeline** > **Track** > **Clips**.
>
> So, a **project** can have several different **timelines**, each timeline can have several different tracks, and each track can contain several different clips.

Track 1 versus track 2

On the **Cut** page, **track 1** (the bottom track) operates differently from **track 2** and above (that is, all the tracks above/on top of **track 1**).

Track 1 will automatically shuffle footage (clips) along the timeline to make room for the new clip – this is called **rippling**. This is great for quickly adding clips to the timeline so that you can get your first overall edit done, also known as a **rough cut**. Any clip that is added to track 2 will overwrite any clips already on track 2. Track 2 is useful for adding additional clips without affecting the duration of your first edit, such as adding cutaways or titles to be shown over existing clips.

For **track 1** to have rippling as a feature, it must be enabled:

1. Select the **Timeline Options** button to the far left of the upper timeline.
2. Select **Ripple On** (*Figure 1.15*). The **Ripple On** button will turn white to show that it has been enabled:

Figure 1.15: The Ripple On and Split Clip buttons

Now, when you add clips to **track 1**, the timeline will ripple to make room for them. Selecting **Ripple On** only changes the functionality of **track 1**; it does not affect any other tracks.

Key concept – cutaway

We will cover **cutaways** in more detail in *Chapter 8*. However, as a brief overview, a cutaway is footage that is added to the edit that illustrates already existing footage in the timeline.

An example of this is when a person is being interviewed, and they refer to a product they are promoting – this is a good place to add a shot of the product on a track on top of the original interview footage, where we continue to hear the interviewee describe the product.

The effect of this would be that the viewer would see the interviewee talk about the product, then see the camera "cut away" to a shot of the product while we still hear the interviewer talking about it. This gives the illusion to the viewer that these shots are happening in real time, as if they are watching a live multi-camera broadcast switching between cameras.

Of course, none of this has to be shot in real time and can all be accomplished in the edit.

Let us see how track 1 rippling works in practice.

Adding footage to the timeline – using track 1

Using the skills you have just learned, use **Source Tape** and **Fast Review** to identify five shots you would like to use for your video:

1. Using **Fast Review**, find and identify the following shots:
    - The **master** shot (a wide shot)
    - Two mid shots of your main subject
    - Two close-ups (either a reaction shot or a cutaway shot)
2. Select your master shot in the **Viewer** window.
3. Click and drag the master shot onto either timeline.

Now, you have a master shot on the timeline that you can use to edit your other shots. All clips can be added to the timeline by either clicking and dragging directly from the **Media Pool** or the **Viewer** window onto the timeline.

Key concept – shot types

When making a video, we use different framing conventions, called **shot types**, that add visual interest to the viewer by changing how much of our subject is in the frame. The closer the shot is to the subject (which is usually a person), the more of an emotional impact it has on the audience.

The three main shot types are as follows:

- **Wide shot (WS)**: This shot contains the whole environment within which our subject is positioned and how they interact with it. For example, it could be a person standing in a room where we see all their body and their relationship to their environment – that is, is this their home or workplace? This shot is too wide to show much emotion. This can also be used as a **master shot** for editing, as it contains all the information in the scene. We can choose to cut this to another closer-framed shot.
- **Mid/medium shot (MS)**: The bottom of the frame starts at the waist of our subject, while the top of our frame ends just above the head of our subject. This is good for formal interviews.
- **Close-up (CU)**: This is a small detail that is magnified, such as framing just the head and top of the shoulders of the subject. This is good for showing intense emotion. It could also be a tight frame of our subject's hands demonstrating a product.

There are many more shot types, but these are the main ones you should use when you are just starting. If you change your mind, you can delete any clip from the timeline by selecting it with the mouse and pressing the *Delete* key on your keyboard. Do not worry – doing this will not delete your original footage as it is still available in the **Media Pool**.

Key concept – non-destructive editing

Editing in Resolve is "non-destructive," which means that you can delete clips from the timeline and even the **Media Pool** and still be able to reimport the same media back in.

When you edit, you are not cutting your original footage but a live preview of it. Resolve stores the editing decisions you make (in a database) and then applies them to your final film when you export it.

The timeline playhead

In the timeline, you will notice a vertical orange line – this is called the playhead (*Figure 1.14*). The **Viewer** window will show a picture of the frame that is under the playhead in the timeline. The **Timecode** display in the bottom-right corner of the **Viewer** window also shows the timecode for the current frame under the playhead.

You can move the timeline playhead just like the playhead in the **Viewer** window – by using the spacebar or the *J* and *L* keys.

You can also use the playhead position to tell Resolve where you want to make a cut. Let us remove the usual dead space at the start of your master shot:

1. Position your playhead just before the main action starts in your story.
2. If there is dialog, you can use the audio waveforms at the bottom of the clip as a guide.
3. Select **Trim Start** from the **Trim** menu (this is called **Trim to Playhead** in earlier versions of Resolve).

Now, your story starts as you can jump straight into the action.

Usually, your master shot will be far too long to use by itself, so we will need to break it up to bring visual interest to the viewer.

Find a part of your master shot where your subject has finished their main thought or action. We are going to cut it here and add a different angle to add visual interest:

1. Move the playhead to where you want to make a cut.
2. Click on the **Split Clip** button (*Figure 1.15*) just above the lower timeline's track headers.

You will notice that the master shot has now been split into two. The dotted vertical line shows that the footage is continuous and has no frames missing – this is called a **through edit**.

Setting in and out points

When editing, we do not have to add a whole clip to the timeline. We can trim the footage down so that it is shorter before we add it to the timeline by adding **in and out points**. These dictate the start (in) and end (out) of the footage we are adding to the timeline.

Now, let us find an alternative clip to insert between the two clips we already have on the timeline and trim out any excess footage from our new clip, using in and out points, before adding it to the timeline:

1. In the **Media Pool**, select a mid-shot clip that matches or enhances the action of the master shot.
2. Play the clip in the **Viewer** window until just before any action or speech. Then, press the *I* key on the keyboard to add an **in** point where the clip will start.
3. Play the clip forward until just after the last words are said, or an action is performed. Then, press the *O* key on the keyboard to add an **out** point where the clip will end.

You will notice that an in and out point marker has been added to the thumbnail of the clip in the **Media Pool**, as well as underneath the **Viewer** window. Now, when we put this clip on the timeline, it will only take the footage in between the in and out points we have marked up on the clip. Now, let us insert this marked-up clip onto the timeline using a feature called **Smart Insert**.

Smart Insert

Traditionally, when we add a clip to the timeline, it will place it where the playhead is on the timeline. There is a feature called **Smart Insert** in the **Cut** page that predicts where we want the new clip to go based on how near the playhead is to a pre-existing cut. Let us use **Smart Insert** to add our marked-up clip to the timeline:

1. Make sure the playhead is near the cut that we made earlier; it does not need to be placed precisely.
2. You will notice some arrows bouncing above the cut point. These are **smart indicators** – that is, a visual cue to show you where the clip is going to be inserted when you click on the **Smart Insert** button.
3. Click on the **Smart Insert** button (the first edit button; see *Figure 1.16*) in the top-left corner of the timeline.

Figure 1.16: The edit buttons

The clip you have chosen has now been trimmed and added to the timeline at the point where you previously made a cut. You should also notice that the surrounding clips have not been overwritten; instead, they have been moved further up the timeline to make room for the new clip – this is called *rippling*.

Append

Now, let us look at the next edit button (see *Figure 1.16*) in the editing toolbar underneath the **Media Pool**: **Append**.

The **Append** button places a new clip at the end of our timeline, regardless of where the playhead is placed. This is great for credits or adding footage quickly to the timeline in chronological order without needing to position the playhead first:

1. In the **Media Pool**, find a new clip that you want to place at the end of the timeline, such as the final shot of the product you are promoting or the final scene of your short film.
2. Click on the **Append** button.

The new clip has now been placed at the end of the timeline, regardless of the position of your playhead.

Ripple Overwrite

If you want to replace a clip in the timeline with another clip in the **Media Pool**, then you can use **Ripple Overwrite** (the third edit button; see *Figure 1.16*). This is great if you want to change your mind about the content of your video. When you use **Ripple Overwrite**, if the new clip is too short, it will ripple the rest of the clips around the new clip to close any resulting gaps. If the new clip is too long, it will ripple the existing clips along the timeline to make room for the new clip.

Let us see this in action:

1. Select the clip in the timeline that you want to replace. You can simply place your playhead on the clip to do this.
2. Select the new clip in the **Media Pool**.
3. Click on the **Ripple Overwrite** button.

You should have noticed that the new clip has replaced the old clip in the timeline, and the timeline has moved the clips to either side (rippled) of the new clip, making the length of the timeline shorter or longer, depending on the duration difference between the two clips.

Adding footage to the timeline – using track 2

There are no problems with performing your whole edit using only the **Smart Insert**, **Append**, and **Ripple Overwrite** buttons. However, there will be times when you will need more advanced functions to solve a particular problem; this is where the following editing tools come in.

So far, all of the edits we have been making have been to track 1 in the timeline. Whatever edit you make to track 1 of the timeline, the clips will always ripple to make room for the new edit. If you want to add clips to the timeline without it rippling to make room for the addition, you can add the clips to track 2. This will not ripple the timeline; instead, it will overlay a clip (on track 2) on top of existing clips (on track 1).

Close Up

The next **Edit** tool, **Close Up** (the fourth edit button; see *Figure 1.16*), uses track 2 to add a close-up of the existing footage on track 1. It does this by taking a zoomed-in view of the clip in your timeline where your playhead is and adding a 5-second duration clip to track 2. If the duration between your playhead and the end of the existing clip is shorter than 5 seconds, it will end the new clip at the end of your existing clip.

It is important to note that this is digitally zoomed, so there might be some loss of quality unless you use a clip that has a higher resolution than the timeline, such as a 4K clip for a 1080p timeline.

This tool does not have to be used only for close-ups; for example, it can also convert a wide shot into a medium shot.

Let us take the medium shot that you placed in the timeline earlier and convert some of it into a close-up:

1. Place your playhead in the timeline over the medium shot clip where you want the close-up to start.
2. Click on the **Close Up** tool button underneath the **Media Pool**.

You will notice that a new close-up shot has been placed on **track 2** above the existing shot on **track 1**.

This is a useful tool to use in an emergency if you are editing footage where there have been no close-ups shot, and there is no time for a re-shoot.

Place on Top

Now that we are familiar with how to place shots on track 2 so that the timeline does not become rippled, let us look at another editing tool that uses track 2 to add alternative footage.

The **Place on Top** edit button (the fifth button; see *Figure 1.16*) adds a new clip to track 2 above the existing clips on track 1. This is good when adding cutaways or inserting shots into the main edit without affecting the duration of the video in the timeline.

By default, the **Place on Top** tool places the new clip on track 2, starting at your playhead position in the timeline.

Let us see this in practice and add one of our cutaway shots to the timeline to illustrate the main dialogue in the video:

1. Place your playhead where you want your new clip (for example, a cutaway shot) to begin in the timeline.
2. Select your new clip in the **Media Pool**.
3. Click on the **Place on Top** button.

You should now have a new clip on track 2 of your timeline that starts where you had your playhead placed.

Once you have completed your main edit and set the final duration of your video, you can use this tool to add extra shots without affecting the length of your video.

Source Overwrite

The final edit tool underneath the **Media Pool** is the **Source Overwrite** button. This button only works if you have more than one clip with overlapping timecodes. If you do not have footage with timecodes, then this button will do nothing. Since this is an editing book for beginners, we will ignore this button.

Feel free to practice using these editing tools until you have mastered them by adding and swapping the footage in your timeline until you are happy with your edit.

In the next section, you will learn how to publish your edited video to social media, such as YouTube or Vimeo.

Publishing your video to social media

Let us see how easy it is to publish an edited video directly from Resolve onto social media platforms such as YouTube or TikTok.

First, we will need to set up Resolve with our social media accounts to enable it to publish directly through them. You will only need to do this once, but it can save a lot of time compared to exporting the video to your computer and then uploading and publishing it to social media separately.

Setting up your social media accounts in Resolve

Resolve can publish videos directly to your YouTube, Vimeo, TikTok, and Twitter accounts. First, you need to sign in to your social media accounts via the **Quick Export** menu:

1. Click on the **Quick Export** button in the top-right corner of the **Viewer** window.
2. From the **Quick Export** screen, select one of the following options:
    - **YouTube**
    - **Vimeo**
    - **TikTok**
3. Click on the **Sign In** button. This will take you directly to your social media login page in your web browser.
4. Sign in to your social media account using your usual login details and authorize Resolve to have access to your account.
5. Repeat *Steps 2* to *4* for your other social media accounts.

> If you want to access the **Internet Accounts** page again to sign Resolve out of your accounts, you can access it from the DaVinci Resolve menu: **Preferences > System > Internet Accounts.**

With that, your social media accounts have been set up, and you are ready to quickly publish your videos to social media.

Publishing to social media within Resolve

Publishing directly to social media is as easy as selecting some options on the **Quick Export** page.

Publishing directly to YouTube

Let us look at the YouTube options first:

1. Click **Quick Export**.
2. Select **YouTube**.
3. Check the **Upload directly** box.
4. Select one of the YouTube **Privacy** options from the drop-down list:
    - **Private**
    - **Public**
    - **Unlisted**
5. Select a playlist option from the drop-down list:
    - **Film & Animation**, **Auto & Vehicles**, **Music**, **Pets & Animals**, **Sports**, **Travel & Events**, **Gaming**, **People & Blogs**, **Comedy**, **Entertainment**, **News & Politics**, **Howto & Style**, **Education**, **Science & Technology**, or **Nonprofits & Activism**.
6. Type the title of your video into the **Title** textbox.
7. Type the description of your video into the **Description** textbox.
8. Click on the **Export** button in the bottom-right corner of the **Quick Export** page.
9. Choose a file location for your exported video.
10. Click on the **Save** button.

Resolve has now saved a copy of your exported video to the location you specified on your computer and uploaded and published a copy of the video directly to YouTube using the settings you specified on the **Quick Export** page.

Publishing directly to Vimeo

Now, let us look at the Vimeo options:

1. Click **Quick Export**.
2. Select **Vimeo**.
3. Check the **Upload directly** box.
4. Select one of the Vimeo **Privacy** options from the drop-down list:
    - **Anyone**
    - **Only Me**

- **People I follow**
- **People with the password**

5. Type the title of your video into the **Title** textbox.
6. Type the description of your video into the **Description** textbox.
7. Click on the **Export** button in the bottom-right corner of the **Quick Export** page.
8. Choose a file location for your exported video.
9. Click on the **Save** button.

Again, Resolve has saved a copy of your exported video to the location you specified on your computer and uploaded and published a copy of the video directly to Vimeo using the settings you specified on the **Quick Export** page.

Publishing directly to TikTok

Finally, let us look at the TikTok export options:

1. Click **Quick Export**.
2. Select **TikTok**.
3. Check the **Upload directly** box.
4. Select one of the TikTok **Privacy** options from the drop-down list:
    - **Public**
    - **Friends**
    - **Private**
5. Type the title of your video into the **Title** textbox.
6. Select the options you want from the **Allow comments**, **Allow Duet**, and **Allow Stitch** check boxes.
7. Click on the **Export** button in the bottom-right corner of the **Quick Export** page.
8. Choose a file location for your exported video.
9. Click on the **Save** button.

As expected, Resolve has saved a copy of your exported video to the location you specified on your computer and uploaded and published a copy of the video directly to TikTok using the description you specified on the **Quick Export** page.

On the **Quick Export** page, Resolve uses common video settings for social media accounts. However, you can change these settings in the **Timeline Resolution** drop-down list (*Figure 1.17*).

Once you change the timeline's resolution, you will notice that the export file settings on the **Quick Export** page will change accordingly. This is useful if you want to, for example, upload your videos in 4K rather than 1080p:

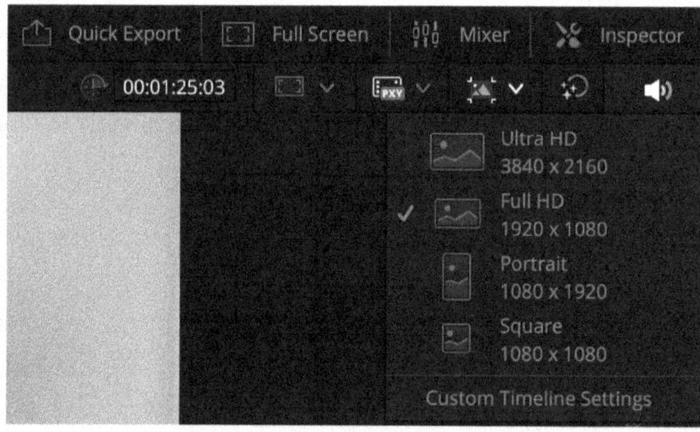

Figure 1.17: The Timeline Resolution drop-down menu

We now know how to publish videos directly to three commonly used social media accounts from Resolve. However, we can also export our videos and upload them separately to other social media accounts. We will learn how to do that next.

Preparing a video to upload to social media outside Resolve

Of course, there are more social media accounts than just YouTube, Vimeo, Twitter, and TikTok. The list keeps on growing, along with their different formatting and aspect ratio requirements. Thankfully, in Resolve, you can quickly reframe and repurpose existing videos so that they can be used for different social media platforms, both current and future ones.

For example, let us take the video you have just edited and prepared for uploading to Instagram. According to Facebook, which owns Instagram, its video requirements are as follows:

Reels Resolution and Size

- *You can upload a reel with an aspect ratio between 1.91:1 and 9:16*
- *Reels should have a minimum frame rate of 30 frames per second (FPS) and a minimum resolution of 720 pixels*

Of course, these requirements can always change, so it is best to check for yourself regularly to be sure (`https://en-gb.facebook.com/help/1038071743007909/?helpref=uf_share`).

Duplicating your timeline

First, let us create a copy of our timeline so that we can make changes to it without losing our original edit:

1. In the **Media Pool**, right-click on your timeline and select **Duplicate Timeline**.
2. Rename the duplicated timeline to something suitable, such as `Insta Edit`, by doing the following:
    - Click on the title below the thumbnail by clicking on it twice and entering a new name
    - Alternatively, if you are in the **List** view, type it directly into the **Clip Name** field
3. Double-click on the new **Timeline** thumbnail or icon (if in the **List** view) to open the new timeline.

Now that we have a copy of our timeline, let us reframe our video for the new **aspect ratio**.

Key concept – aspect ratio

The **aspect ratio** is the ratio of an image's width to its height. It is written as two numbers separated by a hyphen, where the first number represents the width of the image and the second number represents the height.

The aspect ratio is independent of any units of measurement but instead shows the relationship between the width and height of an image.

For example, an aspect ratio of 4:3 could be an old television screen that is 4 feet wide by 3 feet high, or it could be a projector screen that is 4 meters wide by 3 meters high.

To calculate the aspect ratio of any image, you divide the width by the height. So, an aspect ratio of 4:3 could also be described as 1.33:1 (4 divided by 3 is 1.33). This means that for every 1 unit of height, the width will have 1.33 units. So, a screen that is 3 units high would be 4 units wide (3 x 1.33 = 4). Another example is an image that is 3840 pixels wide by 2160 pixels high, has an aspect ratio of 16:9, which is the same as 1.78:1.

Checking your content for a different aspect ratio

First, let us check our content for our new video's **aspect ratio**:

1. Click on the **Safe Area** button in the top-left corner of the **Viewer** window (*Figure 1.18*):

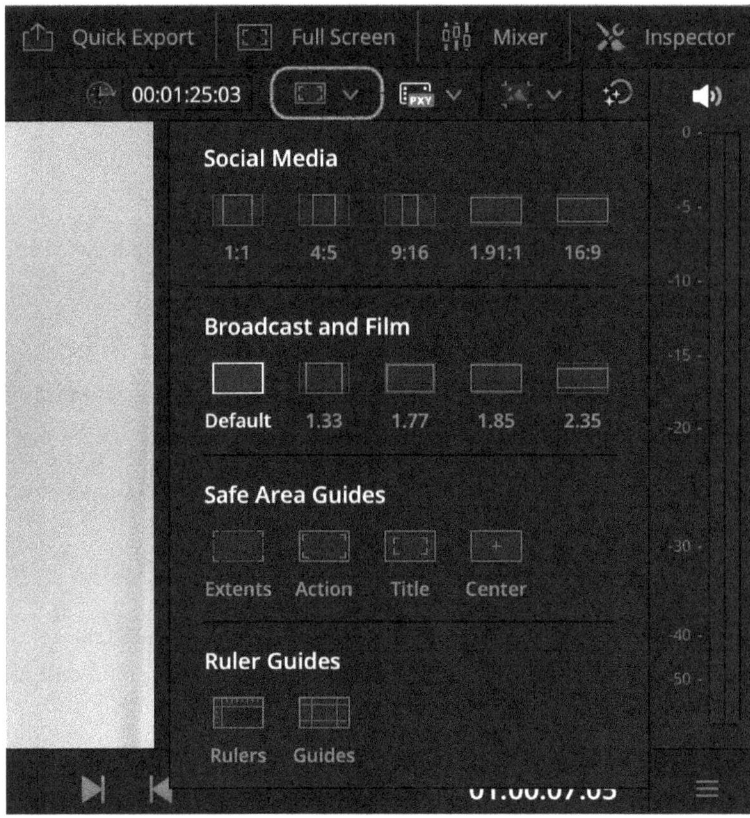

Figure 1.18: The Safe Area button

2. You will see a **Social Media** heading, under which you have the following options:

    - **1:1**
    - **4:5**
    - **9:16**
    - **1.91:1**
    - **16:9**

3. Select the one you prefer. In this case, we will select **9:16** as it is a popular format for Instagram and can also be used for Facebook.
4. You will now see a white box in the **Viewer** window that shows the safe area of our content for it to be seen in the 9:16 vertical format.
5. Scroll through the video in your timeline; you should notice that some of your content will suit the new frame. However, some will not.

You can either use **Ripple Overwrite** to replace the shots that are not framed well for the new **aspect ratio**, or you can reframe the existing footage to suit your needs.

Let us change the framing of the existing clips.

Reframing our video using Transform controls

Let us reframe our video to suit the new aspect ratio:

1. Click on the **Tools** button (highlighted in *Figure 1.19*) in the bottom-left corner of the **Viewer** window. This reveals additional tools that we can use to enhance each clip:

Figure 1.19: The Tools button

2. Select the **Transform** tool (the first button; see *Figure 1.20*). It will be underlined in red to show it has been selected, and the transform controls will be shown underneath.
3. Click and drag the **X** position control (the third transform control from the left) to change the **X** position value of the clip to move it to the left or right until the subject of the clip is inside the white **Safe Area** box:

Figure 1.20: The Transform button and its controls

Feel free to go through each clip and use the **Transform** tool to reframe your video to suit your new aspect ratio.

To see the before and after of any effect, you can toggle the effect on and off by clicking on the red switch to the left of the controls. Anywhere you see this red toggle switch, you can use it to preview what an effect will look like on the video or even disable an effect without deleting it.

Now, let us crop your video so that it suits the new aspect ratio by changing the **Timeline Resolution** property.

Changing the timeline resolution

We now need to change the timeline resolution, which will also change the aspect ratio:

1. Click on the **Timeline Resolution** button (*Figure 1.17*) in the top-right corner of the **Viewer** window to see a drop-down list of common timeline presets:
    - **Ultra HD 3840 x 2160**
    - **Full HD 1920 x 1080**
    - **Portrait 1080 x 1920**
    - **Square 1080 x 1080**
2. Select **Portrait 1080 x 1920** for our 9:16 vertical format.
3. You will notice that the video has now been resized to fit the 9:16 vertical aspect ratio, but Resolve has added black bars above and below the original footage. We do not want this, but there is an easy fix:
    - Select **Custom Timeline Settings** from the bottom of the **Timeline Resolution** drop-down list.
    - Under the **Format** tab, next to the **Mismatched Resolution** options, change the option from **Scale entire image to fit** to **Scale full frame with crop**.

Resolve has now rescaled and cropped the video in the timeline to suit the new aspect ratio. Now, it is time to export our newly reframed video so that it is ready to be uploaded separately to Instagram.

Exporting video using Quick Export

Quick Export is not only used for directly uploading your videos to social media – it can also be used to quickly export videos to your computer.

Quick Export has three main video codec presets: `H.264`, `H.265`, and `ProRes`.

- **ProRes** is a video code only available on Apple computers that is mainly used by professional video editors to edit with, as it has a bigger size and is less compressed to retain image quality. However, due to its large size, it is not so great for social media.
- **H.264** is a universally accepted video codec that compresses video into smaller file sizes efficiently while retaining quality. There are two options for H.264:
    - **H.264 Master** is the standard option for exporting your video using the H.264 codec
    - **Hyperdeck** is used for exporting your video using H.264 settings optimized for recording into a Blackmagic Design Hyperdeck.
- **H.265** is a newer version of `H.264`, so it is not as universally accepted. However, it is more efficient at compressing video for the same quality as `H.264`, so the file sizes can be smaller.

Let us choose `H.264` for our social media uploads:

1. Click on the **Quick Export** button.
2. Select **H.264**.
3. Click on the **Export** button.
4. Navigate to a folder on your computer where you want to save your video.
5. By default, Resolve will name your video after the **Timeline** name. However, you can rename your video before saving it to your computer.
6. Click on the **Save** button to save the file to your computer.

With that, you have repurposed an existing edited video for another social media platform by recomposing shots, cropping the video, changing its aspect ratio, and exporting it to your computer, ready for a separate upload at another time.

Summary

Here is what you did in this chapter:

- Learned about pages in DaVinci Resolve and how to hide them
- Saved your UI as an importable preset
- Imported footage into bins and added, deleted, and exported bins
- Edited a rough cut using track 1-specific editing tools such as **Smart Insert**, **Append**, and **Ripple Overwrite**

- Added cutaways using track 2-specific editing tools such as **Close Up** and **Place on Top**
- Set up your social media accounts, ready for them to be published with Resolve
- Published your video to social media all within Resolve and not even leaving the **Cut** page
- Repurposed existing edits for different social media formats, reframing the footage using the **Transform** controls and adjusting the **Timeline Resolution** property to change the aspect ratio
- Used **Quick Export** to create a copy suitable to be uploaded to other social media accounts outside of Resolve

You now know how to set up DaVinci Resolve to simplify the UI and use the editing tools on the **Cut** page to put together a rough cut and publish it directly to social media. This helps you save time when you are making current and future video edits.

In *Chapter 2*, we will make the video you edited in this chapter look even more amazing by adding titles, transitions, and motion graphics. This will add more visual interest on top of your existing footage. Additionally, we will look at how you can share your work in tandem with others in your team so that they can help you with your edit.

Questions

Answer the following questions to test your knowledge of this chapter:

1. True or false: The **Cut** button on the toolbar splits one clip into two separate clips on the timeline.
2. What social media accounts can you publish videos to directly from within DaVinci Resolve?
3. Which editing tools work specifically with track 1 of the timeline on the **Cut** page?
4. Which editing tools work specifically with track 2 of the timeline on the **Cut** page?
5. True or false: *timecode* is the term used to program time-based effects in DaVinci Resolve.

Further reading

To learn more about the topics that were covered in this chapter, take a look at the following resources:

- Pexels free stock videos: `https://www.pexels.com/videos/`
- PIxabay free stock videos: `https://pixabay.com/videos/`
- Blackmagic Design Pocket Cinema Camera test footage: `https://www.blackmagicdesign.`

com/uk/products/blackmagicpocketcinemacamera/gallery

- Blackmagic Design Cinema Camera test footage: https://www.blackmagicdesign.com/uk/products/blackmagiccinemacamera/gallery
- Blackmagic Design Ursa Cine test footage: https://www.blackmagicdesign.com/uk/products/blackmagicursacine/gallery
- Blackmagic Design Ursa Mini test footage: https://www.blackmagicdesign.com/uk/products/blackmagicursaminipro/gallery
- Sony Cinema Camera test footage: https://sony-cinematography.com/testfootage/, https://pro.sony/en_GB/cinematography/cinematography-tips/x-ocn-burano-8k-downloads, https://pro.sony/en_GB/cinematography/cinematography-tips/x-ocn-8k-download-form?cmp=scl-f23-pse-60094&sf177146761=1
- Arri Alexa Cine Camera test Camera footage: https://www.arri.com/en/learn-help/learn-help-camera-system/camera-sample-footage-reference-image#tab-294300
- Red Cinema Camera test footage: https://www.red.com/sample-r3d-files
- Blackmagic Design Powers More than forty Sundance 2025 Projects: https://www.blackmagicdesign.com/media/release/20250128-01
- More than thirty 2022 Summer Films Created with Blackmagic Design: https://www.blackmagicdesign.com/media/release/20220802-01
- Oscar-nominated films in 2021 that used DaVinci Resolve or Fusion: https://www.blackmagicdesign.com/uk/media/release/20210422-01
- Top Sundance films and TV series that use DaVinci Resolve: https://www.blackmagicdesign.com/media/release/20190129-02
- Indian Tamil-Language Film 'Soorarai Pottru' Graded Using DaVinci Resolve: http://www.content-technology.com/postproduction/indian-tamil-language-film-soorarai-pottru-graded-using-davinci-resolve-studio/
- Resolve used to grade Sundance films: https://magazine.artstation.com/2019/02/behind-the-scenes-sundances-top-films/
- Chinese Blockbuster The Eight Hundred Graded by Zhang Gen Using DaVinci Resolve: https://www.cinematography.world/chinese-blockbuster-the-eight-hundred-graded-by-zhang-gen-using-davinci-resolve-studio/
- Summer 2019's Biggest Film Releases Used Blackmagic Design: https://www.nexttv.com/post-type-the-wire/bmd-2019-summer-films
- Summer movie lineup benefits from Blackmagic Design: https://www.panoramaaudiovisual.com/pt/2021/08/30/summer-movie-lineup-blackmagic-design/

- Behind the scenes of creating the soundtrack for *Fight Club*: http://filmsound.org/studiosound/pp_fightclub.html
- Blackmagic Design Hyperdecks: https://www.blackmagicdesign.com/uk/products/hyperdeckstudio/models, https://www.blackmagicdesign.com/products/hyperdeckshuttlehd
- Aspect ratio: https://en.wikipedia.org/wiki/Aspect_ratio_(image)

Get this book's PDF version and more

2

Adding Titles, Transitions, and Simple Visual Effects

In this chapter, you will open the project you created in *Chapter 1* and learn how to share your project with other computers so that other people can also work on it. You will also enhance your video by adding a basic title and motion graphics using **Fusion FX** and transitions on the **Cut** page. Finally, you will save your favorite effects and transitions so that you can access them quickly for other projects.

In this chapter, we are going to cover the following main topics:

- Opening, saving, and sharing projects
- Transitions – moving from shot to shot
- Adding a title and changing it
- Adding visual effects

Technical requirements

To complete this chapter, you will need to have completed the exercises in *Chapter 1* to edit your first video using your own footage. Later in the book, I will supply you with footage that better illustrates the more advanced techniques in those chapters.

Opening, saving, and sharing projects

Before we start adding titles and effects to our video, let's look at how we can share our project with others so that they can work on it, or even just so that we can open it on another computer.

Whenever we need to save, archive, import, or export a project, we do this in the **Project Manager** (*Figure 2.1*):

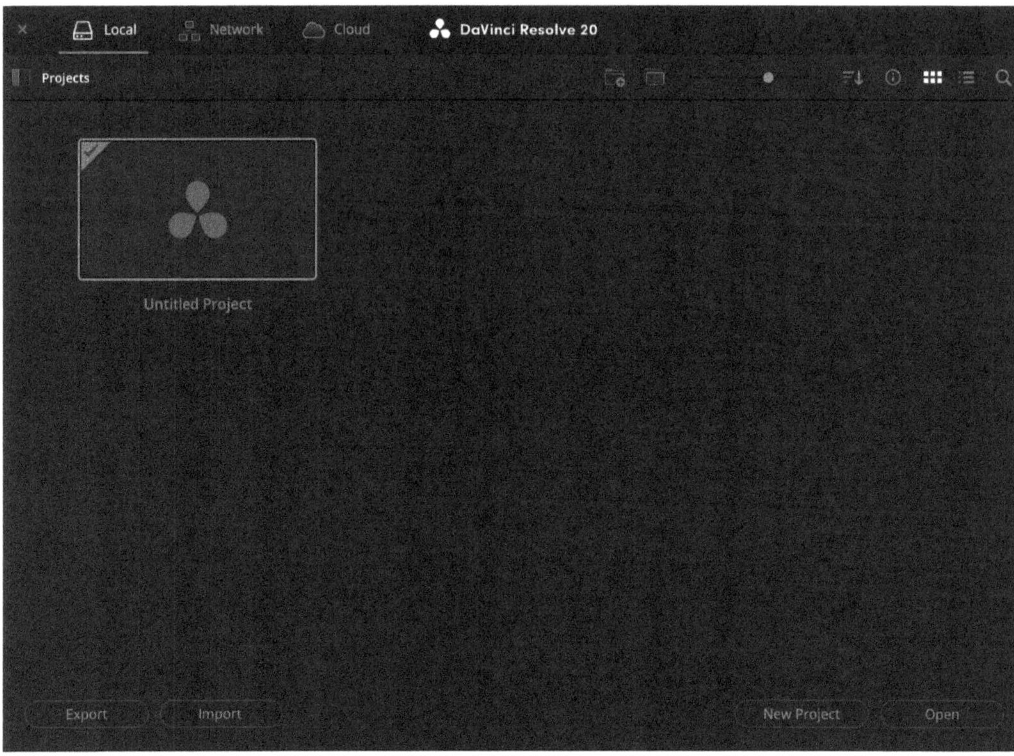

Figure 2.1: The Project Manager

In the **Project Manager**, there are various ways to share our project outside of our computer, each with its strengths and weaknesses. Let us look at each in turn.

> **Chapter requirements**
>
> For the exercises in this chapter, we will continue to work on the project we created in *Chapter 1*. If you have not completed *Chapter 1*, then I suggest that you quickly follow the exercises there so that you can get the most out of this chapter.

Exporting a project

In *Chapter 1*, we looked at how to create and save a new project, but we did not look at how we can access the project so that we can share it with others. You may have noticed that when we saved our project, it didn't ask us where on our computer to save it. That is because Resolve saves our project into a database (which it calls a **Project Library**) that contains all our projects, rather than saving it as a discrete file.

Thankfully, Resolve does let us export individual projects so that we can share them with others rather than sharing our entire database. This is all done via the **Project Manager**, where we can create, name, import, export, and archive our projects. Let us go there now:

1. If you are not already in the Project Manager, click on the **Project Manager** button (it looks like a house; see *Figure 2.2*) at the bottom right of the screen, below the **Timeline**.

Figure 2.2: The Project Manager button

2. Select a project you want to export.
3. Now, do one of the following:
    - Right-click on the project and select **Export Project...**
    - Click the **Export** button at the bottom left of the Project Manager (*Figure 2.1*)
4. Select where on your computer you want to save your project and click the **Save** button.

You have now saved your project, which you can share with others so that they can work on it. You can recognize a **DaVinci Resolve Project (drp)** file on your computer, as it uses the `.drp` file extension. A `drp` file only contains the project, which includes the bins and timelines, but it will not include the media – you will have to share this separately. After, you will need to relink the project to the media stored on another computer. Project files are great if someone else already has access to the media on their computer, since project files that don't contain media are smaller and easier to share via email.

Exporting a project archive

If you do want to share your media with the project file, creating a project archive is the best way to do it:

1. In the Project Manager, select a project you want to archive.
2. Right-click on the project and select **Export Project Archive....**
3. Select where on your computer you want to save your project archive and click the **Save** button.
4. On the **Archive** pop-up screen (*Figure 2.3*), select the checkboxes for the following options for the media you want to include in the archive:
   - **Media Files**
   - **Proxy Media**
   - **Render Cache**
5. Click **Ok**:

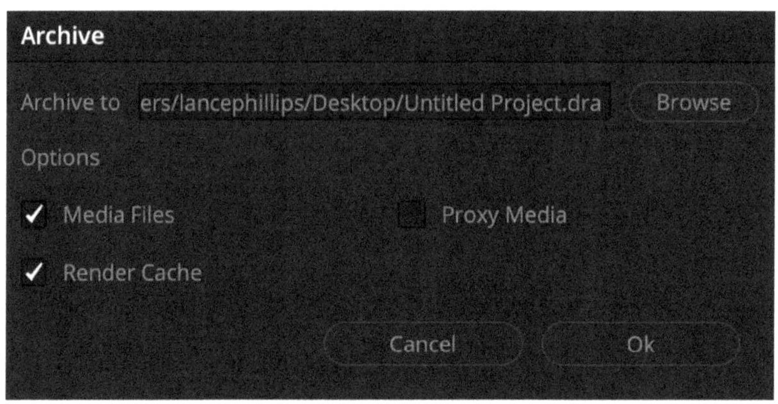

Figure 2.3: The Archive pop-up screen

You have now saved your project archive, which you can also share with others so that they can work on it. You can recognize a **DaVinci Resolve Archive (dra)** file on your computer, as it uses the `.dra` file extension. A `.dra` file contains the project file (`.drp`), which includes the bins and timelines, as well as all the media you imported into your project. So, project archive files are great if someone else does not already have access to the media; however, they can be rather large in file size, so you will need a separate hard drive to share them.

Importing a project

Of course, there is no point in knowing how to export a project if we don't know how to import one back in. Let us look at that now:

1. If you are not already in the Project Manager, click on the **Project Manager** button (it looks like a house) at the bottom right of the screen.
2. Now, do one of the following:
    - Click on the **Import** button at the bottom left of the Project Manager (*Figure 2.1*)
    - Right-click on an empty space in the Project Manager and select **Import Project...**
3. Select where on your computer you have a saved project file, select it, and click the **Open** button.

A copy of your imported project will now appear in the Project Manager.

Importing a project archive

Similarly, there is also no point in knowing how to export a project archive if we don't know how to import one back in. Let us look at that now:

1. If you are not already in the Project Manager, click on the **Project Manager** button (it looks like a house) at the bottom right of the screen.
2. Right-click on an empty space in the Project Manager and select **Restore Project Archive ....**
3. Select where on your computer you have a saved project archive file (`.dra`), select it, and click the **Open** button.

   Make sure to open the DaVinci Resolve Archive (`.dra`) file in DaVinci Resolve, not the project file (`.drp`) that is in the `.dra` folder. That way, all the video files will already be linked to the timeline.

A copy of your imported project will now appear in the Project Manager, complete with the media imported and linked up, ready for it to continue being worked on.

The main difference between a project file and an archive file is that the project file does not contain media, whereas the archive does. So, although the archive file already has all the media linked, how do we do this for a project file if it does not already know where the media is located on your computer?

Well, the solution is easy in Resolve.

Relinking media (version 17 onward)

If your media needs to be relinked, it will show up as red on your **Timeline**, the **Viewer,** and in your **Media Pool**:

1. New to version 17 of Resolve is a **Relink Media** button (*Figure 2.4*) just below the **Media Pool** heading; it will be red if the media is unlinked. Click this button:

Figure 2.4: The Relink Media button, which looks like a chain link

2. A **Relink Media** popup (*Figure 2.5*) will appear, giving you the option of locating the media files on your computer or getting Resolve to do a deep search on your computer to find them:

    - Click **Locate** if you know where on your computer your media is located, navigate to the folder location, select the folder, and click the **Open** button.
    - Click **Disk Search** and select the disk you want Resolve to search if you cannot remember where the media is located. This option will take longer:

Figure 2.5: The Relink Media popup

3. The media will now be relinked, and the red **Media Offline** warning sign on the clips and in the **Viewer** will be gone.

With that, we know how to share our projects with others as either project or archive files and relink the media if necessary.

Next, we will add some transitions to our existing edited video (or someone else's edited video they have shared with us) and customize them.

Transitions – moving from shot to shot

A **transition** is basically how we move from one clip to another. Apart from the basic cut, all transitions consist of two clips that overlap each other slightly.

As we move from one clip to the other, the first one gradually disappears, revealing the second clip underneath it. Transitions only vary in how they reveal the second clip underneath; for example, **Dissolve** slowly dissolves the first clip to reveal the second clip underneath it, whereas **Eye Iris** expands an eye-shaped hole in the first clip until the second clip is fully revealed.

This is an important concept to understand, as if there is no footage to overlap (that is, the edit points have no extra footage to draw upon), then the transition will not work. Resolve will show the edge of a clip as red if there is no room for a transition over that clip.

Our existing edited video used straight cuts as transitions, and 90% of the time, this suits our purposes. However, there may be an occasion when you need to add another type of transition to help enhance your story, such as a **Cross Dissolve** transition to show the passing of time.

On the **Cut** page, open the project you were working on in *Chapter 1*. If you want an extra challenge, import someone else's project so that you can add transitions to theirs.

Adding a **Cross Dissolve** transition is extremely easy on the **Cut** page; there is even a dedicated button for it above the timeline.

Transitions button (Cross Dissolve)

Let us add a **Cross Dissolve** transition to our timeline now:

1. Place your playhead near an existing cut where you want the transition to appear (for example, a transition between scenes). You will see the **Smart Indicators** bouncing up and down, showing you where the transition will go.
2. Select the **Dissolve** button (see *Figure 2.6*) above the timeline.

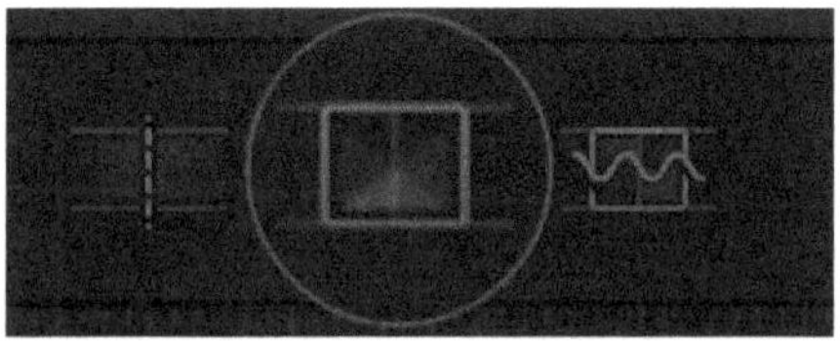

Figure 2.6: The Dissolve button

A **Cross Dissolve** transition will appear on your timeline.

The **Dissolve** button is a quick way to add the default **Cross Dissolve** transition to your timeline. However, if you want to have a more fancy transition, such as a Star Wars-style **wipe** or an 80s TV advert **starburst**, then you can find a variety of extras in the **Transitions** browser, above the **Media Pool**.

Transitions browser

Now, let us add some additional transitions to our timeline:

1. Select the **Transitions** browser (*Figure 2.7*) at the top left of the screen near the **Media Pool**. You will see several different transitions under the **Video** tab, grouped under the following headings:

   - **Dissolve**: The various **Dissolve** options listed here differ based on how they dissolve into the image/clip underneath. For example, **Dip To Color Dissolve** dissolves to a solid color first before dissolving again to the next clip:

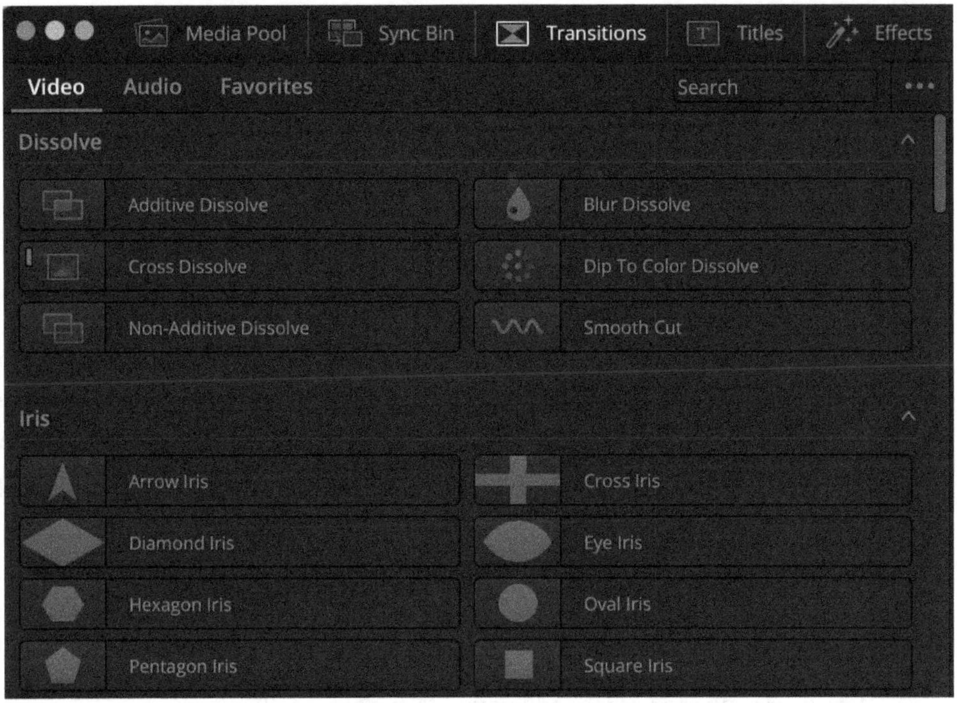

Figure 2.7: Transitions browser

- **Iris**: You can choose different shapes that open up (such as **Eye Iris**) to reveal the second clip underneath.
- **Motion**: Here, you can choose how the first clip moves out of the way to reveal the second clip (or the other way around). For example, using **Slide**, the second clip slides over the first clip to replace the first clip.
- **Shape**: Just like **Iris**, but with additional shapes that open up to reveal the second clip.
- **Wipe**: This is where the first clip is wiped away by the second clip. For example, with **Edge Wipe**, the second clip, starting from one edge, progressively replaces (wipes over) the first clip.
- **User**: This is where you can find your own transitions that you saved after customizing them. We cover how to do this later in this chapter.

- **Fusion Transitions**: These are advanced transitions that use more complex animations created in Fusion. For example, **Zoom In** zooms in on the first clip before dissolving to reveal the second clip. The main advantage of **Fusion Transitions** is that they can be further edited in Fusion by Fusion artists.
- **Resolve FX Color**: This uses effects from the **Color** page. At the time of writing, there is only one transition, called **DCTL Transition**, which uses **DaVinci Color-Space Transform Language** (**DCTL**) to transition between the clips. This is only for advanced users.
- **Resolve FX Stylize**: This uses graphic effects to enhance the transition. However, they cannot be edited on the **Fusion** page as they are not Fusion transitions (they are OpenFX). At the time of writing, there is only one transition, called **Burn Away**, where the first clip is burned away using an animated fire effect, revealing the second clip.

2. Choose a transition that suits the story you are telling. Less is more unless you are trying to emulate the style of a particular television period, such as by using 70s wipes or 80s starbursts.
3. With your playhead near the edit point, do one of the following:
   - Drag the transition directly onto your edit point (the point where two clips meet) on either the upper or lower timeline
   - Double-click the transition you selected in the **Transitions** browser

You will now have the transition you just selected on your timeline. Let us add it as a favorite transition so that we can quickly find it again.

Saving favorite transitions

Scrolling down a long list of transitions to be able to find your favorite one is time-consuming. To remedy this, we can mark transitions as favorites so that we can find them quickly in the future.

Let us add a regularly used transition as a favorite:

1. Select the **Transitions** browser at the top left of the screen near the **Media Pool**.
2. Click on the **Star** icon to the right of the transition you want to save to **Favorites**. The **Star** icon will be highlighted in white to show that it has been saved as a favorite.

At this point, you will notice that a copy of this transition has been added to the **Favorites** section in your **Transitions** browser. You should now be able to find this transition quickly, should you ever need to use it again.

Wouldn't it be great to adjust a transition and then save the changed version to the **Transitions** browser so that it can be used later?

Well, we can do that in Resolve, too.

Customizing transitions

Now that we know about the variety of ways we can apply a transition to our timeline, we can customize the duration and effect of our transition in the **Inspector**.

The **Inspector** is available on every page in Resolve apart from the **Color** and **Deliver** pages. It gives you access to more advanced settings for any element you have selected in the timeline, such as titles, transitions, or clips.

You can also toggle different settings available in the **Inspector** on or off by clicking on the red toggle switch next to each setting. This is great if you want to see the before and after results of a setting.

The reset arrows at the far right of each setting will change the setting back to its default settings in case you make too many changes.

Now, let us use the **Inspector** to customize our transitions:

1. On the timeline, select the transition that you want to change. It will be highlighted in orange to indicate that it has been selected.
2. Select the **Inspector** tab at the top right, above the viewer.
3. You will see options to change the **Video** or **Audio** transition settings.
4. Under the **Video** settings, you will see the following universal options:

    - **Transition Type**: Here, you can change the transition by selecting another transition from the drop-down list. These are the same transitions that are available in the **Transitions** tab.
    - **Duration**: **Seconds** and **Frames** – this is how long the transition lasts in total. You can change **Seconds** or **Frames** depending on what you prefer. Changing your frames will be more precise due to it being based on your timeline's frame rate, since the seconds can only be changed in 0.1 increments (that is, 1/24th of a second based on 24 FPS is a more precise measurement than 1/10th of a second).
    - **Alignment**: This is how the transition aligns between the two clips – covers the clip on the left, covers both clips, and covers the clip on the right.

- **Ease**: This changes the timing for a gradual start (**Ease In**) or end (**Ease Out**) of the transition, or both the start and end (**Ease In & Out**).
- **Transition Curve**: This is for adjusting the **Ease Custom** setting by keyframing the **Ease** animation. This is a more advanced setting and is only for those who want to have total control over the timing of their transition. Since this book is for beginners, it is beyond the scope of this book.

Other settings will also be available that are specific to the transition that is being applied.

5. Change some of the preceding settings to suit the style of your video, such as applying **Ease In & Out** and setting **Duration** to **3 seconds** to provide a smoother, more film-style look.
6. Click on the **Inspector** tab to close the **Inspector**.

Now that you have changed the settings of a transition, let us save this new, altered transition as a user-defined transition in the **Edit** page so that we can use it again later for other videos.

Saving customized transitions (Edit page feature)

Let us save this adapted transition so that we can use it again in the future:

1. Select the **Edit** page.
2. Right-click on the transition you want to save on the timeline.
3. Select **Create Transition Preset**.
4. Name your new transition preset in the **Enter Preset Name** dialog box and click the **OK** button to save it.

With that, you have made a transition on the timeline to suit your video footage and stored it for later use.

You can now find this transition on the **Cut** page in the **Transitions** tab by going to **Transitions** > **User**. It can also be found on the **Edit** page under **Effects Library** > **Toolbox** > **Video Transitions** > **User**.

Now that you have added all these transitions, you may be thinking, "How do I remove the transitions if I just want to go back to the basic cut?"

Removing transitions

There are two approaches to removing transitions. After selecting the transition on your **Timeline**, you can do one of two things:

- Press the *Delete* key on your keyboard

- Click the **Cut** button (*Figure 2.8*) above the timeline next to the **Dissolve** button:

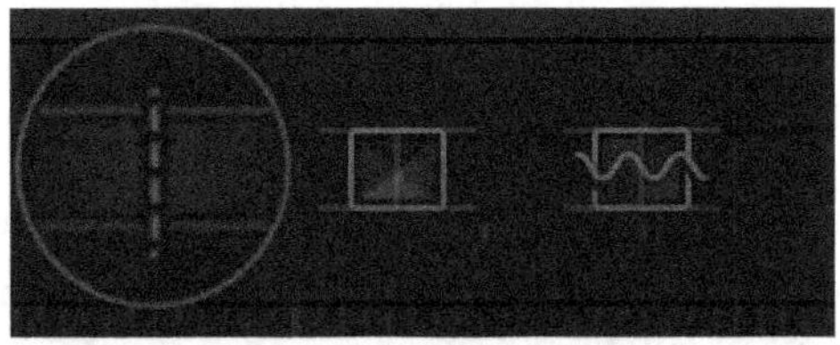

Figure 2.8: The Cut button

Both of these approaches will have the same result: removing the transition and reverting to a straight cut.

You can also remove several transitions at once by doing the following:

1. Press *Cmd* + *click* on several transition points on your timeline, in any order you choose.
2. Then, do either of the following:
    - Press the *Delete* key on your keyboard
    - Click the **Cut** button (*Figure 2.8*) above the timeline next to the **Dissolve** button

With that, you have removed several transitions at once so that you are ready to apply some different ones.

Your video is now flowing a bit better between each shot to help tell the story.

Next, we will introduce the subject of our video by adding a title to our existing edited video (or someone else's edited video) and customizing it.

Adding a title and changing it

On the **Cut** page, open the project you were working on in *Chapter 1*. If you want an extra challenge, import someone else's project so that you can add titles to theirs.

There are many different types of titles:

- Some appear on a black (or a solid color of choice) background before any clips are seen
- Some appear over the top of clips, where we can see the footage behind the title
- Some are called **lower thirds** and appear on the bottom of the screen, introducing the name of the speaker or video location
- Some are called **credits**, where all those who helped make the video are credited by having their name and contributions listed at the end of the video

Whichever title you choose (you are likely to use more than one), adding a title is extremely easy on the **Cut** page; there is even a special tab for it called **Titles**.

Let us add a title to our timeline:

1. Select the **Titles** browser at the top left of the screen, next to **Transitions** (*Figure 2.9*):

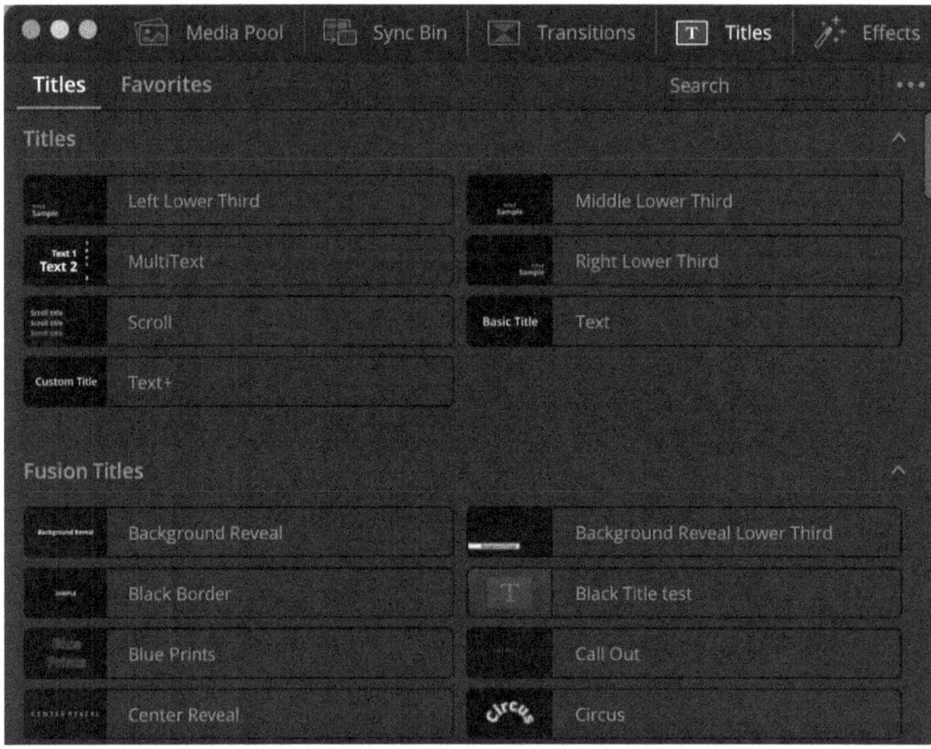

Figure 2.9: Titles browser

2. A list of possible titles will appear:

    - **Titles** contains basic titles that you can use. They are good for low-performing or older computers.
    - **Fusion Titles** contains title templates that use Resolve's powerful animation and compositing tool, Fusion.

3. Select the title you want and drag it down to your timeline:
    - If you drag it onto Track 1, then the title will write over and replace existing clips on the timeline
    - If you drag it onto Track 2, then the title will be overlaid on top of the footage on Track 1

You should now have a blank title on your timeline. Next, we will look at the differences between basic titles and Fusion titles.

Basic titles

Standard titles are less graphically intensive as they have fewer options, so they are good for older, less powerful computers. They are also good if you want to do something basic very quickly or create **temporary** (**temp**) titles for the client while someone else is creating them in Fusion. They will also play back smoother on the timeline. Let us look at the options one of the standard titles, **Basic Title**, provides:

1. Put a regular **Basic Title** on your timeline as described previously.
2. Click on the **Inspector** to reveal the **Basic Title**'s options.
3. In the textbox labeled **Rich Text**, type over **Sample Text** to add your own title (for example, `My First Film`). You will be able to adjust the look of your title's text by changing any of the following **Rich Text** settings (common to any word processing software):
    - **Font Family**: This drop-down list will reveal all the available fonts that have been installed on your computer.
    - **Font Face**: Depending on the font selected, you will also be able to select whether you want it to be **Bold**, **Italic**, and so on.
    - **Color**: Here, you can use a color picker to change the color of your text.
    - **Size**: This is a slider for the font size.
    - **Tracking**: This is for the size of the space between each letter.
    - **Line Spacing**: This is the amount of space between each line of text.
    - **Font Style**: This has buttons to apply underline, overhead line, strikethrough, superscript, and subscript styling.
    - **Font Case**: This is a drop-down list where you can select whether your text is **Mixed** (default setting), **All Caps**, **All Lowercase**, **Small Caps**, or **Title Caps**.

- **Alignment**: You can use various buttons to align the text against an edge – for example, **Left**, **Center**, **Right**, or **Justified** (both left and right edges).
- **Anchor**: You can use various buttons to select how text is anchored to the current position of the text in the frame, which, by default, is the center of the frame. You can adjust the anchor both horizontally (top, centered, and bottom) and vertically (right, centered, and left).
- **Position X, Y**: This adjusts the center position of the block of text. The **X** value moves the block of text left and right, whereas the **Y** value moves the text up and down. The bottom left corner of the frame, in *X, Y* coordinates, is (0,0). Position controls can also be found in the **Tools** button, below the viewer (more on this later).
- **Zoom X, Y**: This adjusts the **Zoom** position of the block of text. The **X** and **Y** values are linked together by default. The value of **1** is the original size of the text, as set under **Font Size**; values higher than **1** are zoomed in, and values lower than **1** are zoomed out. You can click the **Link** button (the small chain symbol between the **X** and **Y** values) to unlink the **Zoom** values. Unlinking the **Zoom** values enables you to stretch or squeeze the text vertically (**Y**) or horizontally (**X**). Zoom controls can also be found in the **Tools** button, below the viewer (more on this later).
- **Rotation Angle**: This slider rotates the text 360 degrees around the center of the textbox. **Rotation Angle** controls can also be found in the **Tools** button, below the viewer (more on this later).

As you can see, there are several ways to adjust the **Title** text in the **Inspector**, but before we look at the options for **Stroke**, **Drop Shadow**, and **Background**, let us look at other ways we can adjust the position, zoom, and rotation of the **Title** text without using the **Inspector**.

Using the Tools button and onscreen text controls

Underneath the viewer, there is a **Tools** button (*Figure 2.10*), which, like the **Inspector**, reveals extra tools you can use to adjust any element on the timeline. We used the **Tools** button in *Chapter 1* to reveal the **Transform** controls so that we could resize our video footage.

In this case, we will look at the tools we can use to move the **Title** text:

1. Make sure the title you want to adjust has been selected on the timeline. It will be highlighted in orange to show that it has been selected.
2. Click on the **Tools** button under the viewer at the bottom left:

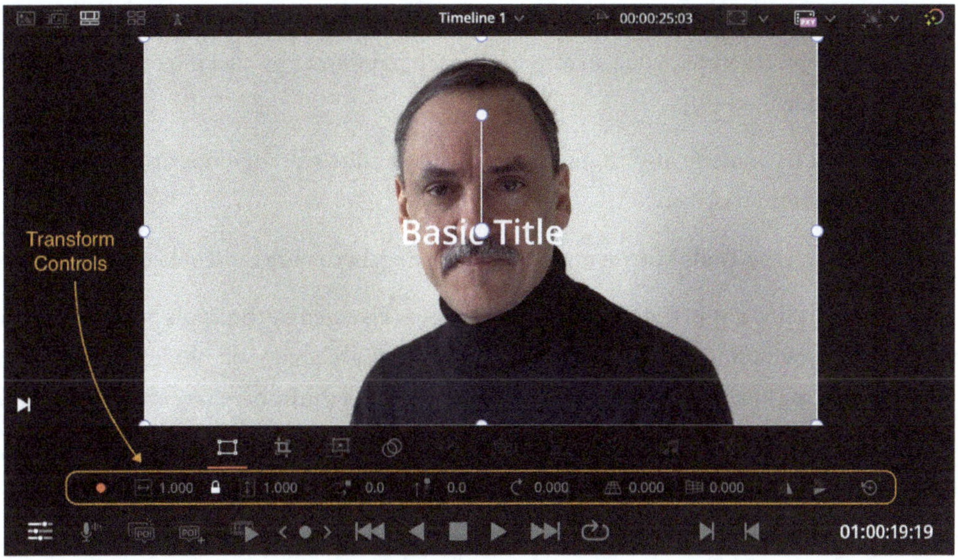

Figure 2.10: Frame bounding box and Transform controls

3. This will reveal different tools under the viewer that you can use to make basic changes to any timeline element that you have selected. Let us look at the first set of tools, called the **Transform** controls (*Figure 2.10*); these can also be found in the **Inspector** under the **Settings** tab.

    - **Toggle switch**: This toggles the controls on and off.
    - **Zoom Width** and **Height**: These first sliders (**Zoom Height** and **Width**) are the **Zoom** sliders and operate the same way as they do in the **Inspector**. Clicking the **Padlock** icon unlinks the **Zoom X, Y** values, enabling you to change the aspect ratio of the text.
    - **Position X**: This slider moves the text left and right along the *X* axis.
    - **Position Y**: This slider moves the text up and down along the *Y* axis.
    - **Rotation Angle**: This slider rotates the text around the center of the text.
    - **Pitch**: This slider changes the vertical angle of the **Title** text (just like the introductory titles in the Star Wars films).
    - **Yaw**: This slider changes the horizontal angle of the **Title** text.
    - **Flip Horizontal**: This button flips the text horizontally.
    - **Flip Vertical**: This button flips the text vertically.

As usual, you can undo all of the changes you made by clicking on the **Undo** arrow on the far right. However, you can also undo each parameter by clicking on its icon just before the slider.

If you have made any changes, you will see a little orange dot at the top right of the **Transform** tool icon.

4. Click on the **Tools** button under the viewer again to hide the **Tools** controls.

When you adjusted any of the **Transform** controls, as revealed by the **Tools** button, you may have noticed that a bounding box (*Figure 2.10*) appeared around the edge of the viewer. You can also use this to adjust the **Position**, **Zoom**, and **Rotation** settings of the frame that contains the whole title.

Independent of the **Transform** controls, you can also change the **Position**, **Zoom**, and **Rotation** value of the **Title** text directly in the viewer. Without needing to use the **Tools** button, click directly on the title in the viewer and use the same onscreen controls to move the text bounding box (*Figure 2.11*):

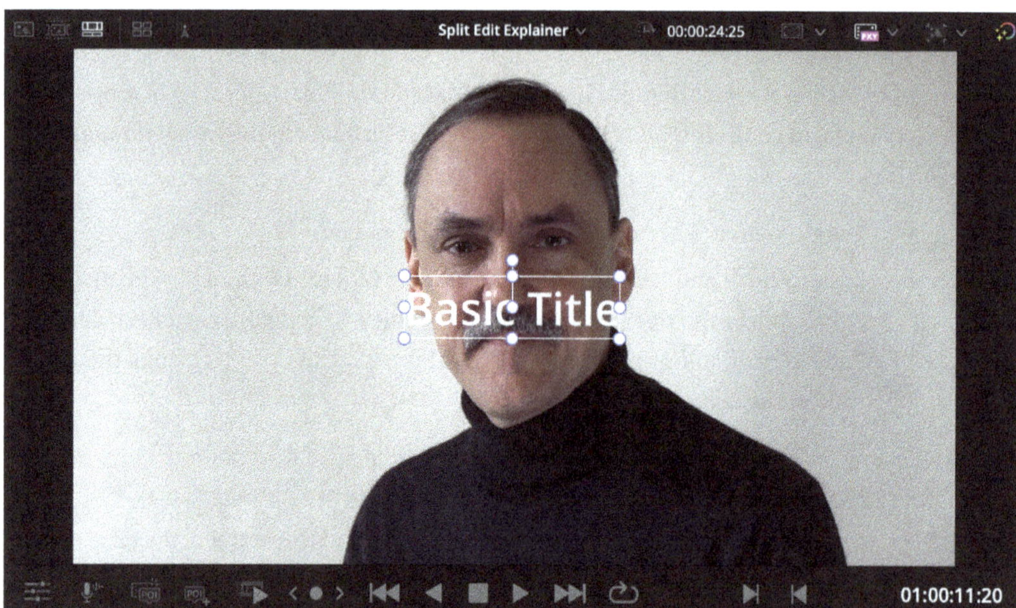

Figure 2.11: Title text bounding box on screen resizing controls

Here are the options that are available when you are using the onscreen controls of whichever method you choose:

- **Position**: Click within the box and drag to move the text's position.
- **Rotation Angle**: Click on the circle above the vertical line coming from the top of the text and drag it to the left or right to rotate the text.
- **Zoom**: Click on a corner and drag to zoom in or out. This will keep the *X* and *Y* dimensions of the text linked.
- **Zoom Height**: Click and drag on the small box or circle on the top or bottom edge of the bounding box to change the zoom height.
- **Zoom Width**: Click and drag onto the small box or circle on the left or right edge of the bounding box to change the zoom width.

> The **Transform** controls in the **Tool** button (and the **Inspector**), and the onscreen viewer controls (and **Rich Text** position controls) operate independently of each other.

This means resetting one will not reset changes in the other. This is because the **Transform** controls in the **Tool** panel and the **Inspector** change the position and size of the whole frame that contains the title, whereas the **Text** controls in the **Inspector** and the onscreen viewer controls affect only the box directly around the text itself.

Now that we have mastered the onscreen viewer controls to resize or transform our title, we can return to the **Inspector**, where we will look at the options to help our title text stand out from its background.

Stroke controls

In the **Inspector** tab, under the **Video** tab and then the **Title** tab, below the **Rich Text** settings, you will find the **Stroke** controls. So, the pathway is **Inspector** > **Video** > **Title** > **Rich Text** > **Stroke**.

If you cannot find the **Stroke** controls, you will need to click **Rich Text** to reveal the **Rich Text** controls, then click **Stroke** to reveal the **Stroke** controls. There are only three **Stroke** controls:

- **Color**: Clicking on the color swatch gives you the option to change the color of the outside edge (stroke) of each character of your text
- **Size**: This slider changes the size of the stroke, making it thicker or thinner (measured in pixels)

- **Outside Only**: Selecting this checkbox adds the stroke to the outside of the text without eroding the shape of the original text

You can use the **Stroke** controls to change the outline border of your text to make it stand out from the background, particularly if it is overlaid over a video image.

Another way to help your title be seen against a video background is to add a **Drop Shadow** effect.

Drop Shadow controls

Beneath the **Stroke** controls, you will find the **Drop Shadow** controls. If you cannot see them, click on the **Drop Shadow** heading to reveal them:

- **Color**: Clicking on the color switch gives you the option to change the color of the shadow of each character of your text.
- **Offset**: This slider and value box change the position of the shadow relative to the text. The default is **0** for both **X** and **Y**, which shows no shadow:
    - **Offset X**: Negative **X** values make the shadow appear from the left, whereas positive **X** values make the shadow appear to the right
    - **Offset Y**: Negative **Y** values make the shadow appear from below, whereas positive **Y** values make the shadow appear from above
- **Blur**: This slider changes the blur of the shadow so that it has a softer or more defined edge.
- **Opacity**: This slider changes how see-through or transparent the shadow is to the image behind it. A value of **0** is completely transparent, whereas a value of **100** is completely solid.

If used well, **Drop Shadow** can help the text stand out from the video background without it being too obvious.

Of course, an even more noticeable way to help your title stand out from your video is to add a block background to mask the video directly behind the **Title** text.

Background controls

Beneath the **Drop Shadow** controls, you will find the **Background** controls. If you cannot see them, click on the **Background** heading to reveal them:

- **Color**: Clicking on the color switch gives you the option to change the color of the background box behind your title.
- **Outline Color**: Clicking on the color swatch gives you the option to change the outline color of the background box behind your title.
- **Outline Width**: This slider changes the size of the outline, making it thicker or thinner (measured in pixels).
- **Width**: This slider changes the width of the background box.
- **Height**: This slider changes the height of the background box.
- **Corner Radius**: This slider changes the roundness of the background box's corners.
- **Center X and Y**: This slider and value box change the position of the background box relative to the center of the text. The default is **0** for both **X** and **Y**.
- **Opacity**: This slider changes how see-through or transparent the background box is to the image behind it. A value of **0** is completely transparent, whereas a value of **100** is completely solid.

Basic Title supports **Rich Text Format** (**RTF**) editing, which means we can change the formatting of individual letters and words in the title as we would in any text editor.

There is another option to create titles, called **Text+**; this enables more options for animation, which is great for motion graphics. However, it does not support RTF editing, so you can only apply one style to the whole block of text. Let us look at **Text+** titles in more detail.

Text+ titles

Although **Text+** is under the regular **Titles** section, it is a **Fusion Title** and, as such, can be edited in Fusion, unlike the rest of the regular titles.

Let us look at some of the extra options the **Text+** title gives us:

1. Put a **Text+** title on your timeline, as described previously.
2. Click on the **Inspector** tab to reveal the title options.

In addition to the settings available for the basic title, a **Text+** title has additional options laid out under tabs to the right of the usual **Text** options (*Figure 2.12*):

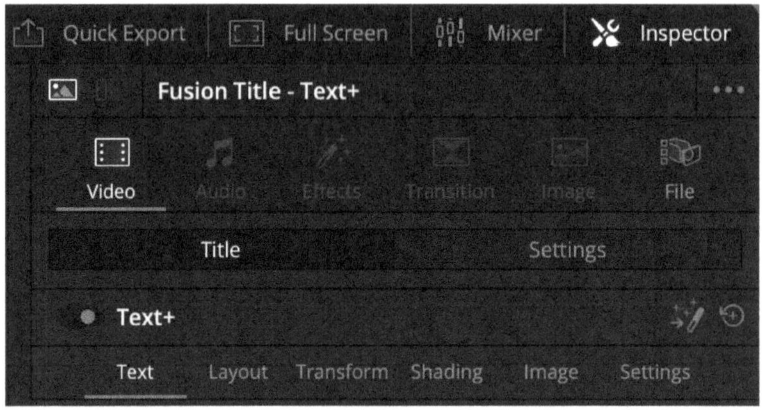

Figure 2.12: Text+ tabs

3. Clicking on a tab will reveal extra options you can use to change your title; the tab will be underlined in orange to show that it has been selected. Here are some of the tabs you will encounter:

    - **Text**: In addition to the same options you found with the basic title, the **Text** tab contains the following:

        - **Direction**: The order in which each character on a line starts. This is great for titles in Asian languages that read from right to left.
        - **Line Direction**: This is the order of each line of the title if it has more than one line – that is, the first line becomes the bottom line, and the title reads from the bottom of the page.
        - **Write On**: Using keyframes, this animates the start and end of the **Title** text that appears on the screen so that individual letters can appear one at a time.

    - **Tab Spacing**: This controls the horizontal positions and alignment of eight separate tab stops, like in any word processor. If you copy and paste text from a word processor document that has tab positions in it, the text will align to these tab settings. This is useful for quickly creating a two-column credits title.

- **Layout**: This tab contains settings that change the layout of the animated text (to a point, frame, circle, or path), rotate the text in a 3D space, or change the color of the background.
- **Transform**: This tab contains controls to change the spacing and pivot point of the title's characters, words, or lines. It also contains controls to change the shear and size of the title on the *X* and *Y* axis, as well as the title's rotation in a 3D space (that is, its *X*, *Y*, and *Z* values).
- **Shading**: This tab contains eight elements that change the text outline, border, shadow, and fill color of the title text. The first four elements (1 to 4) already have presets that you can change or use as-is. The last four (elements 5 to 8) are blank and ready for you to change and name them as you wish. Like the **Transform** controls, there are **Shear**, **Size**, and **Rotation** controls, which control the position of the text outline or fill, shadow, or border, depending upon which element you have selected.
- **Image**: This is an advanced setting that changes the resolution, interlacing, gamma, and color space of each frame "image" of the title.
- **Settings**: These are more advanced settings that allow you to apply masks and **Motion Blur** to your title.

All of these **Text+** settings can be combined and animated using keyframes, which makes this a much more powerful tool compared to the usual **Text Title** generator. In reality, you will probably only change a select few settings to enhance your title. Change one setting at a time to see the effect it has before changing the next one; as they say, "less is more."

The Slider Undo button

If an individual slider has its settings changed from the default value, a little white dot (reset button) will appear under the slider as a visual cue to show that the setting has changed. See *Figure 2.13*, where the reset button has appeared under the text **Size** slider.

If you get too carried away and just want to reset the last setting you changed, you can click on this little white dot underneath the settings slider. This will reset that setting back to its default value. Note that the default value is not always zero. With some effects, such as Fusion FX, the default value is a preset value for the effect as a starting point for when the effect is first applied:

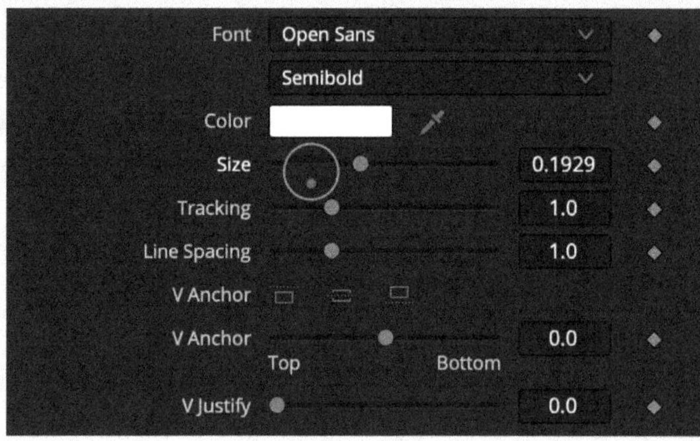

Figure 2.13: Slider value reset button

Now that we have looked at some of the extra functionality that Fusion brings to the **Text+** title, let us look at dedicated **Fusion titles**.

Fusion Titles

Fusion Titles allow us to do a lot more, such as animate titles and create some simple motion graphics. They also have the advantage that they can be edited directly on the **Fusion** page to create even more advanced and customized effects.

You can recognize a **Fusion Title** (including **Text+**) on the timeline by the small **Fusion** icon (*Figure 2.14*) to the bottom left of the title:

Figure 2.14: Fusion Title icon

Let us look at some of the extra options that **Fusion Titles** give us:

1. Put a **Fusion Title** on your timeline as described at the start of the *Adding a title and changing it* section.
2. Click on the **Inspector** tab to reveal the title's options.

   Most **Fusion Titles** will only allow you to change the basic aspects of the text, such as **Font**, **Size**, **Position**, and **Color**. The animation effects are all changed and controlled within Fusion. Think of **Fusion Titles** as presets that are samples of the power you can unlock within Fusion.

   Some **Fusion Titles** will have limited additional options, which is usually due to the specific effect that Fusion is applying to the title.

   Here are some of the options you may encounter:

   - **Large Text**: Change the format of the large text in an animated title or lower thirds
   - **Small Text**: Change the format of the small text in an animated title or lower thirds

> **Key concept – lower thirds**
>
> **Lower thirds** are titles that are placed in the lower third of the screen. They are usually used to display someone's name and job title or the location of a scene. Of course, where you place them is up to you. This is something you can do using the **Transform** controls in the **Inspector**.

Now that you have chosen your title, adjusted it, and helped it stand out from your background, just like transitions, you can save it as a favorite so that you can use it later.

Saving titles as favorites

Let us add a regularly used title as a favorite. This is the same approach regardless of whether it is a standard **Title** or a **Fusion Title**:

1. Select the **Titles** tab at the top left of the screen, near the **Media Pool**.
2. Hover your mouse cursor over the title you want to save to **Favorites**. A *star* icon will appear to the right of the title you want to save.
3. Click on the *star* icon. The *star* icon will be highlighted in white to show that it has been saved as a favorite.

You will notice that a copy of this title has been added to the **Favorites** section in your **Titles** tab. You should now be able to find this title quickly, should you ever need to use it again.

As you can see, there are some basic customization options that we can use on the text of titles. However, if you want to animate your titles, it is better to choose a **Fusion Title**.

Saving titles as templates

Unlike transitions, there is no direct way to save your customized titles for future use on the **Cut** page. To be able to save a title directly in the **Title** tab, you need to open it in **Fusion** and save it as a macro. This does require a more advanced understanding of Fusion, which is beyond the scope of this book and what most videographers have time to learn.

However, there is an easier way to save your customized titles for future use: go to the **Edit** page and drag the title from the timeline into the **Media Pool**. This will create a copy of your title in the **Media Pool**, which you can then drag onto any timeline.

All titles are recognizable on the timeline by the **Title** icon in the lower-left corner of the clip (*Figure 2.14*).

Now that you have gained a better understanding of the differences between regular **Titles** and **Fusion Titles** and put them onto your timeline, let us look at using some Fusion effects to enhance your video even more.

Adding visual effects

Resolve has two types of effects you can use to enhance your videos: **Fusion effects** and **Resolve effects**. Fusion effects are Fusion templates that are created in Fusion and can be further edited in Fusion, whereas Resolve effects are plugins that use the **OpenFX** standard.

So, you don't need to be a visual effects expert to apply some basic effects to your video.

This section will provide an overview of the different types of premade effects available in Resolve. All of these effects can be applied by dragging them onto a clip on the timeline. You can also add effects by clicking the **Add Effect** button that appears at the bottom of the **Effects** browser once it has been selected (*Figure 2.15*):

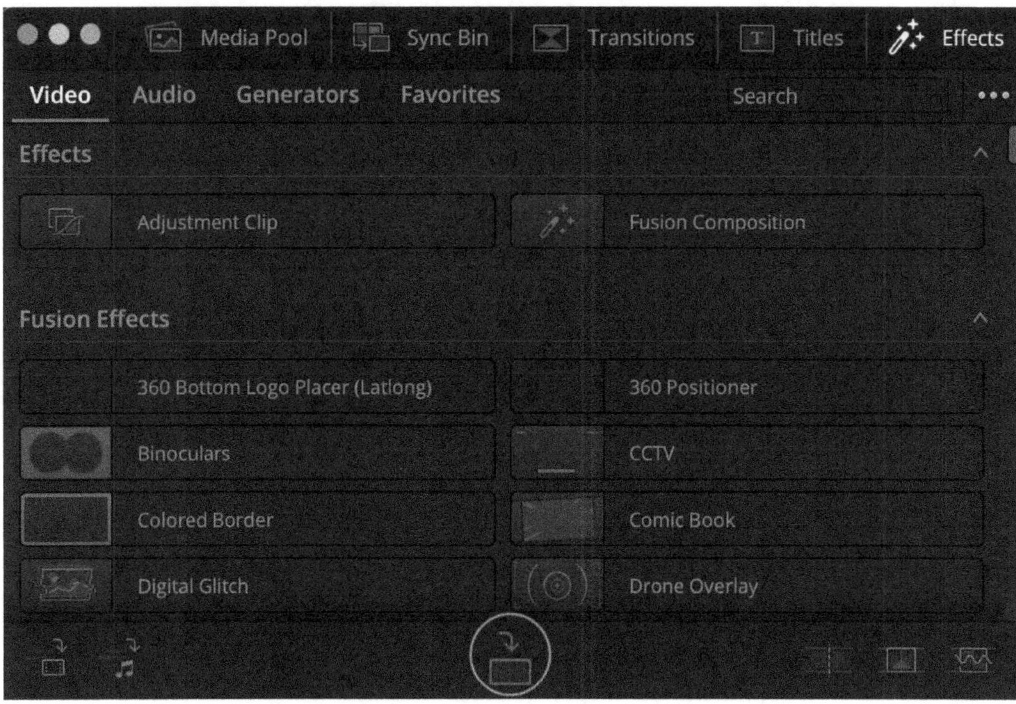

Figure 2.15: The Add Effect button

Select the **Effects** browser tab at the top left of the screen near the **Media Pool**. You will see several different effects under the **Video** tab, grouped under the following headings (*Figure 2.15*):

- **Effects**: These are placeholder clips that can be dragged onto the timeline, just like any other video clip. You can also add effects by clicking the **Add Effect** button that appears at the bottom of the **Effects** browser. There are only two choices here:
    - **Adjustment Clip** allows you to make adjustments to it that will change the underlying tracks. This is good if you want to apply one effect across multiple clips on the timeline, rather than apply the same effect separately to more than one clip. Alternatively, you could add an adjustment clip to apply an effect for only part of a clip by making the adjustment clip shorter than the clip underneath. To do this, you can simply apply (double-click or drag) any effect onto the adjustment clip rather than the clips underneath.
    - **Fusion Composition** is a clip that is edited in Fusion to create a more advanced composite than you can achieve in the timeline. It's great for adding Fusion titles that you create directly in Fusion.
- **Fusion Effects**: As the name implies, these effects are premade in Fusion. You can adjust these effects in the **Inspector**, or for more advanced options, you can edit them directly in Fusion. To apply these effects, you can do either of the following:
    - Place your playhead over a clip on the timeline, and then double-click on a Fusion effect to apply it to the clip
    - Drag a Fusion effect directly onto a clip on the timeline

  The **Fusion** icon (*Figure 2.14*) appears on the clip to show that a Fusion effect has been applied to it.

The following effects are not Fusion effects but Resolve effects (based on the OpenFX standard), which means they cannot be edited in Fusion.

Resolve effects are applied to a clip in the same way a Fusion effect is applied. When a Resolve (or OpenFX) effect is applied to a clip, an **OpenFX** icon is shown (*Figure 2.14*). You can also combine both Fusion and Resolve effects onto the same clip (or even a title) and adjust them both in the **Inspector**:

- **Resolve FX Blur**: These effects apply various styles of **Blur** effects to the clips.

- **Resolve FX Color**: These are various preset **Color** effects borrowed from the **Color** page. This is more useful for professional color processing, as you don't need to use **Resolve Color Management** on the **Color** page.
- **Resolve FX Film Emulation**: New to DaVinci Resolve 19, these are a series of effects that can be applied to your clips to emulate the look of analog film – that is, **Film Grain** or the new **Film Look Creator.**
- **Resolve FX Generate**: These effects generate images that interact with the footage underneath:
    - **Color Generator** generates a single color that can be used as a color filter over the footage by adjusting the blend of the color chosen, with the image below.
    - **Grid** creates a customizable grid overlay.
    - **Color Palette** (Studio version only) creates a color palette overlay from the key dominant colors in the video footage. This is good for analyzing the colors of a scene, so it's great as a starting point for creating graphics that tonally match the footage.
- **Resolve FX Key**: These effects help remove ("key" out) backgrounds and create video layers on top of each other ("composites"). The keyers only differ in the way that they select the background to be able to remove it to make that part of the video transparent to the video layer underneath:
    - **3D Keyer** removes color, such as from a green or blue screen.
    - **HSL Keyer** (**HSL** stands for **Hue, Saturation, and Luminance**) uses a mixture of color (**Hue**), color strength (**Saturation**), and brightness (**Luminance**) to key out the background.
    - **Luminance Keyer** only uses the luminance of an image, not color, to remove the background. For example, this can remove a bright blue sky over a dark blue ocean. A color-based key would not be able to do this successfully because the colors are too similar.
    - **Alpha Matte Shrink and Grow** is used to refine the matte created by the other keyers.

If you do not understand the concept of keyers, mattes, and composites, do not worry – we will explain this in more detail later in this book.

- **Resolve FX Light**: These effects mimic the way that light works with the atmosphere or the camera lens to give a particular look, such as **Lens Flair** (Studio version only) or **Light Rays** (also known to photographers as God rays).
- **Resolve FX Refine**: The **Beauty** effect (Studio version only) allows you to soften the image, much like the **Beauty** filter that photographers use, or in the early days of cinema, where they would smear Vaseline over the lens to soften the image when filming their "leading lady."
- **Resolve FX Revival**: These Studio version-only effects let you fix damaged or poor-quality footage.
- **Resolve FX Sharpen**: These Studio version-only effects give you detailed controls to sharpen specific parts of your video footage.
- **Resolve FX Stylize**: These effects add creative, artistic looks to your footage, such as **Mirrors** to create a kaleidoscope effect in your footage.
- **Resolve FX Temporal**: These effects change the footage over time (temporal). For example, the **Stop Motion** effect creates a stop-motion stuttering effect for live-action footage.
- **Resolve FX Texture**: These effects add textures to your footage. For example, **Analog Damage** recreates the look of an old-style TV, VHS video, or security camera.
- **Resolve FX Transform**: These effects can resize or move (transform) your video either by itself or as a layer over another video. This is good for picture-in-picture effects. We will cover these tools later in this book.
- **Resolve FX Warp**: These effects distort (warp) the image in different ways. For example, **Ripples** will create a water-like ripple through the footage, as if a stone has been thrown into a pond.

With all these effects, you can add more than one effect to the same clip. For example, you could combine the **Binoculars** and **Night Vision** Fusion effects to give the effect of night-vision goggles. You can also use Resolve and Fusion effects together.

You now have an overall understanding of the range of different types of effects available in Resolve. We will show you how to use specific effects from this range in more detail later in this book. However, the best way to understand the wide range of preset effects available is to have fun playing around with them, adding one effect at a time and seeing what they do.

For more advanced users, you can create your own effects in Fusion. However, if you don't have time, you can purchase and import OpenFX plugins into Resolve to add more effects to the effects that are already built into Resolve.

Hopefully, you now have a better understanding of the different options available to you so that you can add titles, transitions, and effects to your video in Resolve.

Summary

Here is what you have achieved in this chapter:

- Learned how to open an existing project and export and import it so that it can be used on other computers or shared with others
- Added a title and customized it
- Added transitions and customized them
- Added visual effects and adjusted them
- Gained an overview of all the effects available and their categories
- Saved your favorite titles, transitions, and effects so that you can access them quickly later

In *Chapter 3*, we will make the video you edited in *Chapters 1* and *2* sound better. We will do this by adding separately recorded sound, syncing it with the video, and fixing and enhancing the sound with built-in and imported audio effects. We will also look at some basic sound theory, such as microphone choice and placement, so that we get the best quality sound in the first place.

Questions

Answer the following questions to test your knowledge of this chapter:

1. True or false? Exporting a `drp` file allows you to work on your Resolve project on another computer without the need to import any media files.
2. True or false? You can only have one font type with **Text** titles, whereas **Text+** titles allow you to use more than one font type in the title.
3. Which default transition is allocated to the **Transition** button? Choose the correct answer:

    a. **Star Burst**

    b. **Star Dissolve**

    c. **Star Wipe**

    d. **Happy Wipe**

    e. **Cross Dissolve**

4. True or false? Saving your favorite title, transition, or effect is as easy as clicking the little *star* icon to the right of its name.

Further reading

More information about the OpenFX standard that DaVinci Resolve uses for visual effects plugins, as well as a list of companies that support it and make plugins for it, can be found here: `http://openeffects.org`.

For some example videos and websites about titles that can inspire you, look at the following:

- Art of the Title: `https://www.artofthetitle.com/`
- The graphic art of film title design throughout cinema history: `https://www.canva.com/learn/film-titles/`
- Get Inspired by 5 Great Film Title Designers: `https://www.ideo.com/journal/get-inspired-by-5-great-film-title-designers`
- The Top 10 Best Designed Movie Title Sequences: `https://www.bluecompass.com/blog/the-8-best-designed-title-sequences`
- Title Design: The Making of Movie Titles: `https://youtu.be/Ggw8Gqi4-Z0?si=FlV9fmAjx6e2vQFd`
- 10 Best Opening Title Sequences of All Time: `https://youtu.be/i8twthdaqB8?si=VrFuwhs5kxat-uRw`
- Opening Credits: How TV's Title Sequences Grew Up: `https://youtu.be/rdtmaqVvWlA?si=iigHbJk_fGQYEar3`
- Saul Bass and the art of movie title design: `https://youtu.be/Q_Mo0MqICXI?si=mdO1elqh2sgEXKKC`
- How Pablo Ferro revolutionized movie title design: `https://youtu.be/OQygyWx0dqs?si=PKhieB6xLBOBErht`
- How Kyle Cooper changed movie credits sequences: `https://youtu.be/knUXwj4Bu1U?si=J_Kmc-kAd3SADGM6`
- The Art of Film & TV Title Design: `https://youtu.be/qbhi-JICKKI?si=zguSB-qsYyACQVX7`
- History of Film Title Design & Typography: `https://youtu.be/fJJwBv4GAQ8?si=Ihf9nCCd1FmEF6Th`

Get this book's PDF version and more

Scan the QR code (or go to `packtpub.com/unlock`). Search for this book by name, confirm the edition, and then follow the steps on the page.

UNLOCK NOW

Note: Keep your invoice handy. Purchases made directly from Packt don't require an invoice.

3

Polishing the Camera Audio – Getting It in Sync

In this chapter, we will look at how recording separate audio can improve your video and how Resolve makes it easy to sync separate sound to your video. We will also look at how we can fix and enhance our audio quickly using **Fairlight** and **AU Effects** plugins.

We are going to cover the following main topics:

- Understanding sound and different ways to record it
- Syncing audio
- Fixing sound using Fairlight FX
- Using AI Dialogue Leveler

Technical requirements

To follow along with the fixing sound exercises in this chapter, download the `Fix_Sound.mp3` sound file and import it into a new project, naming the project `Fixing_Sound`.

You can download the sound file here: `https://packt.link/gbz/9781836208839`

For these exercises, you will be fixing an audio-only file that you have placed on the timeline. The techniques you will learn will apply equally to audio attached to video clips.

Understanding sound and different ways to record it

It is said that sound is the often-forgotten part of the filmmaking process. We often, at our own peril, believe that film is a visual medium and dedicate all our effort to getting the best picture possible, then forget about sound until the last minute. However, video is both a visual and an audio medium. Even the *silent* era of early film was accompanied by live music performed in the cinema to enhance the emotion of the story.

Without sound, a film or video is a lot harder to understand. Poor sound makes it unwatchable. You are more likely to switch off a TV program if the sound is poor or unintelligible than if the visuals are technically poor. Whether it be the low-resolution images of *The Blair Witch Project* or the dimly lit scenes in *Game of Thrones*, we will watch these programs quite happily if we can clearly hear what is going on, even if we can't see it.

At the very least, if sound is 50% of the video experience, then we should dedicate a bit more time to it.

If we start from the shared understanding that sound is important and that it should not be an afterthought, then let us look at what we need to know to capture the best quality sound that we can before we even edit it in Resolve. To do that, we need to understand what sound is.

The properties of sound

Sound is essentially air pressure moving through the space around us as waves.

Just like waves on the sea rise and fall depending upon the amount of force behind them, sound works in the same way. To illustrate this, place your hand over the speaker of your phone or stereo when it is loud and full of bass, and you will feel the pressure of the air being pushed against your hand in time with the loudness of the music.

Let us look at the key terms used to describe the properties of sound:

- **Amplitude**: Like waves in the sea, we measure sound based on the height of the waves, a bit like sonic surfers. The taller the wave, the louder the sound (*Figure 3.1*). The height of a sound wave is called **amplitude**. The word **amplifier** (or **amp** for short) that we use for our car or hi-fi stereos is based on the word *amplitude*. So basically, an amp increases the size (and loudness) of the sound wave.

- **Frequency**: Another way we measure sound is how often those sound waves travel to us in the same time period. Using our sea example, if the waves of the sea only arrive at the beach every other minute, then it would be very calm. However, if several waves crash on the beach within a minute, then we would say it was time to get our surfboard out! How often sound waves travel to us is called **frequency**. A low frequency is fewer waves per minute, and a high frequency means more waves per minute (*Figure 3.1*).

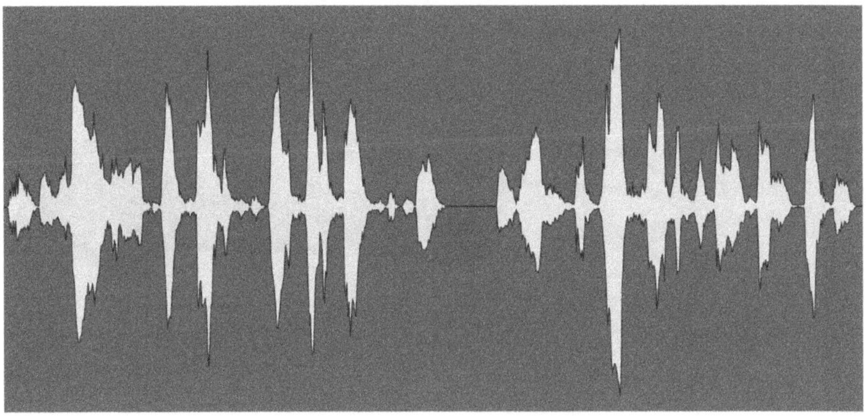

Figure 3.1: A picture of sound waves

It is these sound waves that we see when we edit in Resolve. We use these waves to guide us on where to make the best cut. It is best to cut or trim a sound clip at the point when the wave is at its lowest point (i.e., there is minimal or no sound). Otherwise, we could be cutting someone off halfway through a word, and that would sound jarring to the listener.

Microphone types

Before we talk about which microphone to use, let us understand how a microphone records those sound waves. Regardless of the type of microphone, all microphones essentially work the same way. The air pressure of the sound wave vibrates a very thin material at the same frequency as the sound wave itself. This frequency is converted into an electrical signal, which is then recorded as digital data onto your video or sound tape/disk.

There are two common types of microphones you may come across: **dynamic** and **condenser**. The main way they differ is in how they convert the sound waves into an electrical signal. Rather than go into the mechanics of how each records sound, let us look at what their strengths and weaknesses are:

- **Dynamic microphones** are used in loud concerts and stage work, as they are durable against knocks and bumps. They do not need a power source to work, which makes them less sensitive to picking up different sounds, but more durable.

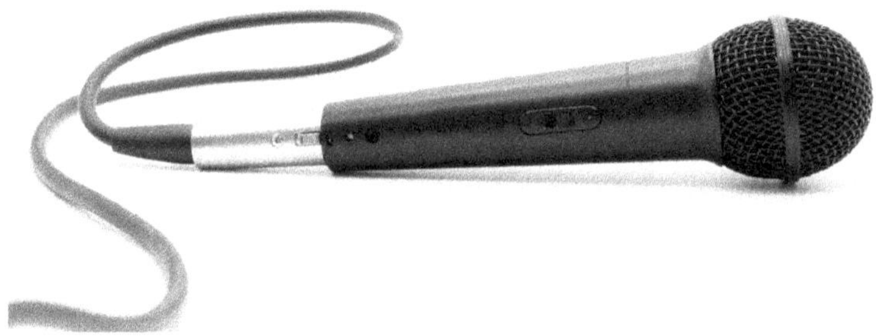

Figure 3.2: A dynamic microphone (image by Juan José Berhó from Pixabay, https://pixabay.com/users/berho-8651687/?utm_source=link-attribution&utm_medium=referral&utm_campaign=image&utm_content=5540787)

- **Condenser microphones** are usually used in film and video work as they are more sensitive to quieter sounds than a dynamic microphone, which does not perceive as much of the subtle sound of the spoken voice. They need a power source to work (such as a battery or a powered feed (*phantom power*) from a mixing desk), which makes them more sensitive but less durable. Condenser microphones can be used outdoors if handled carefully.

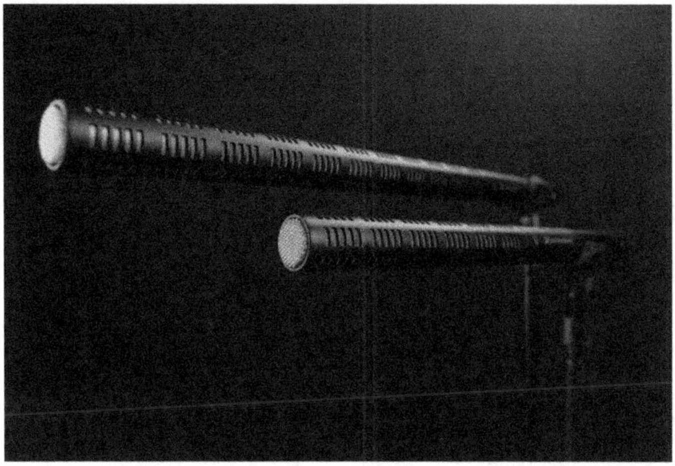

Figure 3.3: A condenser microphone (source: Pexels)

In brief, a dynamic microphone is the least sensitive but most robust of the two; the condenser microphone, regarding its sensitivity and hardiness, is the opposite of the dynamic microphone. Now that we know broadly about the different types of microphones, let's look at the pick-up patterns of different mics, in order to get the best possible sound.

Microphone pickup patterns

Knowing how sensitive a microphone is to sounds from different directions will help us know where to place it in regard to the sound source we are recording.

The directions from which a microphone records sound are called a **pickup pattern**. Pickup patterns are illustrated by a graph showing how sensitive the microphone is to the sound 360 degrees around it. The microphone is in the center of the graph, and the sensitivity is measured in **decibels (dB)**, where a value of 0 dB is the most sensitive to sound and a -25 dB value is the least sensitive. A black line on the graph shows the strength of the microphone's sensitivity to sound from different directions, with 0 degrees being the forward-facing direction of the microphone.

Let us look at the three most common pickup patterns and their variants:

- **Omnidirectional**: Essentially, *omni* is a Latin word that means *all* (e.g., when people say "God is omnipotent," they mean God is all-powerful). So, when a microphone is labelled as **omnidirectional**, it means it picks up sounds from all directions, 360 degrees around the microphone. These microphones are great when you want to record the atmosphere or background noise of the room and give a great sense of space.

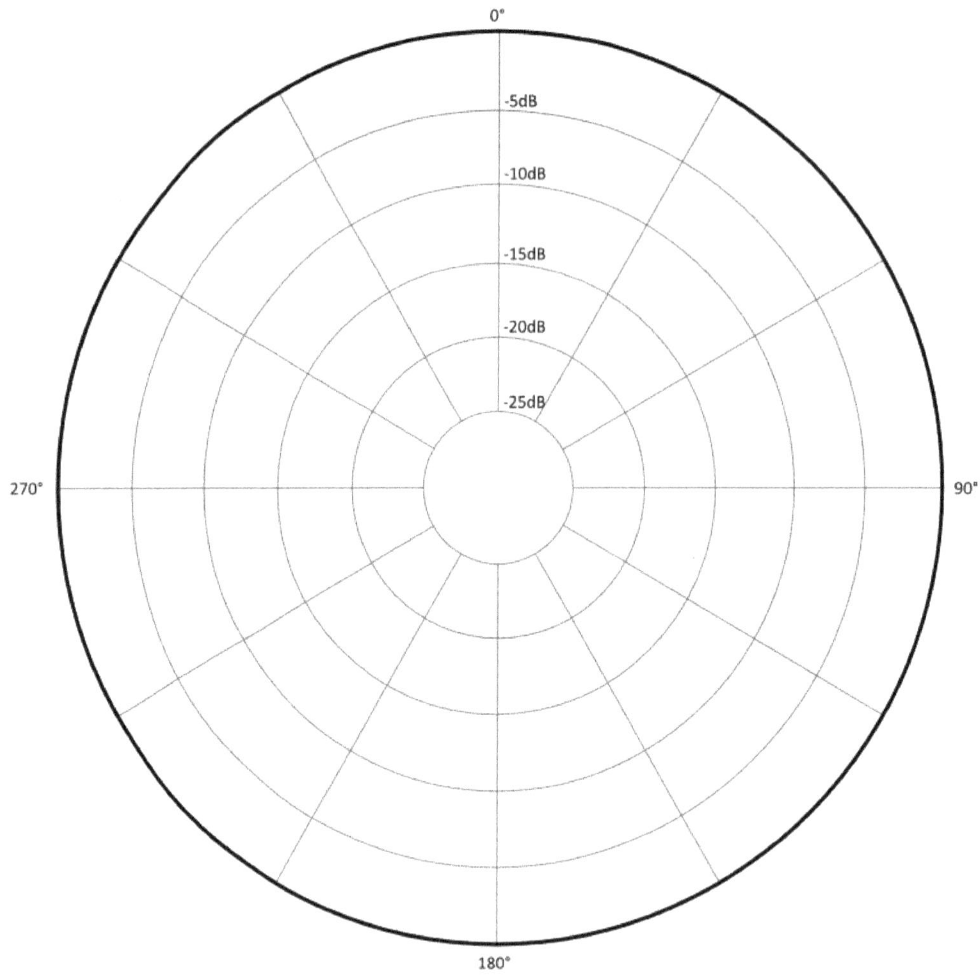

Figure 3.4: An omnidirectional pickup pattern (by Galak76, self-made, Adobe Illustrator, CC BY-SA 3.0, https://commons.wikimedia.org/w/index.php?curid=2025973)

Lapel (lavalier) mics

Lapel mics are tiny microphones that clip onto the lapel of the jacket worn by the person speaking. Lapel mics are not just named after a piece of clothing but also share the name of an item of jewelry called a *lavalier*, which is an ornament hanging from a chain, worn around the neck. This is because early lavalier mics were suspended from a chain/lanyard around the wearer's neck. Lavalier mics now have clips so they can be attached to the lapel of a jacket or anywhere that can be easily concealed in a person's clothing while remaining close (approx. 10 to 15 cm away) to their mouth.

Most lapel mics are omnidirectional mics. It may seem strange that lapel mics are omnidirectional, as we only want to record the voice of the microphone wearer (subject) from one direction.

However, as the person can change the direction of their head when they are talking, an omnidirectional microphone can pick up these changes successfully. Also, an omnidirectional microphone will use the body of the speaker to block unwanted sounds coming from behind.

One thing to consider is clothing noise as the subject moves; this can be eliminated by fixing the mic securely to the clothing so that it moves with it, not against it, or by making sure that the clothing is tight enough that there is no excess movement against the mic.

An advantage of lapel mics being omnidirectional for a sound editor is that they can also pick up the conversation of the other person in the dialogue or conversation. This can then be used in an emergency if the other person's mic failed to record good-quality sound.

- **Unidirectional**: Essentially, *uni* is a Latin word that means *one* or *single* (e.g., a unicycle has one wheel). Unidirectional microphones only pick up sound from one direction (not the UK boy band called *One Direction*). These microphones are great for recording just a specific sound, such as a voice, while eliminating sound from other directions. There are two main types of unidirectional mics based on the shape of their pickup pattern:
    - **Cardioid**: The pickup pattern of these mics is based on a heart shape; it originates from the Greek word for *heart* (e.g., a *cardiac* arrest is a *heart* attack). This pickup pattern is the most sensitive directly in front of the microphone, reducing in sensitivity until directly behind the microphone, where there is no sound pickup. Dynamic microphones use the cardioid pickup pattern to reduce the microphone handling noise from the performer or interviewer.

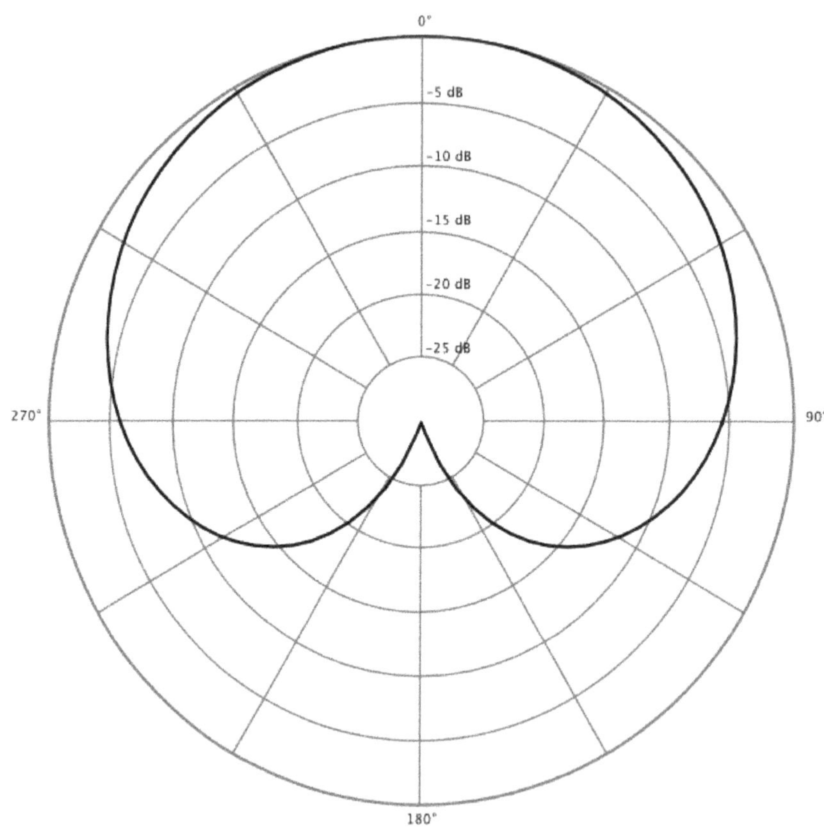

Figure 3.5: The cardioid pickup pattern (by Nicoguaro, own work, CC BY 4.0, https://commons.wikimedia.org/w/index.php?curid=50230608)

- **Hyper-cardioid**: *Hyper* comes from a Greek word that means *over* (e.g., *hyperactive* means *overactive*). Hence, this pickup pattern is a stretched or longer version of the cardioid pickup pattern. This pickup pattern is often used for **boom mics** (microphones held on a boom pole above the talent) as they are the most sensitive to unidirectional sound. However, they can pick up a camera and operator handling directly behind the microphone, so they need to be placed carefully.

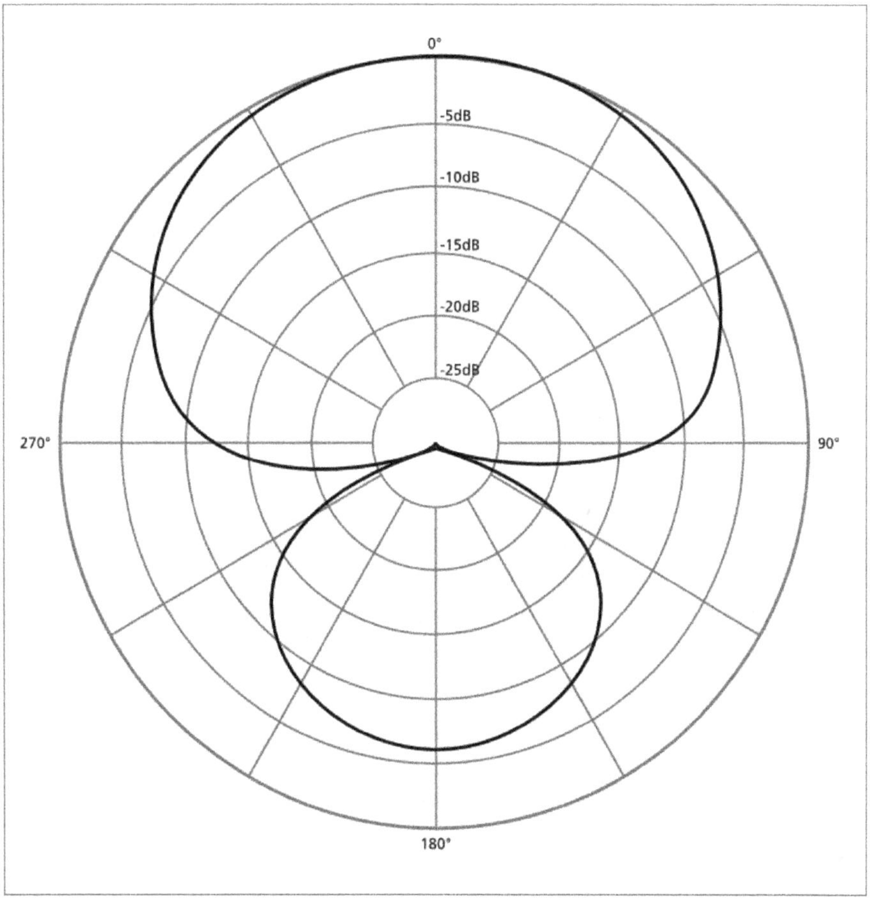

Figure 3.6: The hyper-cardioid pickup pattern (by Galak76, self-made, Adobe Illustrator, CC BY-SA 3.0, https://commons.wikimedia.org/w/index.php?curid=2025973)

- **Bidirectional:** You guessed it! The word *bi* is Latin for *two* (e.g., a bicycle has two wheels). It is also called a *figure of eight* based on the shape of the pickup pattern. These microphones record sound from two different directions. They are less used in filming, but are good if you want to record a conversation between two people and only have one microphone to use. However, this is not a common approach, as using a bidirectional microphone to record two voices makes it harder to separate the voices when we are editing the sound. Also, each voice will have different vocal characteristics (e.g., quieter and louder), so it is better to have a separate microphone for each sound source so that we can adapt the microphone position and gain of each one to suit each sound.

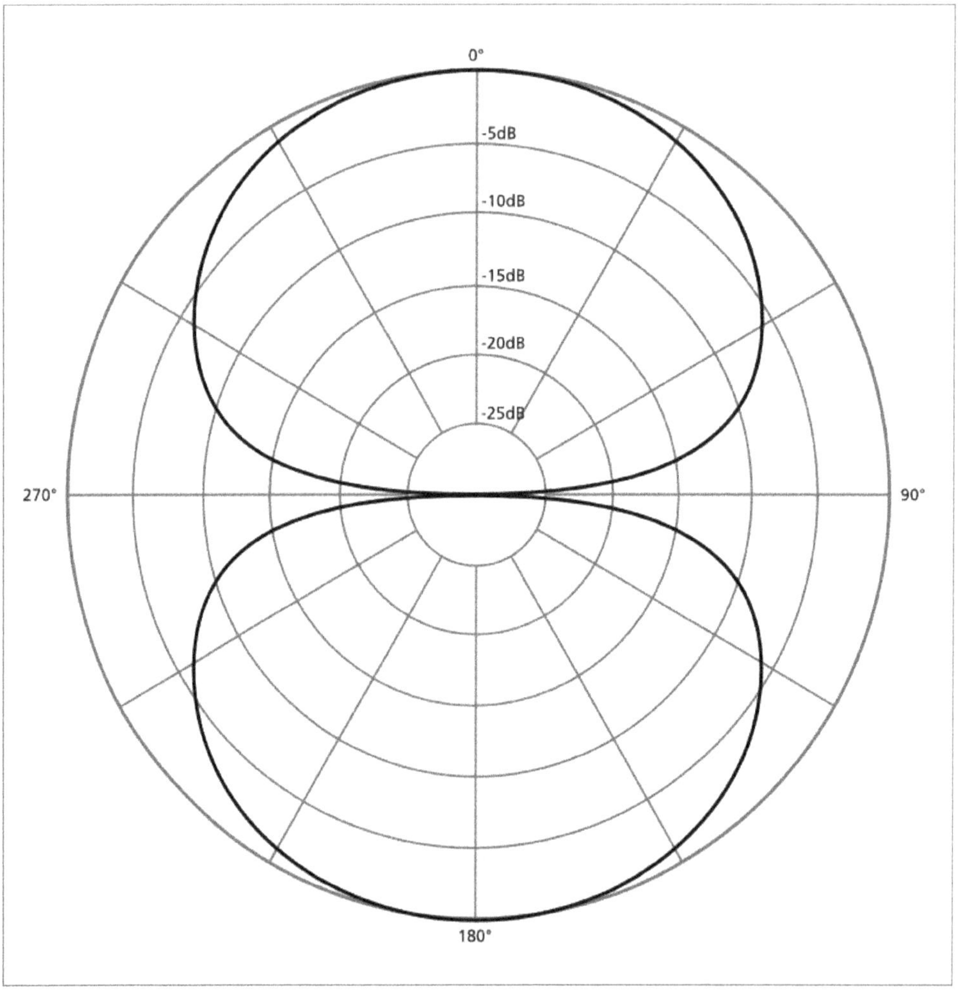

Figure 3.7: Bidirectional pickup pattern (by Galak76, self-made, Adobe Illustrator, CC BY-SA 3.0, https://commons.wikimedia.org/w/index.php?curid=2025973)

Most professional microphones have interchangeable heads to change the microphone's pick-up pattern to suit what you are recording. Even some more affordable microphones can have a switch to change the microphone's pickup pattern to suit.

Now that we know about which microphone to choose for each particular job, let's look at microphone placement to get the best possible sound.

Microphone placement

The best mics to use are the ones closest to the sound source. Usually, this is the lapel mic, as being attached to the lapel of a speaker's jacket places the mic closest to their mouth. Lapel mics can be discreet and easily hidden within clothing.

You may have seen pictures of sound recordists using unidirectional boom mics to record voices in a film. These are great for when a scene is shot in close-up, where the mic is placed just out of frame. However, they are no good in wider shots, as they are too far away and start to pick up more of the ambient noise around them. Most professional sound recordists for cinema use a mix of both boom and lapel mics to get the best of both worlds, and they can be used as backups for each other if one of them should fail. However, when filming a realistic scene or documentary, a boom mic and operator can get in the way of the natural performance of the speaker (or talent), as they are distracting and draw attention to the artificial nature of video recording, resulting in a self-conscious performance. Which you choose to use is, of course, up to you; these are just a few things to consider to help you make your choice.

Because of these considerations, there is a temptation for videographers to use the built-in microphone on the camera. The problem with this approach is that the microphone is usually too far away from the subject and closer to the sound of the handling and operation noise of the camera. Also, most cameras that have on-board mics use cheaper, lower-quality mics to make the cost of the camera more affordable. The camera manufacturers tend to spend their research money on better-quality images, as that is what you are probably buying a camera for in the first place. This all results in poor-quality sound coming from the on-camera microphone, which can be hard to improve upon in any editing software. Unless you are recording a video piece close to a stationary camera, it is much better to record sound separately on a lapel or boom mic closer to the subject. Even using a separate mic plugged into the camera with a very long lead to record directly into the video footage is better than using the on-camera mic.

One problem with long leads is that they can pollute the sound signal going back to the camera with noise. The longer the lead, the more likely it is to introduce this noise. This is usually why microphone cable runs are as short as possible.

Also, microphone cables should never be run parallel to power cables for other equipment, such as lights or cameras; otherwise, they run the risk of picking up electrical hum.

The good news is that Resolve has special tools that can remove electrical hum or noise from poor sound, which we cover later in this chapter.

Now that we know the basics of different microphone types, the direction they record sound from, and their placement, let us look at how to get separately recorded sound into Resolve and sync it up with our video footage.

Syncing audio

One reason that most fledgling filmmakers do not want to record sound separately is that they think it is difficult to match the sound with the video they have recorded. The need to make the audio sync with the mouth movements of the video's subject seems daunting.

Thankfully, it is very easy to sync audio with video in Resolve. There are a few ways to do this, which we will look at now. Firstly, you will need to go to the **Media** page, as you can only sync audio in the **Media** page. If the **Media** page is still hidden from what we did in *Chapter 1*, you can reveal it again by selecting it in **Workspace** > **Show Page** > **Media**.

Auto-syncing audio to video

Even though we will not use the sound recorded by the on-camera microphone, it is useful to help sync our separately recorded sound.

As discussed earlier in the chapter, sound is recorded as waves; the shape of these waves is called a *waveform* (i.e., the shape or *form* of the *wave*). Resolve can take your separately recorded audio and match it up with your video's audio, based on the shape of the waveforms for both pieces of audio. All audio syncing is done in the **Media** page.

The **Media** page in Resolve is where you have more advanced functions to manage your media, such as syncing audio to video. The **Media** page is not to be confused with the **Media Pool,** which is available on every page in Resolve but is limited to arranging media that is already imported into Resolve.

Let us **Auto Sync Audio** based on waveforms in the **Media** page:

1. Go to the **Media** page.
2. Import both the separate audio and the video into the same bin in the **Media Pool** (as described in *Chapter 1*). The audio and video can be imported into the **Media Pool** on any page, not just the **Media** page.

3. To select the audio and video you want to sync, you can do one of two things:
    - Select both the audio and video clips you want to sync. You can either *Cmd* (*Command*) or *Shift*-click on the clips to select them, or press the *Cmd + A* keys on your keyboard to select all the clips in the bin if you want to sync them all at once.
    - Select the bin that contains the video and audio you want to sync.
4. Right-click on any one of the selected clips or bins to reveal a pop-up menu (*Figure 3.8*). Select **Auto Sync Audio...**, as shown in the following screenshot:

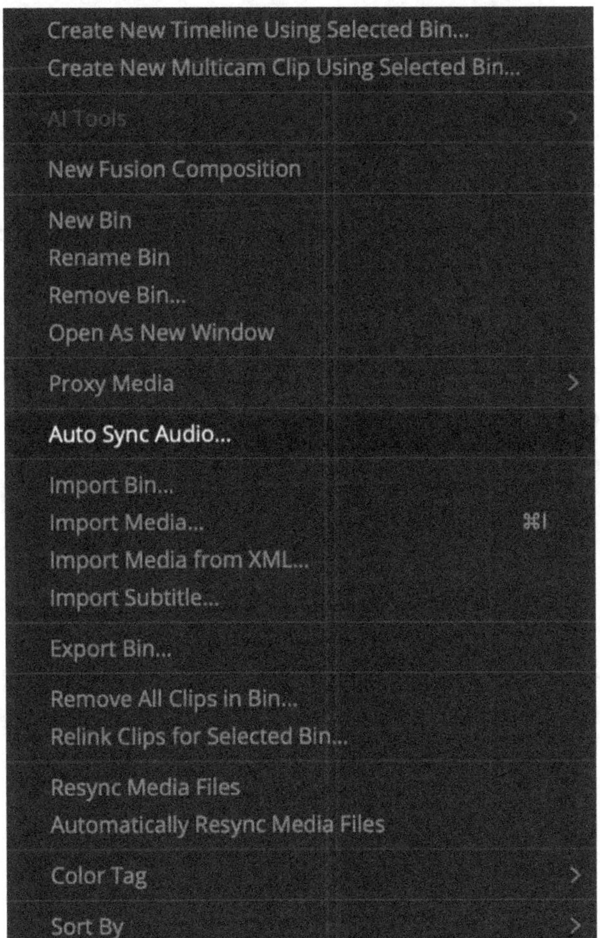

Figure 3.8: The pop-up menu when right-clicking a bin

This will bring up the **Automatically Sync Audio** dialog box:

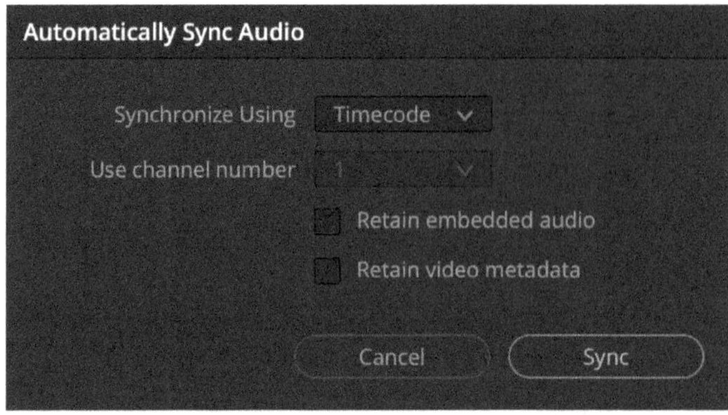

Figure 3.9: The Automatically Sync Audio dialog box

5. Next to **Synchronize Using**, select either **Waveform**, **Timecode**, **In**, **Out**, or **Marker** from the drop-down menu. These five different options will have the following effects:

    - **Timecode**: This option synchronizes the video and audio based on matching timecode.
    - **Waveform**: This option synchronizes the video and audio based on matching waveforms.
    - **In**: This option synchronizes the video and audio based on matching an **In** point on both the audio and video. If no **In** points are on the audio or video, Resolve will use the start of the audio and video clips as an **In** point.
    - **Out**: This option synchronizes the video and audio based on matching an **Out** point on both the audio and video. If no **Out** points are on the audio or video, Resolve will use the end of the audio and video clips as an **Out** point.
    - **Marker**: This option synchronizes the video and audio based on matching a marker on both the audio and video.

> The last three options in the preceding list are only available in DaVinci Resolve version 20.1 onwards.

6. Whichever option you choose, you can select the **Retain embedded audio** checkbox:

   - If this option is selected, the newly synced audio files are added as additional audio tracks below the video clip's existing audio track. This means you can edit the original camera audio and the newly added synced audio separately and mix between them.
   - If you do not select **Retain embedded audio**, the newly synced audio files will replace the video clip's existing audio.

7. The next option is the **Retain video metadata** checkbox. This is more for professional filmmakers, who need the video metadata to be retained to help with their edit. As a beginner, you can safely ignore this option, although it is good practice to retain video metadata, should you ever need it in the future.
8. If you have chosen to sync by **Waveform**, then you will have additional options to select from a drop-down menu next to **Use channel number**. In this menu, you can choose which audio track you want Resolve to perform the waveform analysis on:

   - Selecting **1** will tell Resolve to use Channel 1 to match the audio waveform to. Selecting **2** will likewise select Channel 2 for Resolve's waveform matching.
   - Selecting **Mix** will get Resolve to use a mix of all the available audio channels to perform its waveform match on.
   - Selecting **Automatic** will get Resolve to choose the best audio channel for it to perform its waveform match on.

   If you already know which audio channel has the strongest audio to help make the best waveform match, you can select that channel number instead. However, in most cases, **Automatic** will do the best job.

9. Checking the **Retain embedded audio** checkbox will make sure that your newly synced audio will be added to an additional audio track, and your original camera audio will be kept.
10. Click on the **Sync** button. Your clips will now be synced.

Whichever option you choose, a progress bar dialog box (*Figure 3.10*) will pop up to show you how long the syncing is taking.

Figure 3.10: The Auto Sync Audio progress bar

11. When the syncing is finished, the dialog box will list any video or audio clips that did not sync (*Figure 3.11*).

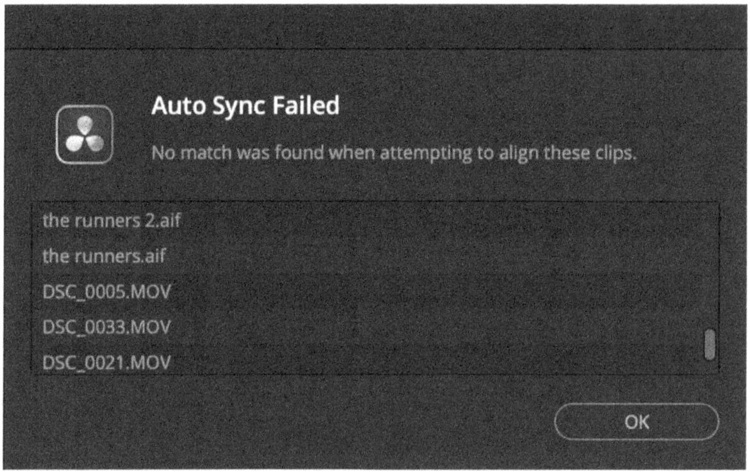

Figure 3.11: The Auto Sync Failed list

Do not worry if you see a list of clips that did not sync; there will be several reasons for this. Resolve will try to match up every clip you selected. If there are any clips with missing audio or timecode (depending upon which auto-sync method you selected), then it will not sync them. Do make a note of these un-synced clips, as you can always manually sync the clips later.

Additionally, if your camera did not record on-camera sound (or you forgot to turn the camera mic on) and it does not have timecode, you can manually sync the audio with the video.

Manually syncing audio to video

This is based on a visual frame of reference for the audio, such as a hand clap within the camera frame or the use of a **clapper board** or even a **digital slate** on an iPad.

Whatever you use as a reference for the video and audio to sync, make sure that you can visually see in the video where the two objects meet to make the sound.

There is no point in using your hands to make a clapping sound if we cannot see the point where your hands meet. I know this sounds obvious, but I have heard of many a frustrated editor trying to sync sound for a student film where the hand clap to sync sound was not visible or just out of the frame.

Let us see how we can manually sync sound if there is no other way to sync it:

1. Follow *steps 1* to *2* in the *Auto-syncing audio to video* section.
2. In the **Media** page bins (named **Master**), select a video clip to sync. In the **Viewer** window, move the playhead to line up with the first visual sync point in the first clip, such as a clapper board or someone clapping.
3. At the top right of Resolve, there is an **Embedded Audio** panel (*Figure 3.12*), which shows the audio **Meters** tab by default. Select the **Waveform** tab next to the **Meters** (*Figure 3.12*). The **Waveform** tab lets you view and scrub along the waveform of audio clips you select in the bins in the **Media** page.
4. Now, in the **Media** page bins, select the audio clip that you want to sync to the video clip that is showing in the **Viewer**. You will see the waveform of the audio clip in the **Embedded Audio > Waveform** tab (*Figure 3.12*).
5. Use the waveform transport controls and scrubber bar in the **Waveform Viewer** to move the playhead to the audio sync point that matches the video sync point. Remember, you can use the right and left arrows to move one frame at a time in either direction to fine-tune your sync point.

   Your sync point may be a hand clap, a clapper board, or any other short, quick sound where we can see a visual reference to the sound source in the video.

   In the **Waveform Viewer**, the bottom half shows the entire waveform for the whole clip. The top half shows an enlarged section of the waveform that follows the playhead. This is useful for finding your sync point.

So basically, you find the visual cue for the sound source in the video, such as where the hand clap meets, then match it with the corresponding peak of the audio waveform of the separate audio clip.

6. Now that you have matched up the audio and video sync points, you just need to lock them together. Click the **Link/Unlink Audio** button (*Figure 3.12*) at the bottom right of the **Embedded Audio** panel to attach the synced audio to the video clip.

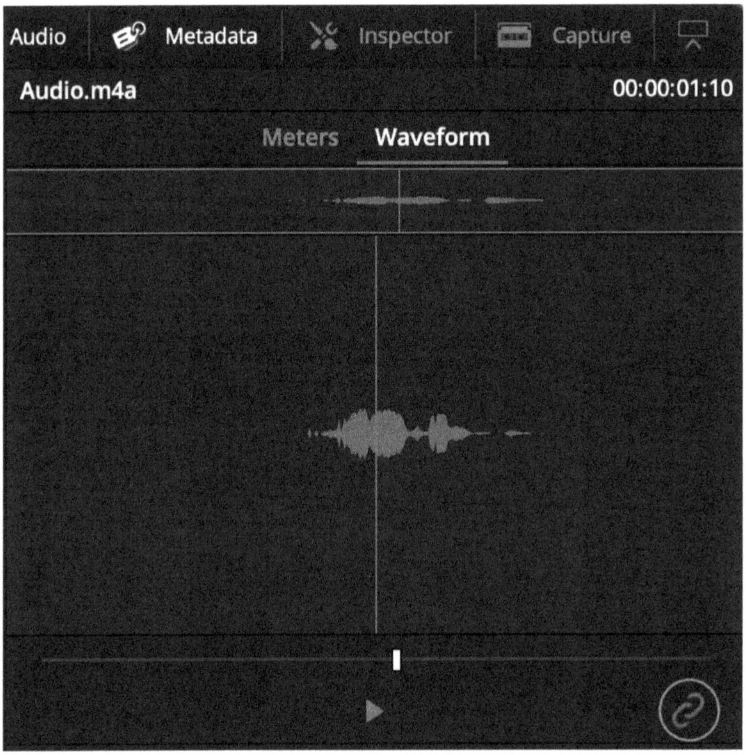

Figure 3.12: The Link/Unlink Audio button.

That's it. Your video and audio are now synced together!

Now that we have synced our separately recorded sound to the video, let us look at how we can enhance the sound further by fixing any quality issues it may have, such as that annoying electrical hum we mentioned earlier.

Fixing sound using Fairlight FX

Now, occasionally, regardless of how much effort you put into choosing the right microphone and positioning it as well as you can, there will still be issues with the sound that you have recorded. Let us look at how we can fix some of these common issues.

These audio fixing tools are **Fairlight FX** plugins built into Resolve and are found in the **Cut**, **Edit**, and **Fairlight** pages. We are going to explore the use of these tools, called **plugins**, from within the **Cut** page. Go to the **Cut** page, and navigate to **Effects** > **Audio** > **Fairlight FX**, where you will find the following built-in audio-fixing plugins.

De-Esser

Sometimes, when recording some people's voices, they sound sibilant. **Sibilance** is when someone overemphasizes the "s" sound in words. It can be jarring after listening to this hissing sound for a long time. Thankfully, Resolve has a plugin to specifically remove this sound from dialogue or other vocals. For this exercise, record your voice saying, "Suzy sells shells by the seashore." This will create a recording with a lot of sibilance. Import your recording into Resolve and place it on the timeline, then follow the next steps.

Let us explore how **De-Esser** works:

1. Drag the `Fix_Sound.mp3` file that you imported at the start of the chapter onto the timeline below the V1 track.
2. On the **Cut** page, navigate to **Effects** > **Audio** > **Fairlight FX** > **De-Esser**.
3. To apply the **De-Esser** effect, you can do one of two things:
    - Select the clip you want to apply **De-Esser** to, then double-click **De-Esser** in the **Effects** > **Audio** > **Fairlight FX** panel
    - Drag it onto the clip to apply it

4. The **De-Esser** control panel (*Figure 3.13*) will open with a graph, showing you the part of the audio signal (frequency) that the controls will affect. To the right of the graph, there are meters that show you the **reduction** (the amount of the sibilant signal being reduced) and the **output** (the overall sound level after the effect has been applied).

Figure 3.13: The De-Esser Fairlight FX plugin

The following options allow you to fine-tune the targeting and reduction of the sibilance:

- **Bypass**: This is an orange toggle switch (labeled **De-Esser**) that turns the plugin on and off. Make sure this is turned on.

- **Listen to Ess Only**: This checkbox at the top right lets you listen only to the "s" sounds (esses) that are being removed. It is good to see how many of the esses are being removed and whether there are any wanted sounds that the **De-Esser** is also removing.
- **Frequency Range**: These two controls let you select the frequency of the "s" sound for an individual's voice:
    - The **Frequency** knob lets you select the frequency of the "s" sound. Sibilant sounds are usually found in the frequency range of 4–8 kHz.
    - The **Range** buttons switch the mode of the **De-Esser**. There are three options (from top to bottom) that let you switch between **Narrow Band**, **Wide Band**, and **All High Frequency**, which reduces all audio above the selected frequency.
- **De-Esser Amount**: This knob adjusts the amount of de-essing that is applied. You will see the notch on the graph go up or down, depending on how much de-essing you apply.
- **Reaction Time**: These radio buttons adjust how quickly de-essing is applied – in other words, how much delay before the effect is applied. There are three options here:
    - **Slow**: This slowly applies the effect
    - **Medium**: This is halfway between slow and fast
    - **Fast**: This applies the effect suddenly

Now that we know how to remove sibilance from a voice recording, we will look at removing another annoying sound in audio recordings, electrical hum.

Removing hum

As mentioned earlier, electrical hum can be introduced to the sound signal through a long cable run or an unshielded or poorly earthed microphone cable. The good news is that this hum is relatively easy to identify and remove, as it exists at a specific frequency based on the electrical phase of the country the cable is used in.

If you are based in the UK, Europe, India, China, Africa, Russia, or Australasia, your electrical frequency will be 50 Hz; if you are based in the USA, Canada, or South America, it is 60 Hz. Regardless, it is best to check what the phase of your country's electrical supply is (there are links to useful websites to do this at the end of the chapter).

Let us look at how the **De-Hummer** plugin works using the same `Fix_Sound.mp3` file that we added to the timeline:

1. On the **Cut** page, navigate to **Effects** > **Audio** > **Fairlight FX** > **De-Hummer**.
2. To apply the **De-Hummer** effect, you can do one of two things:
    - Select the clip you want to apply **De-Hummer** to, then double-click **De-Hummer** in the **Effects** > **Audio** > **Fairlight FX** panel
    - Drag the **De-Hummer** effect onto the clip to apply it
3. The **De-Hummer** control panel will open and show you the following options (*Figure 3.14*):

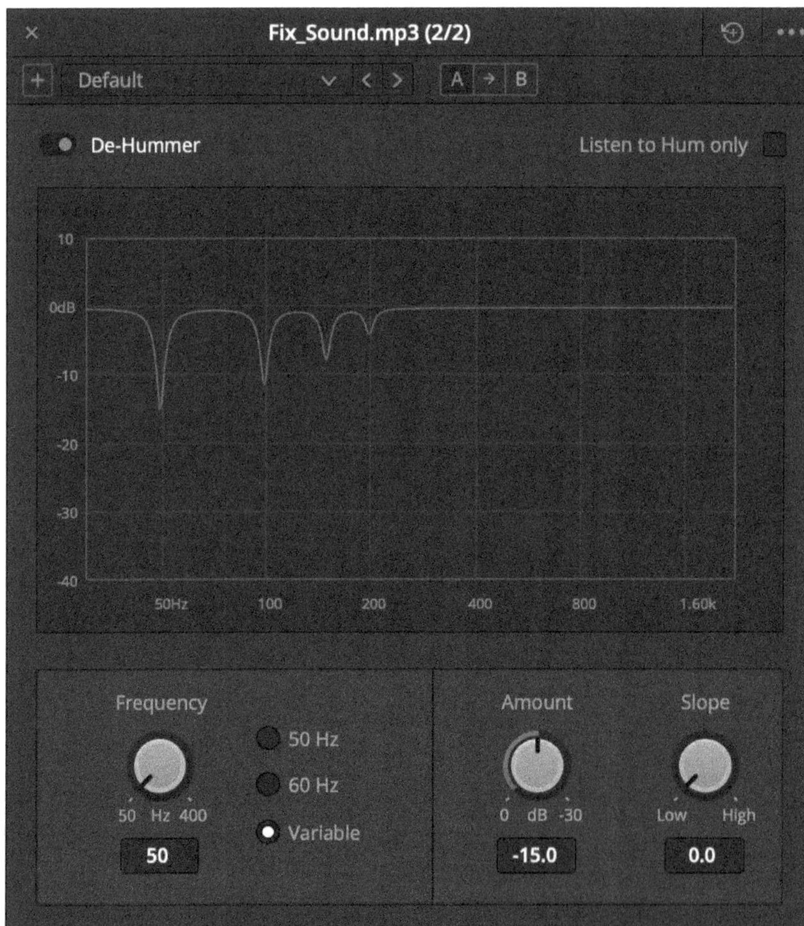

Figure 3.14: The De-Hummer Fairlight FX control panel

- **Bypass**: This is an orange toggle switch (labeled **De-Hummer**) that turns the plugin on and off. This is called the **Bypass** switch, as the audio *bypasses* the effect when turned off, much like a car uses a motorway bypass to avoid going through a city. Make sure this is turned on.
- **Listen to Hum only**: This checkbox at the top right lets you listen only to the hum that is being removed. It is good to see how much of the hum is being removed and whether there are any wanted sounds that the **De-Hummer** is also removing erroneously, such as dialogue.
- **Frequency**: This is the target frequency that the plugin will remove. There are radio buttons that let you select the common electrical mains frequencies of 50 Hz/60 Hz, which most electrical hum is caused by. A knob also allows you to select other frequencies if needed.
- **Slope**: This knob adjusts the slope of the harmonics that are also removed. Harmonics are other secondary frequencies that are double the frequency of the main frequency. So, if the main frequency is 50 Hz, then the harmonics are 100 Hz; if 60 Hz, then they will be 120 Hz. The slope is the ratio of the main frequency to the harmonics or higher secondary frequencies that are being removed. If you set the slope to `0`, then the main frequency is the priority to be removed; if it is set to `1`, then the secondary frequencies are prioritized. A slope value of `0.5` will mean all frequencies will be targeted equally.
- **Amount**: This knob adjusts how much of the selected frequency is removed.

In addition to these controls, a graph lets you see the frequency with which the plugin's controls are targeting.

Changing stereo to mono

This plugin is for fixing stereo sound recordings. As all dialogue sound is usually recorded using mono mics, hopefully, you will not need this plugin. However, occasionally, you may need to fix a sound clip where dialogue has been recorded using a stereo mic.

The problem with stereo sound for the human voice is that it makes the sound feel like it is coming from all around you (which is good for *the voice of God* or narration effects), but in real life, we hear the voice of the person coming from one direction, usually in the center, directly in front of us.

Thankfully, this plugin enables us to convert the clip from stereo to mono. Let us explore this useful feature, as well as briefly look at the other controls it offers. The same `Fix_Sound.mp3` clip has sound only coming out of the left speaker, as it has been incorrectly saved as a stereo clip. We need to fix this by converting the clip to mono so that the sound comes through both the left and right speakers equally:

1. On the **Cut** page, navigate to **Effects** > **Audio** > **Fairlight FX** > **Stereo Fixer**.
2. To apply the **Stereo Fixer** effect, you can do one of two things:
    - Select the clip you want to apply the **Stereo Fixer** effect to, then double-click **Stereo Fixer** in the **Effects** > **Audio** > **Fairlight FX** panel
    - Drag **Stereo Fixer** onto the clip to apply it
3. The **Stereo Fixer** control panel will open and show you the following options (*Figure 3.15*):

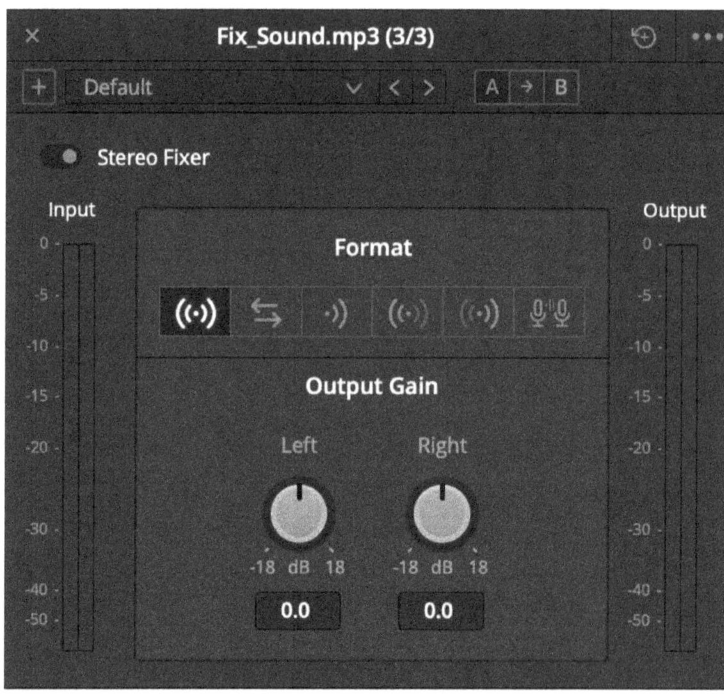

Figure 3.15: The Stereo Fixer Fairlight FX plugin

- **Format**: This is the mode that you want Resolve to use to fix the stereo. The buttons underneath (from left to right) perform the following functions:
    - **Stereo**: No fixing is done (default).
    - **Reverse Stereo**: This swaps the left and right stereo channels.
    - **Mono**: This converts the stereo clip into a mono clip by mixing the two stereo channels. This is the option we want to choose for our `Fix_Sound.mp3` clip.
    - **Left Only**: The left stereo channel is sent to both the left and right stereo channels.
    - **Right Only**: The right stereo channel is sent to both the left and right stereo channels.
    - **M/S**: This is a more advanced tool that converts the stereo recording into the **Mid/Side (M/S)** format used by M/S recording microphones. A mid/side microphone is actually two mics – one mic facing forward and a stereo mic facing sideways in order to record a wider stereo sound.
- **Output Gain**: The **Left** and **Right** gain knobs allow you to apply different levels of gain to the left or right stereo outputs. This gain is applied after the **Format** mode has done its work on the stereo inputs.

There are two volume meters on either side of the plugin. The meter on the left shows the sound levels of the input of the stereo sound (i.e., the original volume levels of the clip). The meter on the right shows the sound levels of the output of the stereo sound (i.e., the new volume levels of the clip after the effect is applied).

Converting to mono

As sound volume levels are accumulative (i.e., one sound on top of another increases the overall volume of the video), converting stereo to mono, by mixing the stereo channels together, will increase the overall volume of the clip. You can compensate for this by lowering the volume levels using the clip's master volume in the **Inspector** or the channel's **Mixer** controls.

Noise reduction

Sometimes when recording audio, we may get noise introduced by a low-quality microphone. The **Noise Reduction** plugin can reduce a range of different types of noise.

Let us explore how the Noise Reduction plugin works using the same `Fix_Sound.mp3` clip already on the timeline:

1. On the **Cut** page, navigate to **Effects** > **Audio** > **Fairlight FX** > **Noise Reduction**.
2. To apply the **Noise Reduction** effect, you can do one of two things:
    - Select the clip you want to apply the **Noise Reduction** effect to, then double-click **Noise Reduction** in the **Effects** > **Audio** > **Fairlight FX** panel
    - Drag the **Noise Reduction** effect onto the clip to apply it
3. The **Noise Reduction** control panel (*Figure 3.16*) will open up with a graph, showing you the range of frequencies that the controls will affect, highlighted in purple.

   Two audio meters, either side of the graph, show you the input sound level (to the left) compared to the output sound level (to the right). This is useful to show how much of the final audio signal is being lost due to the noise reduction being applied.

   In a drop-down menu at the top left, there are three default presets you can select: **De-Hiss**, **De-Rumble**, and **De-Rumble and Hiss,** as well as **Reset Noise Profile** to remove the presets.

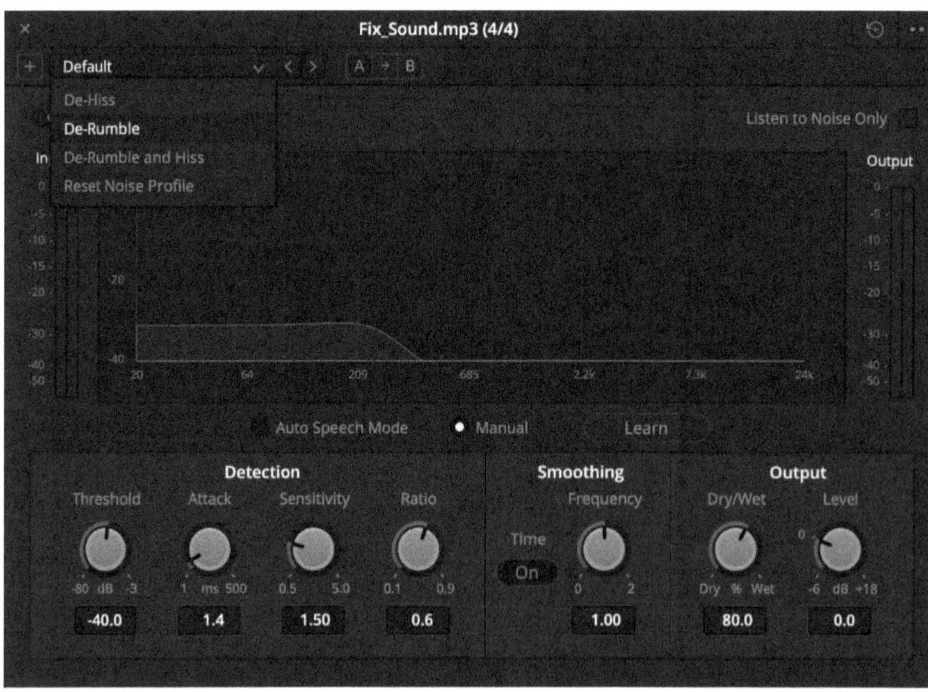

Figure 3.16: The Noise Reduction Fairlight FX plugin

When the noise reduction is being applied, the graph shows a spectral analysis of the audio being targeted, along with a purple overlay that shows what noise is being targeted.

There are two ways to reduce audio noise:

- **Auto Speech Mode**, where Resolve will try to automatically identify and reduce the noise while maintaining speech in the clip
- **Manual** mode, where you teach Resolve what the noise sounds like so that it only removes that sound from the clip

To enable **Manual** mode to work, you select the **Manual** radio button, click the **Learn** button, and then play back a small section of your clip that only contains the background noise that you want to remove. Resolve will listen to the sound of the noise and create a **noise profile** that it uses to identify noise in the clip. When you have finished teaching Resolve what the noise sounds like, unclick the **Learn** button. Resolve will now use the noise profile to remove noise from the input signal of the rest of the clip.

For most people, the default settings for either the automatic or manual noise reduction methods will work perfectly fine.

However, if you want to delve a bit deeper into the controls and tweak the noise reduction results, then the following options allow you to fine-tune the targeting and reduction of the noise to your liking:

- **Bypass**: This is an orange toggle switch that turns the plugin on and off. Make sure this is turned on.
- **Listen to Noise Only**: This checkbox at the top right lets you listen only to the noise that is being removed. It is good to see how much of the noise is being removed and whether there are any other wanted sounds that the **Noise Reduction** effect is also removing erroneously, or whether too little reduction is being applied.
- **Detection**: This is where you tell Resolve what the parameters are within which it will detect noise. The four knobs (left to right) underneath **Detection** (*Figure 3.16*) perform the following functions:
    - **Threshold** (in dB): This is the upper volume level of sound up to which the noise reduction is applied. Any audio below this threshold will have noise reduction applied to it. This level relates to the **signal-to-noise ratio** (**SNR**) in the original clip.

Key concept – Signal to Noise Ratio (SNR)

SNR is the difference between the background noise level of the microphone and the upper level of the sound signal being recorded, both of which are measured in **Decibels Sound Pressure Level (dB SPL)**, where the maximum sound level is 0 dB. For example, for a microphone that has a peak recording signal with a strength of -10 dB and a noise signal starting at and below -80 dB, the SNR will be -10 - (-80) = 70 dB.

Audio recordings with a poor SNR will need a higher threshold value, leading to more noise reduction being applied to a clip.

- **Attack** (in milliseconds): This is how quickly the noise reduction detection responds to variations in noise. If there is consistent noise that doesn't vary much, then a high **millisecond (ms)** value (longer time) of attack can be used. If there is inconsistent noise that quickly varies, then a low ms value (quicker time) of attack can be used. It is particularly useful in **Auto Speech Mode**.

Key concept – Attack

Attack is how quickly any audio effect is applied to the audio. The key concept here is that attack is measured in milliseconds (ms). So, a high attack value (a longer time before being applied) means the effect is applied more slowly, whereas a low attack value (a shorter time before being applied) means that the effect is applied quickly.

- **Sensitivity**: This knob increases the sensitivity of the noise reduction to noise. Higher sensitivity values amplify the amount of noise being detected, but may also remove wanted dialogue sounds.
- **Ratio**: This knob controls the amount of time between the sound signal being detected and when the noise profile is being applied. A longer delay between the signal and the noise profile allows for a better preservation of changes in the human voice, potentially sacrificing noise reduction.

- **Smoothing**: These options smooth the sound of the noise reduction after it has been applied to remove any unwanted sounds created as a byproduct of it:
    - **Frequency Smoothing**: This smooths the signal curve across the frequencies to lessen any hard transitions as a result of the noise reduction
    - **Time Smoothing**: This toggle button enables smoothing across time as well as **Frequency Smoothing**

  Both frequency and time smoothing blend the noise reduction into the rest of the signal. However, these may make the original audio sound a bit muddy or less defined as they smooth out any sound transitions in the audio.

- **Output**: These options affect the output signal after the noise reduction has been applied:
    - **Dry/Wet**: This knob controls the percentage of the output mix of a *wet* or noise-reduced signal to a *dry*, unprocessed signal. So, a value of 0% is completely dry, whereas a value of 100% is completely wet.
    - **Makeup Gain**: This knob lets you make up (by adding gain) to compensate for any sound levels that may be lost due to the noise reduction that you have applied. This gain is applied before the **Dry/Wet** mix.

> **Resetting effects knobs to default values**
>
> It can be easy to get lost with changing the settings of so many knobs at once. Resolve lets you reset each knob to its default value by double-clicking on the middle of the knob.

Now that we have learned how to remove noise, electrical hum, and fix the stereo sound of a clip using Fairlight FX plugins, it is time to reveal a new additional tool in the **Inspector** that can fix all these problems using just one setting.

Using AI Dialogue Leveler

There are many AI audio tools in the paid-for Studio version of DaVinci Resolve; however, there is one free AI audio tool in Resolve called **AI Dialogue Leveler**. You can find it in the **Audio** section of the **Inspector** (*Figure 3.17*). AI Dialogue Leveler uses **artificial intelligence** (**AI**) to analyze the audio clip and enhance the volume levels of dialogue in the clip. Try it with the `Fix_Sound` clip:

1. Select the `Fix_Sound` clip on the timeline on the **Cut** page.
2. Double-click on **AI Dialogue Leveler**.
3. In the **Mode** drop-down menu, select one of the following options based on the volume levels of the original dialogue (*Figure 3.17*):
    - **Allow wider dynamics** is good when there is a range of low and loud sounds in the audio
    - **Optimize moderate levels** is a good option when the original audio has moderate volume levels throughout
    - **More lift for low levels** is good when you want to boost quiet dialogue
    - **Lift soft whispery voices** is good for boosting whispered dialogue
4. Using the toggle switches, select the AI audio processing you want to apply to the clip. Apply any number of the following three options:
    - **Reduce loud dialogue** reduces the peaks of loud dialogue
    - **Lift soft dialogue** increases the volume levels of quiet dialogue without increasing the volume of background sounds
    - **Background reduction** gently reduces the volume of background sounds
5. Adjust the **Output Gain** to boost the overall volume level of the clip from `0.0` to `6.0` dB. The default setting of **2.0** dB is suitable for the majority of needs.

For the `Fix_Sound.mp3` clip, the default mode of **Allow wider dynamics** with only the **Background reduction** toggle selected will be the most suitable setting to further reduce the background hum.

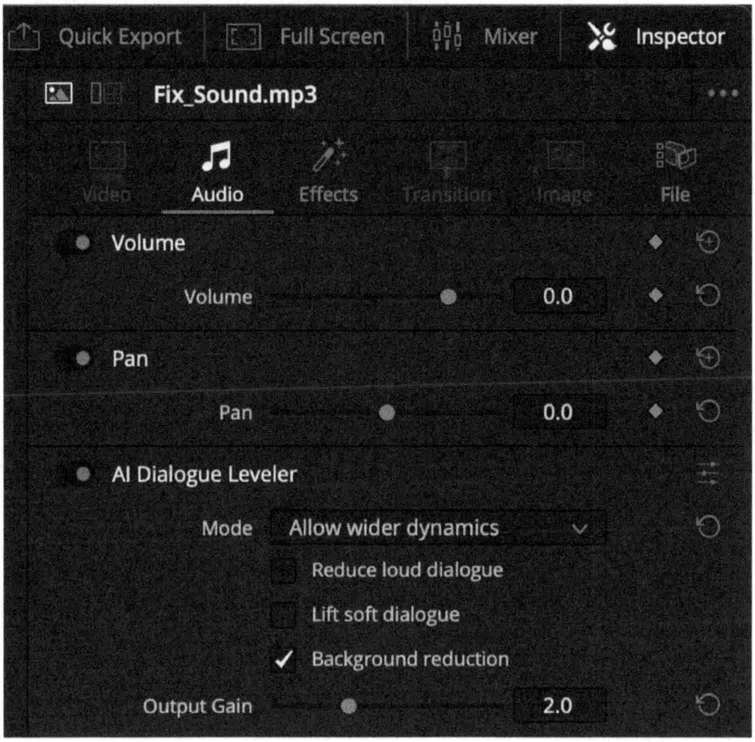

Figure 3.17: AI Dialogue Leveler

AI Dialogue Leveler will not work for every audio problem, but it is a quick and easy place to start before you need to use the more involved Fairlight FX plugins to fix tricky dialogue levels.

There is an additional audio fixing AI tool that is only available in the Studio version of DaVinci Resolve; it is called **AI Voice Isolation**. We will explore this tool further in *Chapter 12*.

Whichever method you choose to fix audio, it is important to fix the audio first before adding any audio enhancements. Otherwise, you will be enhancing and amplifying poor-quality sound, which, of course, we do not want for our video.

So, that's it, you have now explored the range of microphone types and pick up patterns to be able to record better audio, which will save you time in Resolve.

You have also synced, fixed, and enhanced audio in the **Cut** page to get the most out of the audio you have recorded.

Summary

Here is what you have achieved in *Chapter 3*:

- Learned why separately recorded audio is better than in-camera sound and the best practices for recording it
- Synced separate audio to the video footage using waveforms
- Fixed common sound issues using Fairlight FX
- Used AI Dialogue Leveler to fix audio

You now know which microphones to choose to help get the best sound recording. Also, you know how to use the **Media** page to sync separately recorded audio to your video to create a cleaner sound. Additionally, you know how to work with audio in the **Cut** page to fix common audio issues without having to learn how to use Fairlight.

In *Chapter 4*, we will further enhance your video by adding extra audio through recording narration and voice dubbing on the **Fairlight** page, as well as adding subtitles on the **Cut** page, so that your video will be more accessible across different audiences around the world.

Questions

1. True or false? It is always best to use the in-camera mic as it is optimized for the video created by the camera.
2. True or false? You can only sync separate audio to the video if you recorded in-camera sound.
3. True or false? The **Cut** page has access to Fairlight FX audio plugins that enable you to fix and enhance audio.
4. True or false? AI Dialogue Leveler is a Fairlight FX plug-in that isolates the voice from the background noise.

Further reading

This website provides information about the different electricity phases for each country, with a handy downloadable PDF of each country's electrical phases: `https://www.generatorsource.com/Voltages_and_Hz_by_Country.aspx`.

Get this book's PDF version and more

Scan the QR code (or go to `packtpub.com/unlock`). Search for this book by name, confirm the edition, and then follow the steps on the page.

UNLOCK NOW

Note: Keep your invoice handy. Purchases made directly from Packt don't require an invoice.

4

Adding Narration, Voice Dubbing, and Subtitles

With our short film complete, we will look at making the video accessible by adding narration, voice dubbing, and subtitles. To do this, we will start by exploring how to create and import subtitles on the **Cut** page, and then how to add narration and voice dubbing on the **Cut** page using the **Voiceover** tool.

In this chapter, we are going to cover the following main topics:

- Understanding the importance of subtitles and closed captions
- Creating and working with subtitles
- Exporting and importing subtitles
- Recording audio on the Cut page

Technical requirements

For the exercise at the end of this chapter, we will walk through a practical example of how a voice-over recording works, where we will add spoken audio to a short clip from a Buster Keaton silent comedy called *One Week*. You can download the original film here so that you can follow along: `https://archive.org/details/OneWeek512kb`.

We will also use the footage and audio we create in this chapter in *Chapters 5* and *6*.

Understanding the importance of subtitles and closed captions

Subtitles are text at the bottom of the film that translates what is being spoken into the language of the video's audience.

Closed captions are in the main language of the film and are for the text description of the action of the film, as well as what is being said, for those who are deaf or hard of hearing.

There are many reasons to create subtitles or closed captions for our video. All of them relate to making sure our video is accessible to a wider audience, whether it be those who are deaf or hard of hearing, or viewers whose language is different from the language spoken in the video.

Legal requirements to add subtitles to your video

Some countries have made it a law to make your video content as accessible as possible, including to those with a disability.

In the UK, under *The Public Sector Bodies (Websites and Mobile Applications) (No. 2) Accessibility Regulations 2018*, all public sector (government organizations) video content made after September 23, 2020, needs to be accessible, including web- or app-based videos. This also applies to charities that are mostly public-sector funded. Interestingly, it does not apply to the websites or apps of public sector broadcasters such as the BBC.

This is good to know, particularly if you make video content for public sector-funded organizations in the UK.

Check your own country for any legal requirements for your video to be accessible.

Subtitling and SEO

There is another advantage of including subtitles with your video. Search engines such as Google index the text from subtitles to help improve the ranking of your video in search results. So, adding subtitles to your video is an easy way to improve your video's **search engine optimization** (SEO), which will help increase your video's audience.

For example, if your video is talking about surfing and your subtitles have closed captioning that mentions surfing, then when someone is looking for a surfing video, they have a better chance of finding yours. If you have your video subtitled into another language, then surfers from other countries will also be able to find your video.

Thankfully, Resolve makes it incredibly easy to accommodate all kinds of subtitles.

Let us look at the differences between subtitles, closed captions, and lower thirds.

Comparing subtitles, closed captions, and lower thirds

A **lower third** is text in the lower third of the image (hence the name) that is permanently burned onto the video image and cannot be turned off. An example of this would be the presenter's name appearing for a few seconds when they are first introduced in the video. Some movies (for example, spy films) use lower thirds to show the translation of the language being spoken by a character when it is not their main language.

Lower thirds are applied just like any other title and are found on the **Cut** page, in the **Titles** panel. There, you will find standard lower thirds in the **Titles** section, as well as a variety of animated **Fusion** lower thirds grouped under the **Fusion Titles** section.

Unlike lower thirds, subtitles and closed captions can be turned on and off by the viewer of the video. Let's look at these in more detail.

As subtitles or closed captions need to be able to be turned on or off by the viewer of the video, we need to create them in a different format from our usual titles in Resolve.

As the only difference between subtitles and closed captions is the textual information you include, when we refer to subtitles in Resolve, it also applies to closed captions as well.

Let us look at how to add our own subtitles next.

Creating and working with subtitles

Subtitles can be created and edited on both the **Edit** and **Cut** pages. However, for simplicity, we will look at how to add subtitles on the **Cut** page.

Creating and editing your own subtitles

On Resolve's **Cut** page, you can create subtitles and edit them in a variety of ways. Let us look at the most common methods.

As with other titles, subtitles can be found in Resolve on the **Cut** page in the **Titles** panel. Here are the steps to create your own subtitles:

1. On the **Cut** page, navigate to **Titles> Titles** (*Figure 4.1*) and scroll down to the bottom of the panel.

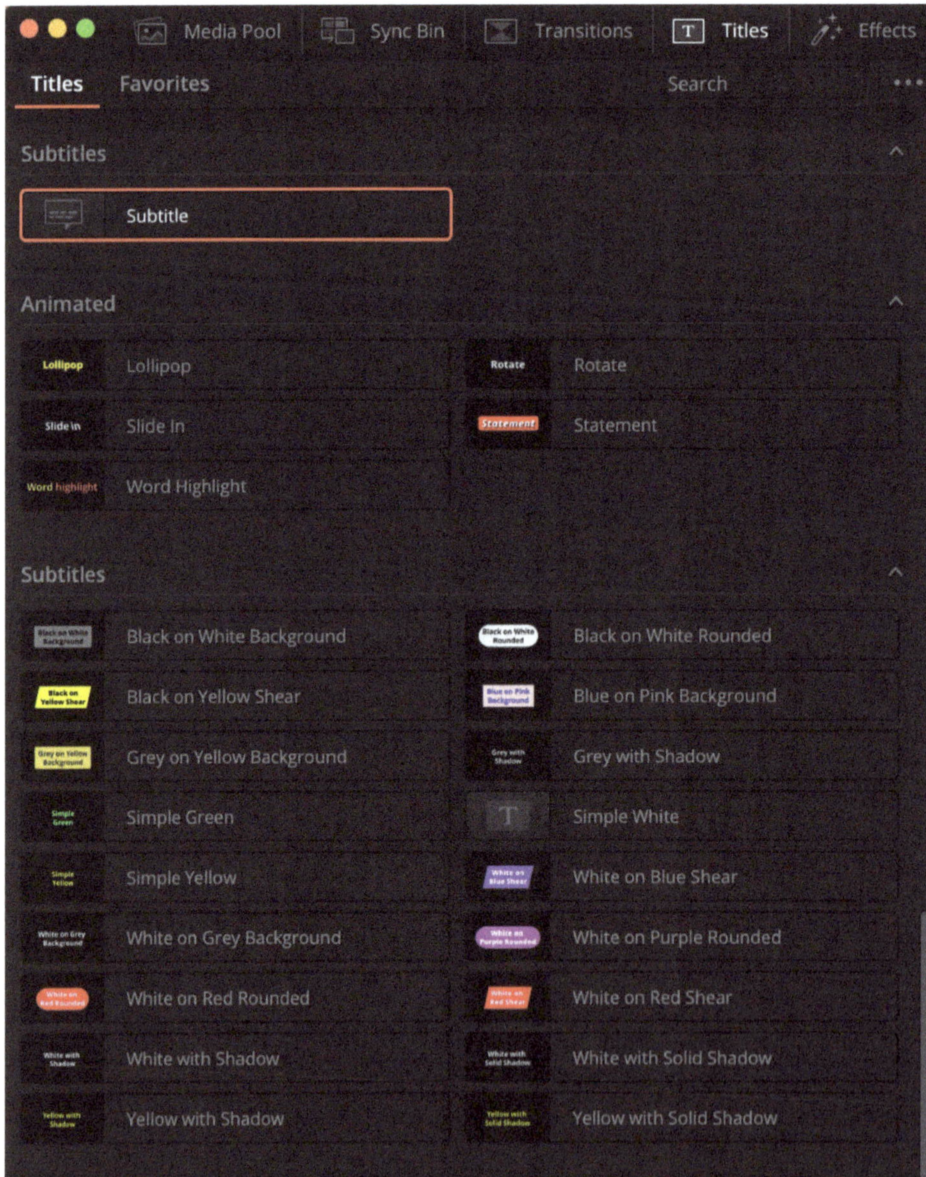

Figure 4.1: Titles panel on the Cut page

There, you will see the **Subtitles** dropdown, under which there is only one option – **Subtitle** (*Figure 4.1*).

2. Apply this **Subtitle** by dragging it onto either timeline. A new **ST1** (*Subtitle 1*) track (*Figure 4.2*) will be automatically created to accommodate the new subtitle you have just added:

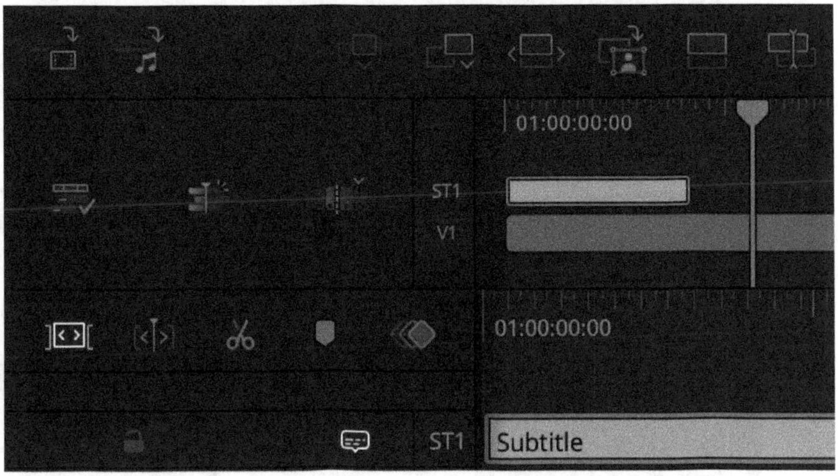

Figure 4.2: Subtitle track and clip on both timelines

Let's see how we can edit our subtitles now.

Just as with any text title, you can edit the text and format of the subtitle in the **Inspector**:

3. On the timeline, select the subtitle you want to edit.

4. Open the **Inspector**. You will now see the following options in the **Inspector** (*Figure 4.3*):

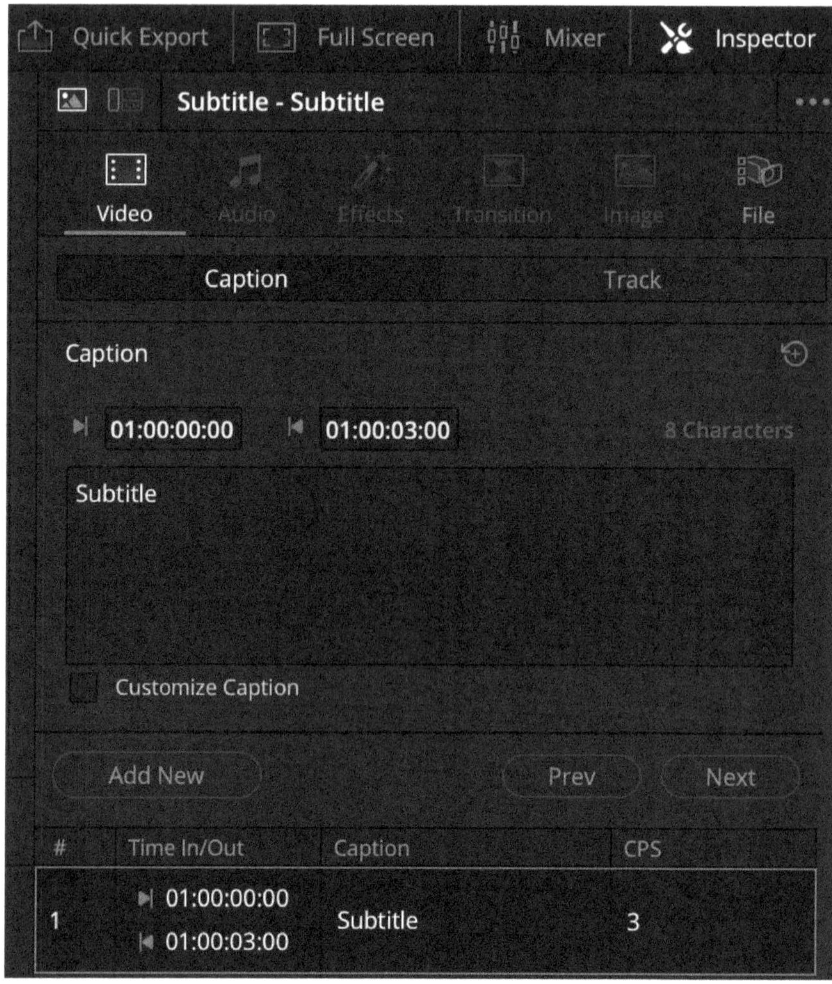

Figure 4.3: Subtitle Inspector options

Let us go over what these options mean:

- **Start timecode** and **end timecode**: These are the beginning and end of the subtitle appearing on the screen based on the timeline's timecode.
- You can either manually enter new timecode numbers here or just extend or shorten the subtitle clip's duration as you would with any other clip by dragging the edges of the clip in the timeline to change its length.

- **Textbox:** This is where you can change the text of the subtitle from the default text **Subtitle** to the text being spoken in the video. **8 Characters** (as seen in *Figure 4.3* and to the right of the textbox) is the number of characters in our default **Subtitle** text. This number will increase as we add text to our textbox.
- **Customize Caption:** This is a checkbox that changes the subtitle clip's text style between an individual style (box checked) and a style that is applied to all the subtitle clips on the subtitle track (box unchecked).

  Checking the **Customize Caption** box will reveal **Caption Style** drop-down options that allow you to change the text style of the selected subtitle clip without affecting the style of the other clips on the track.
- The **Track** tab reveals the usual text style options that we can apply to the text of all of our subtitles on the track when we leave the **Customize Caption** checkbox unchecked. We will look at these options later in the chapter.
- **Subtitle list:** This is a list of the subtitle clips on the track, which you can navigate between using the **Prev**(ious) and **Next** buttons just above the list. Let us look at what the subtitle list headings mean:
  - #: Subtitle clip number.
  - **Time In/Out:** The start and end timecode for the subtitle clip – that is, its duration.
  - **Caption:** The actual text of your subtitle or closed caption.
  - **CPS:** This stands for *characters per second*. This is the audience's reading speed of the subtitle text in your video.

  This reading speed is determined by the number of characters (individual letters) in your text and the duration of your clip. You will notice that as you type in the textbox, the **CPS** number will increase to accommodate the extra characters you are adding. You can lower the **CPS** number by stretching out the clip on the timeline. You can do this by clicking on the edge of a clip and dragging it as we would any other video, audio, or title clip. Stretching or shortening a subtitle clip to fit the length of our video clip is also how we sync the clip up to fit the action in the video.

Of course, we cannot add all of our subtitle text into one clip – that would be impossible to read! We can add more subtitle clips to lower the **CPS** to make our subtitles easier to read. There are several ways to add a new subtitle clip, as we will see next.

Adding a new subtitle clip

Clicking the **Add New** button (*Figure 4.3*) in the **Inspector** will add a new subtitle clip starting where the playhead is placed on your timeline.

This is the same as what we did earlier, where we dragged the **Subtitle** effect onto the timeline from the **Titles** panel.

As with many things in Resolve, there is also another way to add a new subtitle clip. If you have an empty subtitle track, you can add a new subtitle clip by clicking on the **Create Caption** button in the **Inspector**. This adds a new subtitle clip to the empty subtitle track, starting from where your playhead is on the timeline.

This last method of adding a new subtitle clip will only work if you have selected an empty subtitle track on the timeline by clicking on the track name.

Let us now create a new empty subtitle track on our timeline to give our audience an option for viewing subtitles in an extra language.

Adding a new subtitle track

Having only one subtitle language supported in your video will limit your audience. Ideally, we will need to add a new subtitle track for each additional language's subtitles.

This is easy enough to do:

1. Right-click on the header of any existing subtitle track in your lower timeline.
2. Choose **Add Subtitle Track** from the pop-up menu.

A new empty subtitle track (**ST2**) will appear at the top of your timeline.

If there is no existing subtitle track on your timeline, you can create a new one by doing the following:

1. Click the **Timeline Actions** icon to the left of the upper timeline (*Figure 4.4*).

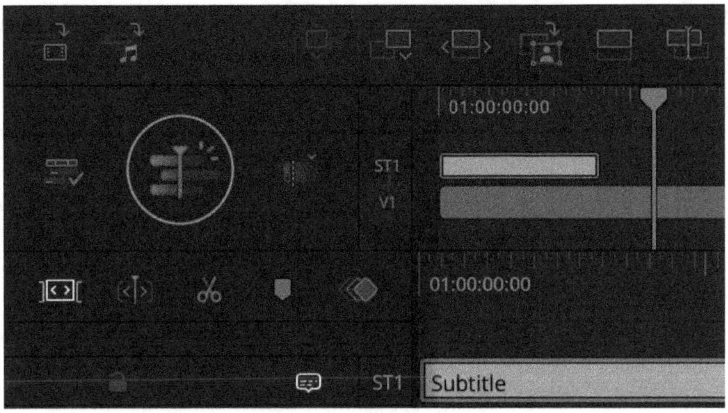

Figure 4.4: The Timeline Actions icon

2. Choose **Add Subtitle Track** from the pop-up menu (*Figure 4.5*).

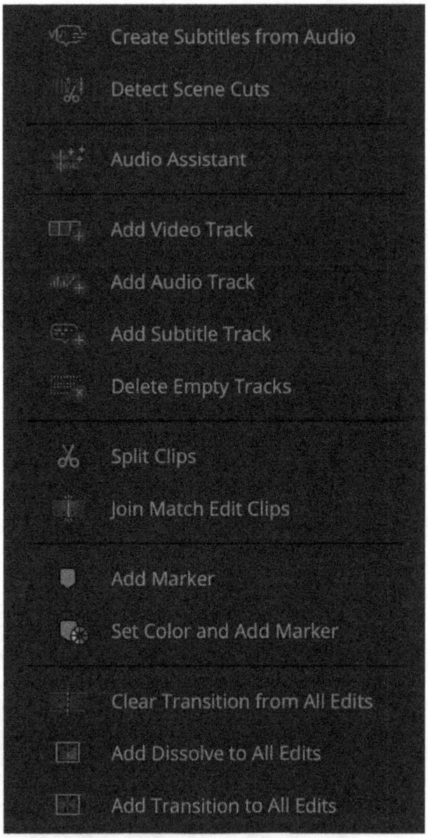

Figure 4.5: The Timeline Actions menu

So far, we have two subtitle tracks on our timeline, named **ST1** and **ST2**. Let us look at how we can format the look of the subtitles.

> **Subtitle broadcasting standards**
>
> Looking at the broadcaster's standards for subtitles will help us create a standard look for our own subtitles that viewers are used to.
>
> There are established broadcast guidelines as to how many characters of text we should have for each subtitle and what their CPS should be to make them readable.
>
> Although you may not be creating your video for television or video-on-demand broadcast, reading their subtitling guidelines can be useful as a starting point for creating your own.
>
> In the *Further reading* section, I have given links to some of the popular broadcasters' subtitles standards.
>
> There is no international standardized subtitle format between broadcasters, so just use these guidelines as a starting point.
>
> Resolve allows you to change the default subtitling settings to meet the standard you are aiming for.

Changing default subtitle settings

We can change the default settings for our subtitles to match the subtitle standard we are aiming for in the **Project Settings** section (*Figure 4.6*).

Here's how to go to the subtitle section in **Project Settings**:

1. Click on the **Project Settings** icon (which looks like a gear wheel) in the bottom right-hand corner of Resolve (*Figure 4.6*):

Figure 4.6: Project Settings icon

2. Click on **Subtitles and Transcription** in the list on the left of the **Project Settings** window (*Figure 4.7*).
3. Change your settings based on your target values for your subtitle, then click the **Save** button (*Figure 4.7*) at the bottom right of the **Project Settings** window:

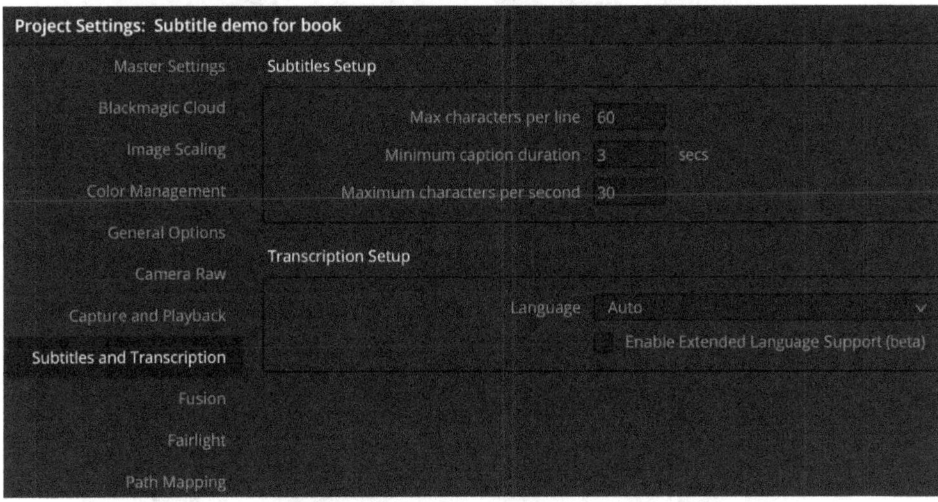

Figure 4.7: Project Settings – Subtitles

The **Subtitles Setup** settings in **Project Settings** have the following options:

- **Max characters per line**: This is the maximum number of characters allowed on one line in a subtitle – the default is `60` characters. When you type in more characters than the line limit allows, Resolve will automatically add the new characters on a new line for the subtitle.
- **Minimum caption duration**: The default is `3` seconds. This is the minimum duration allowed for subtitles in the timeline.
- **Maximum characters per second**: The default is `30` characters. This value is the maximum allowable CPS.

Resolve automatically calculates the subtitles' CPS based on the subtitle clip's duration and character count. Resolve then shows this CPS value in the subtitle's **Inspector**, rounded up or down to the nearest whole number.

If this calculation is higher than the maximum CPS in **Project Settings**, Resolve highlights in red the value in the **Inspector** (*Figure 4.8*).

In the following example (*Figure 4.8*), the duration of the subtitle clip is 3 seconds, and the subtitle is `140` characters long, which means that the CPS value is `47`. That is, `140` characters divided by 3 seconds gives us 47 CPS (rounded up to the nearest whole number):

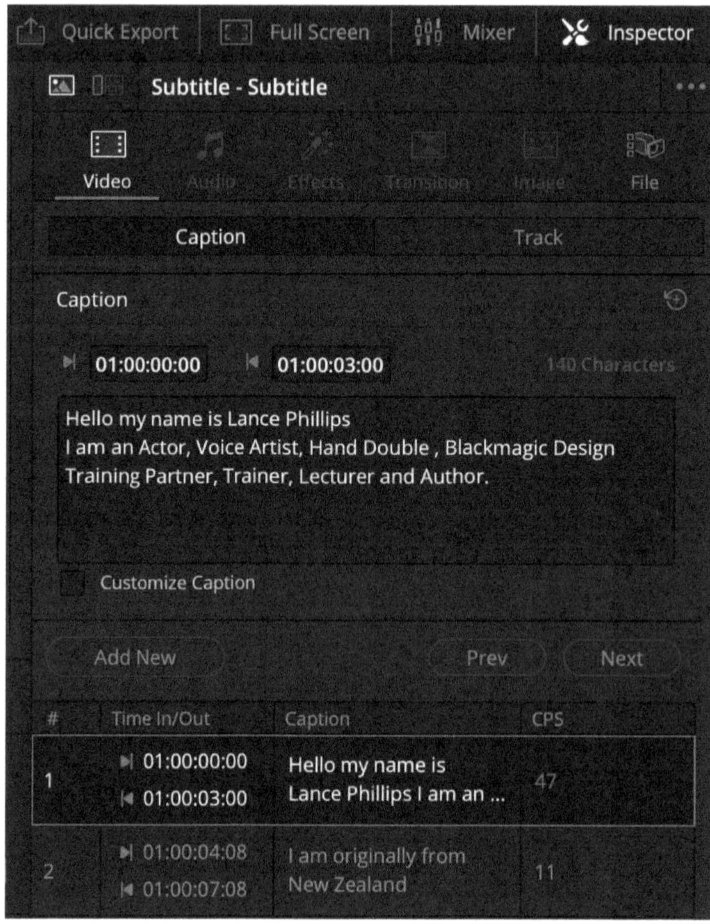

Figure 4.8: Red-highlighted CPS value in the Inspector

To correct this red **CPS** value, I would have to do one of the following:

- Make my subtitle clip on the timeline longer.
- Reduce the number of characters in my subtitle clip. If someone is speaking too fast for the length of the clip, I would need to shorten what they are saying in the subtitles to make it readable.

Either of these options will reduce the **CPS** number, and the number will turn white to show that it is within the target you have set in **Project Settings**.

The other option is to override the **Project Settings** for the whole track by deselecting the **Use Project Settings** checkbox in the **Inspector> Video> Track> Subtitle Settings** (*Figure 4.9*). This will allow you to change the **Max Line Length, Min Duration**, and **Max CPS** settings just for the selected subtitle without affecting the rest of the subtitles on the timeline.

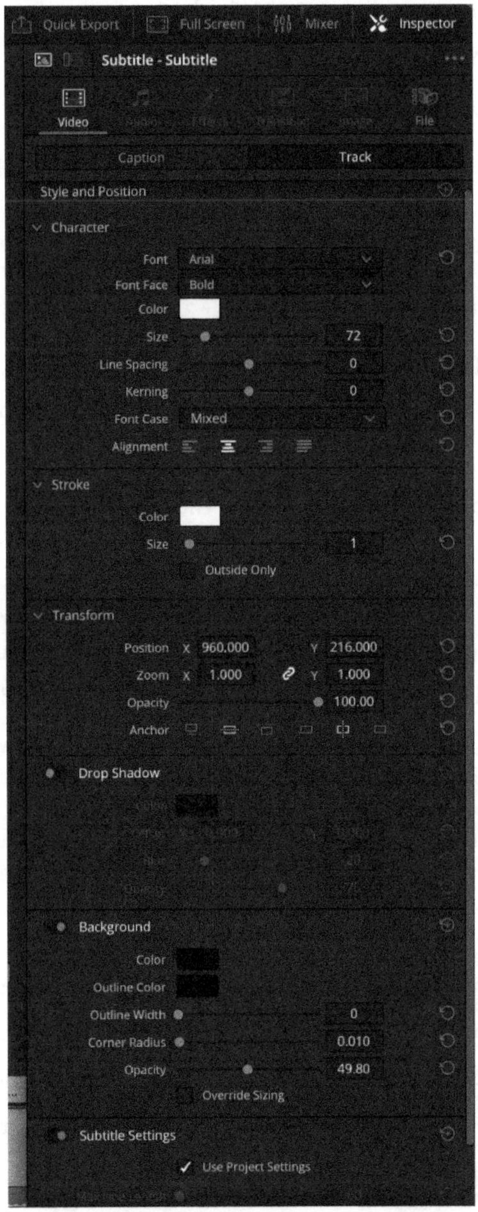

Figure 4.9: Subtitle Track style settings in the Inspector

Let us look at how to change the subtitle font and style to meet our chosen subtitle formatting standards.

Formatting our subtitles

Resolve gives us a range of text-styling controls in the **Inspector** that will change the styling of all subtitles on the subtitle track.

To do this, complete the following steps:

1. Select a subtitle clip or subtitle track (click on the track header).
2. Open the **Inspector** panel and select the **Track** tab.

   The **Track** tab has several text formatting options, under **Style and Position**, which we already explained the function of in *Chapter 2*.

However, we have two additional formatting options, **Drop Shadow** and **Background** (*Figure 4.9*), to help the text stand out from the video background. Both options can be toggled on or off with the red toggle switch to the left of the settings:

- **Drop Shadow**: Provides a shadow behind the text where we can change the following properties:
    - **Color**: A color picker to select the shadow's color.
    - **Offset**: *x/y* coordinates to change in which direction the shadow is being cast.
    - **Blur**: A slider to define how sharp the edges of the shadow are.
    - **Opacity**: A slider to define how see-through the shadow is. A value of `100` is 100% solid, and `0` is completely transparent.
- **Background**: Creates a rectangular box behind the text where we can change the following properties:
    - **Color**: A color picker to select the background's color.
    - **Outline Color**: A color picker to select the background's outline edge color.
    - **Outline Width**: A slider to define how thick the edges of the outline are.
    - **Corner Radius**: A slider to define how rounded the corners of the background are.
    - **Opacity**: A slider to define how see-through the background is. A value of `100` is 100% solid, and `0` is completely transparent.

- **Override Sizing**: A checkbox that turns off the automatic background resizing. In Resolve, the background will automatically resize to fit just around the text. Checking this checkbox will reveal the **Background Controls** section, where you can change the following:
    - **Width**: A slider to change the width of the background across the screen.
    - **Height**: A slider to change the height of the background across the screen.
    - **Center**: *x*/*y* coordinates to change the center position of the background.

The **Track** tab formats all subtitles on the same subtitle track.

If you want to change the style of an individual subtitle without affecting the other subtitles, check the **Customize Caption** checkbox (at the bottom of the **Caption** tab) to reveal the **Caption Style** dropdown for basic text formatting options such as **Font Family**, **Font Style**, **Color**, **Size**, **Font Case**, **Alignment**, and **Position**. You can only override the font options using **Caption Style**, not the **Background** or **Shadow** options.

Now that we have finished making and formatting our subtitles, we are ready to export them to be used on a social media platform.

Exporting and importing subtitles

Not only can you create subtitles within Resolve, but you can also export your subtitles to share with someone else or import subtitles created elsewhere to use in your project.

Exporting subtitles to upload to YouTube or Vimeo

Resolve supports two common web- and social-media-friendly subtitle file formats: **SRT** (`.srt`) and **WebVTT** (`.vtt`).

SRT is a basic, universally recognized subtitle file format used on the internet. This subtitle file format is the preferred format for Facebook.

WebVTT is a more advanced subtitle file format that adds more functionality to your subtitles than **SRT**, such as supporting text formatting. The **WebVTT** subtitle file format is used by YouTube and Vimeo.

There are also options to export subtitles as **IMSC 1** (`.ttml`) and **DFXP** (`.dfxp`) file formats for more advanced users.

There are a couple of ways that Resolve can export the subtitles we created on the **Cut** page as a separate subtitle file.

Exporting subtitles in the File menu

Like most applications, Resolve allows you to export your subtitles from the **File** menu:

1. In Resolve's **Menu** bar, choose **File> Export> Subtitle....**
2. Use your computer's **Export Subtitle** dialog to choose a location to save your subtitles to and whether you want to use the **VTT** or **SRT** format.

   The **Without Formatting** option for **SRT** subtitles saves the subtitles without any formatting attached.

Exporting subtitles on the Edit page

You can use the **Edit** page to export subtitles.

To do this, go to the **Edit** page, right-click on the subtitle track header, and select **Export Subtitle...** from the pop-up menu (*Figure 4.10*).

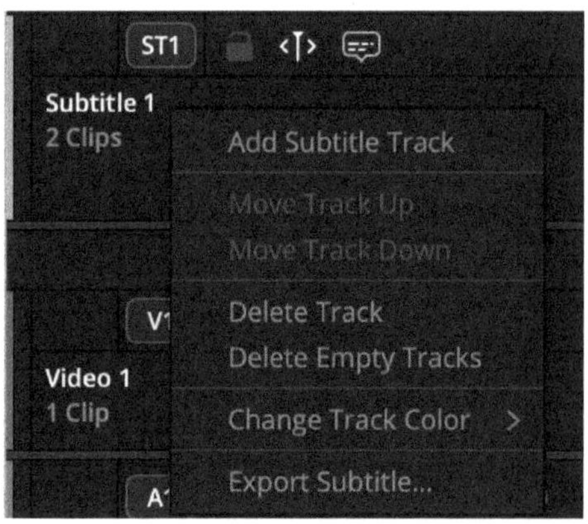

Figure 4.10: The Track header with pop-up menu

Exporting subtitles on the Deliver page

You can also export any subtitles you have created when you export your completed video from the **Deliver** page. Selecting the **Subtitle Settings** (*Figure 4.11*) drop-down menu at the bottom of the **Video** tab in the **Render Settings** panel will reveal more advanced options for exporting subtitles, including exporting as the broadcast-friendly **IMSC1** or **DFXP** file formats, as well as the usual **WebVTT** or **SRT** web-friendly subtitle formats:

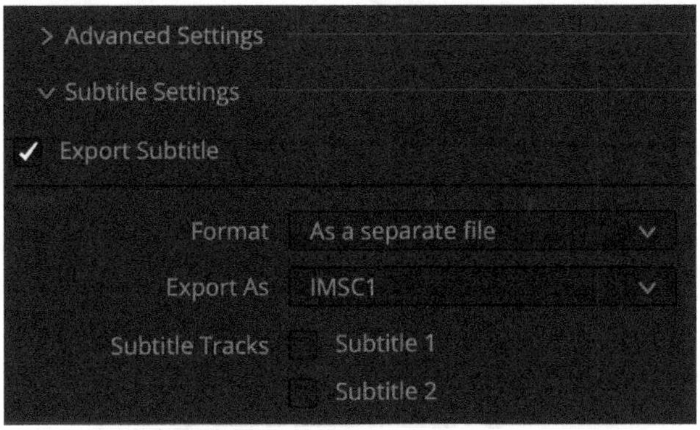

Figure 4.11: The Deliver page's Export Subtitle options

We will not go into these more advanced options here, as this is a beginners' book; however, it is useful to know there are more advanced subtitle export options available in Resolve should you ever need them (should you have the need to produce subtitles for Netflix, the BBC, or other broadcasters).

Of course, sometimes, to save time, we can get someone else to create the subtitles for us and then import them into Resolve.

Importing subtitles into Resolve

DaVinci Resolve supports importing subtitle files in the **SRT, WebVTT, IMSC1**, or **DFXP** formats. To import a subtitle file, do the following:

1. In the **File** menu, select **Import> Subtitle...**:
2. Use your computer's file manager to locate the subtitle file that you want to import (you can use the one you have just exported) and click the **Open** button.

3. The subtitle file will appear as a subtitle clip in the bin you selected. A speech bubble icon (*Figure 4.12*) at the lower left of the clip shows that it is a subtitle:

Figure 4.12: Subtitle clip in Media Pool

Alternatively, you can also import subtitles on the **Edit** page by right-clicking in the **Media Pool** and selecting **Import Subtitle...** from the pop-up menu.

With that, let's move on to the positioning of subtitle clips on our timeline.

Positioning subtitle clips on the timeline

Now that you have imported a subtitle clip into the **Media Pool**, you can add it to the timeline as you would with any other clip:

1. Select, drag, and drop the subtitle file above the video track on either timeline. A new subtitle track will be created for your subtitle clip.

   If you already have a subtitle track you want to put subtitles on, you can just drag the subtitle clip directly onto it.

   Once the subtitle clip has been dragged onto a subtitle track, it will open up and convert into a series of individual subtitle clips on the subtitle track.

2. You can reposition the subtitle clips just like any other clip by selecting them and dragging them to line up with the other clips on the timeline.
3. You can now reformat the subtitles you have imported just like you did when manually creating your own subtitles.

Now that we have added subtitles to make our video more accessible, let us look at how we can use the **Cut** page to add a voice dub or narration to our video to help it reach a wider audience.

Recording audio on the Cut page

Sometimes, in addition to adding subtitles, we may need to overdub our video into another language, add narration, or add a voice-over to our video to further illustrate the story we are trying to tell. Rather than doing this in separate audio software and then importing it into our edit, we can do this all within Resolve on the **Cut** page.

Previously, we needed to use the **Fairlight** page to do this; however, since DaVinci Resolve version 20, we can now do this directly on the **Cut** page using the **Voiceover** tool.

1. Click the **Voiceover** tool icon in the toolbar (*Figure 4.13*).

Figure 4.13: Voiceover tool icon

2. This reveals several controls (*Figure 4.14*) to set up and record your voice-over on the **Cut** page timeline.

Figure 4.14: Voiceover controls

Before you record a voice-over, you need to connect a microphone to your computer. If you have a built-in microphone on your computer, such as on a laptop, or if you have already connected a microphone to your computer before starting Resolve, then it should be recognized in the following steps.

Connecting a microphone

If you are using an external microphone, then you will need to save your work and restart Resolve to force it to recognize the microphone connected to your computer.

If your microphone is still not recognized, then make sure it is recognized by your computer first. If your computer does not recognize it, then restarting your computer with your microphone plugged in should fix the issue.

Your computer and software apps look for connected hardware devices (such as microphones) when they are first started. Restarting Resolve (as with any software) will often solve any hardware connection issues. If this doesn't work, restarting your computer after connecting external hardware should resolve the problem. This is the case for most hardware.

Once your microphone is connected and recognized by your computer (you can check for this in your computer's sound settings), we can look at **Voiceover Settings**.

Voiceover Settings

Clicking on the **Voiceover Settings** icon reveals the following settings (*Figure 4.15*):

- **Audio Input**: Select the microphone you want to use to record your voice-over. By default, Resolve will select the same microphone you have allocated in your computer system settings.
- **Record Track**: Select the audio track you want to record to. By default, Resolve will create a dedicated **Voiceover Track** labelled **VO** to record your voice-over to.
- **Monitoring**: These are the options for how you would like to monitor your audio as you record.
    - **Timeline & Microphone**: This setting allows you to hear both the microphone audio input and timeline audio as you record.
    - **Timeline Audio Only**: Allows you to hear just the timeline audio as you are recording.
    - **Microphone Audio Only**: Allows you to just hear your microphone input and mutes the timeline while you are recording.

    - **Mute Monitoring When Recording**: Mutes all audio playback while you are recording. This setting is useful to avoid audio feedback that can occur when recording without headphones.

- **No Countdown**: When you click **Record**, start talking without a visual countdown.
- **3 Secs Countdown**: A numerical counter that appears in the timeline viewer that counts down to the start of the recording. This visual three-second countdown appears on the viewer before the recording begins, giving you a little time to get ready. It's a visual cue only, with no audio beeps.
- **5 Secs Countdown**: Like **3 Secs Countdown**, this visual five-second countdown appears on the viewer before the recording starts, allowing you to prepare. It's a visual cue only, with no audio beeps.
- **Voiceover Recording File Location**: Select where you want to save your new voice-over audio files.

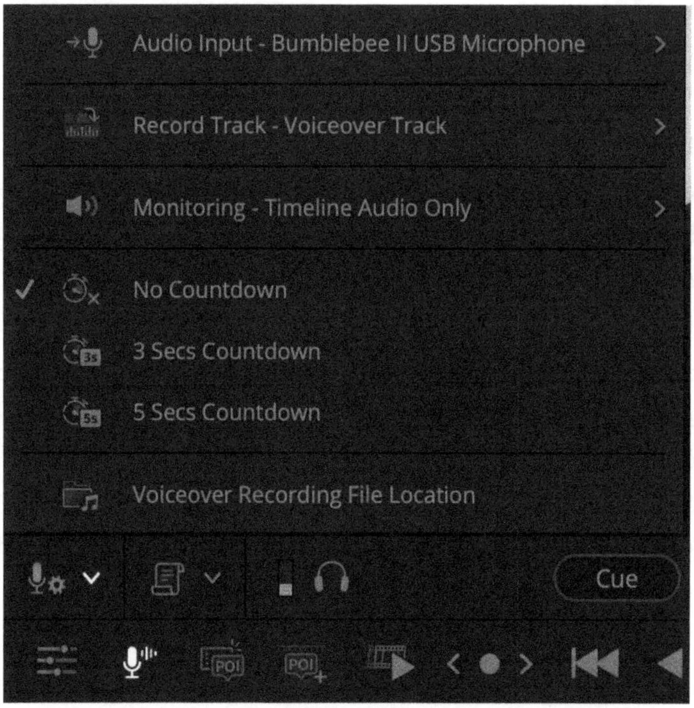

Figure 4.15: Voiceover Settings

Now that you have set up your recording and audio monitoring settings to suit your personal preferences, we can import a script into Resolve to use as a teleprompter in the **Script Menu**.

> **Key concept – teleprompter**
>
> A teleprompter is a mechanical or digital device that projects a script over a screen so that an actor or presenter can read their lines without having to memorize them or rely on cue cards.
>
> The name comes from the TelePrompTer Corporation, which made the first teleprompter for television programs in 1950.

Let us look at the **Voiceover** tools that enable us to adjust the look of our teleprompter.

Script Menu

Before you record your voice-over, you can import a **plain text** `.txt` file to use as a teleprompter script and adjust how this appears on the screen. You can access these script settings in the **Script Menu** (*Figure 4.16*):

- **Enable Prompter Overlay**: This option turns on or off the text overlay for the loaded script.
- **Load Script File**: This opens your computer's file selector to choose a text (`.txt`) file to load into the prompter.
- **Clear Script File**: This removes the text (`.txt`) file from the prompter.
- **Font Size**: This allows you to choose the font size of the onscreen text.
- **Line Spacing**: This lets you choose the line spacing of the onscreen text.
- **Side Margin**: This allows you to choose how big a margin to use for the left side of the onscreen text.
- **Background Opacity**: This lets you choose the transparency level of the onscreen text background so that you can read the text. A setting of 100% background opacity will result in not being able to see the underlying video.

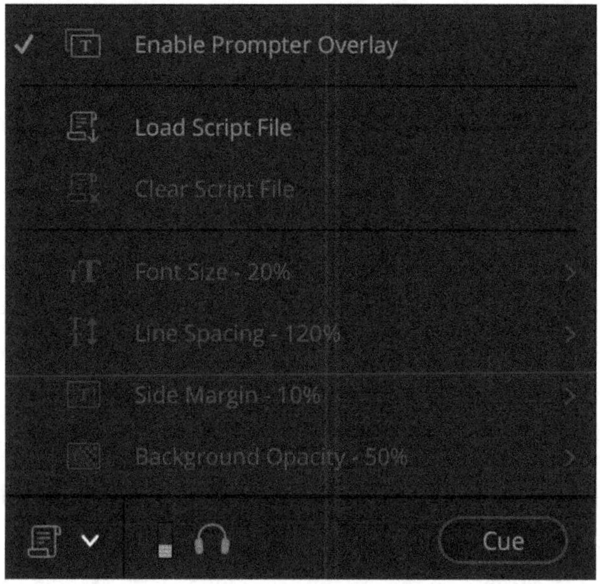

Figure 4.16: Script Menu settings

Now that we have set up the **Cut** page for recording audio and loaded our script, let us record a voiceover.

We will add spoken audio to a short clip from a Buster Keaton silent comedy called *One Week*. You can download the original film here so that you can follow along: `https://archive.org/details/OneWeek512kb`.

We will also use this footage in *Chapter 6*.

Practice what you learned in *Chapter 1* by creating a new project for this exercise:

1. Create a new project and name it `Chapter_4_VO`.
2. Import the `OneWeek512kb` file into the **Media Pool**.
3. Drag `OneWeek512kb` from the **Media Pool** onto the timeline.

We are now going to add some dialogue to the breakfast scene in *One Week*. Let us select the footage we want and create a new timeline with it next.

Creating a new timeline using selected footage

Rather than use a whole lengthy clip on the timeline, which is often the case with archival footage, we can create a new timeline with only part of the footage that we want to use, selected from our original timeline:

1. Go to the timeline we just created on the **Cut** page.
2. Place your playhead on the timeline at the clip that shows the **Monday 9th** calendar roughly at `01:03:18:14`. Add an **In** point by typing *I* on the keyboard.
3. Place your playhead at the end after Buster's wife kisses him, roughly at `01:04:23:04`. Add an **Out** point by typing *O* on the keyboard.
4. We will now create a new timeline for our clips by doing either of the following:
    - Right-clicking in the **Media Pool** and selecting **Create New Timeline Using Selected Bin...**
    - Right-clicking on the timeline thumbnail in the **Media Pool** and selecting **Create New Timeline Using Selected Clips...**
5. In the resulting **Create New Timeline** dialog box (*Figure 4.17*), name the timeline and make sure that **Use Selected Mark In/Out** is checked. We have named it `Breakfast Scene`.
6. Click on the **Create** button:

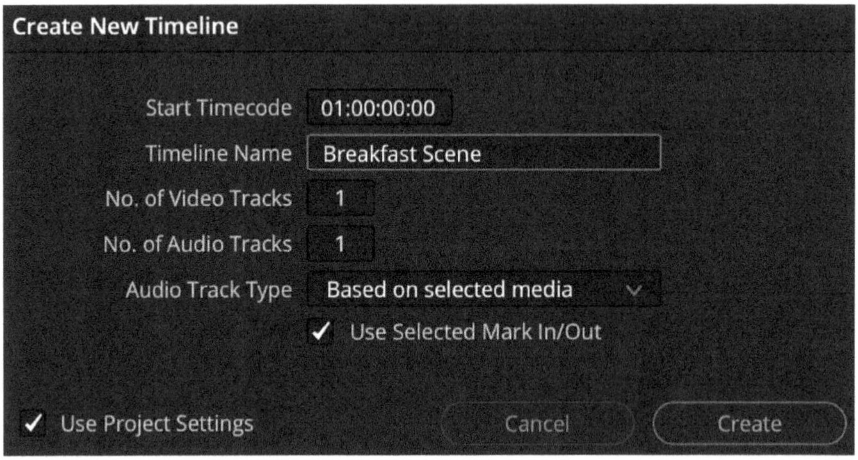

Figure 4.17: Create New Timeline dialog box

You now have a new timeline in the **Media Pool** that only contains clips that have just the breakfast scene.

Before we can start to add our voice-over to the footage, we need to prepare it for the edit. As it is one single clip with no cuts between the shots, we need to divide up the clip into individual shots so that we have more control over the timings of each shot.

Adding scene cuts

Rather than manually adding cuts to the footage, we can use the **Detect Scene Cuts** feature in the **Studio** version of DaVinci Resolve. Here's how to do this:

1. Select the **Timeline** menu in the menu bar.
2. Select **Detect Scene Cuts** in the drop-down **Timeline** menu.

A progress bar will show (*Figure 4.18*), as Resolve looks for any sudden changes in the footage and adds cuts where the changes are:

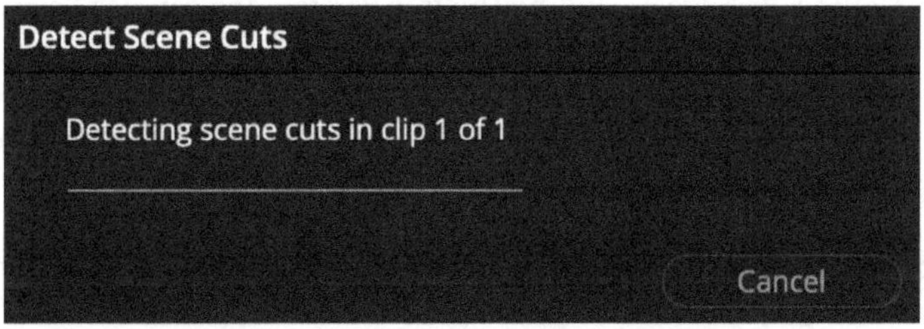

Figure 4.18: Detect Scene Cuts progress bar

The original clip on your timeline will now be separated into individual clips for each shot.

Occasionally, Resolve will not recognize a shot change due to a dissolve between the shots. You can always add a cut manually where Resolve has not created one.

If Resolve has added a cut where there should not be one, you can remove it by following these steps:

1. Place your playhead on or just after the cut you want to remove.
2. Select the **Timeline** menu in the menu bar.
3. Select **Join Clips** in the drop-down **Timeline** menu.

The two clips will now be merged into one.

If you do not have the Studio version of Resolve, there is another way to add cuts between shots. We will now discuss that.

Scene Detect on the Media page

If you are sent a video to edit (such as archive footage) with no access to the original clips, it can be time-consuming to manually add your own cut points to every shot to separate the scene. Thankfully, Resolve has another function, called **Scene Detect**, that can automatically detect individual shots and separate them by adding cuts between each shot.

The advantage of **Scene Detect** over **Detect Scene Cuts** is that with **Scene Detect**, you can change Resolve's sensitivity in being able to detect scene cuts. You can also use **Scene Detect** to manually add scene cuts that Resolve did not identify, rather than having to add the clips to the timeline to cut them, as we did in the preceding method.

Let us look at how **Scene Detect** does this.

In all versions of DaVinci Resolve, including the free version, we can use **Scene Detect** on the **Media** page, as follows:

1. Create a bin in the **Media Pool** called `Scene Detect Clips`. **Scene Detect** will put the clips it creates into the currently open bin.
2. Open the **Media** page and select the **One_Week_512kb** video file on your hard drive in the **Media Storage** panel.

   Scene Detect will not work on clips already imported to the **Bins** section in **Media Pool**.
3. Right-click on the **One_Week_512kb** video file and select **Scene Cut Detection...** in the pop-up menu.

   The **Scene Detect** window (*Figure 4.19*) will open with the video file you selected, ready to divide it into individual clips.

4. Click the **Auto Scene Detect** button:

Figure 4.19: Scene Detect window

Resolve will now play back the video and begin detecting the cuts automatically. Resolve analyzes the video, looking for sudden visual changes between frames. The **Scene Detect** window (*Figure 4.19*) will show one large viewer with a mini viewer inset on the left and right of the main one. The mini viewer on the left will show the frame before the detected cut, the main viewer will show the frame following the detected cut, and the mini viewer on the right will show the second frame after the detected cut. Each potential cut is placed on the timeline of **Scene Detect** as a vertical line. The taller the line, the more confident Resolve will be that it has detected a cut.

Let's look at this in more detail:

- The *vertical green lines* represent each cut that Resolve has detected as a potential cut.
- The *vertical white lines* are where Resolve has detected a change in the footage between frames but has not marked them as cuts.

- The *horizontal purple line*, called the **confidence bar**, can be adjusted up or down to change the level of confidence Resolve has in detecting cuts. Moving the bar up will make green bars shorter than the confidence bar white, eliminating them as cuts. Moving the bar down will make the white bars taller than the confidence bar green, adding them as cuts.
- The numbered list on the right-hand side of the window is a list of all the cuts that Resolve has accepted. This **Cut List** functionality will show the **Scene** number, **Frame** number, and timecode (**Start TC**) for each cut. You can click on any of these listed cuts to navigate to that cut in the timeline.
- The **Delete** button will remove the selected cut from **Cut List**.
- The **Add** button will add a cut where the playhead is. Sometimes, Resolve will be confused by a transition between cuts, such as a gradual fade, and not detect it as a cut. In this case, you will need to use the viewers to find and align the cut to your playhead, and then click the **Add** button to manually add the cut to the **Cut List**.
- The slider (at the bottom right of the window) zooms the view of the timeline in or out to show the detected cuts in more detail.

5. Click on the **Add Cuts to Media Pool** button to add the cuts in the **Cut List** to the **Media Pool**.

   Unlike using **Detect Scene Cuts** on the timeline, **Scene Detect** will add our new clips to the **Media Pool**, where we can choose which clips to add to our timeline.

   If we want to use **Scene Detect** rather than **Detect Scene Cuts** to detect our cuts in our breakfast scene and add them to our timeline, then we will need to do the following:

   a. Go to the **Cut** page.
   b. Click on the **Metadata View** icon (*Figure 4.20*) at the top of the **Media Pool** to reveal the clip's timecode:

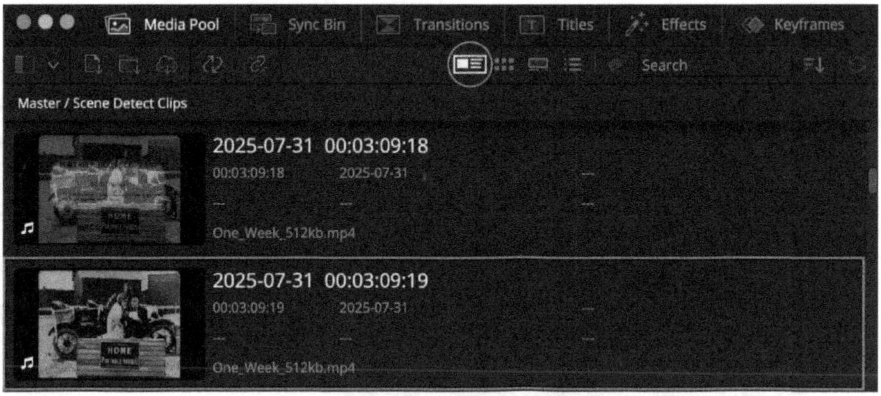

Figure 4.20: Metadata View

c. Select all clips starting from `00:03:09:19` and finishing before `00:04:23:06`, by *Shift*-clicking on them. Your timecode may be different, depending on where **Scene Detect** decided to make the cuts. If that is the case, use the thumbnail in *Figure 4.20* to guide you.

d. Right-click a selected clip and select **Create New Timeline Using Selected Clips....**

e. Name your new timeline `Breakfast-Scene`.

Let us now remove the title cards from the timeline, as we are replacing them with audio.

Ripple-deleting clips on the Cut page

An easy and quick way to ripple-delete clips on the timeline is to enable the **Ripple On** function of the timelines on the **Cut** page:

1. Select the **Ripple On** icon (*Figure 4.21*) to the left of the timeline. The icon will turn white when it is enabled.

2. Delete the **Breakfast is ready!** and **I'll be right down!** title card clips.

Figure 4.21: Ripple On icon

Now, we are going to record the missing dialogue to replace our title cards.

If you already have audio that you want to keep on **Track A1** (such as music), then first create a new audio track (**A2**), as outlined in the next section.

Creating a new audio track

To create a new audio track on the **Cut** page, right-click on the black area below the **A1** track on the lower timeline and select **Add Audio Track**.

Or, you could select the **Timeline Actions** icon and select **Add Audio Track** from the **Timeline Actions** pop-up menu.

Let us now return to the **Voiceover** tool and record our voice-over.

Recording audio

Whenever you record live audio (whether it be via a microphone, keyboard, or MIDI instrument) in Resolve, it does two things:

- It stores it as a new audio file on your computer
- It puts a copy of the recorded clip in whichever bin you selected when you started recording

In the following subsections, we take a deeper look at some of the steps involved in recording.

Choosing where to save recorded audio clips

You can change where on your computer Resolve stores your new recording in **Project Settings**. Here's how:

1. Open **Project Settings**.
2. Open the **Master Settings** panel in **Project Settings**.
3. In the **Working Folders** section, next to **Project media location**, use the **Browse** button to choose a new location on your computer to save all your video and audio recordings.

When you record audio in Resolve, the recording begins at the position of the playhead on the timeline. This is so that you can record audio in a specific position in your edit – for example, in reaction to an audio cue.

Begin recording

Once you have placed your playhead where you want your recording to start, it is a simple case of clicking the **Record** button in the **Voiceover** controls above the timeline to begin recording, as follows:

1. Put the playhead on the timeline where you want the recording to start.
2. Click the **Record** button in the **Voiceover** controls above the timeline. The button will turn red to show that it is recording.

A recording will start immediately, and a new audio waveform will be drawn underneath the playhead on the track you have selected.

Stop recording

To stop recording, you can do either of the following:

- Click the **Stop** button in the **Voiceover** controls above the timeline
- Press the spacebar on the computer keyboard

Although we can determine the start of the recording based on where our playhead is on the timeline, this does not affect the start of the script prompt in the viewer. By default, the script prompt will appear at the start of the timeline and finish at the end. To have more control over when the script prompt appears in the viewer, you will need to create a **Cue** point on the timeline.

Creating cues

To create a **Cue** point for the start of the prompt script, we put an **In** point (*I* key) on the timeline.

To create a **Cue** point for the end of the prompt script, we put an **Out** point (*O* key) on the timeline.

Clicking the **Cue** button will snap the playhead back to the initial record **In** point. If you do not set an **In** point on your timeline, Resolve will use the start of your timeline as the **Cue** point to snap to.

Let us look at how we can create our own prompt script cue for our Buster Keaton video:

1. On the timeline, line up the playhead just before the bride opens her mouth to speak at `01:00:49:00`.
2. Mark an **In** point on the timeline by pressing the *I* key on your keyboard.
3. On the timeline, line up the playhead just after the groom finishes speaking at `01:00:55:00`.
4. Mark an **Out** point on the timeline by pressing the *O* key on your keyboard.

The distance on the timeline between the **In** and **Out** points will determine the playback speed of the prompt script in the viewer.

What appears in the viewer will depend on what is in our prompt script. You can create your own script using any text editor as long as you save it as a **plain text file** (`.txt`). Saving your script in **rich text format** (`.rtf`) will not work.

I have included a sample script for you to load into Resolve if you don't want to create one yourself. I have called it `DR Chapter 4 VO.txt`. Feel free to load this script into Resolve as outlined earlier in the chapter, and play around with the script prompter to see what it can do.

Finally, there are some additional tools that we can use while recording our voice-over to help improve the quality of the recording.

Recording tools

Once we start recording, the background of the **Voiceover** toolbar turns red to indicate that we are recording (*Figure 4.22*).

Figure 4.22: The Voiceover toolbar during recording

We can see a little green audio levels bar to the left of the tools, which shows the microphone's audio levels.

We can also click the **Input Monitoring** icon (it looks like a pair of headphones next to the audio levels bar) to allow us to hear the microphone input. This is useful to listen to the noise the microphone may be picking up.

There are also some additional AI tools to the right of the **Cue**, **Record**, and **Stop** buttons that allow us to improve the recorded audio as we are recording. The tools from left to right are as follows:

- **Voice isolation**: This is a Studio-only tool to remove background sounds.
- **Dialog Leveler**: This is the same as the similarly named **AI Dialogue Leveler** in the **Inspector** (even though it is spelled differently), which we used in *Chapter 3*. In this case, we are applying it to the clip as we are recording it, to help keep a constant volume for the track. You can always adjust the settings in the **Inspector** after the clip has been recorded.
- **Stereo Fixer**: This tool fixes common issues when translating audio between stereo and mono. If you are recording from a stereo microphone, it will help translate the audio so that the channels work correctly on a mono track.

That's it! You now know how to use the **Voiceover** tool to add a voice-over or overdub other languages over your original audio recording.

Of course, it is beyond the scope of this book to teach you any foreign languages, so you will need to find your own voice-over artists fluent in the language you require for your video's audience.

Summary

Here is what you have achieved in *Chapter 4*:

- Learned about the different subtitle formatting requirements
- Added different format subtitles to your video and edited them
- Exported and imported subtitles into and out of your video project
- Used **Scene Detect** to automatically cut a single video into several clips based on the original video's edit points
- Used the **Voiceover** tool to record a narration or voice-over on the **Cut** page

In *Chapter 5*, we will look at creating a sound library and importing sound effects into **Fairlight**. We will also look at how to audition sound effects and how to apply them to a video in the timeline. We will then change their speed and timing to fit the video.

Questions

1. True or false? You cannot record audio on the **Cut** page; to do this, you need to use the more advanced audio features of the **Fairlight** page.
2. True or false? Resolve only supports SRT subtitle files, so this is the only file format you can export your subtitles in.
3. True or false? Pressing the *M* key on your computer keyboard will mute an audio track on the **Cut** page.
4. True or false? To record from a microphone on the **Cut** page, you will need to first patch the microphone, arm the track, and then record.

Further reading

More information about subtitles' broadcast standards:

- BBC:
  - `https://www.bbc.co.uk/accessibility/forproducts/guides/subtitles/`
  - `https://www.bbc.co.uk/academy-guides/how-do-i-create-subtitles`
- Netflix:
  - `https://partnerhelp.netflixstudios.com/hc/en-us/categories/1500000000781-Timed-Text-Resources`
  - `https://partnerhelp.netflixstudios.com/hc/en-us/articles/217350977-English-Timed-Text-Style-Guide`
- Amazon:
  - `https://videodirect.amazon.com/home/help?topicId=G201979140`
- Channel 4:
  - `https://www.channel4.com/media/documents/corporate/foi-docs/SG_FLP.pdf`
- Subtitle file naming standards:
  - `https://loc.gov/standards/iso639-2/php/code_list.php`
- Facebook subtitle naming standards:
  - `https://www.facebook.com/help/1528795707381162`

- SRT file info:
    - `https://en.wikipedia.org/wiki/SubRip#SubRip_text_file_format`
- WebVTT file info:
    - `https://w3c.github.io/webvtt/`
- YouTube instructions on adding subtitles:
    - `https://support.google.com/youtube/answer/2734796?hl=en-GB&ref_topic=7296214#zippy=%2Cupload-a-file`
- Vimeo instructions on adding subtitles:
    - `https://vimeo.zendesk.com/hc/en-us/articles/224968828-Captionsand-subtitles#h_01FPAZ98X0B9ESFP23KMXGVTYB`
- Accessibility requirements for UK public sector videos:
    - `https://www.gov.uk/guidance/accessibility-requirements-for-public-sector-websites-and-apps`
    - `https://www.legislation.gov.uk/uksi/2018/852/contents/made`
- Archive videos to practice with:
    - `https://archive.org/details/OneWeek`

Get this book's PDF version and more

Scan the QR code (or go to `packtpub.com/unlock`). Search for this book by name, confirm the edition, and then follow the steps on the page.

UNLOCK NOW

Note: Keep your invoice handy. Purchases made directly from Packt don't require an invoice.

5

Creating Additional Sound

In this chapter, we will look at enhancing the vocals you created in *Chapter 4*, using **Fairlight FX** on the **Cut** page. We will also explore how to import third-party audio FX plugins to add more functionality. Additionally, we will create a **sound effects** (**SFX**) library into which we can import SFX into Fairlight. We will then look at how to audition those SFX and how to apply them to the video in the timeline.

In this chapter, we are going to cover the following main topics:

- Enhancing the vocals
- Importing audio effects plugins
- Navigating the Fairlight page
- Importing an SFX library
- Auditioning and adding SFX to the Fairlight timeline

Technical requirements

For the exercises in this chapter, we will continue to work on the audio project we created in *Chapter 4*. If you have not completed *Chapter 4*, then I suggest you quickly follow the exercises there so that you can get the most out of this chapter.

Enhancing the vocals

In the previous chapter, you learned how to use the tools on the **Cut** page to record your voice directly into Resolve from a microphone connected to your computer. Now that we have recorded our voiceovers directly into Resolve, we can enhance the sound quality of the vocals by lifting the frequencies that we want people to pay attention to and lowering other unwanted frequencies into the background; this is called **sweetening**.

Here, we are going to look at three Fairlight FX audio plugins that enhance the vocals, as our listeners will often switch off if they cannot hear what is being said or if it is difficult to listen to. Like the audio fixing plugins, all of these plugins can be found on the **Edit**, **Fairlight**, and **Cut** pages. For our examples, we are going to use the **Cut** page. On the **Cut** page, navigate to **Effects** > **Audio** > **Fairlight FX**, and then to the specific plugin. You can have fun applying these plugins to the voiceover clips you recorded in the `Chapter_4_VO` project you created in *Chapter 4*. Let's take an in-depth look at each of these vocal-enhancing plugins, starting with the **Pitch** plugin.

Pitch

This audio plugin changes the audio pitch without changing the clip speed. It is great to add slightly more bass to a person's voice, which will add a bit more authority.

Figure 5.1: The Pitch Fairlight FX

Let us explore how the **Pitch** plugin works:

1. On the **Cut** page, navigate to **Effects** > **Audio** > **Fairlight FX** > **Pitch**.
2. To apply the **Pitch** effect, you can do any of the following:
    - Select the clip you want to apply the **Pitch** effect to, then double-click the effect in the **Effects** > **Audio** > **Fairlight FX** panel
    - Drag it onto the clip to apply it
    - Click the **Add Effect** button at the bottom of the **Effects** panel

The **Pitch** control panel (*Figure 5.1*) opens with the following controls:

- **Bypass**: An orange toggle switch at the top left of the window, which turns the plugin on and off. Make sure this is turned on.
- **Pitch**: These knobs control the selection and direction of the pitch change:
    - **Semitones**: This knob changes the pitch by whole semitones. Negative values lower the pitch, and positive values increase the pitch.
    - **Cents**: This knob is for more subtle pitch changes. It changes the pitch up or down in increments of 1/100th of a semitone. This is great if you want the effect to be more subtle and less noticeable.
- **Output**: This knob affects the output signal after the pitch has been applied:
    - **Dry/Wet**: This knob controls the percentage of the output mix of the *wet* or noise-reduced signal to the *dry* or unprocessed signal. So, a value of `0` is completely dry, whereas a value of `100%` is completely wet. Mixing in some of the dry/unaltered voices will add more depth and naturalness to the change.

Next, we will talk about another popular vocal-enhancing plugin: **Vocal Channel**.

Vocal Channel

This plugin is for all-purpose changes to the human voice, whether it be singing or the spoken word. The controls for **High Pass** filtering, **Equalizer**, and **Compressor** are combined within this one plugin.

Let us explore how the **Vocal Channel** plugin works:

1. On the **Cut** page, navigate to **Effects** > **Audio** > **Fairlight FX** > **Vocal Channel**.
2. To apply the **Vocal Channel** effect, you can do any of the following:
    - Select the clip you want to apply the **Vocal Channel** effect to, then double-click **Vocal Channel** in the **Effects** > **Audio** > **Fairlight FX** panel
    - Drag it onto the clip to apply it
    - Click the **Add Effect** button at the bottom of the **Effects** panel

3. The **Vocal Channel** panel (*Figure 5.2*) opens with the following graphs. The graph on the left lets you see the frequency that the **High Pass** and **Equalizer** controls are targeting. The **Dynamics** graph (called this as it shows the **dynamic range** of the audio) on the right shows you the effects of the **Compressor** controls. An audio meter to the right of the graphs will show you the **Output** sound level to enable you to monitor the final output of all the controls.

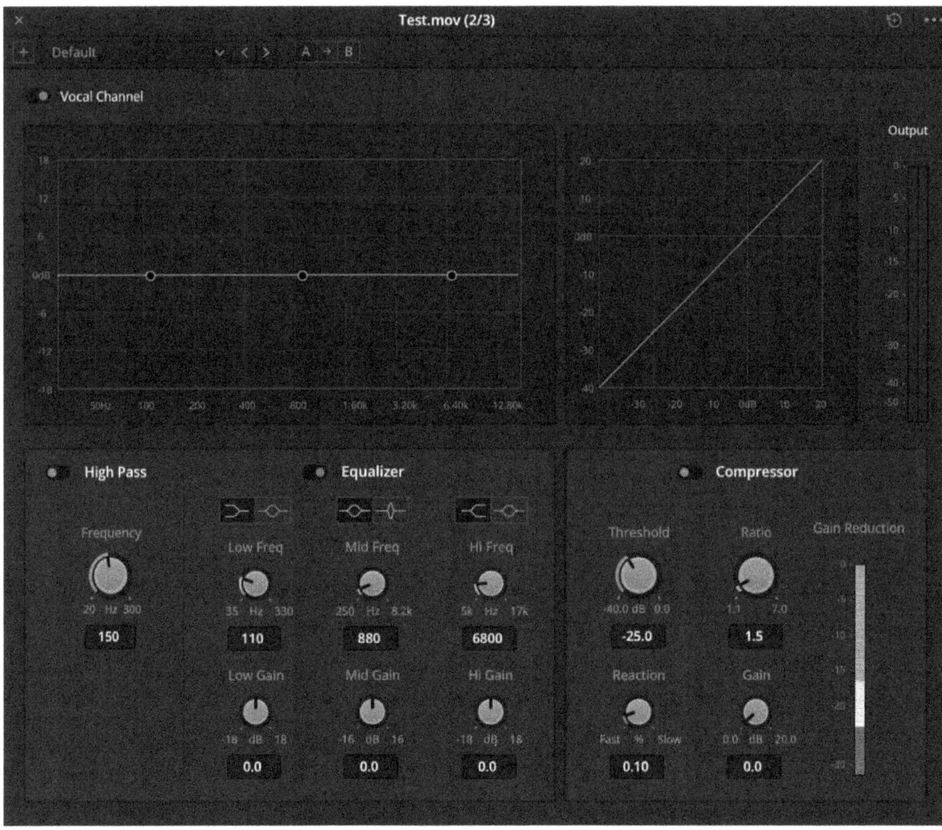

Figure 5.2: The Vocal Channel Fairlight FX

Let us explore the **Vocal Channel** controls in more detail:

- **High Pass**: This is a filter that reduces the lower-end bass frequencies. A toggle switch turns it on (it is off by default), and a knob sets the frequency level below which the bass reduction is applied. It is called a **High Pass** filter as it allows higher frequencies through but stops lower-end frequencies. It is effective to remove the *boominess* or heavy bass sound from some mics created when the singing or speaking talent gets too close to the mic.

- **Equalizer**: A three-band graphic equalizer (toggle enabled by default) for adjusting specific frequencies for speech. The controls are split for **Low**, **Mid**, and **Hi Freq** (frequency) and **Gain** adjustments:
    - **Low/Mid/Hi** selection mode: These selection buttons change the shape of the frequency selection based on the selection curve shown on the button (*Figure 5.2*).
    - For example, the **Mid** range selection buttons allow you to broaden or narrow the frequencies included on either side of the core frequency selected.
    - The **Low** and **Hi** range selection buttons allow you to toggle between a threshold selection (where all frequencies above (for **Hi**) or below (for **Low**) the selection are affected) or a more targeted frequency selection:
        - **Low/Mid/Hi Freq (Hz)**: These knobs allow you to select the core frequency for which you want to change the gain for
        - **Low/Mid/Hi Gain (dB)**: These knobs allow you to raise or lower the level of the selected frequencies
- **Compressor**: This (toggled off by default) takes the loud sounds and compresses them down to be closer to the quieter sounds. This is good if a person's speech volume levels often alternate between high and low, and it makes it easier to listen to. Common examples of the use of compression are in radio commercials or film trailers, where the sound of the speaker's voice stays steady in volume throughout. **Compressor** has the following controls to select and adjust the compression effect:
    - **Threshold (dB)**: The **Threshold** knob sets the frequency level above which compression occurs.
    - **Reaction**: The **Reaction** knob adjusts how fast the compression is applied when the audio frequency goes above the threshold. **Fast** quickly applies compression, whereas **Slow** takes longer before applying compression.
    - **Ratio**: This knob adjusts the compression ratio, which is the amount of compression applied above the threshold set. The first number in the ratio is the strength of the input signal before compression, whereas the second number is the strength of the output signal after compression. So, a compression ratio of 4:1 means that for every 4 dB of sound input, the compressor allows 1 dB of sound output. So, a 1:1 compression ratio means no compression is being applied (for every 1 dB, 1 goes through), whereas the max setting of 7:1 is heavily compressed.

- **Gain (dB)**: The **Gain** knob compensates for any audio levels lost due to the compression by raising the gain of the output audio levels. This effectively raises the volume level of all the sounds in the clip after lowering the lowest sounds using compression. The result is that the average sound level is higher.

Next, let's look at the **Dialogue Processor** plugin to enhance our audio.

Dialogue Processor

Dialogue Processor contains a mixture of audio-fixing and enhancing tools associated with speech.

The **De-Rumble**, **De-Pop**, **De-Ess**, **Compressor**, **Expander**, and **Excite** controls each have simplified controls that focus on common adjustments needed for dialogue.

Let us explore how the **Dialogue Processor** works:

1. On the **Cut** page, navigate to **Effects** > **Audio** > **Fairlight FX** > **Dialogue Processor**.
2. To apply **Dialogue Processor**, you can do any of the following:
    - Select the clip you want to apply **Dialogue Processor** to, then double-click **Dialogue Processor** in the **Effects** > **Audio** > **Fairlight FX** panel
    - Drag it onto the clip to apply it
    - Click the **Add Effect** button at the bottom of the **Effects** panel
3. The **Dialogue Processor** panel (*Figure 5.3*) opens with two audio meters on either side of the controls to show you the **Input** sound level (to the left) compared to the **Output** sound level (to the right). This is useful to show how much of the final audio signal is being lost due to the **Dialogue Processor** controls being applied.

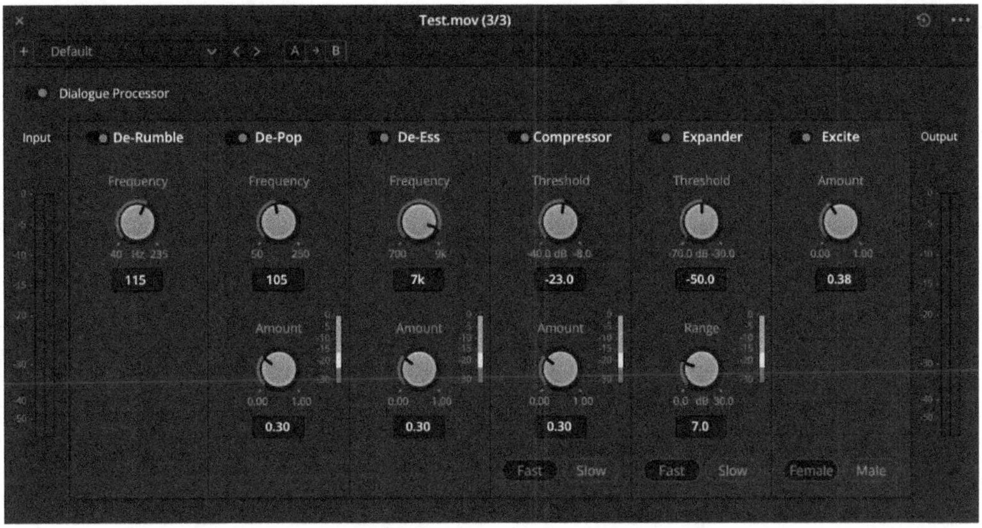

Figure 5.3: The Dialogue Processor plugin

Dialogue Processor shows the following controls, each with their own individual toggle switch to enable or disable them:

- **De-Rumble**: The **Frequency** knob selects the audio frequency that **De-Rumble**, as the name suggests, will target to reduce the bass tones of the input signal. Good for reducing the rumble from mic handling or the lav/lapel mic rubbing on clothes.
- **De-Pop**: This tool, as the name suggests, will reduce the *popping* sounds created by air blowing across the mic when somebody speaks into it. This is good for when someone particularly emphasizes the "p" and "b" sounds in their speech. It has two knobs:
    - **Frequency**: This knob selects the audio frequency that **De-Pop** will target to reduce the popping sound.
    - **Amount**: This knob changes the amount of the de-popping applied to the target frequency. A dB-level meter to the right of the knob shows the amount of dB reduction being applied. The meter is color-coded to help you set your target reduction: green is good, whereas the red levels of -25 dB and below are excessive.
- **De-Ess**: This is essentially the same as the **De-Esser** effect covered in the *Fixing sound using Fairlight FX* section in *Chapter 3*.

- **Compressor**: This is a simplified version of the **Compressor** in the **Vocal Channel** plugin covered in the previous section about the **Vocal Channel**. The **Fast** and **Slow** buttons select the speed of attack.
- **Expander**: This is the opposite of **Compressor**. Where **Compressor** reduces the dynamic range (the difference between the loud and quiet sounds) of the audio, **Expander** increases the dynamic range of the audio. So, in effect, **Expander** makes quiet sounds quieter and loud sounds louder. **Expander** has the following controls:
    - **Threshold**: This knob selects the audio frequency around which **Expander** will target to expand the dynamic range of the audio. It turns down the volume when the signal level falls below the threshold and turns up the volume when the signal level goes above the threshold.
    - **Range**: This knob changes the extra dynamic range that **Expander** applies around the target threshold. So, a value of `0.0` dB means that the dynamic range has not changed, whereas a value of `30.0` dB means that the dynamic range between the quietest and loudest sounds is increased by 30 dB. The meter is color-coded to help you select your target expansion range: green is good, whereas the red levels of -25 dB and below are excessive.
    - **Fast** and **Slow** buttons: These select the speed of the attack.
- **Excite**: This effect adds more treble to the audio to add more vocal interest if the speaker's voice is monotone. It has the following controls:
    - **Amount**: This knob selects the amount of **Excite** applied to the audio
    - **Female/Male**: These buttons select which target frequencies to excite, depending on whether the target voice is male or female

We have now covered a good range of the Fairlight FX audio plugins built into Resolve. I trust you had fun applying these plugins to see how they affected the voiceover clips you recorded in *Chapter 4*. However, Resolve does not limit you to just using its own plugins; it also has the feature of importing third-party plugins to add extra functionality.

Importing audio effects plugins

One advantage of using Resolve is that, like any other **digital audio workstation** (**DAW**), it can import extra audio plugins to expand its audio capabilities.

Resolve supports two common audio plugin formats, AU and VST:

- **AU plugins**: The **Audio Unit** (**AU**) plugin was created by Apple. So, if you are using an Apple Mac, you will find that Resolve automatically recognizes the AU plugins already installed on your Mac.
- **VST plugins**: The **Virtual Studio Technology** (**VST**) plugin is a standard audio effect plugin created by Steinberg.

  VST plugins come as either effects plugins or instrument (VSTi) plugins, where you can play a virtual instrument or synthesizer.

> **Finding VST and AU effects**
>
> There are plenty of independent third-party plugin developers on the internet who offer both free and paid VST and AU plugins you can download. Just do a quick web search to discover pages of results.
>
> Make sure you try out their free samples first before purchasing one to ensure that they work with your version of Resolve.

Let us look at how we can import extra VST or AU plugins into Resolve.

For the following section on installing a plugin, you can either download your own plugins to install or install the free **Protoverb** plugin I found here: `https://u-he.com/products/protoverb`. This Protoverb plugin has presets that simulate the reverb of different room sounds, as well as the ability to create your own room reverb presets.

Installing AU or VST plugins into Resolve

The following example uses an Apple Mac interface; however, the steps for a PC are very similar and the same as installing any other software you have already installed on your computer. If you are unsure about how to install software on your computer, please consult your **operating system's** (**OS's**) help file or user manual:

1. In the **Finder** (*Figure 5.4*), navigate to the `.pkg` file for the plugin you just downloaded.

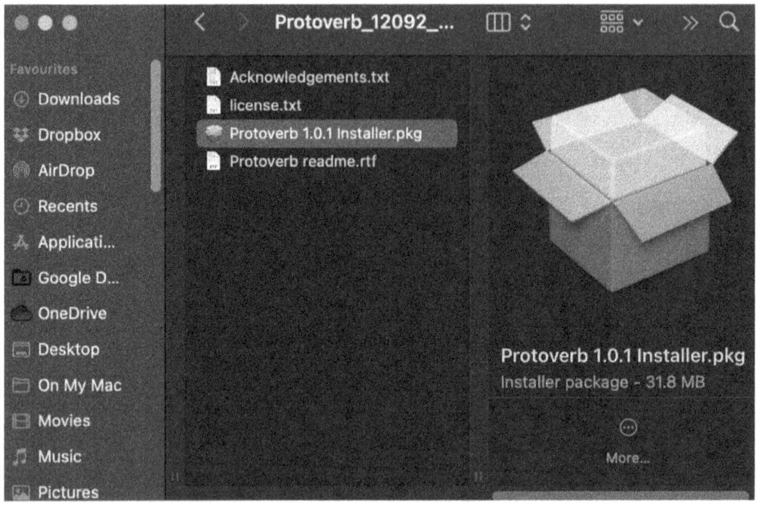

Figure 5.4: Package installer

2. Double-click the `.pkg` file (*Figure 5.4*) to open the installer.
3. Follow the instructions in the package installer (*Figure 5.5*) to install it on your Mac or PC.

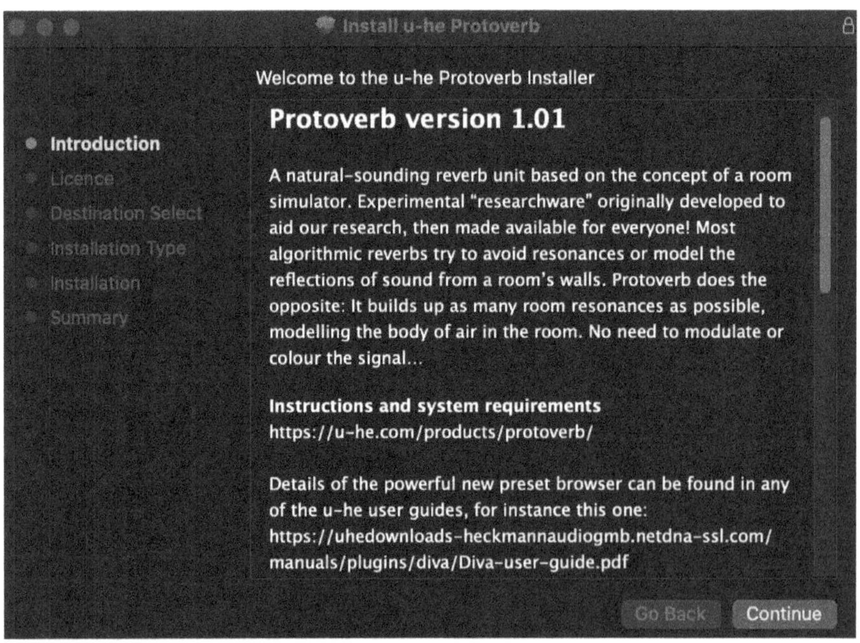

Figure 5.5: Package installer instructions

4. Select the installation options for the plugin you want to install (*Figure 5.6*) and click **Continue** to progress through the pages for the rest of the installation.

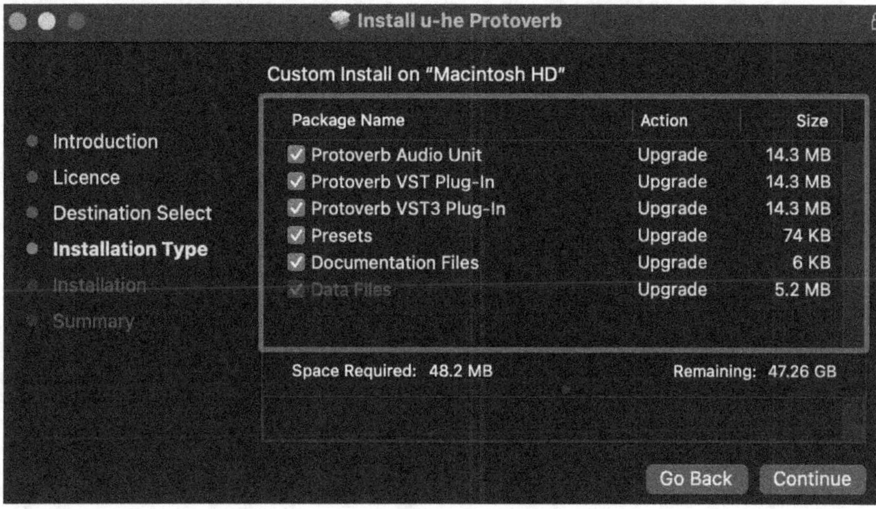

Figure 5.6: Installation options

5. The plugin is now installed on your computer.
6. Close DaVinci Resolve and re-open it to make it search for any new plugins installed on your computer. If this does not work, you may need to restart your computer so that your computer can recognize any new plugins you have just installed.

Now, let us check to see whether your plugin is installed correctly:

1. On the **Cut** page, navigate to **Effects** > **Audio** and choose either **AU Effects** or **VST Effects** (*Figure 5.7*).

2. You should now see your plugin installed and ready to be applied.

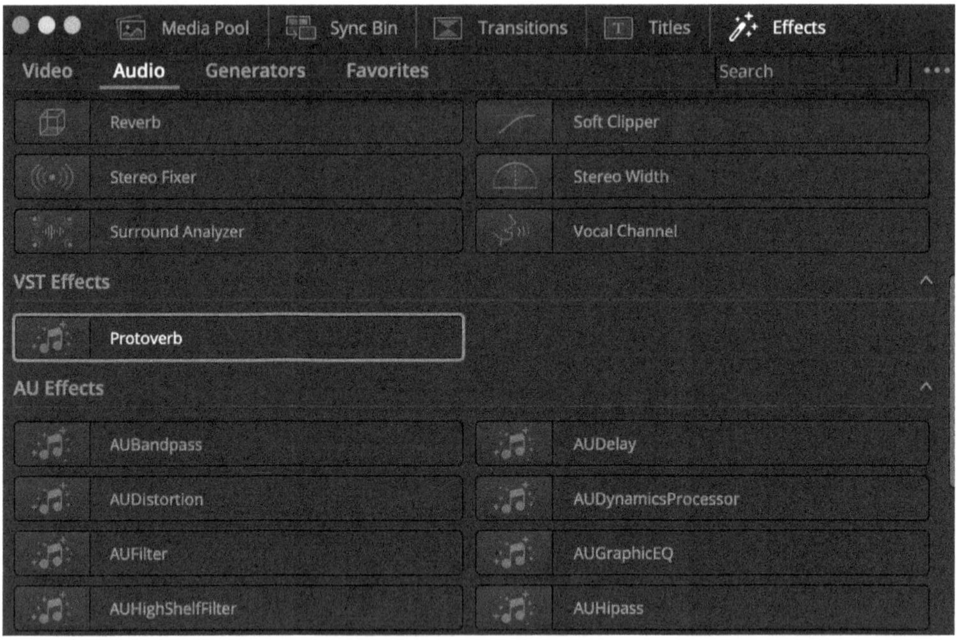

Figure 5.7: Installed plugin

Now that we have imported some plugins, let us apply one to our footage.

Applying plugins

Applying a VST or AU plugin to your audio is exactly the same as applying a Fairlight FX plugin:

1. On the **Cut** page, navigate to **Effects** > **Audio** and choose either **AU Effects** or **VST Effects** (*Figure 5.7*).
2. Choose the plugin you want to apply, and then you can do any of the following:
    - Select the clip you want to apply the effect to, then double-click the effect in **Effects** > **Audio** > **AU/VST Effects**
    - Drag the selected effect onto the clip in the timeline to apply it
    - Click the **Add Effect** button at the bottom of the **Effects** panel

Importing plugins that can fix or add effects to audio is great, but sometimes we want to add short audio clips, called SFX or Foley, to enhance the ambiance of the story we are telling, such as the sound of a door slamming, footsteps, or the background sound of a busy cafe.

> **Key concept – Foley**
>
> SFX that are created artificially, especially for a film, are called **Foley**, compared to just recording a real sound. For example, recording the sound of gloves flapping to represent the sound of bird wings flapping is Foley. Foley, in this example, would be used instead of the hassle of trying to record a bird's wings in flight.
>
> Foley is often used when recording the actual sound would be technically impossible (e.g., bird wings flapping) or has a fantasy element (such as laser fire).
>
> Foley effects are named after Jack Foley, who pioneered their use for Universal Pictures in the early days of audio cinema in the 1920s. A person who creates Foley sounds is called a Foley artist.

The good news is that we can import an SFX library directly into Resolve to use in **Fairlight** for this purpose.

But first, we will quickly look at the **Fairlight** interface so that we can find our way around it.

Navigating the Fairlight page

To use more advanced audio techniques, we will need to visit the **Fairlight** page.

Fairlight is a fully functional DAW and is powerfully more capable than audio-editing plugins you may encounter in other video-editing software.

When you click on the **Fairlight** page, all your audio edits from the **Cut** and **Edit** pages, including audio effects, are instantly accessible on the **Fairlight** page.

Let us first look at the **Fairlight** page interface to see the similarities with and differences from the **Cut** page:

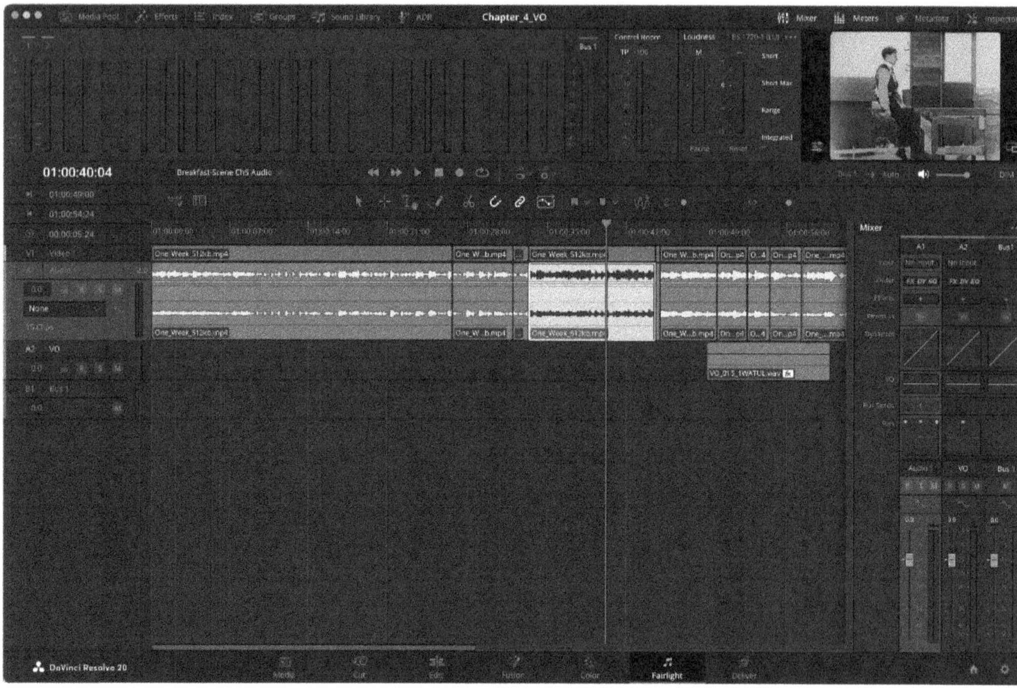

Figure 5.8: The Fairlight page

As you can see, the **Fairlight** page (*Figure 5.8*) has the same access to the **Media Pool**, **Effects**, and **Inspector** panels, which are in the same places as on the **Cut** page.

Additionally, it also has the **Sound Library**, **Index**, **Mixer**, and **Metadata** tabs, which are the same as on the **Edit** page.

There are also some changes: there is only one **Viewer**, and the **Mixer** has more advanced controls in it. Like the right-hand **Viewer** on the **Edit** page, the **Fairlight** page's **Viewer** (*Figure 5.8*) shows you a view of the media under the playhead on the timeline.

There are also new tabs: the **ADR** tab at the top left, and the **Meters** tab at the top right.

Let us look briefly at these extra features and outline what they do.

Meters

Meters are on by default. Clicking on the **Meters** tab will hide or reveal the audio meters and **Viewer**, which are along the top of the timeline. The audio meters show the volume levels (in dB) for each of the tracks and are useful when mixing the audio levels between the tracks.

Automated Dialogue Replacement

Automated Dialogue Replacement (**ADR**) is a tool that we use to replace the original video's dialogue with audio recorded afterward. This may be necessary due to poor-quality original sound needing to be replaced or, as we will explore later in the chapter, dubbing another language over the original video.

Now that we have a brief understanding of the **Fairlight** interface, let us import a free SFX library to use for our sound effects.

Importing an SFX library

One of the great things about the **Fairlight** page in Resolve is that it allows you to add SFX from within Resolve without having to clutter your **Media Pool**.

Blackmagic Design helpfully provides over 500 royalty-free SFX for you to use in your projects, even commercial ones.

Let us download these free SFX to use in future exercises.

Importing the Fairlight Sound Library

Here are the links from where you can download the SFX, depending on your computer's OS:

- **Mac:** `https://www.blackmagicdesign.com/uk/support/ download/05acbc36dbba4519a4972b7ddce31810/Mac%20OS%20X`
- **PC:** `https://www.blackmagicdesign.com/uk/support/download/05acbc36dbba4519a4972b7ddce31810/Windows`
- **Linux:** `https://www.blackmagicdesign.com/uk/support/download/05acbc36dbba4519a4972b7ddce31810/Linux`

Figure 5.9 shows the web page for downloading the free SFX:

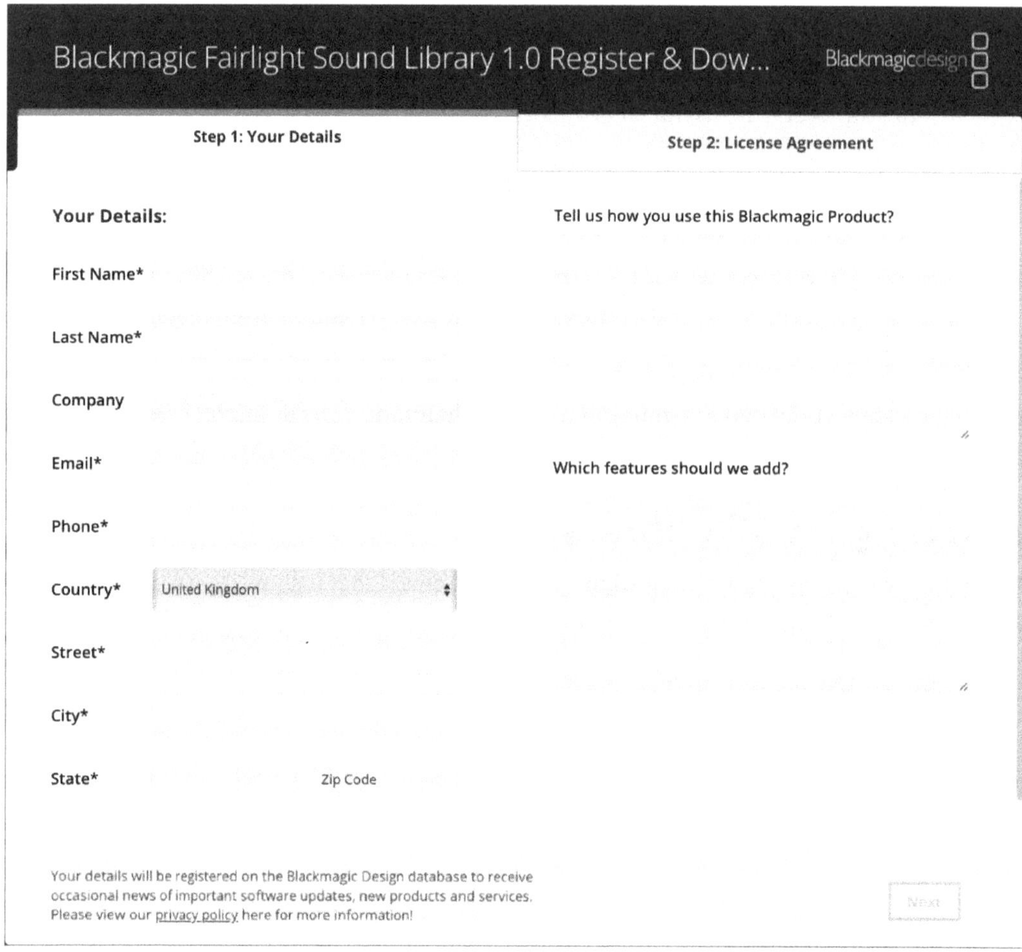

Figure 5.9: Blackmagic Fairlight Sound Library download page

Once you have registered your details, agreed to the **Sound Effects License Agreement** (*Figure 5.9*), and downloaded the free SFX, you can now import them into Resolve:

1. You will now have a software installer file on your computer called `Blackmagic_Fairlight_Sound_Library_Mac`. Double-click this to open the installer (*Figure 5.10*).

2. Double-click the **Install Fairlight Sound Library 1.0** icon (*Figure 5.10*).

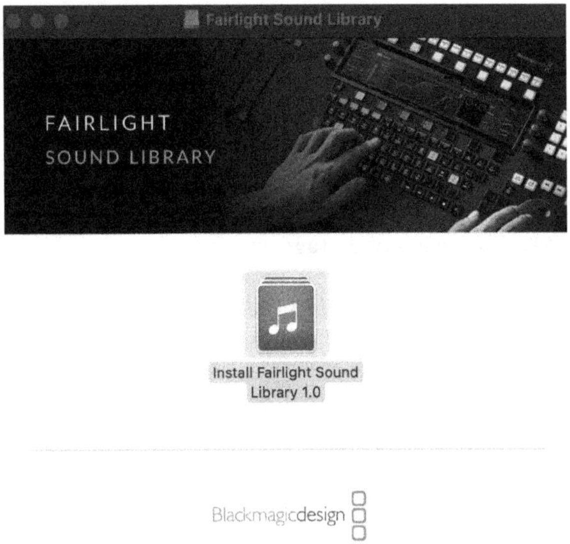

Figure 5.10: Fairlight Sound Library installer

3. Follow the instructions on each page of the installer (*Figure 5.11*). Remember where on your computer you install the Fairlight Sound Library, as this will be useful to know for later.

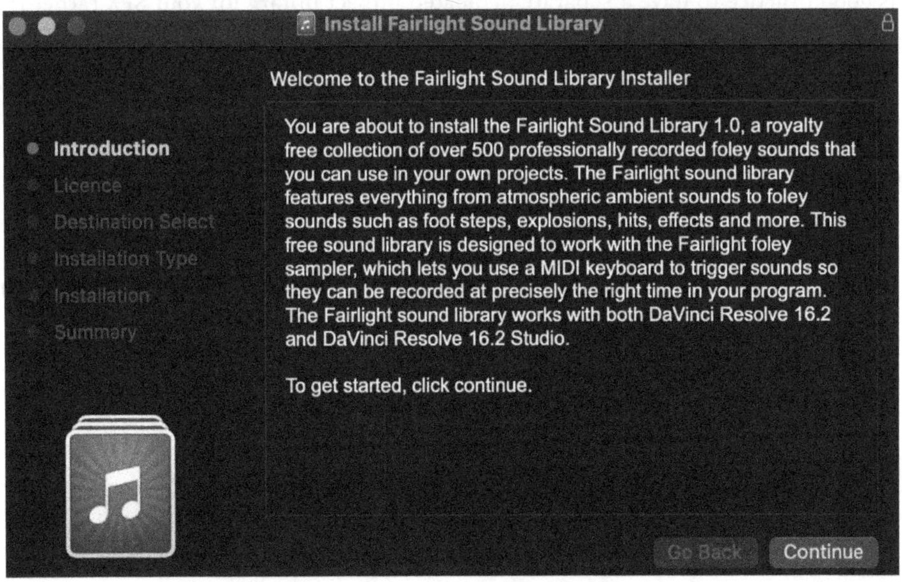

Figure 5.11: Sound Library installer pages

You now have over 500 Foley SFX installed in Resolve that you can use in your projects.

However, what do you do if you want to import your own SFX that you have found elsewhere? How do you get individual Foley sounds into Resolve without an installer?

Let us answer those questions now.

Creating your own SFX library

Creating your own SFX library is a two-stage process.

First, you need to create a database, called a **project library** in Resolve, within which to store your SFX library; then, you can create an SFX library within that database.

One advantage of creating a project library for your SFX, instead of just importing sounds into the **Media Pool**, is that it is indexable (hence, searchable) and you can share it across different projects and computers.

Creating a new project library for SFX

As of Resolve version 18.1, databases are now called project libraries. So, if you are using an older version of Resolve, substitute the term *project library* for *database* as they are essentially the same thing.

It is good practice to have a separate dedicated project library for your SFX rather than using your current project's database. This prevents your project library from becoming too large. It also means you can easily identify where all your SFX are, rather than trying to remember which project you imported them into.

Let us create a dedicated SFX project library now:

1. Go to **Project Manager** (house icon, bottom right).
2. Open the **Project Libraries** sidebar by clicking the **Show/Hide Project Libraries** icon (*Figure 5.12*) at the top left of the **Projects** window.

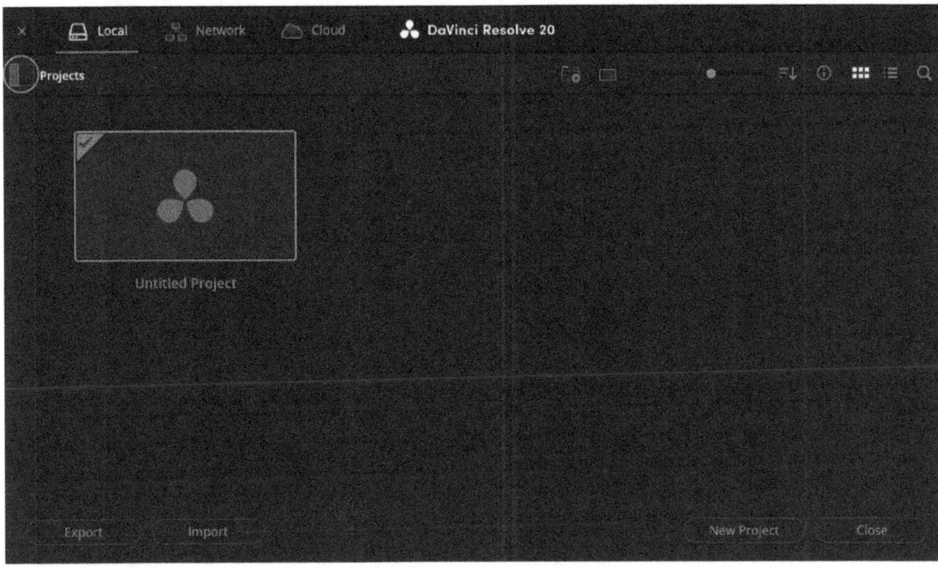

Figure 5.12: The Show/Hide Project Libraries icon

3. Click the **Add Project Library** button at the bottom of the **Project Libraries** sidebar (*Figure 5.13*).

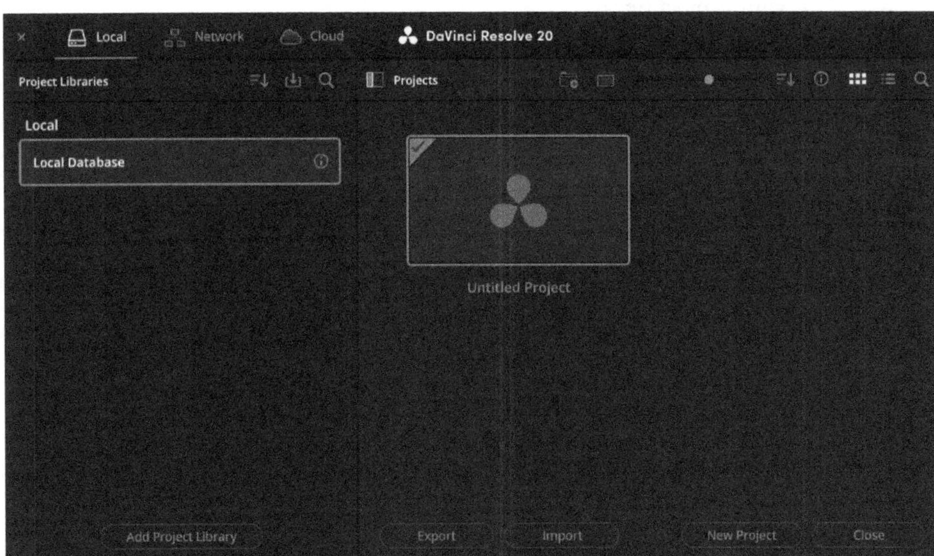

Figure 5.13: The Project Libraries sidebar

4. An **Add Project Library** window will appear (*Figure 5.14*). In the **Add Project Library** window, click the **Create** tab if it is not already selected.

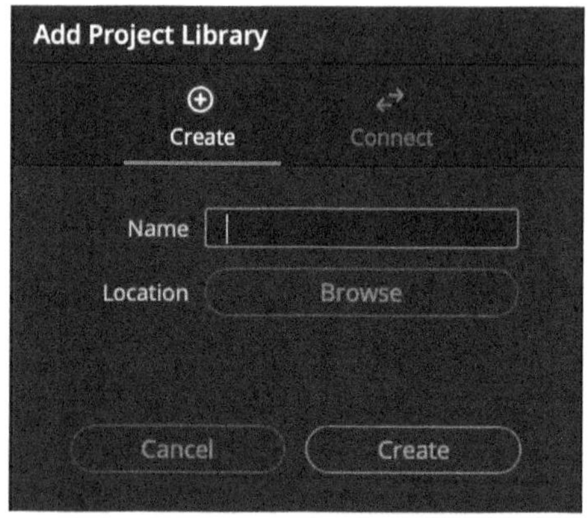

Figure 5.14: The Add Project Library window

5. In the **Add Project Library** window, complete the following information:

    - **Name**: Type the name of your database (e.g., `My Sound FX`).
    - **Location**: This is the location on your computer to which you are going to save your project library:

        a. Click on the **Browse** button to open your computer's file manager.

        b. Navigate to where on your computer you want to store your project library, create a new empty folder, and give it a recognizable name (e.g., `Resolve Sound FX Library`). Resolve will only store a new project library in an empty folder.

        c. Select the new project library folder you have just created, and if prompted by your computer's file manager, open it.

    - **Create**: At the bottom of the **Add Project Library** window, click the orange-highlighted **Create** button (*Figure 5.15*).

Figure 5.15: The completed Add Project Library window

A new project library called `My Sound FX` (if you used my example in *Figure 5.15* will appear in the **Project Libraries** sidebar under the **Local** section.

6. In the **Project Libraries** sidebar of **Project Manager**, select the project library where the project you are working on is stored. If you haven't created any new project libraries before now, your projects will be stored in the default local project library called **Local Database**.
7. Close the **Project Libraries** sidebar by clicking the **Show/Hide Project Libraries** icon (*Figure 5.12*) at the top left of the **Projects** window.

Naming project libraries

Before DaVinci Resolve version 19, database names could only accept lowercase characters with no spaces. To make database names more understandable, you had to use an underscore (_) to separate words in the database name. From version 19 onward, you no longer have these restrictions when naming your project libraries.

One advantage of having a separate project library for the SFX is that you can name it based on where you sourced your SFX from. This can help when tracking down licensing agreements for the SFX you use in your project (e.g., `freesfx` or `bbc_licensed_sfx`).

Creating new project libraries in Resolve can also be useful for keeping your different projects or client work separate from each other.

Using separate project libraries for each client makes **Project Manager** less cluttered, and your projects become easier to find rather than scrolling through other clients' work.

Also, having many smaller project libraries results in Resolve being able to operate faster, as it doesn't have to search a large project library to find your project.

We are now ready to create our own sound library.

Creating a new sound library

Now that we have a project library for our SFX, let's add some to it.

First, you will need to have some new SFX in a folder already downloaded onto your computer, ready to import into Fairlight.

If you don't have any new SFX, a simple web search will reveal a multitude of royalty-free SFX that you can try out. Try web searching for `Free SFX` or `Free Foley`.

Or you can download some SFX from the links in the *Further reading* section at the end of this chapter.

Once you have downloaded the SFX onto your computer, let us import them into Fairlight:

1. Go to the **Fairlight** page.
2. Click the **Sound Library** tab to open the Sound Library (*Figure 5.16*).
3. Click the **Database** button at the top right of the **Sound Library** panel to reveal a drop-down menu.

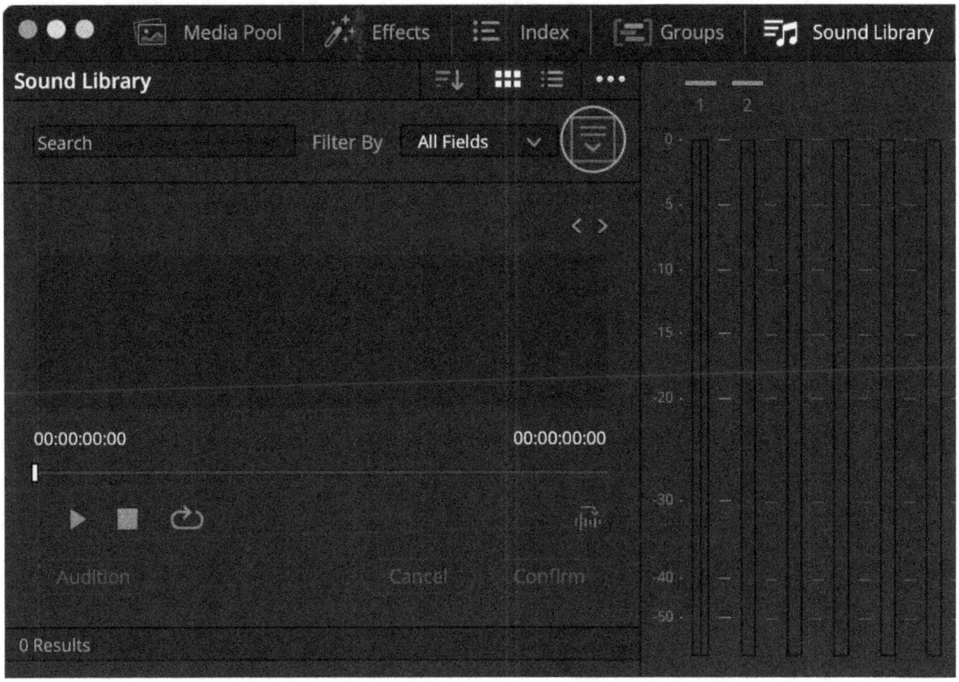

Figure 5.16: The Sound Library (Database button circled)

4. In the **Database** drop-down menu, select the project library you created in the last exercise (e.g., `My Sound FX`).
5. Now that you have selected a project library in the **Sound Library**, you can add sounds to it. Depending upon whether you have already installed a sound library, you can do either of the following:

   - If you have not added any SFX libraries before, you will notice that you can choose to **Download DaVinci Resolve's Free Sound Library** into your project library. To do this, click the **Download** button at the center of the **Sound Library** panel (*Figure 5.17*). However, on this occasion, we don't want to do this as we already have our DaVinci Resolve free sound library in our **Local Database**.

Figure 5.17: The Download button

- In this case, we want to add our own sound library. In the upper-right corner of **Sound Library** above the **Database** button, click the **Options** menu (three dots). Select **Add Library...** from the drop-down menu.

6. In your computer's file manager, navigate to the folder that contains the SFX files that you want to import and open it. For us, we will go to the folder where the **Fairlight Sound Library** installer put our SFX files.
7. An import progress dialog box will appear as Fairlight indexes the audio files. Once it is finished, click the **OK** button to close the dialog box.

You have now imported your new SFX into your **Sound Library** database.

Now, we are going to search for, audition, and add our newly imported SFX to the timeline.

Auditioning and adding SFX to the Fairlight timeline

One of the advantages of using the Sound Library in Fairlight rather than the **Edit** page is the ability to **audition** our SFX on the timeline before committing them to the edit. Let us now add some of our imported SFX to our `Chapter_4_VO` project to explore this **audition** feature:

1. In Fairlight, select the audio track you want to add the SFX to by clicking on its header. The audio track header will turn from black to mid-gray to show that it is selected (*Figure 5.18*).

Figure 5.18: Audio track header

2. Move your timeline playhead (*Figure 5.18*) to where you want the SFX to start. This is usually where you see the visual source of the sound in the timeline viewer (e.g., a door closing SFX should start on the timeline when a door closes in the **Viewer**).

3. Open the **Sound Library** panel (*Figure 5.19*).
4. In the search bar of **Sound Library** (*Figure 5.19*), type the description of the SFX you are looking for (e.g., `footsteps`). Resolve will search the name and description of the SFX files and list matching SFX entries as you type your search term.

> **Searching for SFX in Sound Library**
>
> Fairlight uses the filename and description to match the SFX clips to your search term. This means it is important to make sure that your SFX filenames reflect their content. So, a sound recording of footsteps on gravel should be renamed from, say, `Zoom000034.wav` to something such as `footsteps_gravel.wav`.

If you are unsure what to look for, you can always list all the SFX files alphabetically in the selected Sound Library database by typing three asterisks, ***, into the search field in Sound Library (*Figure 5.19*). Then, you can manually scroll through them and play each one to find a sound you like.

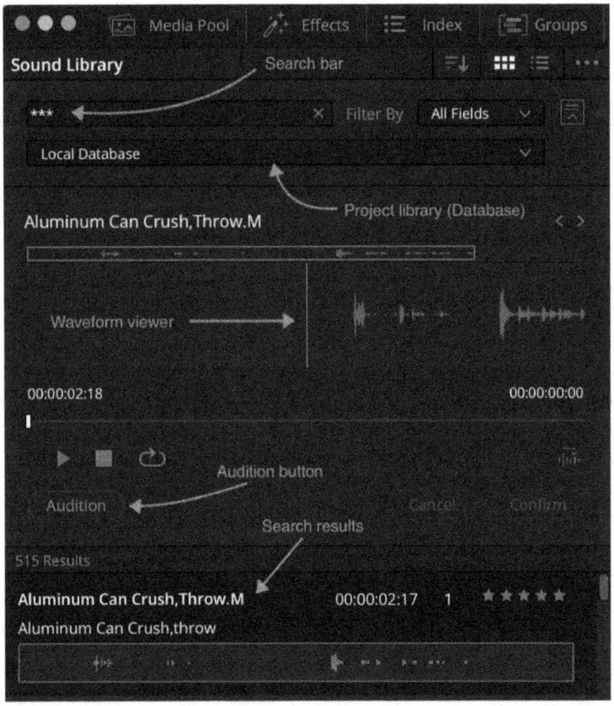

Figure 5.19: Sound Library showing three asterisks in the search bar

5. Select an SFX from the list and play it back to preview it. To play the selected SFX, do either of the following:
   - Click the **Play** button underneath the waveform viewer (*Figure 5.19*)
   - Press the spacebar on the keyboard
6. Play each SFX in the list until you find a couple that you like. Select any one of them. For example, you could select **Carving Wood with Metal** to line up with the groom sawing wood.
7. Click the **Audition** button (*Figure 5.19*) to temporarily place the selected SFX onto the selected track on the timeline, starting at the position of your timeline playhead.
8. Play the timeline to hear the auditioned clip in the context of the rest of the project. To play the selected SFX on the timeline, do either of the following:
   - Click the **Play** button above the timeline
   - Select the timeline, then press the spacebar on the keyboard
9. To remove the SFX clip from the timeline, do either of the following:
   - Click the **Cancel** button in the **Sound Library** panel (*Figure 5.19*)
   - Select another SFX clip in the search results list
10. Once you have found a suitable SFX clip for your project (by repeating the preceding steps), click the **Confirm** button in the **Sound Library** panel (*Figure 5.19*) to keep the selected SFX clip on the timeline.
11. Click the **Sound Library** tab to hide the Sound Library (*Figure 5.19*).

You now know how to create an SFX database and use the Sound Library to import and audition your own SFX for your projects.

Plus, you have added extra audio effects plugins from third-party developers to expand the functionality of Fairlight within Resolve.

Summary

Here is what you have achieved in this chapter:

- Adjusted the volume of different frequencies and enhanced the vocals using **Fairlight FX**
- Imported your own AU and VST effects and applied them
- Discovered the unique layout of the **Fairlight** page

- Created a sound library and imported new SFX into it
- Used the sound library to audition SFX and add them to the **Fairlight** timeline

You now know how to work with some audio-editing techniques on both the **Cut** and **Fairlight** pages and import audio effects and plugins to expand Resolve's audio-editing functionality.

You have now completed *Part 1* of the book. *Part 2* begins with *Chapter 6*, where we will look at restoring and fixing archive footage.

In *Chapter 6*, we will also look at different file types and what video codecs are. We will look at importing and preparing different file types traditionally associated with old video footage into Resolve. We will then fix the video using FusionFX and the audio using Fairlight.

Questions

1. True or false? DaVinci Resolve accepts AU and VST plugins to add extra audio effects.
2. True or false? You are limited to only using **Fairlight FX** on the **Cut** page and need to use **Fairlight** to apply AU or VST effects.
3. True or false? The **Cut** page has access to **Fairlight FX** audio plugins that enable you to fix and enhance audio.
4. True or false? In order to import SFX into Fairlight, you need a dedicated SFX database to import the clips into.
5. True or false? An auditioned sound effect will not stay on the timeline unless you click the **Confirm** button in the **Sound Library**.

Further reading

Here is the official Steinberg website, which has some free VSTi instruments to download (filter to show the free ones): `https://is.gd/5P0gli`.

Here is the link where I downloaded the free **u-he Protoverb VST/AU Effects** plugin: `https://u-he.com/products/#effects`.

Here are some websites where you can download free SFX:

- `https://freesound.org/browse/`
- `https://pixabay.com/sound-effects/`
- `https://freesfx.co.uk`

Get this book's PDF version and more

Scan the QR code (or go to `packtpub.com/unlock`). Search for this book by name, confirm the edition, and then follow the steps on the page.

UNLOCK NOW

Note: Keep your invoice handy. Purchases made directly from Packt don't require an invoice.

Part 2

Fixing Audio and Video

Building on Part 1, which introduced us to completing a first video edit using Resolve's Cut page, in this part, we will look at fixing audio and video files in Resolve. We will start by importing archive footage and fixing common issues with poor-quality footage. We will also look at stabilizing handheld or action-cam footage. Finally, we will look at adding cut-ins or cutaways to hide jump cuts and other edits.

This part of the book includes the following chapters:

- *Chapter 6, Working with Archive Footage*
- *Chapter 7, Stabilizing Shaky Footage*
- Chapter 8, *Hiding the Cut – Making Our Edits Invisible*

6

Working with Archive Footage

In this chapter, we will look at using Resolve FX to restore the quality of the old video footage we first imported in *Chapter 4*, to make it easier to view for a modern audience. We will also use Fairlight to change the timing of our dubbed audio, which we created in *Chapter 4*, to match the timing of the actor's mouth in the video using **Elastic Wave**.

We will also use Fairlight to **normalize** the audio levels of our audio clips so that the sound volume of our video is consistent and easy for our video's viewers to listen to, by removing any loud, unexpected changes in volume.

In this chapter, we are going to cover the following main topics:

- Restoring video using Resolve FX Revival (Studio only)
- Changing audio speed
- Using Elastic Wave
- Normalizing audio

Let's begin our journey into working with archive footage by learning how to restore videos using Resolve FX.

Technical requirements

For the exercises in this chapter, we will be continuing to work on the audio project `Chapter_4_VO` (`https://packt.link/gbz/9781836208839`) we created in *Chapter 4* and continued to refine in *Chapter 5*.

In *Chapter 4*, we used **Scene Cut** to detect cuts in archive footage and added scenes to a new timeline. We also dubbed in our own audio over the silent film. If you have not already completed *Chapter 4*, I highly recommend that you do so before you continue this chapter.

Restoring video using Resolve FX Revival (Studio only)

Often, when we use old archive videos in our projects, they can be scratchy, missing frames, and possibly have flicker. Of course, the amount of damage that will have occurred to archive footage will depend upon when it was originally recorded and how successfully it was converted into a digital format. Videos with scratches, missing frames, or flicker can be distracting to modern audiences. It can also seem out of place when mixed with modern video footage. Thankfully, Resolve has dedicated tools to restore old archive footage so that it is compatible with our audience's tastes.

To showcase just that, we will now restore a short clip from a 1920s *Buster Keaton* silent comedy called *One Week*.

Open the project named `Chapter_4_V0` that you created in *Chapter 4*.

There are several useful FX plugins to restore old footage included in the Studio version of DaVinci Resolve. You can find the **Resolve FX Revival** plugins in the **Effects** panel on either the **Cut**, **Edit**, **Fusion**, or **Color** pages.

In this example, we will apply the **Resolve FX Revival** plugins to our footage in the **Cut** page. To find the plugins, navigate to **Effects** > **Video** > **Resolve FX Revival** (*Figure 6.1*).

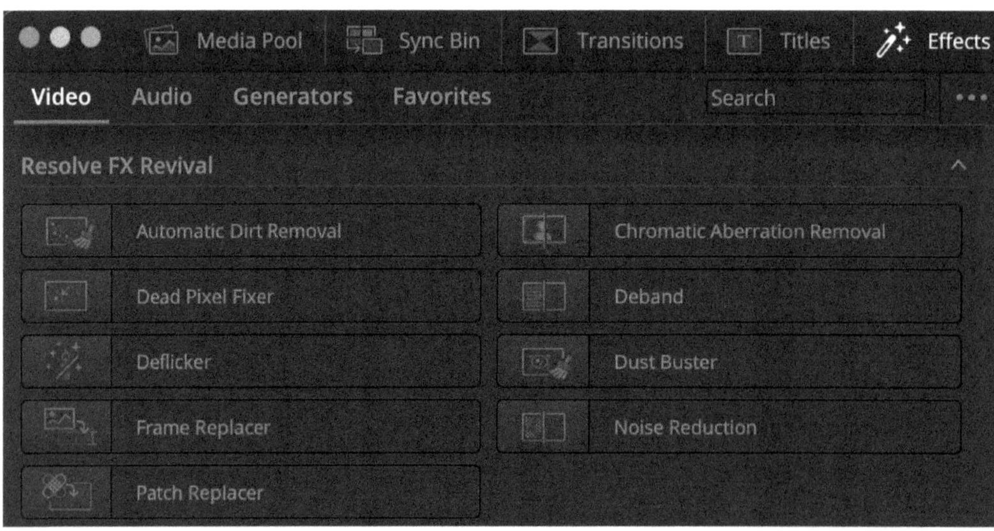

Figure 6.1: Resolve FX Revival plugins

We will look at three of the most useful Resolve FX plugins for restoring old film footage. These plugins are the following:

- **Deflicker**: To remove the flicker created by old cinema projectors
- **Automatic Dirt Removal**: To remove scratches and dirt from a frame
- **Frame Replacer**: To replace completely damaged frames with an undamaged copy

Let's start with **Deflicker**.

Using Deflicker

When we play back Buster Keaton's *One Week* on the timeline, we can see the shots have a slight flicker, as if the lights in the room are flickering. We will use the **Deflicker** plugin to remove this flicker:

1. Drag the **Deflicker** plugin onto any clip on the timeline.
2. Open the **Inspector** window and select the **Effects** tab to reveal the **Deflicker** controls (*Figure 6.2*).

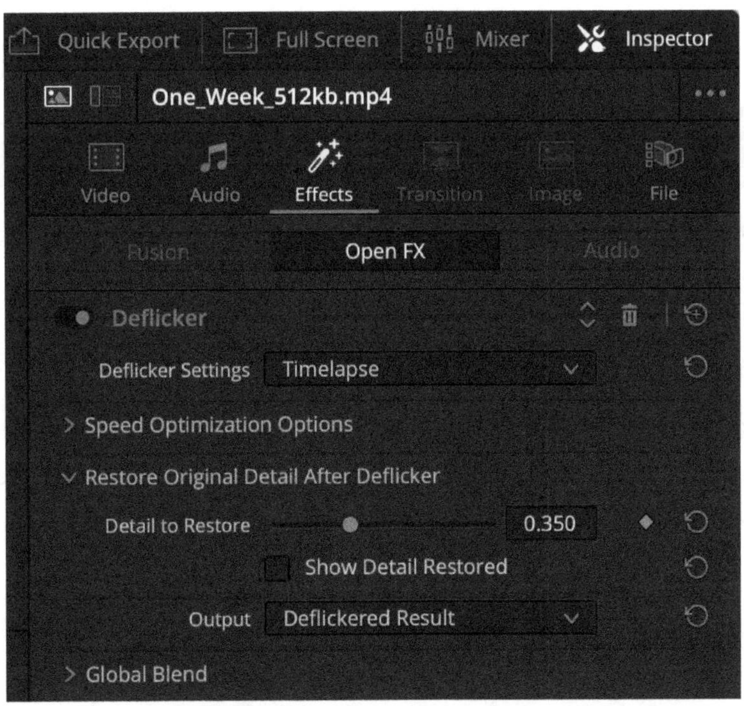

Figure 6.2: Deflicker controls in the Inspector window

3. In the **Output** drop-down menu, select **Detected Flicker** so that we can see the flicker we are removing.
4. Click on the **Restore Original Detail After Deflicker** dropdown, then change **Detail to Restore** to get a balance between flicker removal and the amount of detail lost. You can do either of the following:
   - Move the **Detail to Restore** slider to the left or right
   - Type a numerical value between `0.00` and `1.00` directly into the number box (where `0.00 is` no detail restored and `1.00` is the maximum amount of detail restored)
5. Select **Deflickered Result** in the dropdown next to the **Output** settings so that we can see the result of the **Deflicker** effect.
6. Play back the clip to allow the plugin to analyze the clip and apply the **Deflicker** plugin.
7. Play back the clip again to review the results.
8. If necessary, repeat *steps 3* to *8* until the flicker has been removed.

Now that we have removed the flicker, it looks a lot better, and the film looks like it could have been shot on a modern camera. However, there are still bits of dust, dirt, and scratches that appear on the film. Let us remove these using the **Automatic Dirt Removal** plugin.

Automatic Dirt Removal

The **Automatic Dirt Removal** plugin looks for dirt in the frame by comparing the dirty frame with clean frames on either side of it. It then removes the dirt and replaces it with new pixels generated from parts of the clean image surrounding it.

Let us apply it to our clip:

1. Play back the clip after the wife calls her husband down for breakfast.
2. Note an *S*-shaped scratch in front of the fence to the right of the clip. We need to remove this (*Figure 6.3*).

Figure 6.3: The clip before Automatic Dirt Removal is applied

3. Drag the **Automatic Dirt Removal** FX plugin onto the clip on the timeline.
4. Play back the clip to allow the plugin to analyze the clip and apply the **Automatic Dirt Removal** effect.
5. Play back the clip again to review the results. The *S*-shaped scratch has mostly disappeared (*Figure 6.4*).

Figure 6.4: The clip after Automatic Dirt Removal is applied

The footage looks a lot cleaner. However, elsewhere in the video, there is still some video damage that covers a whole frame, which is where the **Frame Replacer** FX plugin can be used.

Key concept – keyframes

Keyframe is a term used in animation. The word *keyframe* comes from hand-drawn animation. Historically, a lead animator would draw the first and last frame of a movement, which were the *key* or important frames, and the junior animators would then fill in all the missing frames between those two positions.

With computer animation, the word refers to a keyframe of a video where a change is made by you (i.e., to a position of an object, such as point A). Further along the timeline, a second keyframe is then altered by you (i.e., to a different position, such as point B). The computer (like the junior animator) then animates the changes between these two keyframes (i.e., the computer calculates the movement of the object between points A and B).

Resolve has a feature called **auto keyframing**. First, you need to add a keyframe to a frame by clicking on the gray keyframe diamond at the end of the setting. The gray keyframe diamond turns orange to show that a keyframe has been applied. This first keyframe becomes your base value for the change to start from. If you then play the video further on and change the same setting to a different value, Resolve will automatically apply a second keyframe and animate the changes between the two.

You can jump the playhead from one keyframe to another by clicking on the arrows on either side of the keyframe diamond. This means you can easily go back and tweak the settings after applying the keyframe to adjust the animation to your liking.

Most of Resolve's settings in the **Inspector** can be keyframed. Any setting that has a gray diamond at the end of the setting can be keyframed.

Frame Replacer

Sometimes, a frame in the film we want to restore is so damaged that the **Automatic Dirt Removal** plugin will not be able to restore the damage. An example of this is in the video frame of the frying pan on the stove. Even though **Automatic Dirt Removal** is applied, we can still see a distortion of the stove and frying pan (*Figure 6.5*).

Figure 6.5: The clip with Automatic Dirt Removal applied, showing the warped stove

In this situation, we can use the **Frame Replacer** plugin to delete the frame and replace it with a single frame or a blend of non-damaged frames on either side of it. This is how you can do it:

1. Drag the **Frame Replacer** plugin onto the damaged clip on the timeline. In my edit, it is about `01:00:48:16` on the timeline.
2. Open the **Inspector** window and select the **Effects** tab.
3. Move your playhead to the frame you want to replace.
4. Check the **Replace This Frame** checkbox to select the frame you want to replace. A key-frame (*orange diamond*) is placed on this frame to mark it for removal (*Figure 6.6*).

Figure 6.6: Frame Replacer applied

1. Select your **Replacement Method** option from the drop-down box to tell Resolve how to recreate the missing frame. These are the methods to choose from:
   - **From Previous:** This copies the previous frame and writes it over the current frame.
   - **From Next:** This copies the next frame and writes it over the current frame.
   - **Blend Prev/Next:** This creates a new replacement frame out of a blend of the previous and following frames.
   - **Optical Flow:** This uses DaVinci Resolve's optical flow technology to create a replacement frame from a blend of the previous and following frames. This usually creates the best results but requires more processor power from your computer.

   For our example with the warped stove, we will choose **Optical Flow** as our **Replacement Method** option.
2. Play back the clip to allow the plugin to analyze the clip and apply the **Frame Replacer** effect.
3. Play back the clip to review the results.

As you can see from the finished result (*Figure 6.6*), **Frame Replacer** can sometimes achieve a better result than **Automatic Dirt Removal** if there is significant damage. The stove now looks brand-new!

The order of FX plugins in the Inspector window

The order in which you apply any FX plugin is important, as each plugin analyzes an image based on what effects have already been applied to it. In brief, the plugins' effects are cumulative. This means you can apply several instances of the same plugin to see the effect magnified.

Try applying plugins that affect the overall image first – for example, you can apply **Deflicker** and then progressively apply other plugins that remedy/enhance finer and finer detail in stages within the frame, such as **Automatic Dirt Remover.**

You can always change the order of the plugins in the **Inspector** window after they have been applied by clicking on the up or down arrows at the end of the plugin name (*Figure 6.6*), to move the plugin up or down in the **Inspector** window.

The plugins are applied in order, starting with the plugin listed at the top of the **Inspector** window.

Now, our footage looks a lot more visually pleasing. Next up, we will look at some audio editing techniques. In *Chapter 3*, we already looked at fixing audio, but here we will look at changing the speed of the audio we dubbed in *Chapter 4* to match our actor's speech.

Changing audio speed

When we are dubbing audio, no matter how hard we try to match the original actor's lip movements, our dubbed version will still be out of sync with the original visual.

This is where it is useful to change the speed of our audio without changing the pitch. There are two methods to do this:

- Changing the audio speed in the **Inspector**
- Changing the audio speed using the **Cut** page tools

Let's look at both methods.

Changing the audio speed in the Inspector

First, we will look at changing audio speed in the **Inspector** on the **Cut** page; this will also work on the **Edit** page. This is how we can do it:

1. On the timeline, select an audio clip you want to change the speed of.
2. Move the clip so that the start of the audio matches the start of the actor opening their mouth in the viewer.
3. Open the **Inspector** panel and click on the **Audio** tab to reveal the audio controls (*Figure 6.7*).

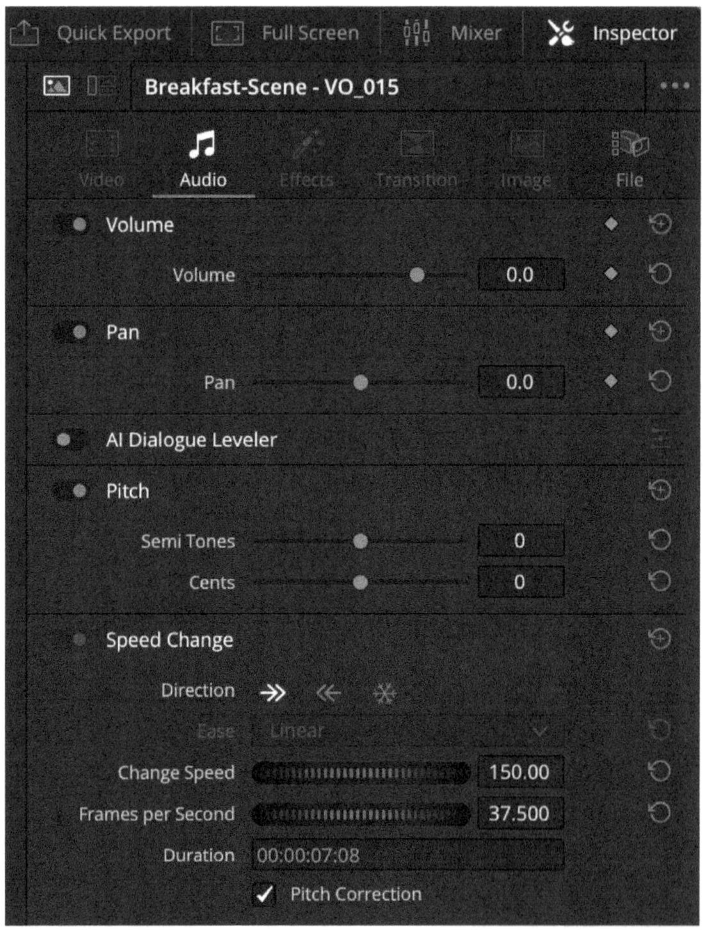

Figure 6.7: Speed Change controls in the Inspector

4. Click on **Speed Change** to reveal the speed change controls (*Figure 6.7*).

5. Keeping the **Pitch Correction** box ticked, move the **Change Speed** dial (*Figure 6.7*) in either of these ways:
    - Move it to the right to speed up the audio and hence shorten the audio clip
    - Move it to the left to slow down the audio and hence lengthen the audio clip
6. Adjust the speed of the audio clip until the end of the audio matches the actor closing their mouth in the timeline viewer.

Another way to change the audio speed is to use dedicated tools only found on the **Cut** page.

Changing the audio speed using the Cut page tools

The **Cut** page has a simplified **Tools** interface that we can use to change an audio clip's speed, rather than using the **Inspector**. Changing the audio speed using the **Tools** interface has the exact same effect as using the **Inspector**; which method you choose is up to you:

1. Reveal the **Speed Change** tools by doing either of the following:
    - Clicking the **Tools** icon (white slider bars) in the toolbar under the viewer above the timeline (*Figure 6.8*)
    - Right-clicking the audio clip on the timeline and selecting **Change Speed** in the pop-up menu
2. Click on and drag the **Speed** slider (highlighted by an orange box) to the left to reduce the audio speed or right to increase it. A value of `1.00` is the original speed, `1.50` is one and a half times the original speed, and `0.50` is half the original speed.

   Once any change has been made, an orange dot will appear above the icon of the tool that has been used, indicating that a change has been applied to the original clip (*Figure 6.8*).

Figure 6.8: The Cut page tools with Speed Change selected

3. Click on the **Tools** icon again to hide the tools.

Now, the audio better matches the speed of the actor's speech. However, there will be words in the middle of their speech that do not match. So, let's fix this by using the **Elastic Wave** tool in Fairlight.

Using Elastic Wave

Elastic Wave is a keyframe-based method of changing the timing of audio without changing the pitch. Audio keyframes are placed at points in the audio clip where you do not want the audio waveform to move or stretch. The audio between the keyframes can be stretched or compressed to fit key timings in the actor's performance.

We will now use **Elastic Wave** to match our **voiceover (VO)** to Buster Keaton's performance in our project:

1. To enable **Elastic Wave**, first, go to the **Fairlight** page.
2. Right-click on the audio clip you want to enable **Elastic Wave** for and choose **Elastic Wave** from the pop-up menu. From there, select the **Voice** option and then the **Elastic View** option.

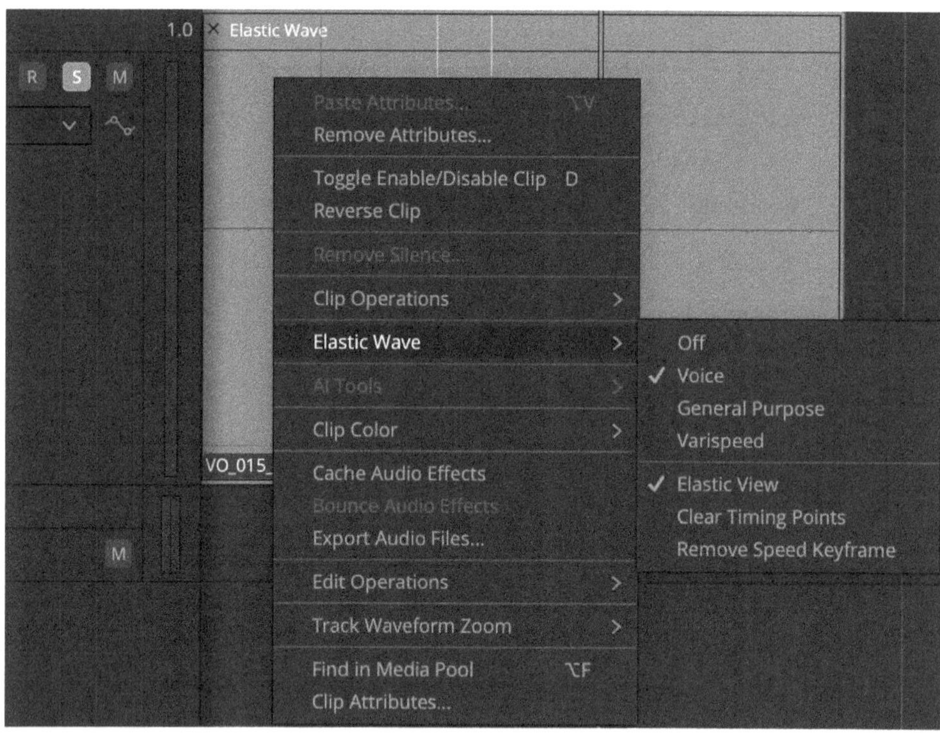

Figure 6.9: The Elastic Wave pop-up menu

This will reveal the **Elastic Wave** controls, shown by the words **Elastic Wave** now written across the top of the audio clip (*Figure 6.9*).

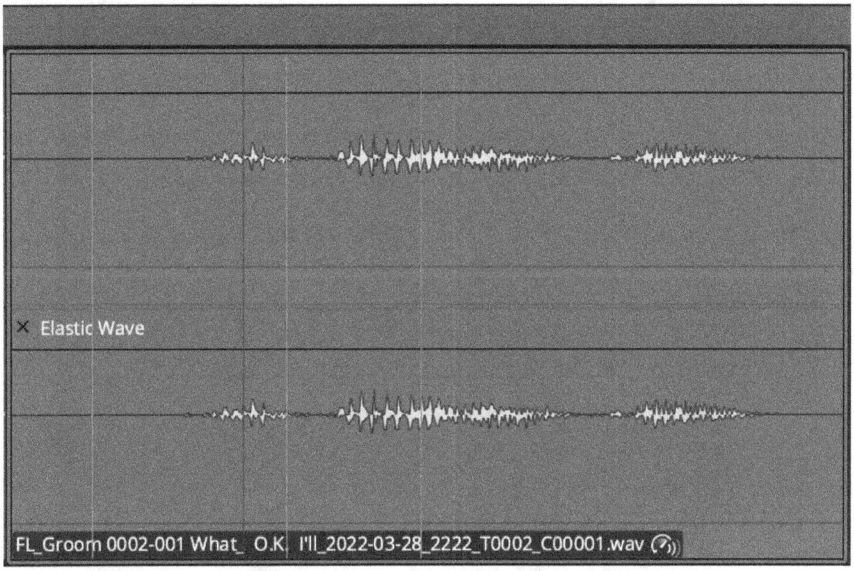

Figure 6.10: The Elastic Wave keyframes

3. Press *Command* (*Cmd*) + click on the audio waveform where you want to add a keyframe. A green vertical line will appear on the waveform to show where the audio keyframe has been applied (*Figure 6.10*).

   You will also see a **Speed Change** icon at the bottom right of the audio clip name to show that an **Elastic Wave** keyframe has been applied (*Figure 6.10*).

4. Apply audio keyframes at the beginning and end of the audio waveform you want to shorten or lengthen the timing of (*Figure 6.10*).
5. Drag the keyframe to either end of the waveform to lengthen or shorten the audio waveform to match the length of time the actor is speaking in the viewer. The keyframe will turn red to show which one you have selected for adjustment (*Figure 6.10*).
6. Close the **Elastic Wave** controls by clicking on the **X** button next to the **Elastic Wave** heading at the top of the clip (*Figure 6.10*). Once **Elastic Wave** has been enabled, double-clicking on the far left of the clip name at the bottom left of the audio clip will toggle between revealing and hiding the **Elastic Wave** controls.

We have now adjusted our dubbed ADR audio to match the lips of the actor talking in the video clip. We just need to make sure that all our audio clips are at a consistent volume level.

Normalizing audio

Staying on the **Fairlight** page, we will now use Resolve to automatically change all the audio levels of the clips to a specified maximum volume. Normalization stops drastic changes in the peak volume, which can deafen your viewer and have them constantly reaching for the volume control.

Rather than individually adjusting the volume of each clip to match the others, you can instruct Resolve to automatically adjust the clips so that the peak (loudest) volume of each clip is the same.

This automatic volume leveling of the clips is called *normalizing audio*. To do this, follow these steps:

1. Right-click the selected audio clip or clips you want to normalize and select **Clip Operations > Normalize Audio Levels** from the pop-up menu.

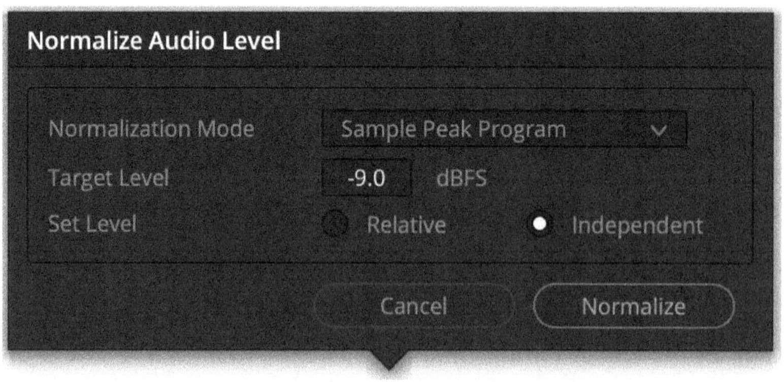

Figure 6.11: The Normalize Audio Level control pop-up box

> **Normalize Audio Level – alternative method**
>
> You can also access the **Audio Normalization** controls on the **Edit** page, just like on the **Fairlight** page.

2. This reveals a **Normalize Audio Level** control pop-up box (*Figure 6.11*) with the following options:

   - **Normalization Mode**: This is the method used by Fairlight to analyze audio. The default **Sample Peak Program** option is fine for most uses, particularly social media. The other normalization modes are more useful when delivering audio for television broadcasts or streaming services, such as Netflix.

- **Target Level**: This is the target peak volume level that the normalization will match. This is measured in **decibels relative to full scale (dBFS)**.
- **Set Level**: This setting only appears when you have selected two or more clips on which you will normalize the audio. It has two options:
    - Selecting **Relative** will change the audio across all the clips collectively to be relative to the clip with the highest audio peak. In practice, all the clips together are treated as one clip. So, for example, if the loudest clip needs to be reduced by 10 dB, then all the clips will be reduced by 10 dB.
    - Selecting **Independent** will change the audio of each clip independently to meet the **Target Level** setting. Therefore, some clips will need to be lowered, and others raised to meet the dBFS **Target Level** setting. This is useful if you want to ensure all the clips have similar volume levels.

Key concept – dBFS

With dBFS, `0` is the maximum volume of your audio system before distorting or clipping occurs. A value of `-12` dBFS is 12 dB lower than the system maximum. Hence, the larger the negative number, the quieter the sound will be.

For example, a dBFS value of `-12` (e.g., human speech) will be quieter than a dBFS value of `-9` (e.g., shouting).

Common target level values include the following:

- **Human speech**: -12 dBFS
- **SFX**: -10 dBFS to -30 dBFS
- **Music**: -20 dBFS to -30 dBFS

From these settings, keep your **Target Level** value as `-9` dBFS as a rough target for the loudest human speech, which is shouting.

3. Click the **Normalize** button.

Note that the waveforms of the selected audio clip(s) will now become higher or lower to match the selected dBFS target level.

We have now normalized all our audio clips to reach a target level of -12 dBFS so that it is easier for our audience to hear what is being said without being deafened or having to strain to hear what is being said.

Summary

Here is what you have achieved in *Chapter 6*:

- Used a range of Resolve FX Revival tools to restore old footage
- Changed the speed of audio clips
- Used **Elastic Wave** to change the timing of dubbed audio clips to fit your video
- Normalized audio levels in Fairlight

In *Chapter 7*, we will look at different tools we can use to stabilize video footage in the **Cut**, **Edit**, and **Color** pages. We will use these tools to stabilize our Buster Keaton archive footage from *One Week*.

Questions

1. True or false? You need the Studio version of Resolve to use Resolve FX Revival.
2. True or false? You can only change the speed of audio clips on the **Fairlight** page.
3. True or false? **Elastic Wave** controls can only be accessed on the **Fairlight** page.
4. True or false? Normalizing audio can only be done on the **Fairlight** page.

Further reading

Here are some archive footage websites:

- `https://archive.org/details/movies`
- `https://media.nationalarchives.gov.uk/index.php/category/video/`
- `https://www.britishpathe.com`
- `https://www.ap.org/content/archive/archive-video/`
- `https://publicdomainreview.org/collections/film`

Get this book's PDF version and more

Scan the QR code (or go to `packtpub.com/unlock`). Search for this book by name, confirm the edition, and then follow the steps on the page.

UNLOCK NOW

Note: Keep your invoice handy. Purchases made directly from Packt don't require an invoice.

7

Stabilizing Shaky Footage

In *Chapter 6*, we looked at common methods of restoring archive footage using Resolve FX. A typical problem that can plague both archive and modern footage is shaky video.

Although it is always preferable to capture stable video footage with our camera, this is not always practical. For example, we may be creating a *run-and-gun-style* documentary where there is no time or space to attach expensive stabilization equipment to our camera. It could also be that the batteries on your hand-held camera stabilizer failed, or you filmed the action on a mobile phone with no tripod for support.

Whatever the reason for having shot shaky video footage, there are times we need to fix the shaky footage in post-production to make it easier for the viewer to watch. DaVinci Resolve has an excellent stabilizer that you can use to convert unstable footage into footage that could have been created on a tripod.

In this chapter, you will learn how to stabilize shaky footage on the **Cut**, **Edit**, and **Color** pages, which you can apply to both your archive and recent footage.

We are going to cover the following main topics:

- How video stabilization works
- Stabilizing video on the Cut page
- Stabilizing video in the Inspector on the Cut and Edit pages
- Stabilizing video on the Color page

Technical requirements

For the exercises in this chapter, we will be starting a new project where we stabilize a wedding video. You can download the `The Wedding.dra` file here, which contains the wedding video media required for the next few chapters: `https://packt.link/gbz/9781836208839`.

How video stabilization works

It is important to understand the basic principles of how video stabilization works in post-production software so that we can understand how to use controls to fine-tune the software's video stabilization.

Outlining the steps of video stabilization

As with all editing software stabilizers, Resolve will compensate for camera movement by cropping the video. So, as with all video stabilization, there will be a slight loss of resolution and the image will be slightly zoomed in, due to the need to crop the image. Let us look at how and why video stabilization crops the image.

1. The first step in video stabilization is to enable the software to detect and track movement in our video clip. We can select which type of movement the software detects by selecting options such as **Perspective**, **Similarity**, and **Translation**. These movement detection options will be described in further detail in the following sections.
2. The next step is for the software to stabilize the clip by moving it in the opposite direction to the camera movement to counteract the shaky movement.

   So, for example, if the camera moves to the left, causing the subject to be placed to the right of the frame, the software will move the frame to the left to keep the subject of the video in its original place (*Figure 7.1*).

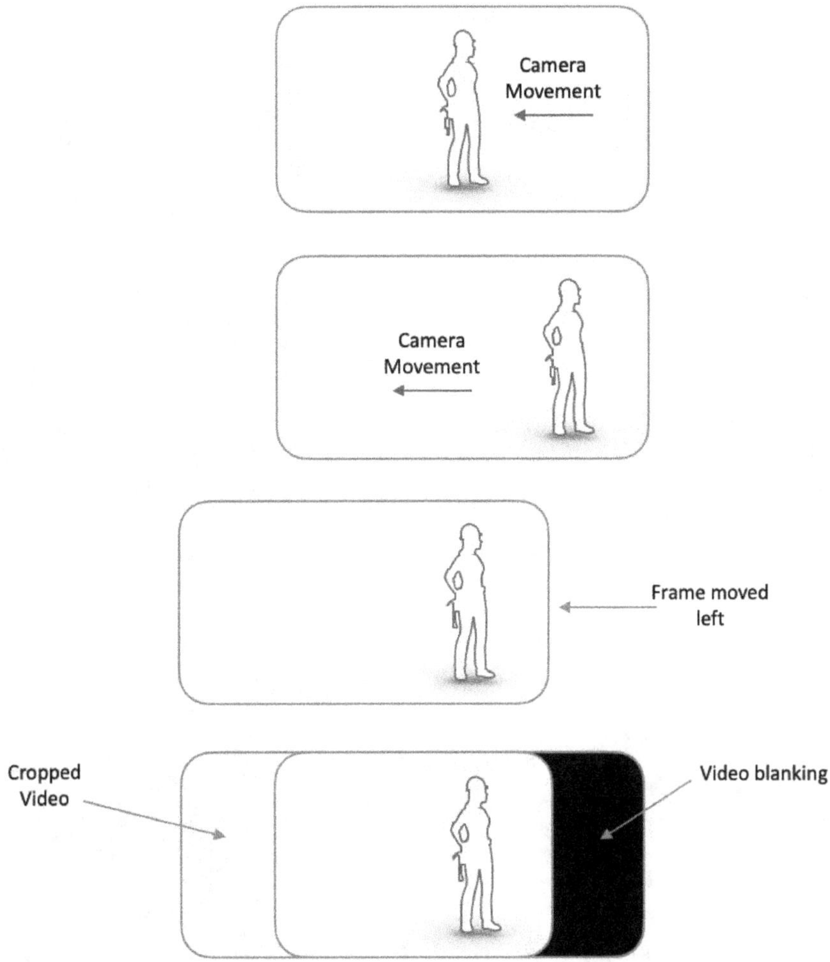

Figure 7.1: Software compensating for camera movement

Unfortunately, this leaves a black edge (video blanking) within the frame, as there is no video information to show because we have moved the clip within the frame.

3. So, the final step is for the software to crop the clip by zooming in to remove the black edges.

This is difficult to illustrate using drawings, so let's demonstrate this using Resolve itself. *Figure 7.2* shows a clip in Resolve before it has been stabilized.

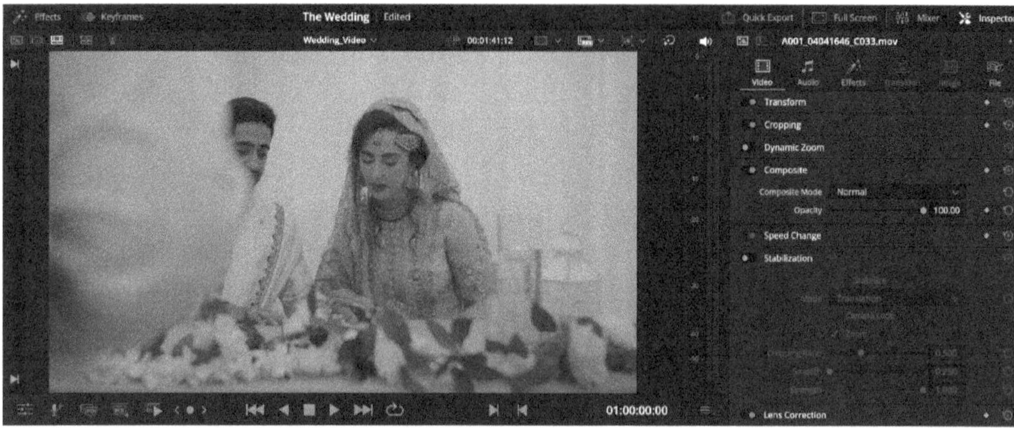

Figure 7.2: The pre-stabilized clip

Figure 7.3 shows the same clip in Resolve after it has been stabilized.

Figure 7.3: The zoomed-in stabilized clip

Note that although the clip is now stabilized, it has also zoomed in to hide the black bars of the video blanking. This will result in the subject taking up more of the frame, some of the background being cropped out, and a slight loss of video resolution.

For this reason, it is better to use software stabilization sparingly and record video as stably as you can.

Otherwise, you can record video at a higher resolution than your video's intended final output resolution and frame the video so that there is room to crop the clip later. For example, shooting in 4K to deliver a 1080p video will allow room for cropping without a loss in video resolution.

Now that we know how software stabilization works, let us look at the different ways that you can stabilize video using DaVinci Resolve, starting with the **Cut** page. You can always try these different techniques on the wedding video footage to see how each one works.

You can use your own shaky footage for these techniques or use the wedding video footage in the `The Wedding.dra` file, which we will continue to improve in *Chapter 8*. In the following exercises, we will assume you are using the `The Wedding.dra` footage.

Creating a new timeline and reviewing our footage

This is how you can create a new timeline and review the footage:

1. Let us set up our new project and review the footage before we stabilize the video. Import `The Wedding.dra` into Resolve, just like we covered in previous chapters.

   On the **Cut** page, the footage is already separated into bins for the timelines and video files. You can use the existing timelines to compare your version with the final version.

2. Create a new timeline in the **Timelines** bin by right-clicking on an empty section of the bin and selecting **Create New Timeline...**; rename it to something appropriate (e.g., `My Wedding Stabilized`) following the steps to create a timeline we outlined in *Chapter 4*.
3. Drag the clip named `A001_04041646_C033.mov` from the **Video** > **BMPCC4K** bin onto the new timeline you just created on the **Cut** page.
4. Select the clip on the timeline you want to stabilize (e.g., `A001_04041646_C033.mov`) and play it to review the camera movement.

Now that you have quickly reviewed your footage, note that there are some shaky camera moves as well as out-of-focus shots that we need to remove. We will need to replace them with stable footage.

As it is wedding video footage, we cannot reshoot the video without asking the bride and groom to repeat the whole ceremony, so we will need to be able to fix what we have. Thankfully, Resolve has some easy-to-use tools that help us stabilize existing footage.

Stabilizing video on the Cut page

Often, through no fault of our own, we are working with video footage that is too shaky and needs to be stabilized. Whatever the reason for the shaky footage, DaVinci Resolve has an excellent stabilizer you can use to convert unstable footage into footage that could have been created on a tripod.

First, let us look at how we can stabilize video footage on the **Cut** page:

1. Select the clip on the timeline that you want to stabilize.
2. Click on the **Tools** button (the sliders in *Figure 7.4*) to reveal the **Clip** tools.

Figure 7.4: The Tools button

3. Click on the **Stabilize** icon (which resembles a *shaky camera*) to reveal the stabilization controls (*Figure 7.5*).

Figure 7.5: The Stabilize icon

4. Choose your stabilization method in the drop-down menu box (*Figure 7.5*). The options are listed from the strongest stabilization method (**Perspective**) to the least complex method (**Translation**):

    - **Perspective**: This option enables Resolve to analyze the footage for changes in perspective, pan, tilt, zoom, and rotation, and compensates for this movement.
    - **Similarity**: This option is the same as **Perspective**, but without analyzing for changes in perspective. Therefore, this stabilization method only compensates for changes in pan, tilt, zoom, and rotation. This is a good option to choose if the **Perspective** option caused unwanted motion artifacts.

- **Translation**: This option only analyzes the video for changes in pan and tilt movements. It ignores changes in perspective, zoom, and rotation. If the **Similarity** option did not work, then choosing **Translation** instead may be a better option, as it limits the stabilization to just up-and-down and left-and-right movement on a 2D plane parallel with the camera, ignoring any movement in depth, such as zooming. Of course, choosing **Translation** is a good option if you want to stabilize a shot without affecting the intentional zoom of the camera lens.

5. Click on the **Stabilize** button to stabilize the clip using the method you have just selected. Resolve will analyze the clip for movement (*Figure 7.6*) and apply stabilization to remove the movement, based on the stabilization method you chose.

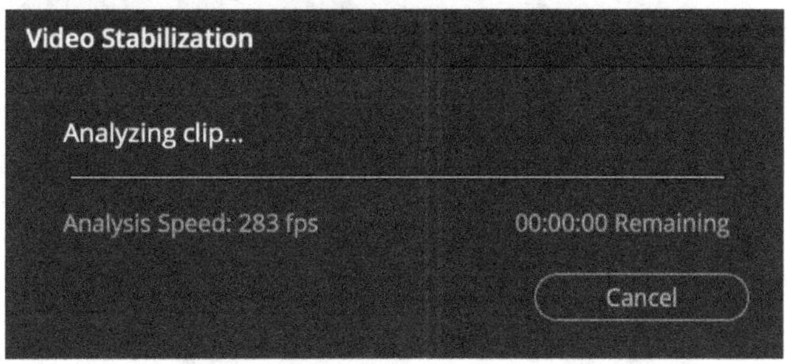

Figure 7.6: The Video Stabilization progress bar

If you do not like the results of the stabilization method you selected, you can select a different stabilization method and click again on the **Stabilize** button to get Resolve to re-analyze and stabilize the clip, based on the newly selected method.

The stabilization tool used on the **Cut** page is the same tool that is used on the **Edit** and **Color** pages. The main difference is that there are more controls available on the **Edit** and **Color** pages to fine-tune the stabilization result.

One place to reveal these additional stabilization controls is in the **Inspector** on both the **Edit** and **Cut** pages.

Stabilizing video in the Inspector on the Cut and Edit pages

Let us now look at the stabilization controls in the video stabilizer, which can be found in the **Inspector** panel on both the **Cut** and **Edit** pages. As the stabilization controls are exactly the same, we will stay on the **Cut** page to look at these extra controls in the **Inspector**:

1. Select the clip on the timeline that you want to stabilize.
2. Click on the **Inspector** tab to reveal the **Video Inspector** controls.
3. Double-click on the **Stabilization** tab to reveal the **Stabilization** controls (*Figure 7.7*).

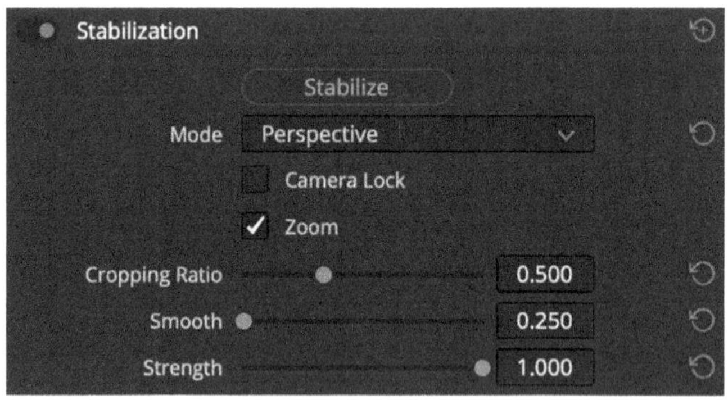

Figure 7.7: The Stabilization section of the Video Inspector panel

4. The **Mode** drop-down menu allows you to select your stabilization method, just like we did with the other simplified stabilization controls on the **Cut** page.
5. The extra controls in the **Inspector** window, which are not in the basic controls on the **Cut** page, allow us to control the power or amount of stabilization. Every time you change one of these settings, you will need to click the **Stabilize** button again to apply the change:
   - **Camera Lock**: Selecting this checkbox disables the **Cropping Ratio**, **Zoom**, and **Smooth** controls. The stabilizer will attempt to lock the shot as if the video were filmed on a *locked-off* tripod, where there is absolutely no camera movement.
   - **Zoom**: Selecting this checkbox zooms the video in to eliminate the black edges created by stabilization:
     - The **Cropping Ratio** slider (with values from `0.250` to `1.000`) determines how aggressive the stabilization will be and, hence, the amount of zooming that Resolve will need to apply. A value of `1.000` means that no zooming will occur. The lower the number, the more zooming will occur.

- **Smooth**: The **Smooth** slider (values `0.250` to `1.000`) determines how much smoothing to apply to the original camera movement. A value of `1.000` means that maximum smoothing will be applied, and very little camera movement will be retained. A low **Smooth** value will allow more of the original camera movement to be applied to the clip.
- **Strength**: This slider (values `-1.000` to `1.000`) allows you to choose the strength of the stabilization, where `1.000` is maximum stabilization, and `0.000` is no stabilization. A value under `1.000` and above `0.000` allows some of the original camera movement to be mixed in with the stabilization. A negative value is used in more advanced match moving of shots (where two video clips are overlaid and need to have the same video movement), so this is safe to ignore for most users.

The **Smooth** and **Strength** controls are used together to get a balance of smooth, stabilized shots while retaining a blend of some of the original camera movement. Try different combinations of the **Smooth** and **Strength** settings until you get the result you like.

As you can see, the two different video stabilization controls on the **Cut** page do not differ in function; the **Inspector** on the **Edit** and **Cut** pages just has more advanced controls to tweak the strength of the stabilization applied to the video clip.

Let us now look at how video stabilization works differently on the **Color** page.

Stabilizing video on the Color page

Stabilizing video on the **Color** page uses the same tools as the **Cut** and **Edit** pages, but the interface is very different.

As the **Color** page interface is so different and can be confusing for even advanced editors, we will only look at how the **Color** page stabilizes video and not the vast number of other tools we can access there:

1. Place the playhead over the clip you want to stabilize on the timeline.
2. Go to the **Color** page; the clip you selected on the timeline will already be selected.

3. Open the **Tracker** palette (*Figure 7.8*).

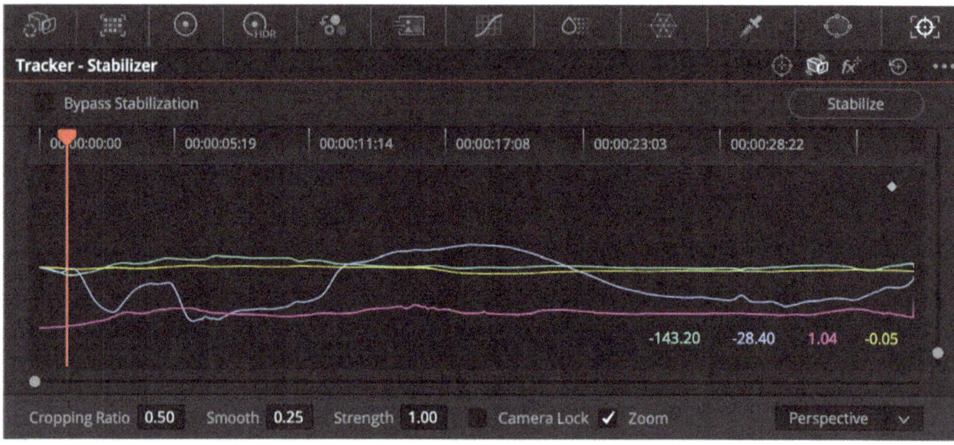

Figure 7.8: The Tracker palette

4. Select the **Stabilizer** icon (which looks like a camera shaking in *Figure 7.8*).
5. The drop-down menu at the bottom right of the palette (*Figure 7.8*) allows you to select your stabilization method, just like we did on the **Edit** and **Cut** pages.
6. Along the bottom of the **Tracker** palette (*Figure 7.8*) are the same stabilizer controls from the **Inspector** window on the **Cut** and **Edit** pages. They work in the same way. The only difference is that the interface for the controls looks slightly different.
7. Click the **Stabilize** button (*Figure 7.8*).

Resolve will now analyze the clip with camera movement and track the movement.

The clip will be stabilized, just like on the **Cut** and **Edit** pages. However, uniquely to the **Color** page, the tracking data will be represented in a graph (*Figure 7.8*) by four colored (pink, green, blue, and yellow) lines:

- The *pink* line shows the **Zoom** tracking data
- The *green* line shows the **Pan** tracking data
- The *blue* line shows the **Tilt** tracking data
- The *yellow* line shows the **Rotate** tracking data

If the line is completely flat, this means that there was no tracking data recorded.

Numerical tracking data is also shown for each color graph by the corresponding color number at the bottom right of the graph (*Figure 7.8*).

More than one way to change a number

Most number entry boxes in Resolve act like sliders when you change the numerical value in them.

If you hold your left mouse button down and drag left or right, you will change the number values in the box up or down, just like you would with a visible slider interface.

We know that selecting **Translation** only tracks the **Pan** and **Tilt** data to stabilize the shot. Let us see what the graph shows when we stabilize a shot using **Translation** mode. In theory, only the green and blue lines should show any movement, and the pink and yellow lines will remain completely flat:

1. On the **Color** page, open the **Tracker** palette.
2. Click the **Stabilizer** icon.
3. Select the **Translation** mode.
4. Click the **Stabilize** button.

You should now see that the pink and yellow lines are completely flat, and there will be some movement up and down the blue and green lines (*Figure 7.9*).

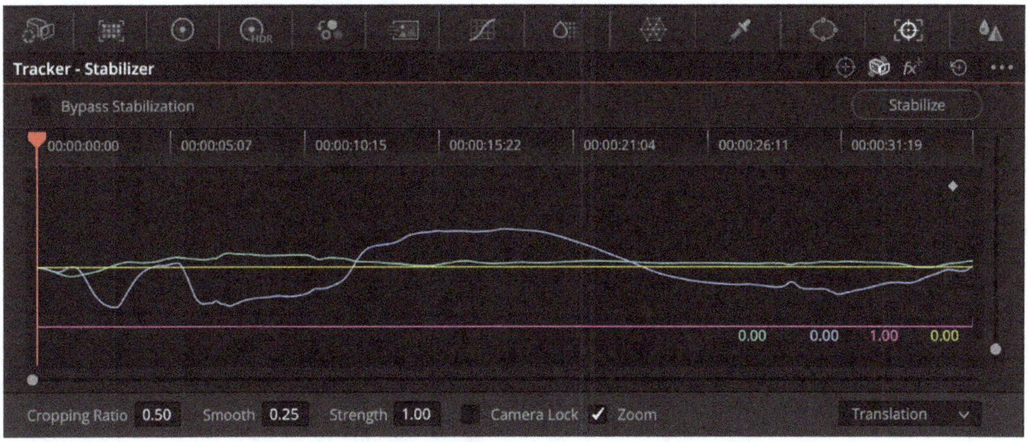

Figure 7.9: Tracker palette showing Translation mode

To see how the different stabilization modes work, select them on the **Color** page and compare the results of the graphs.

> Any tracking that is performed on the **Cut** and **Edit** pages will show on the **Color** page.
>
> So, if you performed a track on the **Edit** page, you could still go to the **Color** page and see the results of the tracking data in the **Tracker - Stabilizer** graph without having to re-stabilize the clip on the **Color** page.

Now, if you really want fine control of stabilization in Resolve, you can select **Classic Stabilizer**. **Classic Stabilizer** was the main way to stabilize video footage in DaVinci Resolve version 12.5 and earlier. With DaVinci Resolve version 14 onward, you have the simplified stabilizers, as described earlier in this chapter, where you only have three stabilization presets to choose from: **Perspective**, **Similarity**, or **Translation**. **Classic Stabilizer** is still included, as it has the option to individually select each of the **Pan**, **Tilt**, **Zoom**, and **Rotate** options and turn them on or off, allowing you to have more control over your stabilization. If using the new stabilization controls doesn't work, you can always try your own combination of stabilization using **Classic Stabilizer**. Let us look at how **Classic Stabilizer** works.

The Classic Stabilizer

Classic Stabilizer separates stabilization into three distinct steps. So far, all the techniques we have covered on the **Cut**, **Edit**, and **Color** pages combine these three steps.

1. The first step is to analyze the clip for movement.
2. The second step is to select what stabilization settings to apply.
3. The third step is to stabilize the clip.

Let us see how this works in practice using the default **Cloud Tracker** settings.

Classic stabilizing using the Cloud Tracker

Classic Stabilizer, by default, generates a cloud of tracking points to help us stabilize our video footage:

1. In the **Tracker - Stabilizer** palette, select the **options** button (looks like a row of three dots ...).

2. Select **Classic Stabilizer** in the drop-down menu (*Figure 7.10*). A check mark will show next to it in the menu to show that it is selected.

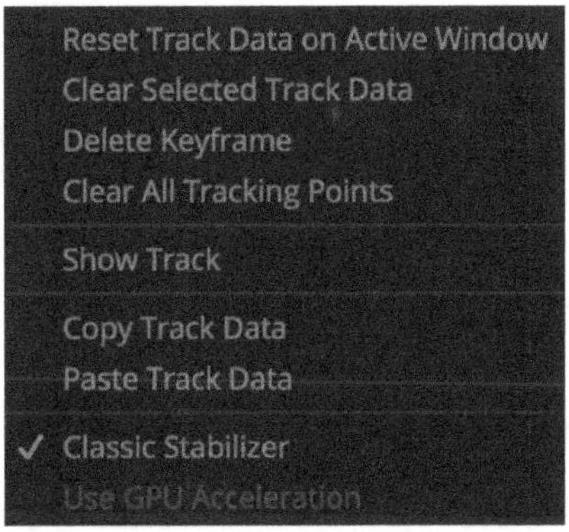

Figure 7.10: The Tracker options drop-down menu

The **Tracker** palette interface will change to show different tracking controls for **Classic Stabilizer** (*Figure 7.11*).

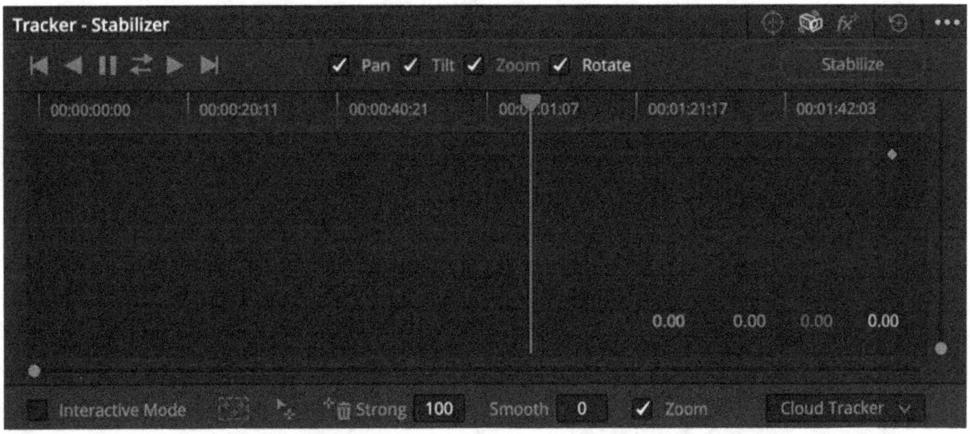

Figure 7.11: Classic Stabilizer

3. Analyze the clip for movement as follows:

    a. Select the movement you want Resolve to look for by selecting any combination of the **Pan**, **Tilt**, **Zoom**, and **Rotate** checkboxes, located at the top of the **Classic Stabilizer** palette.

b. Start tracking the clip for movement by selecting one of the following:

   - The **Track Forward** button (looks like a play button)
   - The **Track Forwards and Reverse** button (looks like arrows pointing in both directions)
   - The **Track Reverse** button (looks like a reverse play button)

4. Select the stabilization settings. Like in the previous stabilization methods, you can choose the **Strong**, **Smooth**, and **Zoom** settings. There are no options for **Camera Lock** or **Cropping Ratio**.
5. Click the **Stabilize** button to perform the stabilization.

When analyzing the clip for movement, by default, Resolve uses **Cloud Tracker**, which creates a cloud of tiny white crosses (you can see them on the bride's dress in *Figure 7.12*) on distinguishing features in the starting frame of the video. These crosses are then tracked for changes in their position within the frame.

Figure 7.12: Tracking points

You can select a **Point Tracker** instead of the **Cloud Tracker** if you want more control over what points in the video you want Resolve to track.

Now, let us show you how to use a **Point Tracker**.

Classic stabilizing using the Point Tracker

To make Resolve track and stabilize using a selected point in the video, we need to follow these steps:

1. Select **Point Tracker** in the **Cloud Tracker** drop-down menu.
2. Click on the **Add Tracker Point** icon to add a tracker point (*a blue cross*) to the current frame shown in the viewer.
3. Click and drag the tracker point in the viewer to reposition it to the point in the frame you want to track. When you click on the tracker point, it will turn *red* to show that you have selected it.
4. Repeat *steps 2* to *3* until you have positioned as many tracker points as you need.
5. Now, complete the remaining *steps 5* to *7* as if you were completing cloud stabilization (analyze the clip, select the stabilization settings, and stabilize).
6. Analyze the clip for movement exactly as we did in *step 3* for **Cloud Tracker**.
7. Select the stabilization settings exactly as we did in *step 4* for **Cloud Tracker**.
8. Click the **Stabilize** button to perform the stabilization.

Point Tracker

When selecting a point to track, select a high-contrast point that is easily identifiable from the rest of the clip that represents the motion that you want to track. Select at least four points if you want to stabilize **Pan**, **Tilt**, **Rotation**, and **Zoom** together.

Keep the tracker points at the same depth from the camera as the subject being tracked, as points in the background move more slowly than points in the foreground. Also, choosing several points on the object being tracked will help the tracking be more successful. Do not put tracker points on different objects moving in different directions, as this will confuse **Point Tracker**.

If you apply too many tracking points, you can delete some by selecting one (turns *red*) and then clicking on the **Delete Tracker Point** icon (the *trash can*).

When adding tracker points, they will all appear in the center of the frame. This means that if you click the **Add Tracker Point** icon several times, they will all stack upon each other, making it appear as if there is only one tracker point. Move the topmost tracker point, and you will see more underneath.

Now, we know how to stabilize a video in Resolve using stabilization controls on the **Cut**, **Edit**, and **Color** pages. We also understand how stabilization works and how to add tracker points manually. This brings us to the end of the chapter.

Summary

You now know about the range of stabilization tools available in DaVinci Resolve, whether it's quick and easy video stabilization on the **Cut** page or more involved stabilization on the **Color** page. You can now choose the best stabilization for the needs of your footage, always knowing that you have access to some advanced stabilization tools should you ever need them.

Here is what you have achieved in *Chapter 7*:

- You learned how video stabilization works in editing software
- You learned how to stabilize footage on the **Cut** page
- You learned how to stabilize footage on the **Edit** page
- You learned how to stabilize footage on the **Color** page using both cloud and point trackers

In *Chapter 8*, we will look at using cutaways and cut-ins on the **Cut** page to hide bad edits. We will also look at how to do this on the **Edit** page.

Questions

1. True or false? When shooting footage, it is always better to stabilize footage in post-production rather than worry about capturing stable footage.
2. True or false? There is just one way to stabilize a clip on the **Cut** page.
3. True or false? Stabilization on the **Edit** page works completely differently from the **Cut** page.
4. True or false? There is more than one way to stabilize a clip on the **Color** page.

Further reading

An overview of the different types of stabilization for video production and post-production: `https://moviola.com/technique/dslr-filmmaking-stabilizing-techniques-production-and-post/`.

Get this book's PDF version and more

Scan the QR code (or go to `packtpub.com/unlock`). Search for this book by name, confirm the edition, and then follow the steps on the page.

UNLOCK NOW

Note: Keep your invoice handy. Purchases made directly from Packt don't require an invoice.

8

Hiding the Cut – Making Our Edits Invisible

So far, we have only really covered the basics of editing, such as introducing basic cuts to trim down our content. However, editing is more than just cutting out unwanted video footage. It is also a way to help tell a story seamlessly.

Our task as editors is to choose clips and put them together in a sequence that helps tell a story. To ensure our audience can connect with the story we are telling, it is important that the editing process itself is not noticeable, as this can distract from the content of the video.

One editing technique that both helps tell the story and hides obvious or jarring edits is the use of cut-ins and cutaways inserted from B-roll video footage.

In this chapter, we will look at how to use **cutaways** and **cut-ins** on the **Cut** page to hide bad edits. Additionally, we will look at how to use the **Smooth Cut transition** to make a cut invisible. Finally, we will look at how to hide jarring cuts on the **Cut** page using a **split edit**.

In this chapter, we are going to cover the following main topics:

- Understanding cutaways, cut-ins, and the editing process
- Understanding continuity editing
- Creating cut-ins
- Creating cutaways
- Using Smooth Cut to hide an edit
- Hiding cuts with a split edit

Technical requirements

To follow along with the exercises in this chapter, download the wedding footage (`The Wedding.dra`), as described in *Chapter 7*, and stabilize the clip named `A001_04041646_C033.mov` if you haven't done so already. You can download the required video clips from: `https://packt.link/gbz/9781836208839`.

Before we begin our first exercise, we need to explain some editing terms, such as cutaways, cut-ins, and B-roll.

Understanding cutaways, cut-ins, and the editing process

To understand what **B-roll** is, let us uncover where the term first came from.

In the film industry, the main camera team (the **main unit**) shoots the central action of the film's key characters with *Camera A*, and a second camera team (called the **second unit**) will shoot other footage with *Camera B*, where you do not need the main actors present. The footage from Camera A is called A-roll, and the footage from Camera B is called B-roll. Both were named in the early days when movies were exclusively shot using rolls of film (*Figure 8.1*):

Figure 8.1: Image of rolls of film (LDGE at English Wikipedia): https://commons.wikimedia.org/wiki/File:35mm_cinema_release_print.jpg#mw-jump-to-license

Since B-roll from the second unit is used to capture elements of the story where the main actor is not needed, this frees up time for the main unit to focus on the main story, while the second unit captures other shots for the edit, such as cut-ins or cutaways. Cut-ins and cutaways are two types of B-roll footage that can be used by the editor to hide an obvious edit, which we will demonstrate in a later exercise in the *Understanding continuity editing* section, where we will edit a short wedding video.

So, what is the difference between a cut-in and a cutaway? Let's find out together.

Cut-ins

Generally, **cut-ins** are close-up shots of the main action within the scene. For example, if the main actor is making an origami bird, then the second unit would film a tight close-up shot of a hand double who is an origami expert (with similar hands to the lead actor) making the origami bird. This would be a cut-in as it illustrates the main action of the central character; hence, the name cut-in as we are *cutting in* to the main action.

Cutaways

Cutaways are different from cut-ins in that they *cut away* from the main action of the key actor in the scene. Cutaways can often show other visual information that can help illustrate the main action of the scene or give a different interpretation to it.

For example, the main actor might be making an origami bird; however, if we cut away to a ticking clock, then we will assume that there might be a time limit to the origami, such as a contest. If using the same example, where we cut away to a Japanese serenity garden, we would assume that the actor is making the origami bird to unwind or relax.

Now that we understand the difference between cut-ins and cutaways, let us look at the overall editing process and how cuts are not just used to hide mistakes in the footage.

The editing process

A good cut-in or cutaway will not only be used to hide an unwanted edit, but it will also be used to help enhance or tell the story better.

Some examples of how they can be used to enhance a story are listed as follows:

- **Extend or slow down time**: Cutting out surplus footage, such as long pauses, and covering the edits with cutaways, cut-ins, or shots from a different camera angle, can speed up time. On the other hand, adding cuts into the footage, without removing any footage, and adding cutaways, cut-ins, or other angles will slow down time.

- **Show the internal thoughts of the main character in the scene**: A cutaway can be used to illustrate what the character is thinking about, such as a flashback to a childhood memory.
- **Create suspense or tension**: Cutting away to an image of a threat (such as an approaching train or tidal wave) that the main character is oblivious to can create tension in the audience. Alternatively, cutting into the main character holding a weapon under the table can add tension to the conversation being had above the table.
- **Reveal a comedy gag or punchline**: The main character might be saying something profound, but we cut away to something to illustrate that what they are saying lacks any credibility, causing the audience to laugh. One example would be the main character saying that they were cool and collected in an emergency, and we then cut away to them panicking in the emergency.
- **Add visual interest**: If we filmed the whole scene with one shot, the viewer could get bored and lose interest. Adding a shot of the same scene but from another angle can keep the viewers' attention by adding visual interest.

Now we are going to illustrate how to use cut-ins and cutaways to both enhance the story in a wedding video and hide some poor footage.

Understanding continuity editing

One use of cut-ins and cutaways is to help with **continuity editing**. Continuity editing is an editing technique where we aim to maintain the timing of the clips on the timeline as if the action is happening in a continuous moment in time (even if the clips were shot at different times or on different days). Rather than try and understand it with a definition, it is easier to demonstrate it in the following exercise using the *TheWedding* project that we downloaded in *Chapter 7*.

Even though we have stabilized the wedding video footage, there are still parts of the clips that we cannot fix, such as the camera drifting in and out of focus.

We will need to cut these out and hide the resulting **jump cut** with other B-roll footage, which was shot at a different time by a wedding guest. I have already color-coded the B-roll footage we are going to use as a **Lime** green color and the master footage as a **Navy** color to make them easier to find and differentiate. If you want to change the clip colors yourself, you can do so by right-clicking on any clip, and from the drop-down menu, selecting **Clip Color**, and choosing your color. This can be done to the clips in either the **Media Pool** or those directly on the timeline.

Key concept – jump cut

A jump cut is where a piece in the middle of the same shot is cut out, leaving a jump in time.

For example, say a person walks from left to right in a single shot, cutting out the middle part of the shot between the start and the end of the walk will create a jump in time. As we don't see them move between the start and end points of their walk, this will create a shortening of time for the scene.

Jump cuts are often seen in YouTube tutorial videos where the subject has edited out their mistakes (for example, "umms" and "Ahhs") but keeps talking in the same shot.

Jump cuts are often avoided as they throw the viewer off watching the video due to the jarring effect they create. However, sometimes, they can be used for good effect if you want the viewer to feel uneasy, such as in horror or action sequences during a film.

Now that we know more about jump cuts and clip colors, we will jump into the exercise. Using our stabilized wedding video clip in the timeline of the **Cut** page, we are going to remove the shaky and out-of-focus camera moves and replace them with some B-roll footage, and make it seem that it was all shot in the same moment:

1. Move the playhead on the timeline to timecode `01:00:37:02`.
2. Add a cut using the **Split Clip** tool, which looks like a pair of scissors, to the left of the timeline. The *Cmd* + *B* key combination is the shortcut for **Split Clip**. A cut will appear under the playhead on the timeline.
3. Move the timeline playhead to the following timecode: `01:00:45:00`.
4. Add another cut by pressing *Cmd* + *B*.
5. Turn off **Ripple On** (as described in *Chapter 1*) so that the timeline will not ripple when we delete our clip.
6. Select this new clip in between the two cuts (between `01:00:37:02` and `01:00:45:00`) and delete it by pressing the *Backspace* key on your keyboard.

Deleting this section of the video has created a gap in your timeline on video track 1 (**V1**), which we need to cover (*Figure 8.2*):

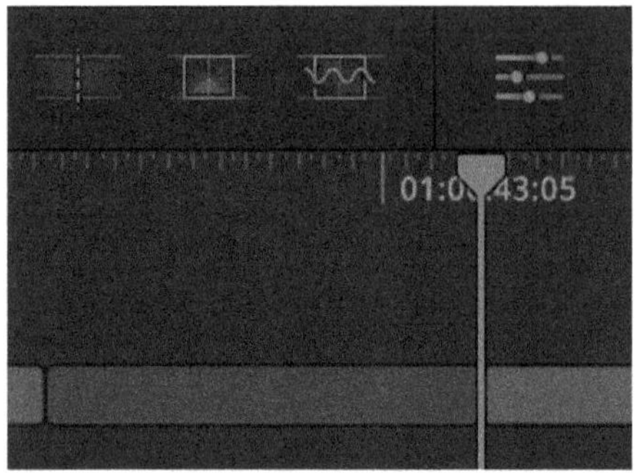

Figure 8.2: Gap in the timeline

> **Deleting clips**
>
> The two easiest ways to delete a clip on the timeline are to select it and then use either the *Delete* or *Backspace* key on your keyboard to remove it. These keys both operate in the same way on the **Cut** page. However, these two keys delete the clip in different ways on the **Edit** page and have different effects on your edit.
>
> The *Backspace* key will delete a clip and leave a gap in the timeline. This is good if you want to leave the timing of the video intact without creating a jump cut. The clip can be easily covered over with another clip from the B-roll, as we demonstrate in this chapter.
>
> The *Delete* key will delete the clip and ripple all the other clips along the timeline to close the gap; this is called a **ripple delete**. This will create a jump cut if it is used to delete the middle section of a clip. A **ripple delete** is best used when removing clips that are no longer needed to shorten the length of the video.

7. Go to the `BMP4K` bin in the **Media Pool** and find a different angle of the bride and groom looking at each other (i.e., `A001_04041647_C034.mov`). Double-click on it to see it in the viewer.

8. This clip is too long to use in its entirety, as we are only using it as a cutaway of the bride and groom looking at each other, so let us shorten it before we add it to the timeline. We also need to find a part of the clip that matches the action of the existing clips on the timeline.

   The end of the first clip on the timeline has both the bride and groom looking down at the paper they are about to sign. We need the start of the new clip in the **Media Pool** to start with the couple in a similar position.

   Add an *In point* (where our new clip will start) by pressing the letter *I* on your keyboard at `16:51:05:15` (*Figure 8.3*). A gray marker will appear under your viewer's playhead to mark the In point:

Figure 8.3: In and Out points marked up on the source clip in the viewer

Key concept – In and Out points

We used In and Out points when using **Fairlight** to dub audio in *Chapter 4*. In and Out points are also used in video editing, and we first used them in *Chapter 1*. An **In point** is the point where we want our new clip to start. The keyboard shortcut to create an In point is the *I* key, which is short for "In." An **Out point** is where we want our clip to end. The keyboard shortcut to create an Out point is the *O* key, which is short for "Out." In and Out points can be created for clips in the **Media Pool** to mark up what part of a clip to keep before they are added to the timeline. Conversely, they can also be used to mark up part of a clip on the timeline to be removed from the timeline.

9. The start of the second clip that we have on the timeline has both the bride and groom looking at each other, so we will need the end of our new clip in the **Media Pool** to also match this.

   Add an Out point (where the clip will end) by pressing the *O* key at `16:51:12:19` just before the groom pokes his tongue out.

10. Drag the clip down from the viewer onto the timeline just above video track 1. A new track (video track 2) will be automatically created, where we can drop our newly prepared B-roll clip (*Figure 8.4*):

Figure 8.4: B-roll on Video Track 2

11. Position the clip on the timeline in track 2 so that it covers the missing clip on track 1.
12. There is still a gap between our B-roll clip on track 2 and our master shot on track 1, so drag the start of the second clip on track 1 to line up with the end of our first B-roll clip on track 2.

Now we have covered up the shaky camerawork at the start of the master shot by adding some B-roll to cover up the edit. The B-roll I have used is just a suggestion, so feel free to find your own part of the clip to use if you prefer a different angle.

Key concept – master shot

Although we referred to the master shot in *Chapter 1*, we haven't needed to explain its use until now.

A **master shot** is the main shot that tells our story, as it shows most of the scene in that one shot. Usually, a master shot is a wide shot, but it can be closer if the widest shot in the scene is a mid-shot, in which case, the mid-shot will be the master shot.

Other shots are then added to the master shot, such as cut-ins, cutaways, or B-roll, to help add to the story.

The main learning point from this exercise is that when covering up a missing clip with a shot from another angle, we need to make sure that the action at the end of the previous clip matches the start of the new clip, and the end of the new clip matches the start of the next clip on the timeline. If we do not do this, it will create a jump in the action, which will be jarring for the viewers. This principle of hiding obvious edits, to help maintain the timing of the story, is the basis of *continuity editing*.

Key concept – three-point editing

The process of adding an In Point marker and an Out Point marker to a clip and then inserting the clip on the timeline from a set point marked by the playhead is called **three-point editing.**

Once you have mastered the basics of drag-and-drop editing, as covered in this book, you can use your understanding of three-point editing to progress on to using the more advanced editing tools in the toolbar, such as inserting a clip – *F9*, overwriting a clip – *F10*, or placing a clip on top – *F12*.

Without going into too much detail (as that is beyond the scope of this book), you mark up your three points using In and Out points and your playhead, then use either the **Insert** clip option (by clicking the **Smart Insert** icon or using the *F9* key on your keyboard) or the **Overwrite** clip option (by clicking the **Ripple Overwrite** icon or using the *F10* key on your keyboard).

What we just did by dragging the clip from the viewer onto a new video track can also be achieved by clicking the **Place on Top** icon or using the *F12* key to place the new clip on a new track starting at the playhead position on the timeline. This will do the same job as drag-and-drop editing but more quickly, as you don't need to use your mouse.

There are other variations of three-point editing, such as marking one point on your source media and two points on your timeline using In and Out points. The main concept to remember is that we use three points to mark our source and timeline edit points. To fully understand three-point editing, I suggest you try the various combinations to see what they do. For now, the basic three-point edit is sufficient for a beginner's book.

The footage we have just added is not really a cut-in, as it is a shot of the same subject from a different camera angle. Now we are going to add a cut-in to help emphasize a certain part of the story.

Creating cut-ins

Here, we will use the same clip to show how cut-ins work. We need to add a close-up of the groom signing the marriage certificate as a cut-in to help tell the story. We want to emphasize this part of the story, and getting closer will draw our audience's attention to this key moment:

1. Move the playhead to the following timecode of the timeline: `01:00:57:23`. This is the point where we will add our cut-in.

2. Now, let us mark up our cut-in on clip `A001_04041647_C034.mov`:
   a. Double-click on the clip in the **Media Pool** to load it in the viewer.
   b. Move the playhead in the viewer until `16:48:37:11`, and mark an In point (*I*).
   c. Move the playhead in the viewer until `16:48:40:11`, and mark an Out point (*O*).
3. Drag the marked-up clip down from the viewer onto video track 2 of the timeline. Line up the start of our cut-in with the playhead on our timeline that we just placed in *step 1*. Or, you can use the **Place on Top** edit – *F12* to do the same thing.
4. Play back the clips on the timeline to review your cut-in to see if the action flows. If it does not flow, you can trim the start and end points and reposition the clips on tracks 1 and 2 until you get a closer match that you are happy with.

As you can see, adding cut-ins can require the back-and-forth trimming needed for continuity editing until it feels right.

Now, let us add a cutaway, which is usually a shot that does not affect the continuity of the scene but can reveal some internal thoughts the subject might be having.

Creating cutaways

When inserting a cutaway, it is useful to find a part of the main shot that motivates the cutaway. Play through the edit on the timeline and mark any key moments where the subjects look away off-camera or seem to be thinking. Here's an example of how to do that:

1. Move the playhead to the following timecode of the timeline: `01:01:15:13`. Both the bride and groom see something outside the shot (off camera) that attracts their attention. Notice that their eye lines are looking to the lower-left part of the frame. We will need to find a B-roll clip where the action matches the direction of their eye lines.
2. In the **Media Pool**, locate clip `A001_04041629_C028.mov` and load it into the viewer.
3. Play it until you reach `16:29:09:02`, where the B-roll is of a little boy and a girl walking up the steps. This shot matches your couple's eye lines.
4. Add an In point.
5. Add an Out point at `16:29:13:07` before the children reveal they are walking up to the couple in a different location.

6. Drag the marked-up clip down from the viewer onto video track 2 of the timeline (*Figure 8.5*). Line up the start of our cutaway with the timeline playhead we just positioned in *step 1* (or just press *F12* to do a **Place on Top** edit):

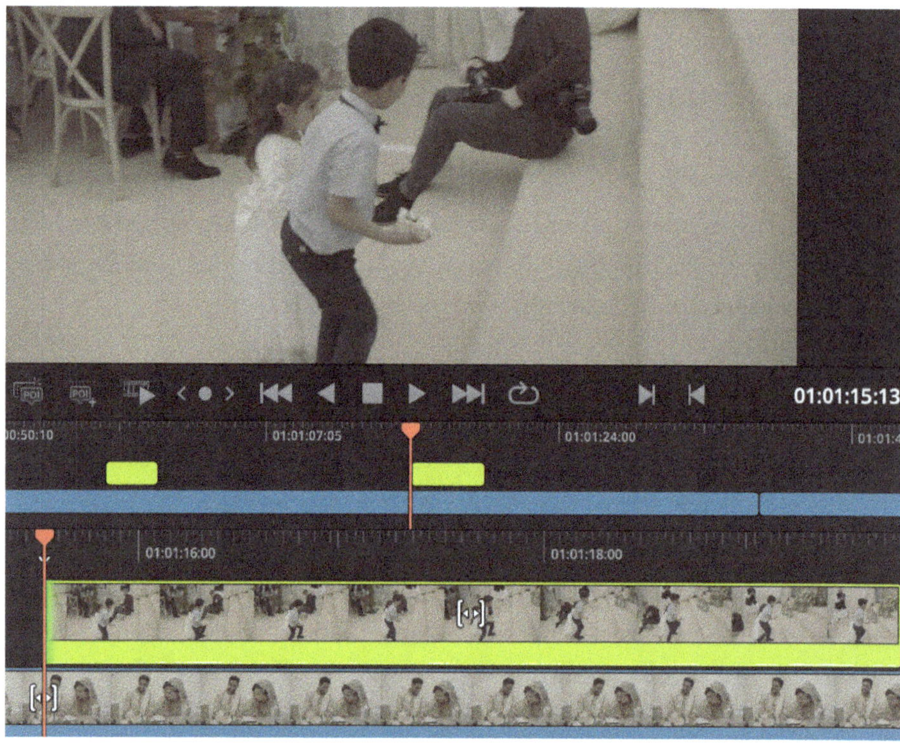

Figure 8.5: Cutaway lined up on the timeline

7. Play back the footage on the timeline from the newly added cutaway to review it. It now looks like the bride and groom are looking at the children approaching them.

Now that we have added both cut-ins and cutaways to our edit, let us look at other ways we can add an invisible edit.

As an optional exercise, see whether you can add an additional shot from the B-roll to add some more visual interest. Once you have done this, compare your edit with the edit I have included in the `Wedding_Video` timeline, which is part of the media download for *Chapter 7*.

Sometimes, there are occasions where we need to cut out a section of a clip, but don't have any suitable B-roll footage to hide the edit. How do we then hide the resulting jump cut? Well, DaVinci Resolve has a solution to remove subtle jump cuts in the same clip – it is an effect called **Smooth Cut**.

Using Smooth Cut to hide an edit

Smooth Cut works best when there is not too much movement within the frame.

Much like the **Frame Replacer FX** plugin we used in *Chapter 6*, to replace a missing frame for the archive footage, the **Smooth Cut** video transition takes information from frames on both sides of the cut and blends them to hide the cut.

In this exercise, we are going to cut out the section of the clip where the groom looks at the camera, as this can be distracting for the audience and can break them out of the intimacy of the scene. Then, we will be removing the resulting jump cut with the **Smooth Cut** transition:

1. Move the playhead to timecode `01:00:52:19` of the timeline and add a cut.
2. Move the playhead to timecode `01:00:55:24` of the timeline and add a second cut.
3. Ripple delete this section of the clip by doing the following:
    a. Click the **Ripple On** icon (next to the **Split Clip** icon) (*Figure 8.6*). The icon will turn white to show it is enabled.
    b. Select the clip and press the *Delete* or *Backspace* key on your keyboard. The section of the clip will be deleted, and the rest of the clips on the timeline will be rippled up to fill the gap.
    c. Remember to disable the **Ripple On** setting by clicking on it. The **Ripple On** icon will turn gray to show that it is disabled.

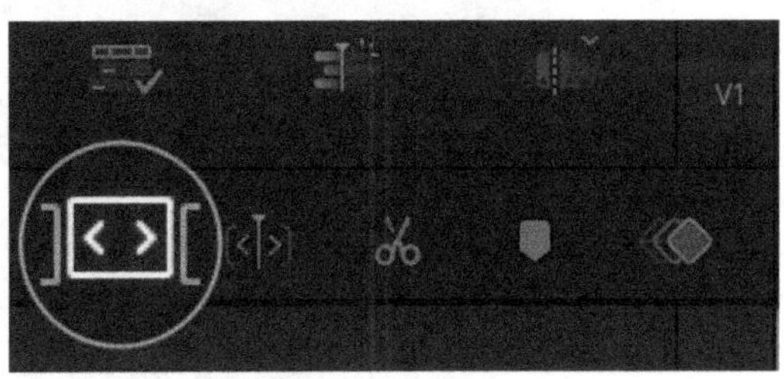

Figure 8.6: Ripple On icon enabled

4. Play back this new cut (see the *Play around* tip box), and you will notice a small jump cut, like a glitch in the Matrix. We will now fix this.

Play around (/)

A quick way to review a transition is to use the **play around** command, which is the / key on the keyboard. The play around command will play the timeline from 2 seconds before the playhead or what you have selected on the timeline (either a clip or a transition) to 2 seconds after. Play around is good for quickly reviewing edits you have made to see whether the edit has worked.

5. Click on the **Smooth Cut** icon in the toolbar (*Figure 8.7*):

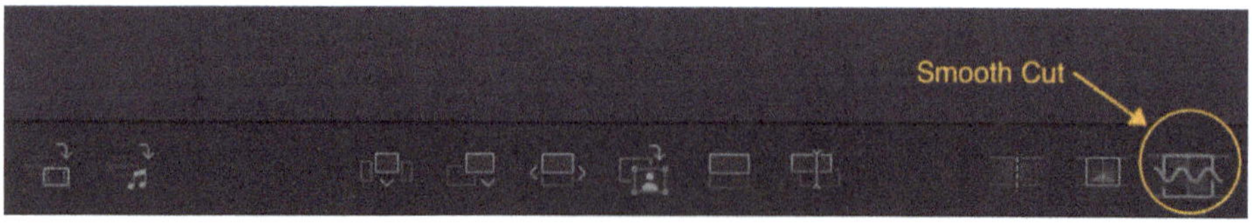

Figure 8.7: Smooth Cut in the toolbar

A transition will be applied to the edit point with a red line on the timeline above it. This red line shows that the **Smooth Cut** transition has not been rendered yet (*Figure 8.8*).

Figure 8.8: The Smooth Cut transition applied before rendering

Once the **Smooth Cut** transition has been rendered, this red line will turn blue (*Figure 8.9*), then disappear.

Figure 8.9: The Smooth Cut transition after being rendered

6. Play back the **Smooth Cut** transition, and you will notice that the transition is very stuttery in playback. Let us make sure that the playback performance of any transition is optimal.
7. To do that, in the menu bar, select **Playback > Render Cache > Smart**. This will mean that the transition will be automatically rendered when we play it back to help it play smoothly:
   - A red bar (*Figure 8.8*) on the timeline above the transition means it needs to be rendered
   - A blue bar (*Figure 8.9*) on the timeline above the transition means that the effect has been rendered and will play back smoothly

8. Play back the transition, and you will notice that, although it has improved, it is still a bit jumpy. The groom's face seems to have morphed (*Figure 8.10*). This is because **Smooth Cut** works best when there is little movement in the frame. In this clip, the groom moves his head, and the bride barely moves. You will notice that the glitch is at the start of the **Smooth Cut** transition, where it overlays the first clip. After that, where the transition overlays the second clip, it plays back flawlessly. This gives us a clue on how to fix it:

Figure 8.10: The groom's face showing an unwanted morph effect

We can fix this by changing the **Smooth Cut** settings.

9. Select the **Smooth Cut** transition (an orange border will appear to show it has been selected; *Figure 8.8*).
10. Open the **Inspector** panel to reveal the transition controls (*Figure 8.11*).

Figure 8.11: The Smooth Cut controls in the Inspector panel

11. Change the **Transition** > **Video** settings until you get a smooth result.

    These are the settings I chose for my **Smooth Cut** transition for this edit (*Figure 8.11*):

    - **Duration: Seconds** and **Frames:** By default, this will be **1 Seconds** or **25 Frames**, as this clip has a frame rate of *twenty-five* **frames per second (fps)**. You can change the duration of the clip by changing either the **Seconds** or **Frames** value. I am going to change the transition to **9 Frames** (**0.4 Seconds**) long, as a shorter **Smooth Cut** transition often produces better results.

- **Alignment**: There are options here to choose whether to apply **Smooth Cut** only to the clip to the left of a cut (the left-hand button), over the clips on both sides of the cut (the middle button), or just the clip to the right of the cut (the right-hand button). I chose the right alignment, as, if you remember, the glitch was to the left of the cut, so we can avoid this glitch altogether.
- **Mode**: This drop-down menu selects the quality of the render:
    - **Faster** renders faster but with a slight drop in quality
    - **Better** is the highest quality render, but takes longer to do so

  I have left this at the default **Better** setting.
- **Ease**: This drop-down menu selects the following:
    - **None**: This is the default setting that applies a linear transition
    - **In**: This eases in the start of the transition
    - **Out**: This eases in the end of the transition
    - **In & Out**: This eases in the start and the end of the transition
    - **Custom**: This is where you can add your own keyframes to the transition curve to modify how gently or suddenly you want the transition to be applied

  I have changed this to the **In & Out** setting.

12. There are options to change the settings for the audio transition; however, I have left these all at the default values as I am more interested in the visuals of this clip.
13. Now you can play back the transition on the timeline.

If it is still a bit jittery, you can change the settings in *Step 11* to your own preference until it looks right to you.

Smooth Cut transitions are great for removing jump cuts that have appeared when we have edited out all those "umms" and "aahs" in our online videos.

The next way to disguise a cut is not with any additional footage but to use audio to smooth over the transition. This is called a split edit.

Hiding cuts with a split edit

A **split edit** is a cut where the transition between the audio and video is split to happen at different times.

There are two types of split edit: a *J Cut*, where we hear the audio from the next clip before we see the video, and an *L Cut*, where the audio from the previous clip is heard over the video of the next clip. They are named *J* and *L* cuts after the shape they make on the timeline. The bottom of the *J* and *L* cuts is the audio, and the upright shape of the letter is the video, as the audio appears below the video on the timeline.

Split edits are good for hiding an edit, as there is a softer transition than a straight cut (**through cut**), as our brains only notice one sensory change at a time. With a through cut, the video and audio change at the same time, whereas with a *J* or *L* cut, the audio changes at a different time in the video, which softens the edit and makes it less obvious.

With this exercise, we need some audio to play with, and as the wedding video does not have any good audio, I have created some clips especially for this exercise.

You can download the project files (`Split_Edit_Explainer.dra`) with the clips in them here:

`https://packt.link/gbz/9781836208839`.

> Remember to open the archive (`.dra`) file in DaVinci Resolve, not the project file that is in the `.dra` folder. That way, all the video files will already be linked to the timeline. How to import a `.dra` file is outlined at the start of *Chapter 2*.

We are going to use the `Split Edit Explainer` video clips on the **Cut** page timeline to demonstrate how a split edit works:

1. Open the timeline called **Split Edit Explainer** on the **Cut** page. You will notice that all the clips are already on the timeline, with cuts already applied. Now we are going to add some split edits.
2. First, make sure **Ripple On** is disabled, as described in the previous section.

3. Enlarge the video track by clicking on the **Enlarge Track** icon (*Figure 8.12*). This will enlarge the track so that we can adjust the video and audio tracks separately.

Figure 8.12: Enlarge Track icon

4. On the **V1** track, drag the top-right edge of the title clip to the right over the audio until the phrase *J Cut ...* is underneath the title clip.
5. Play back the edit. When you play this back, you will hear me describing what a *J* cut is before you see me talking.
6. After the third clip, where I describe an *L* cut, drag the edge of the video from the end title to the left-hand side so that it covers some of the third clip. Move the video until the phrase *whilst we hear the audio from the previous clip* is heard underneath the end title clip.
7. Play back the edit. When you play this back, you will continue to hear me describe what an *L* cut is after the video has cut to the next clip.
8. Once you have finished, remember to click the **Collapse Track** icon (the reverse of the **Expand Track** icon) to stop you from accidentally making split edits when moving clips on the timeline.

That's it; we have now done our first split edits. It is best to use a split edit if there is a motivation to do so in the scene; otherwise, it can come across as a mistake.

Split edits are great to show a back-and-forth conversation, as real-life conversations usually overlap.

For instance, let us say that I am watching two people, person A and person B, have a conversation. I am looking at person B when I hear person A talking to person B. I hear person A speak first (while I am looking at person B). Then, I turn to see person A speaking, pretty much just like a *J* cut. If I want to see person B's reaction to what is being said, I will look at them while person A is still talking, just like an *L* cut. In this situation, we would be showing the audience that we are interested in the emotional journey of person B during the conversation.

We have now used a variety of editing techniques to help the flow of a story and to hide our editing. This brings us to the end of this chapter.

Summary

Here is what you have achieved in *Chapter 8*:

- Learned what cutaways and cut-ins are and why they are used
- Learned what continuity editing is
- Learned how to create a cut-in on the **Cut** page
- Learned how to create a cutaway on the **Cut** page
- Used a **Smooth Cut** transition to hide a jump cut
- Learned what a split edit is (*J* and *L* cuts) and how to create them

Learning how to edit using B-roll and split edits gives us a greater opportunity to tell a seamless story where the viewer is more immersed in our story and not distracted by our editing techniques.

In *Part 3* of the book, we start with *Chapter 9*, where we will explore creating composite images by adding split-screen and picture-in-picture effects.

Questions

1. True or false? A cutaway or cut-in is another name for a split edit.
2. True or false? Continuity editing is when we add the audio of a continuity announcer.
3. True or false? A cut-in is used to emphasize closer details within the action.
4. True or false? A cutaway is when we remove unnecessary video footage.
5. True or false? **Smooth Cut** is a type of transition.
6. True or false? There are two types of split edits, a *J* cut and an *L* cut.

Further reading

Here is a list of some useful articles on editing theory, such as cutaways and cut-ins, to help add a deeper understanding of what we have covered in this chapter:

- `https://www.masterclass.com/articles/cutaway-shot-explained`
- `https://www.studiobinder.com/blog/cutaway-shot/`
- `https://nofilmschool.com/cutaway-shot-definition-examples`

Get this book's PDF version and more

Scan the QR code (or go to `packtpub.com/unlock`). Search for this book by name, confirm the edition, and then follow the steps on the page.

UNLOCK NOW

Note: Keep your invoice handy. Purchases made directly from Packt don't require an invoice.

Part 3

Advanced Techniques with DaVinci Resolve 20

The objective of this part is to familiarize you with more advanced techniques that can further enhance your footage. We will do this by enhancing colors, applying split-screen or green screen effects, and using Studio-only, AI-based tools to speed up your video editing workflow.

This part of the book includes the following chapters:

- *Chapter 9, Split Screens and Picture-in-Picture*
- *Chapter 10, Enhancing Color for Mood or Style*
- *Chapter 11, Adding Greenscreen Effects*
- *Chapter 12, Studio-Only Techniques – Mostly AI*

9

Split Screens and Picture-in-Picture

Have you ever wondered how sports broadcasts can overlay one video over another so that you can watch a close-up of a footballer's tackle in a small window, while you see the commentators' reactions in the video behind? This effect is also used in news broadcasts and even some movies to show the action happening concurrently. If you are making a wedding video, you can show the groom waiting and show the bride preparing at the same time to show two different sides of the same story. This can be achieved with the help of a split screen.

In this chapter, we will look at creating similar split-screen effects using composite footage and video resizing, as well as **picture-in-picture** effects using the *Resolve FX Transform Video Collage plugin* on the **Cut** page.

In this chapter, we are going to cover the following main topics:

- Creating a simple split-screen effect
- Creating compound clips
- Picture-in-picture effects using Video Collage | Create Background
- Picture-in-picture effects using Video Collage | Create Tile

DaVinci Resolve has several different ways we can create split screens by layering videos on the **Cut** page. We will begin with the simplest and progress to the more involved techniques toward the end of the chapter. For each of these techniques, we are going to use additional wedding video footage beyond what we used in *Chapters 7* and *8*.

Technical requirements

To follow along with the exercises in this chapter, download the following project archive, which contains all the clips needed: `Ch 9 Split Screen.dra` (`https://packt.link/gbz/9781836208839`)

Creating a simple split-screen effect

Creating a simple split-screen effect is not unique to Resolve and has been used for decades in cinema to show two perspectives of a story at the same time. For example, in early cinema, it was often used to show two characters in different locations having a phone conversation with each other. You can equally use split-screen effects to show a close-up of a product at the same time that a presenter talks about it.

The following approach can be used in any editing software and is a good way to understand how layering video works. Let us take the video of our bride and groom and show them cutting the cake with different camera angles, side by side as a split screen, to highlight the event to our audience:

1. Open `Ch9 Split Screen.dra` (remember, opening a `.dra` file was described in *Chapter 2*) and go to the **Cut** page.
2. Create a new timeline (*Cmd* + *N*) in the **Media Pool** and call it `Split_Screen`. Then, select two video and two audio tracks in the **Create New Timeline** pop-up window (*Figure 9.1*).

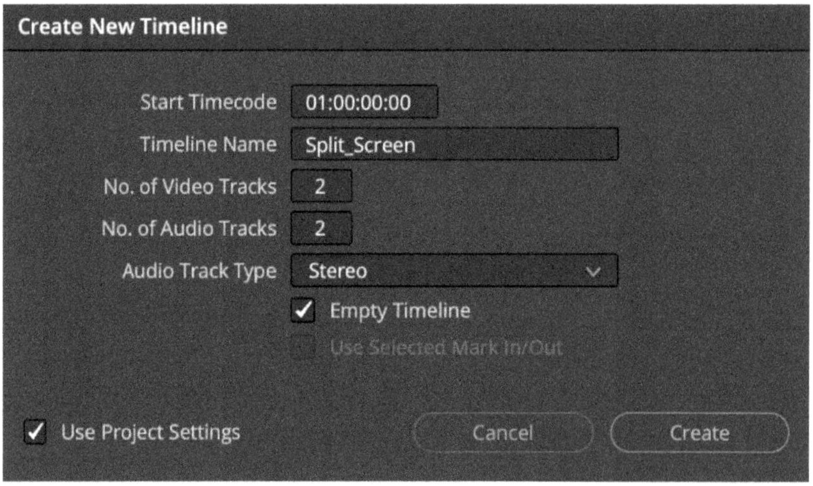

Figure 9.1: The Create New Timeline Window

3. In the **Media Pool**, navigate to the **Media** > **The Wedding** > `C70` folder.

4. Drag the clip of the groom and bride cutting the cake (`MVI_2580.mov`) onto track 1 on the timeline (or use the **Append** button on the toolbar).
5. Drag the second clip of the groom and bride cutting the cake (`A002_04042018_C039.mov`) from the **Media Pool** (**Media** > **The Wedding** > **BMP4K** > **A002**) onto track 2 above track 1 on the timeline (or use the **Place on Top** button in the toolbar). This will hide the first clip. There's no need to worry about the first clip; the next steps will reveal it again.
6. We now need to resize the second clip so that we can see the first clip underneath. Select the clip in track 2. To help us frame the top clip, move the playhead on the timeline to `01:01:42:00` so that we can see the bride and groom (*Figure 9.2*).

Figure 9.2: Playhead placement

7. Click the **Tools** button to reveal the tools under the viewer.
8. Select the **Transform** tool (*Figure 9.3*).
9. Move the top video layer to the left by changing the *x* position slider to have a negative value (such as `-288.000`, as shown in *Figure 9.3*). This will move the top clip to the left, revealing the clip underneath. We now need to crop the right-hand side of the top clip to reveal more of the clip underneath.

Figure 9.3: The Transform tool

10. Select the **Crop** tool (*Figure 9.4*).
11. Move the **Crop Right** slider until it crops the right-hand side of the top image, allowing the image underneath to fill half of the frame (a value of approximately `31.000` should be fine, as shown in *Figure 9.4*). This has now created a split-screen effect, where we see the action happen side by side from two different angles. Remember those 1970s cop shows? They used a very similar effect.

Figure 9.4: The Crop tool

12. Click the **Tools** button again to hide the tools.
13. Play back the timeline to review the effect.

Although we have successfully created a split-screen effect, the two clips play back out of sync with each other. This would be fine if they were totally different scenes; however, it is confusing, as both clips were filmed at the same time.

This presents us with an opportunity to show another feature in Resolve, called **auto align**.

Auto-aligning clips on the timeline

To be able to sync the timing of two clips that are already on the timeline, we need to pop over to the **Edit** page:

1. On the **Edit** page's timeline, select both clips that you want to sync.
2. Right-click on one of these clips and select **Auto Align Clips....** You can also find this function in the **Clip** menu – **Clip** > **Auto Align Clips**.

3. In the **Automatically Align Clips** dialogue box, make sure the **Waveform** option is selected in the drop-down menu. Then click on the **Sync** button (*Figure 9.5*).

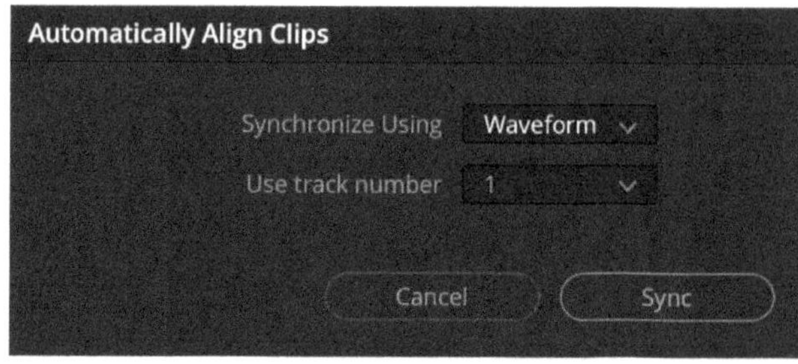

Figure 9.5: Automatically Align Clips

4. A progress bar will appear to show the progress of Resolve matching up the clips on the timeline, based on the audio waveform (*Figure 9.6*).

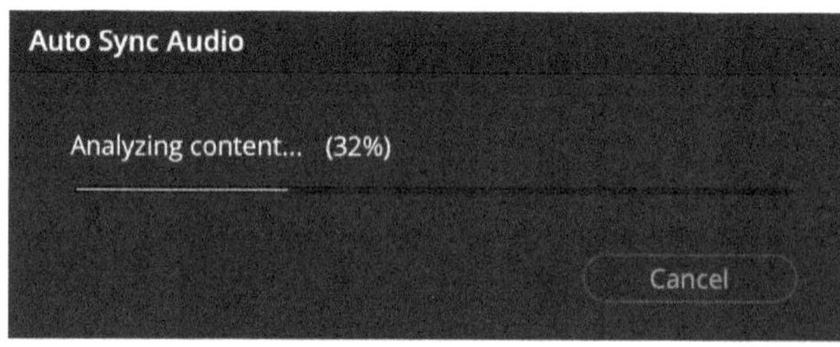

Figure 9.6: Auto Sync Audio

That is it – you are now done. You should now see that the clip on track 2 has moved along the timeline to match up with the clip on track 1. If you play them back, you will see that both videos (including their audio) match up frame by frame.

However, the clip on the right does not have the cake in the center. You can use this opportunity to practice using the **Transform** tool on the clip on track 1 to center the cake in the frame. If you change the **Transform Right** value to `420.000`, that should work.

You can tidy up this composite by trimming the end of the clip on track 1 to be the same length as the clip on track 2. The colors between the two clips are different from each other, but we can fix this in the next chapter.

Now that we have synced the clips together, we do not want to separate them by mistake. We may also want to apply effects to both of the clips at once, rather than tweak each clip individually in the composite. One way to both protect a composite and edit it as a whole is to create a compound clip.

Key concept – composite

A composite is where a single image is a combination of more than one image. So, the split screen we have just completed is a composite, as well as the picture-in-picture effects in the rest of this chapter. In *Chapter 11*, we will create more video composites using greenscreen effects.

Creating compound clips

You can take a series of clips on the same track on the timeline, or clips stacked on top of each other on different tracks on the timeline, and merge them into a single clip. This single clip that has been created from various video and audio files combined into one is called a **compound clip**. The advantage of working with a compound clip is that you can apply effects and transitions to it as if it were a single clip, without having to apply the same effect several times to its parts. So, anything you can do to a normal clip, you can do to a compound clip.

Creating a compound clip is easy:

1. Select all the audio and video clips on your timeline that you want to turn into a compound clip. You can *Shift* + *Click* on each one to select them or, in our case, use *Cmd* + *A* (Mac) or *Control* + *A* (Windows) to select all the clips on the timeline.
2. On the **Edit** page, right-click on any of the selected clips and choose **New Compound Clip...** at the top of the pop-up menu. Or, if you are on the **Cut** page, you can select **Clip > New Compound Clip...** in the menu.
3. Name your compound clip in the dialog box (*Figure 9.7*).

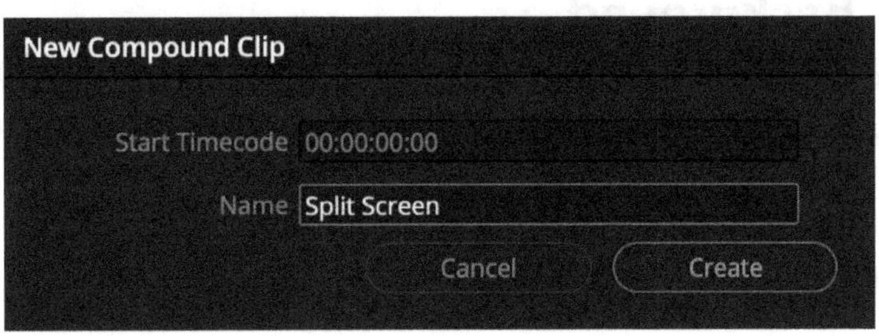

Figure 9.7: The New Compound Clip dialog box

Let us rename ours from `Compound Clip 1` to `Split Screen`. Click the **Create** button (*Figure 9.7*).

We now have a compound clip on the timeline, replacing all the clips we selected. There is a new icon at the bottom left of the clip (it looks like a stack of video frames on top of each other, as shown in *Figure 9.8*) to show that this clip is a compound clip.

Figure 9.8: Compound Clip icon

Resolve has also automatically created a copy of our compound clip and placed it in the **Media Pool**.

You may be concerned that we can no longer access our individual clips. Don't worry – we can access the individual clips by right-clicking on our compound clip on the **Edit** page timeline and selecting **Decompose in Place > Using Clips Only** from the pop-up menu. This will return all of the clips to their original state on the timeline before we turn them into a compound clip.

There is a Resolve FX effect called **Video Collage** that can be used to create more complex picture-in-picture effects. **Video Collage** can be found in the **Effects** panel on either the **Cut** or **Edit** page. Let us look at the two different options that **Video Collage** gives us to create these split-screen effects.

Picture-in-picture effects using Video Collage | Create Background

In the **Video Collage** effect, the **Create Background** option uses a top layer of video as the background layer and punches holes in this layer to show the video on the layers underneath (*Figure 9.9*). These holes appear as video tiles on the final video.

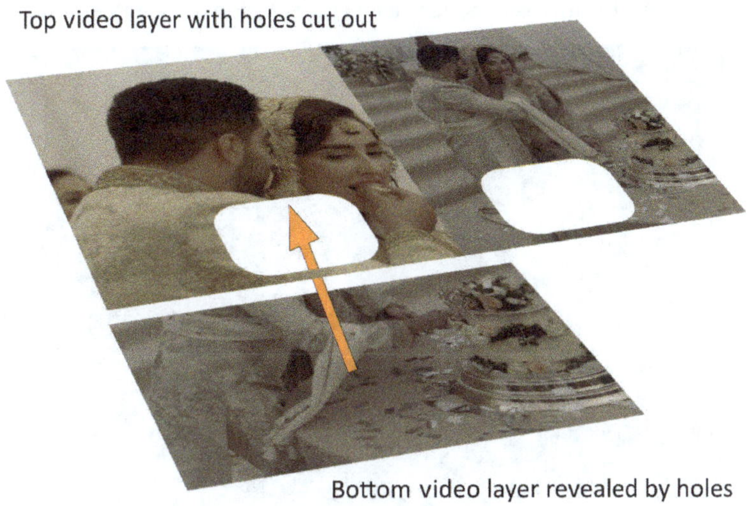

Figure 9.9: A Create Background example

We will be using the split-screen compound clip we created in the last exercise to overlay close-up shots of the cake being eaten.

We are going to use the **Cut** page for the following exercise; however, the effect works in exactly the same way on the **Edit** page.

Preparing our timeline for Create Background

First, we need to add all the video clips we will use for the picture-in-picture effect:

1. Right-click on the `Split_Screen` timeline in the **Media Pool**, select **Duplicate Timeline**, and rename it `Create_Background`. We will use this new timeline for our new effects without losing our original split-screen effects.
2. With the `Create_Background` timeline open, right-click on the video track header and select **Add Video Track** to add a third video track.

3. Drag the composite clip from video track 1 (**V1**) to video track 3 (**V3**) (*Figure 9.10*).

Figure 9.10: The composite clip on video track 3

We have now made space to add our new video clips to the timeline. Let us now add the new clips.

4. In the **Media Pool**, find both clips named `MVI_2573.mov` and `Cake Tile` (a compound clip of various resized cake shots I created for this exercise). Drag each clip onto a separate empty track on the timeline (*Figure 9.11*).

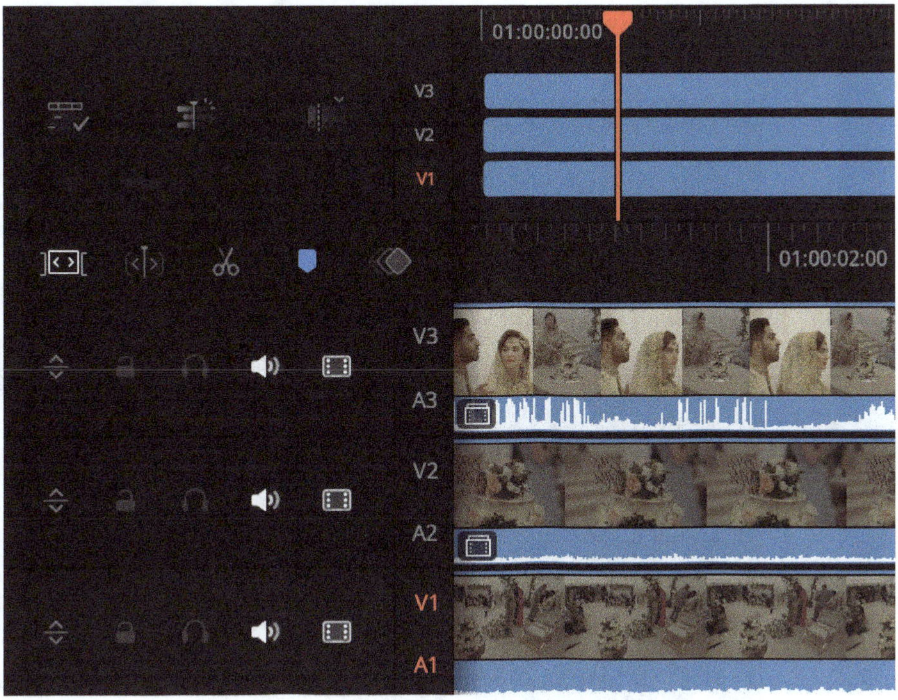

Figure 9.11: The timeline with all clips added

Now that we have prepared our timeline for **Video Collage | Create Background**, let us apply it to the timeline.

Applying the Video Collage | Create Background effect

Make sure that you have selected the topmost video clip on the timeline before applying the **Video Collage** effect, as you will be punching holes in this video layer to reveal the other clips on the video tracks underneath.

Locate the **Video Collage** effect in **Effects > Video > Resolve FX Transform > Video Collage**. From here, you can apply the **Video Collage** effect as described in *Chapter 2*, to the selected clip in the timeline by any of the following methods (*Figure 9.12*):

- Double-click on **Video Collage** in the **Effects** panel
- Drag and drop **Video Collage** from the **Effects** panel to the selected clip in the timeline

- (On the **Cut** page only) Click the **Add Effect** button (located at the bottom of the **Effects** panel)

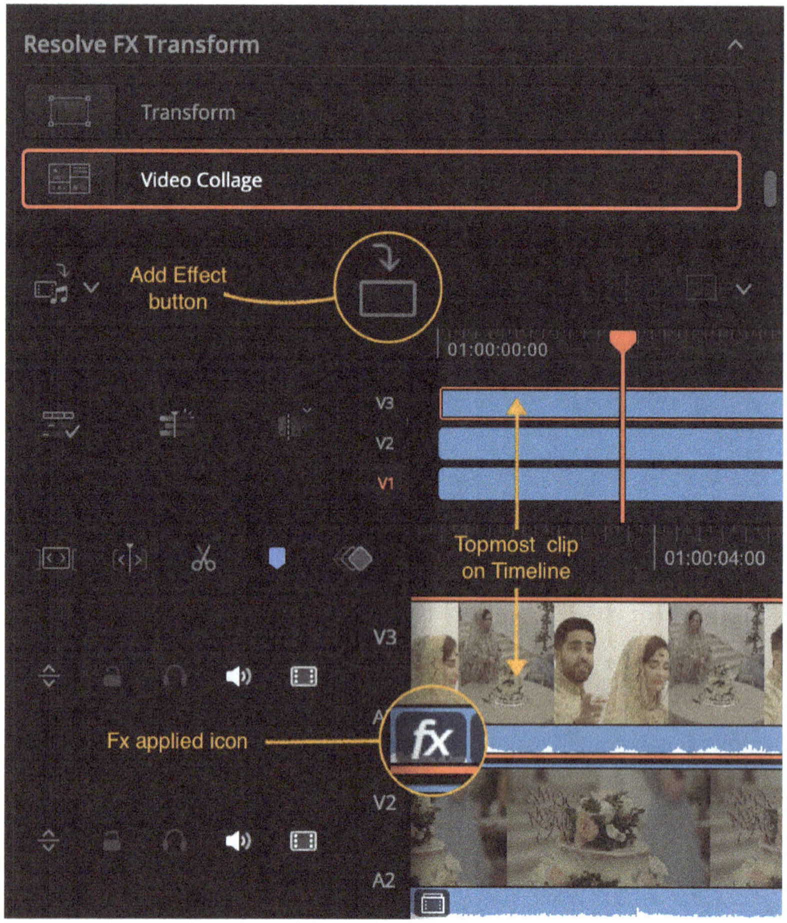

Figure 9.12: Applying effects on the Cut page

Once the video effect has been applied, note that a grid of four tiles appears, showing the video that is on the track directly below.

Let us adjust the number and position of these tiles to get the effect we want.

Adjusting Video Collage | Create Background

Now that we have applied our video collage, it shows four video thumbnails by default. As we only need two images of the cake, let us change the settings in the **Inspector** window to only show two video thumbnails of the cake from different angles:

1. Open the **Video Collage** control panel in the **Inspector** window (**Inspector** > **Effects** > **Open FX** > **Video Collage**), as shown in *Figure 9.13*.

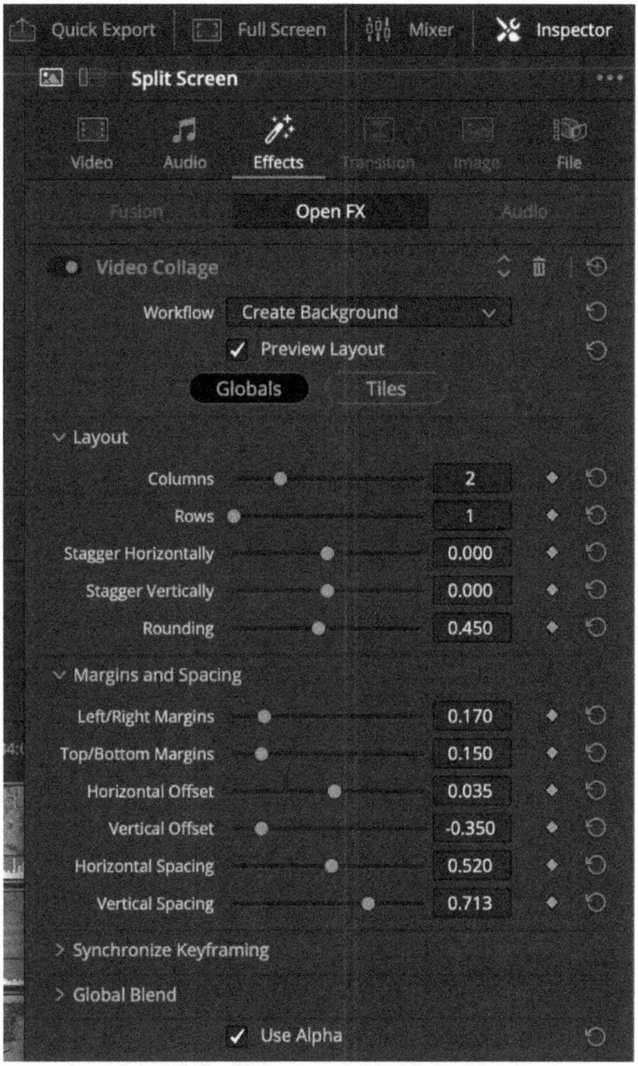

Figure 9.13: The Video Collage control panel

2. With the **Globals** button selected, under **Layout**, move the **Rows** slider to the left to reduce the rows from two to one. You will now have only two tiles rather than four (*Figure 9.13*).
3. Move the **Rounding** slider to the right to make the corners of the tiles rounder and less square (*Figure 9.13*).
4. Select the **Preview Layout** checkbox to make it easier to see the tiles against the background. This turns the tiles into yellow layout placeholders.
5. Under **Margins and Spacing**, move both the **Horizontal Spacing** and **Vertical Spacing** sliders to make both tiles smaller.
6. Move the **Vertical Offset** slider to the left to move both tiles to the bottom third of the video frame.
7. Move the **Horizontal Offset** slider to line up the tiles so that they are spaced evenly on either side of the vertical line in our `Split Screen` compound clip.
8. Select the **Tiles** button. This will give us the controls to change the tiles individually (*Figure 9.14*).

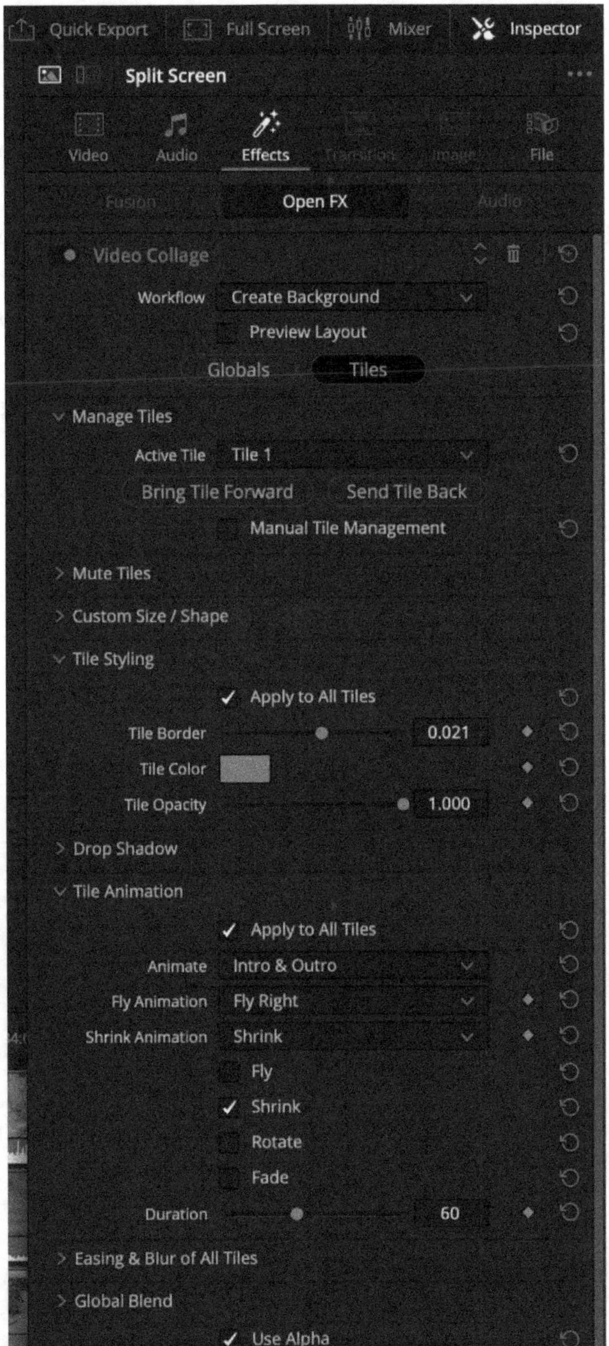

Figure 9.14: The Video Collage Tiles controls

9. Under **Tile Styling**, move the **Tile Border** slider to the right to create a border around your tile (*Figure 9.14*).
10. Click on the **Tile Color** swatch (*Figure 9.14*) and choose a color from your computer's color picker that suits the video. I have chosen a cream color to go with the color scheme of the cake.
11. Under **Tile Animation** in the **Animate** dropdown, select **Intro & Outro**. Under it, select any combination of the **Fly**, **Shrink**, **Rotate**, and **Fade** checkboxes to choose how to animate the appearance of the tiles at the start and end of the video clip (*Figure 9.14*).
12. Deselect the **Preview Layout** checkbox to reveal how the tiles look on your video and play back the video to test the tile animations. After reviewing your video, make any adjustments that are necessary.

Globals versus Tiles

The controls with the **Globals** button selected allow you to change the position and look of all the tiles at once, whereas the **Tiles** button reveals controls that allow you to change the properties of each individual tile.

Now that we have your tiles appearing how you want them to look (*Figure 9.15*), we need to line up the video underneath to fill the tile frames.

Figure 9.15: The tiles in their final position

Repositioning the videos under the tiles

To do this, we will use the same **Transform** tools (*Figure 9.16*) we used to create our first split-screen effect earlier in the chapter:

1. Select the clip on video track 2 (**V2**) and use the **Transform** and **Crop** tools as described at the start of this chapter to reposition the video on track 2 to line up with the left-hand video tile.
2. Select the clip on video track 1 and use the **Transform** and **Crop** tools as described at the start of this chapter to reposition the video on track 1 to line up with the right-hand video tile.

Figure 9.16: Repositioning the video clips using the Transform controls

Now you have a video with two tiles showing two separate videos in miniature at the bottom of your video frame (*Figure 9.17*).

Figure 9.17: The final result

This is just the starting point of how to use **Video Collage** | **Create Background.** Feel free to explore the other controls in the **Inspector** window to change the look and feel of the tiles to your own taste.

We will now look at another way of using **Video Collage** to create picture-in-picture effects, using the **Create Tile** workflow option.

Picture-in-picture effects using Video Collage | Create Tile

In the **Video Collage** effect, **Create Tile** uses a layout that you design rather than the pre-made layout design of **Create Background. Create Tile** is a bit more work to set up; however, it gives you more options for the design of your layout.

Preparing our timeline for Create Tile

This time, when preparing our timeline for **Create Tile**, we will put our background video on the bottom video track and lay our other clips on tracks above it.

1. Duplicate `Split_Screen` (timeline) and rename it `Create_Tile`.
2. In the timeline, add two extra video tracks (Tracks 2 and 3) above the composite clip that is already on track 1.

   With **Create Tile**, we leave the background video layer (i.e., our `Split Screen` compound clip) on the lowest track (**V1**), as shown in *Figure 9.18*.

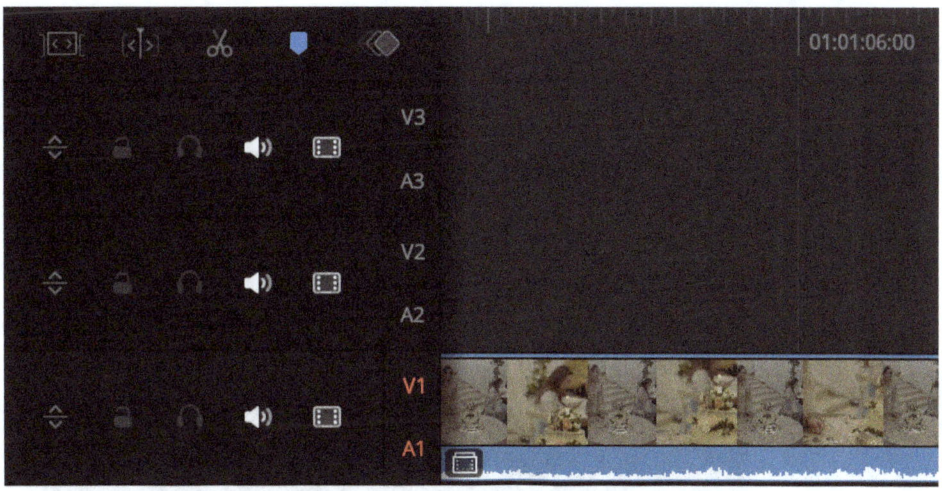

Figure 9.18: The compound clip left on Track 1

3. In the **Media Pool**, find the other clips as before – `MVI_2573.mov` and `Cake Tile`. Drag each one onto a separate empty track on the timeline.

Now that we have prepared our timeline for **Video Collage** | **Create Tile**, let us apply the effect to the timeline.

Applying the Video Collage | Create Tile effect

Applying the **Create Tile** effect is exactly the same as applying the **Video Collage** | **Create Background** effect:

1. Make sure that you have selected the topmost video clip on the timeline before applying the **Video Collage** effect.
2. Apply the **Video Collage** effect, just like we did for the **Create Background** effect.

3. Once the **Video Collage** effect has been applied, note that the usual grid of four tiles appears, showing the video that is on the track directly below.

Let us adjust the number and position of these tiles to get the effect we want.

Adjusting Video Collage | Create Tile

Now that we have applied **Video Collage**, let us change the settings in the **Inspector** window to only show two video thumbnails of the cake from different angles:

1. Open the **Video Collage** control panel in the **Inspector** window (**Inspector** > **Effects** > **Open FX** > **Video Collage**).
2. With the **Globals** button selected, select **Create Tile** in the **Workflow** drop-down menu.

   You will now see that our grid of four tiles has disappeared and been replaced with only one tile, which is a thumbnail version of the current video track, using the video track directly below as the background.

   Let us disable video track 2 so that we can see video track 1 as the background.

3. Select the **Disable Track** button (the *white film strip* icon) on the video track 2 header (*Figure 9.19*). We can now see our bottom track as the background. The **Disable Track** button will now turn red with a diagonal line through it, and the clips on the disabled timeline track will be grayed out as a visual reminder that the track has been disabled.

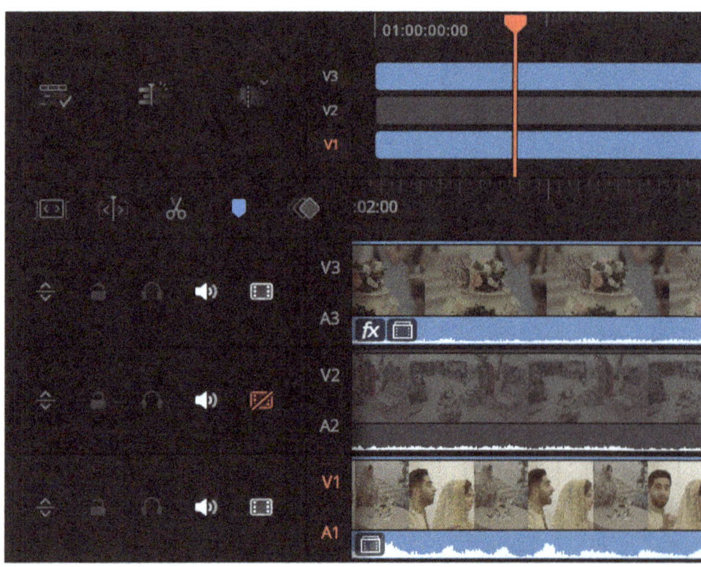

Figure 9.19: Video track 2 disabled

4. Select the **Preview Layout** checkbox in the **Video Collage** panel in the **Inspector** window so that we can design our new layout.
5. Still with the **Globals** button selected, under **Layout**, move the **Rows** slider to the left to reduce the rows from two to one. You will now have only two tiles rather than four.
6. Move the **Rounding** slider to the right to make the corners of the tiles rounder and less square.
7. Under **Margins and Spacing**, move both the **Horizontal Spacing** and **Vertical Spacing** sliders to make both tiles smaller by the same amount.
8. Move the **Vertical Offset** slider to the left to move both tiles to the bottom third of the video frame.
9. Move the **Horizontal Offset** slider to line up the tiles so that they are spaced evenly on either side of the vertical line in our `Split Screen` clip.
10. Select the **Tiles** button. This will give us the control to change the tiles individually.
11. Under **Tile Styling**, move the **Tile Border** slider to the right to create a border around your tile.
12. Click on the **Tile Color** swatch and choose a color from your computer's color picker that suits the video. As before, I have chosen a more muted golden yellow color to go with the color scheme of the bride and groom.
13. Under **Tile Animation** in the **Animate** dropdown, select **Intro & Outro** and any combination of the **Fly**, **Shrink**, **Rotate**, and **Fade** checkboxes to choose how to animate the appearance of the tiles at the start and end of the video clip.
14. Deselect the **Preview Layout** checkbox to reveal how the tile you just created looks on your video and play back the video to test the tile's animations. After reviewing your video, make any adjustments that are necessary.

So far, all of the adjustments we have made to our layout have been the same as we did for the **Create Background** workflow, except for needing to disable video track 2.

We now need to create a second tile. Instead of adjusting all the settings all over again, we can copy them from the first tile and apply them to our hidden video track to create a new tile.

Assigning video tracks to tiles using Paste Attributes

Now that we have perfected the layout and look for our first tile (on **Track 3**), we need to copy these settings and apply them to our clip on video track 2.

To do this, we will use the **Paste Attributes** function on the **Cut** page.

1. Staying on the **Cut** page, select the clip on video track 3 and copy it by pressing *Cmd* + *C* (Mac) or *Ctrl* + *C* (Windows).
2. Re-enable track 2 using the **Enable Track** button (*Figure 9.20*).

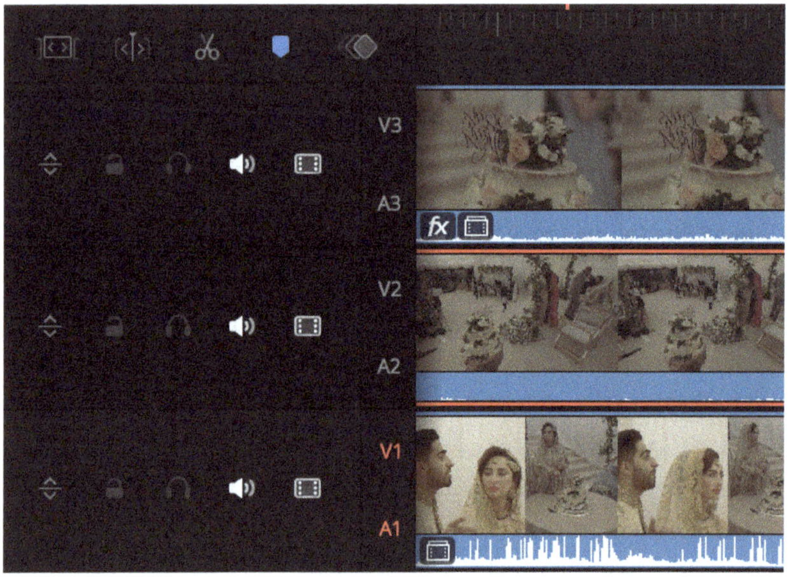

Figure 9.20: Re-enabling track 2 on the Cut page

3. In order to copy the tile from track 3 to track 2, we need to access the **Paste Attributes** settings. You can do this by any of the following methods:
    - Right-click the clip on track 2 and select **Paste Attributes...**
    - Select the clip on track 2 and press *Option* + *V* (Mac) or *Alt* + *V* (Windows)
    - In the **Edit** menu, choose **Edit** > **Paste Attributes...**

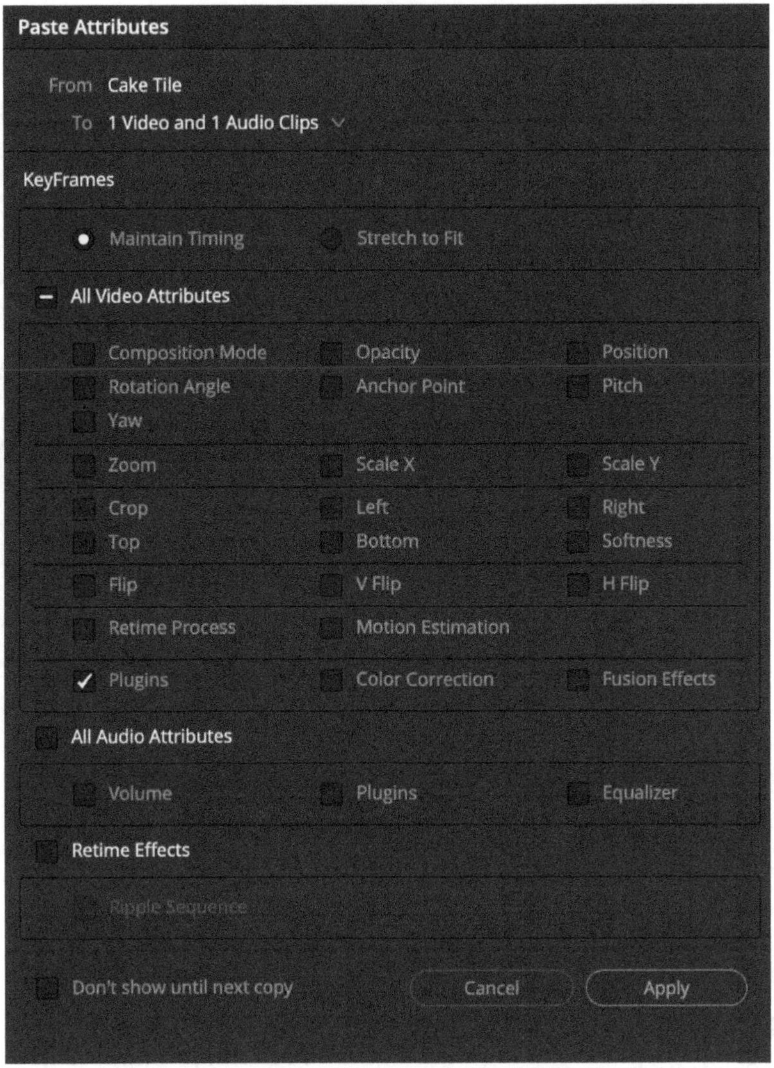

Figure 9.21: The Paste Attributes window

4. In the **Paste Attributes** window that appears, select **Plugins** under the **Video Attributes** section and click **Apply** (*Figure 9.21*). The tile effect plugin from track 3 has now been applied to track 2. We now need to reposition the tile on track 2 to its final position to be able to see it.
5. With track 2 still selected, open the **Effects** panel in the **Inspector** window again.
6. Click on the **Tiles** button to reveal the tile controls.

7. Under the **Manage Tiles** section, select **Tile 2** in the **Active Tile** drop-down menu (*Figure 9.22*).

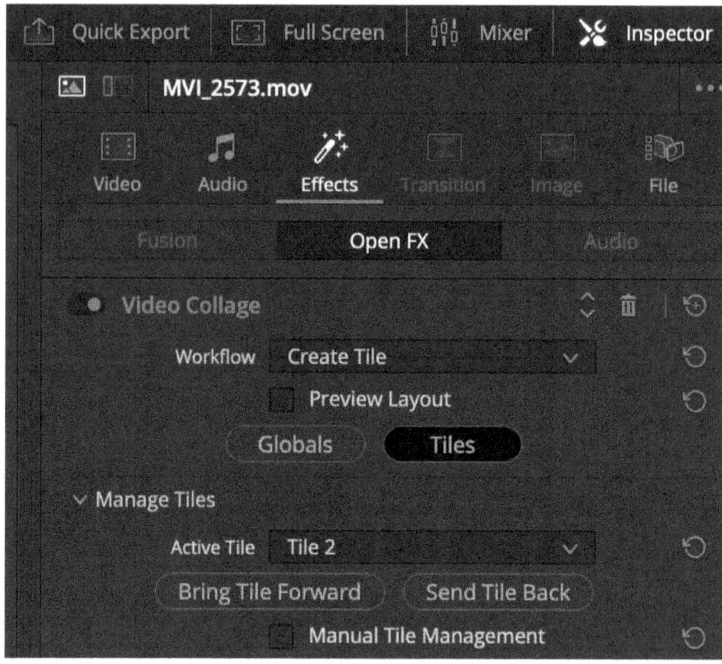

Figure 9.22: The Active Tile selection

You can now see both tiles, but when you play the video back, the second tile's outro transition is missing. That is because the track is too long.

8. Trim the clips on track 2 and track 3 to be the same length as track 1, and you are done!

Repositioning the videos in the tile frames

With **Create Background**, we shrunk and repositioned video clips to fit into the frames created by holes in the top layer. **Create Tiles** differs in that a whole clip is shrunk down to the size of a tile. We don't need to do anything else.

However, if we want to adjust what we see in each tile, then we can use the **Transform** tools, just like we did with the clips in **Create Background**.

You now have two ways you can add tiles to a video to create picture-in-picture effects using the **Video Collage** plugin. As with all effects plugins, it is a good idea to play the **Timeline** back to test the effect and then make any necessary adjustments in the **Inspector** window until you are satisfied with the final result.

Now that you have explored the many ways that you can create split-screen effects in Resolve, you will be able to explore how to use split screens in your own videos to enhance your storytelling.

Summary

We now know how to create split-screen and picture-in-picture effects. These effects are useful for how-to videos where we want to show a picture of the presenter and a close-up of their hands at the same time. Other uses for split screens are shown in the *Further reading* section at the end of the chapter.

We also know how to create compound clips, which are useful for applying effects to a whole group of clips at the same time.

Here is what you have achieved in this chapter:

- You have learned how to create a split screen by resizing and recomposing composite video footage on the **Cut** page
- You have learned what a **compound clip** is and how to create one
- You have learned how to create a picture-in-picture effect using Resolve FX's **Video Collage | Create Background** effects
- You have learned how to create a picture-in-picture effect using Resolve FX's **Video Collage | Create Tile** effects

In *Chapter 10*, we will look at how to adjust the color of our clips so that they match and create a visual style for our video.

Questions

1. True or false? You can't create a split-screen effect on the **Cut** page. You will need to use the **Edit** page instead, as it is a more advanced effect.
2. True or false? Once you have created a compound clip, you can no longer access the individual clips.
3. True or false? The Resolve **Video Collage | Create Background** effect is applied to the bottom video layer.
4. True or false? The Resolve **Video Collage | Create Tile** effect can be copied from the top track to each clip on the different video tracks underneath using **Paste Attributes**.

Further reading

Here are some extra web links that look at practical uses for split-screen effects:

- `https://www.premiumbeat.com/blog/split-screen-editing-and-composing/`
- `https://nofilmschool.com/2018/03/split-screens-watch`
- `https://www.theguardian.com/film/2022/apr/29/youve-been-reframed-how-playing-with-split-screen-and-aspect-ratio-went-mainstream`

Get this book's PDF version and more

Scan the QR code (or go to `packtpub.com/unlock`). Search for this book by name, confirm the edition, and then follow the steps on the page.

UNLOCK NOW

Note: Keep your invoice handy. Purchases made directly from Packt don't require an invoice.

10

Enhancing Color for Mood or Style

One of the most common aspects of filmmaking that sets professional-looking videos apart from beginner ones is the use of color to tell a story.

Color is important for filmmaking on so many different levels, and there are whole books written about it. Rather than replicate what is written in those books, I aim to summarize the color theories so that you can begin to understand how to use color in your videos.

So, in this chapter, we will introduce color theory as used in Hollywood films. We will then introduce you to the automatic color tool on the **Cut** page and look at the **Color Management** setting in **Project Settings** to help automatically optimize your image there. Then, we will use **Resolve Color FX** on the **Cut** page to manually adjust the color of shots from different cameras to help them match each other.

Understanding the tools you can use to correct color between different cameras and add a particular feel to your footage will help you to elevate the quality and emotional impact of your videos. This can also help give a more cinematic feel to your videos.

In this chapter, we are going to cover the following main topics:

- Understanding basic color theory
- Applying Auto Color
- DaVinci Resolve Color Management
- Using Chromatic Adaption FX
- Using Color Compressor FX

Technical requirements

To follow along with the exercises in this chapter, download the following project archive, which contains all the necessary clips: `Split Screen.dra` from `https://packt.link/gbz/9781836208839`.

Let us begin with a basic understanding of color theory.

Understanding basic color theory

Color can be measured and described in many ways, probably more than any other medium. There are whole topics dedicated to color: science, psychology, sociology, and, of course, technology. Let me explain each of these in relation to color and why they are important.

Color science

Color reaches our eyes through visible waves of electromagnetic radiation from the sun and is measured in **nanometers (nm)**. Our eyes, along with our brains, translate light into color. The perception of each color we see is based on a different wavelength of this radiation, with red (740 nm) being the longest wavelength we can see and violet (380 nm) being the shortest (*Figure 10.1*):

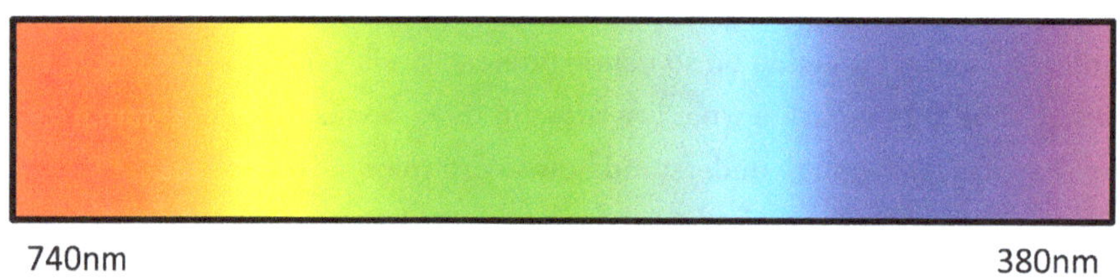

Figure 10.1: Wavelengths of visible light (image: Lance Phillips)

Artificial light mimics these wavelengths of the sun. All the colors that we see with our eyes are light either reflected off surfaces or emitted by a light source.

The retina in our eyes is most sensitive to the red, green, and blue wavelengths of light. Our brain processes these wavelengths and mixes them together to create all the other colors we see.

Additive (RGB) color model

The way we see color is called the **Additive Color Model**, as we add different strengths of **Red, Green, and Blue** (**RGB**) light together to create the colors we see. Red, green, and blue light mixed equally gives us pure white light. This is also the basis of the technology of how our cameras capture color (red, green, and blue light sensors) and how our screens portray color using red, green, and blue pixels. Essentially, any technology that emits images using light uses the RGB additive color model. The following diagram shows how the RGB colors mix to create other colors (*Figure 10.2*):

Figure 10.2: The RGB color model (image: Lance Phillips)

Now, let us look at the subtractive color model, which is the complete opposite of the additive color model.

Subtractive (CMYK) color model

You may think, well, the color ink in my printer is not RGB; it is cyan, magenta, and yellow. This is the **Subtractive Color Model** and uses **Cyan, Magenta, and Yellow** (**CMY**) to create colors on printed images, where the RGB light reflects off the image for us to see it. This subtractive color model is labelled **CMYK** for short, where the "K" stands for black ink, as it is the key color used in printing.

CMYK is a subtractive color model. So, in the printer using the CMYK model, the ink absorbs (subtracts) some colored light while it reflects the remaining colored light. For example, magenta ink absorbs green light and reflects blue and red light; so, blue and red mixed give us magenta. The following diagram shows how the CMYK colors mix to create other colors (*Figure 10.3*). Essentially, CMYK is a color model used to describe any image that uses ink to create colors. As ink is not a light source, it needs reflected light to create these colors for us to see them:

Figure 10.3: The CMYK color model (image: Lance Phillips)

If you look at *Figure 10.2* and *Figure 10.3*, you will notice that the RGB and CMYK color models combine to create a rough diagram of the full spectrum of visible light.

Color temperature

Not all white light is pure white. As all light is energy transmitted as radiation, the hotter and more powerful the light source, the bluer the light. This is evident when you turn on a gas burner: the flame starts orange and then moves from yellow to blue as you increase the strength of the flame and the temperature. Hence, color temperature is the color a white light gives based on its heat output.

For example, the light a slow-burning campfire emits is orange, an indoor house lamp is yellow, and the sun on an overcast day is blue. Our brains compensate for this slight color tint and give us the perception that all these sources of light are white.

However, a camera records the color of this white light as it sees it. To compensate for this, most cameras will have a **White Balance** setting that, when enabled, will remove the color tint from the whole image to show white objects in the image as pure white (i.e., if an image is too blue, the camera will compensate by adding orange and vice versa). Additionally, we can use **Resolve** to compensate for this change in color temperature with tools such as **Color Stabilizer**, which we will describe how to use later in this chapter.

Essentially, the color of white light is described as its *color temperature* and is measured in degrees Kelvin (or °K):

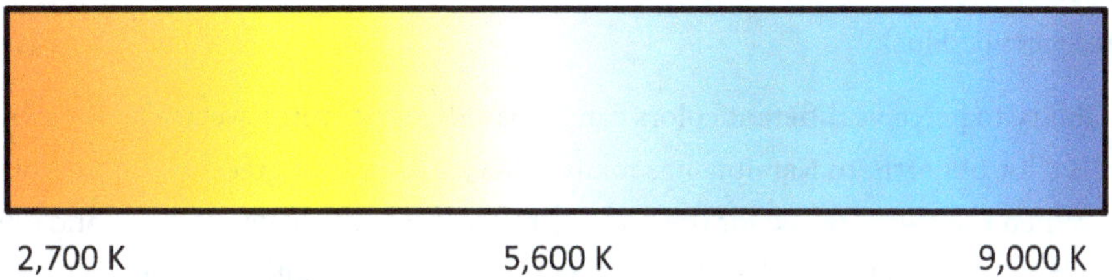

Figure 10.4: Color temperature in degrees Kelvin (image: Lance Phillips)

You may not have noticed, but even modern household bulbs now have their color temperature written on them to help us buy a light that suits what we use it for. A yellow lightbulb will have 2,700 K (degrees Kelvin), and a more neutral, whiter light will have 5,600 K (*Figure 10.4*).

All film lights are also measured in degrees Kelvin; some allow you to even adjust a dial to set the color temperature of the light to match any other lights (such as household lights) at the film location.

Color psychology

Color influences our mood and can change how we feel and think. This is because color has symbolic meanings that our brain subconsciously interprets.

Unlike the science of color, where blue is hot and red is cold, we attach different symbolic meanings to these colors. We perceive blue as a cold color and red as a hot color. That is why we use these colors to label hot and cold-water taps.

Out of the most recognizable symbolic meanings of color, the most common is that red represents danger. Therefore, stop signs, brake lights, traffic stop lights, and warning signs are all red. However, red can also represent love and passion, hence why Valentine's Day cards are often red. Green represents calm, nature, safety, and peace, hence why it is used in green traffic lights to say "go" or in eco packaging to show it is good.

How we use color in our videos can affect the emotional response of our viewers, so it is an important consideration when designing the look of our film.

Color sociology

Our ability to perceive different colors is also based on our culture. For example, in China, red represents good luck.

Our ability to perceive different colors can be based on the words we use to describe color. The Himba tribe of northern Namibia has many different words for green, but hardly any words for blue. When they were tested for their ability to see different shades of green and blue, they correctly recognized all the shades of green but could not see the difference between cyan and blue.

This shows that the words we culturally use to differentiate color influence our perception of color.

Color technology

Increasingly, as technology has improved, so has our ability to show a wider range of colors on our computer screens, TVs, and mobile phones. We now even have a name for the number of colors our screens can show: **Dynamic Range**.

Standard Dynamic Range (**SDR**) screens can show 16.67 million colors, whereas the latest **High Dynamic Range** (**HDR**) screens can show 1.07 billion colors. That means that an HDR screen can show almost 100 times more color than an SDR screen.

The range of colors a screen can display is often called a **Color Gamut** (gamut is a Middle English word for range). You might have also heard of the term **Color Space**. Color space and gamut are terms that are often used interchangeably. However, color gamut (which only refers to the range of colors) is actually a subset of color space (which, as well as color, includes luminance and tonal ranges).

Color space

A color space is exactly that: a three-dimensional model (space) showing the number of colors and luminance values that a device can record or display. All color spaces used for videos are based on the RGB color model and show the range of colors and brightness levels associated with that color model. However, it is hard to show a 3D space on a 2D piece of paper, so color spaces are often shown as 2D diagrams, which show a cross-section of the color space where the colors are at their strongest. The most commonly used color space is the CIE 1931 chromaticity diagram (*Figure 10.5*)

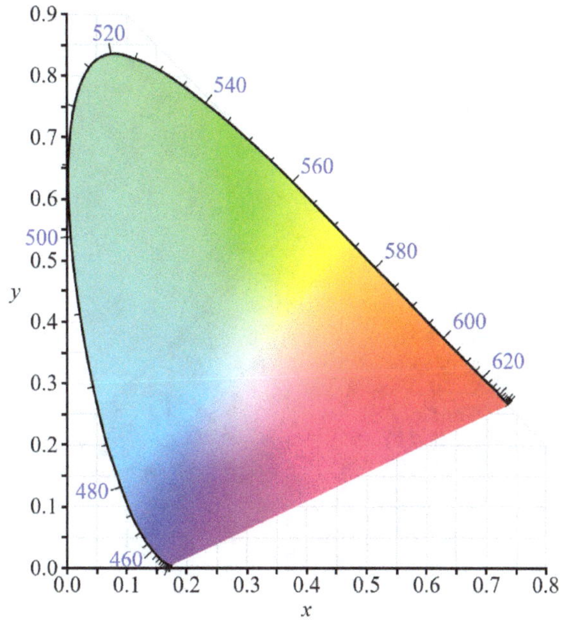

Figure 10.5: CIE 1931 color space. (2025, February 13). BenRG, Public domain, via Wikimedia Commons In Wikipedia. https://en.wikipedia.org/wiki/CIE_1931_color_space

This diagram was created in 1931 by the **Commission internationale de l'éclairage** (**CIE**) as a standard to measure the range of colors the average human eye can perceive. The 3 corners represent the red (740nm), green (520nm), and blue (380nm) wavelengths of light that the retina in our eyes can perceive. All other color spaces use this CIE 1931 diagram as a comparison and are often shown as a triangle within the larger CIE 1931 diagram (*Figure 10.6*).

One popular color space for old TVs and computer monitors is the Rec.709 color space, which contains 16.67 million colors and a luminance of 100 nits, which is 35% of all the colors that the human eye can see. In comparison, a Rec. 2020 color space can contain at least 1.07 billion colors at a minimum of 1,000 nits luminance, which is 75% of the total colors that the human eye can see.

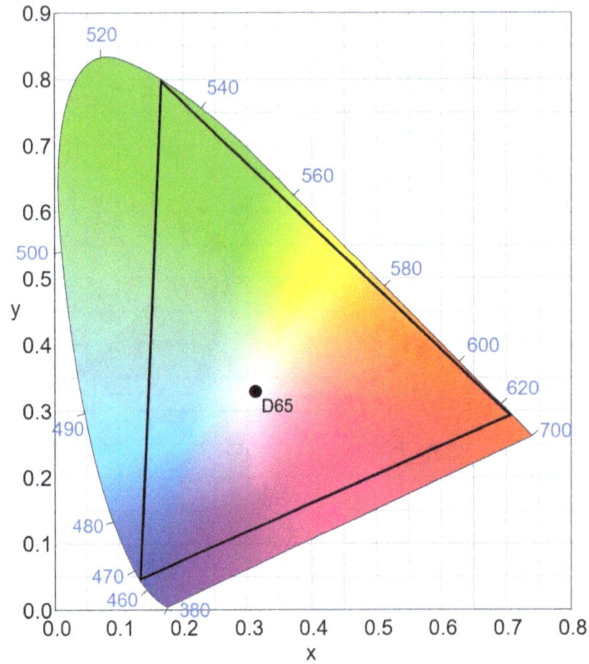

Figure 10.6: CIE 1931 color space that shows the Rec. 2020 color space within it. By File:CIExy1931.svg: Sakuramboderivative work GrandDrake - File:CIExy1931.svg, CC BY-SA 3.0, https://commons.wikimedia.org/w/index.php?curid=21864661

So, the Rec. 2020 color space (the standard against which HDR televisions are measured) is closer to what the human eye sees than SDR (Rec. 709) televisions (*Figure 10.6*).

Key concept – luminance

Luminance is the measurable light output of an image. It is measurable and can be used to compare the brightness of one digital image to another.

The term brightness, by comparison, is how we as humans perceive the strength of light, and it cannot be used as a comparison tool, as it is not measurable.

Luminance is measured in **candelas per square meter (cd/m2)**. This is the light emitted by the number of candles in a square meter. So, 100 cd/m^2 is the light of 100 candles in a square meter. This measurement is commonly referred to as nits. So, 100 cd/m^2 is the same as 100 nits.

7. Click on the **Auto Color** button (*Figure 10.8*).

Both clips have now been corrected, and there is now a noticeable improvement in both color and contrast. The clips now look more similar, as they both have whites that look white and are not tinted. The wedding dress and the tablecloth now look more consistent in color across both clips.

Auto Color is particularly well-suited for color correcting videos for social media as it is optimized for the **Rec. 709** color space, which is the range of colors most consumer cameras and phones capture their video in.

So far, we have limited ourselves to the only color correction tool that we can find on the **Cut** page. However, there is a tool, outside the **Cut** page, that we can quickly use to help us enhance the colors in our video. This tool is called **DaVinci Resolve Color Management (DRCM)**. Let's take a look at it next.

DaVinci Resolve Color Management

Now, I know plenty of professional colorists who find this topic too scary to mention. However, *Blackmagic Design* has made color management in DaVinci Resolve easy to use for all levels of experience.

So, what is **Color Management**? Well, firstly, it is much more than a tool; it is a different way of working. It is where we match the color space the camera recorded to our computer monitor's color gamut, and then to the color space of the final video. So far, we have been correcting the color of our video based on what we see in the viewer, with no regard for the color the camera captured. This is not always the most accurate approach, as our video could look different on various computer screens and may not look like what the camera saw.

Earlier, we mentioned the Rec. 709 color space, which is the range of colors a consumer camera usually records in. Rec. 709 (the input color space from a camera) is also the same color range as an SDR monitor using the standard sRGB color gamut (the output color space for graphics). As social media videos (e.g., YouTube) are currently optimized for display on SDR devices such as phones and computer screens, Rec. 709 is also the ideal color space for our final video (the output color space for our exported video).

However, even though this pathway of color from the camera to our computer screen to final output on social media (which could be any form of screen, such as phones, tablets, computers, and more) seems roughly the same, there can be subtle differences in how the color is processed at each stage. For example, in our project, we are mixing video footage from two different cameras, both using their own camera-specific color spaces optimized for a more cinematic look. Some footage was from a Blackmagic Design camera using their own **Film Gen 4** color gamut, and the rest was from a Canon camera using **Canon Cinema Gamut** with **Canon Log 3** applied. Neither of these was captured in the standard Rec. 709, so tools such as **Auto Color** will not have the desired effect. We will need to change the color gamut of these clips into Rec. 709 so that our automatic tools will work properly.

This is where DRCM comes in. It reads the color space of the camera from the imported video clips and changes the color of our video clips on the timeline to suit our display's color space (in this project, we will be using Rec. 709 as our **output color space**, as this is our monitor's color space). DRCM does this to better show on our computer monitor what the original camera saw by adjusting for the differences between the two cameras. If we do not use color management, then our display might not be showing us the most accurate version of what the camera recorded.

Color management is good when we have images recorded from more than one camera (all cameras record color differently). DRCM will recognize the color space that each camera used to record the video clip and adjust the color of each clip on the timeline to display the color on the computer monitor correctly. Essentially, DRCM will convert both cameras' different color spaces into one color space.

I know this is an oversimplification of color management and that there is more to it than that, such as using a color-accurate and calibrated monitor. However, using DCRM can get our colors closer to the right look, especially for social media videos.

Now that we know why using Resolve **Color Management** is useful, let us see how we can enable it:

1. Click on the **Project Settings** icon (the small cog in the lower-right corner of the screen; *Figure 10.9*) to open it:

Figure 10.9: The Project Settings icon

2. Select **Color Management > Color Space & Transforms** (*Figure 10.10*):

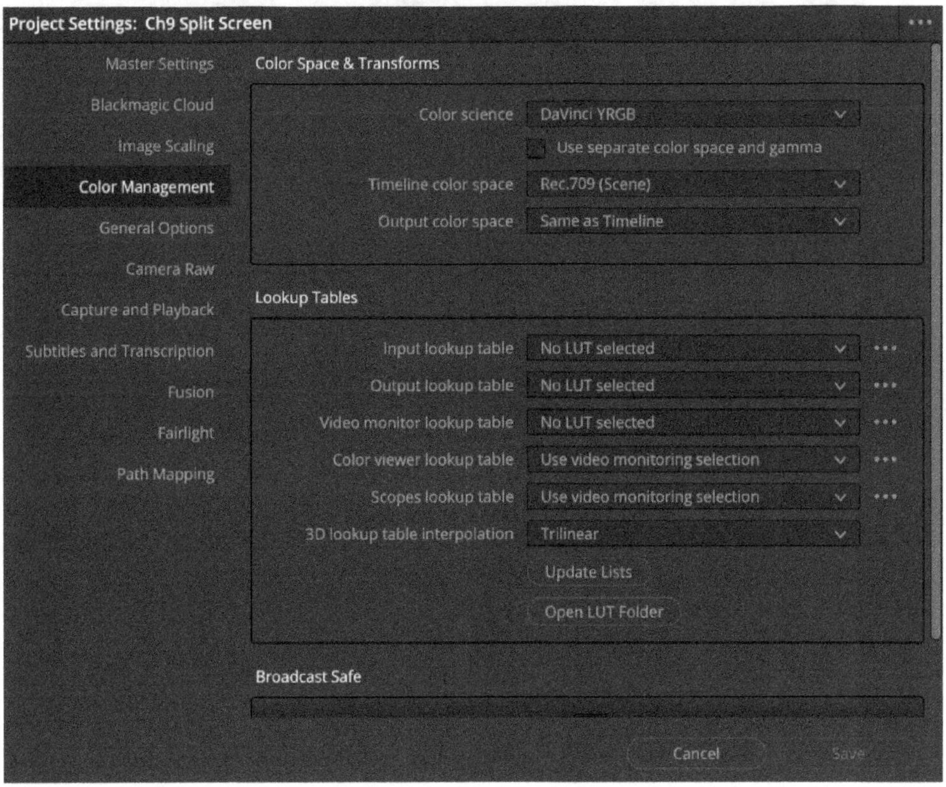

Figure 10.10: The Color Management settings

3. In the **Color science** drop-down menu, select **DaVinci YRGB Color Managed** (*Figure 10.11*). Leave the **Automatic color management** checkbox selected and the **Color processing mode** option set to **SDR**. Leave **Output color space** as **SDR Rec.709**:

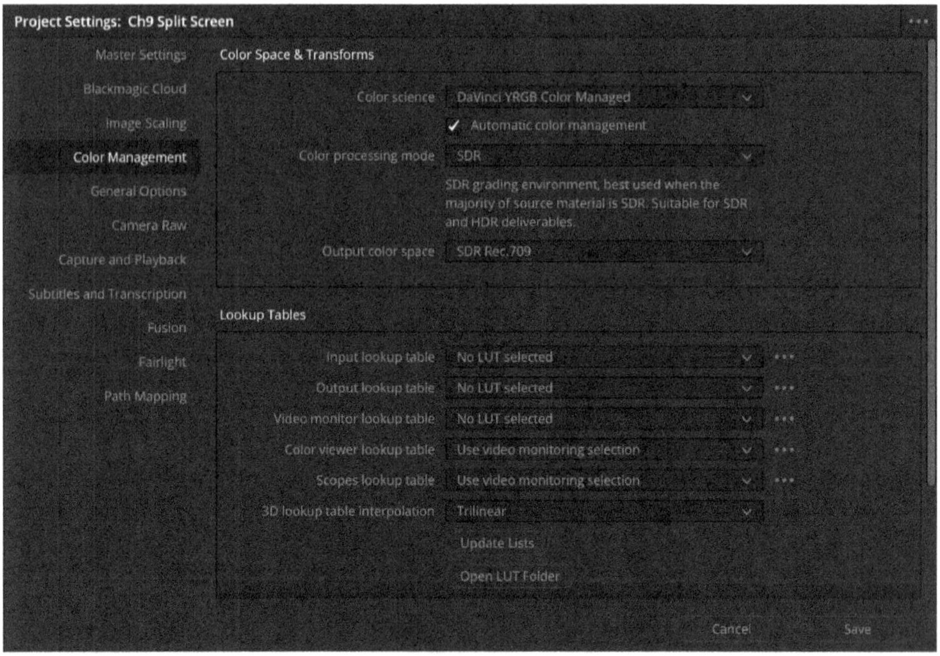

Figure 10.11: After selecting DaVinci YRGB Color Managed

4. Click on the **Save** button.

You will notice that the clip has now changed to be ever more colorful and vibrant, as we had already applied **Auto Color** before the camera color spaces were converted (*Figure 10.12*):

Figure 10.12: After Color Management has been enabled

DRCM can be enabled at any time; however, it will change how your previous color corrections will look (*Figure 10.12*), so it is best to enable this feature before you start to make any other color changes. For example, the **Auto Color** tool (which is optimized for Rec.709) will now need to be re-applied so that the image does not have too much color and contrast.

Using Chromatic Adaptation FX

Sometimes, when editing video footage, we might have camera shots that did not have the correct white balance applied in camera.

Resolve has a Resolve FX Color plugin called **Chromatic Adaptation** that corrects this and any other unwanted changes in color and exposure within a single clip. Let us see how it works on the clips we have been working on.

I have chosen to apply the following effects after enabling **DRCM**. If you choose to apply these effects without first applying **DRCM**, you may get different results. I have also removed **Auto Color** from my clips.

Applying the Chromatic Adaptation effect

Now, let us apply the **Chromatic Adaptation** effect to the clips we have on the timeline to even out the color temperature difference between the two clips.

1. Open the *Split_Screen* **Timeline** on the **Cut** page.
2. Apply the **Chromatic Adaptation** FX plugin to both clips on tracks 1 and 2 of the timeline, as we have done in previous chapters. You will find the plugin in **Effects** > **Video** > **Resolve FX Color** > **Chromatic Adaptation.**

Even though we have applied the **Chromatic Adaptation** effect, it will do nothing until we tell it what color temperature light to use.

From our **Auto Color** results, the image was too contrasty. Disabling **Auto Color** and using just DRCM fixes the contrast issue; however, there is still a yellowish tone to the whole image, which implies that the white balance is off (as shown in *Figure 10.13*). This is still a good frame to use as the exposure is roughly average for the whole clip.

Figure 10.13: DRCM applied with no Auto Color

We are now ready to use the **Chromatic Adaptation** controls to cool down the shot.

Adjusting the Chromatic Adaptation controls

Now that we have chosen our reference frame for color and exposure, let us look at the **Chromatic Adaptation** controls and how to use them to correct the changing color and exposure of light in our clip to make it cooler (*Figure 10.14*):

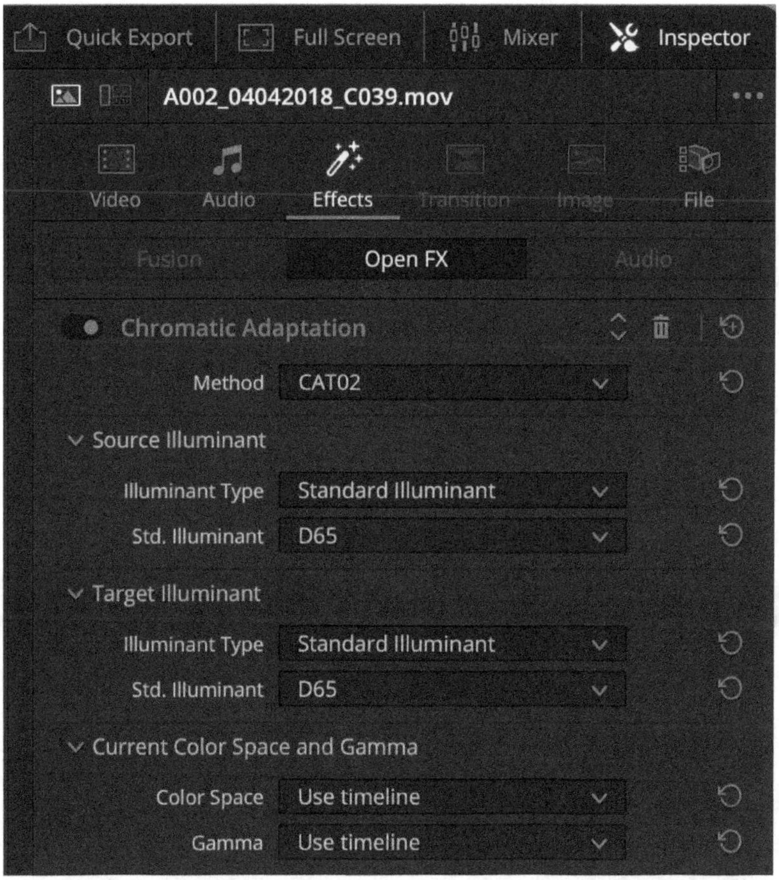

Figure 10.14: The Chromatic Adaptation controls

1. Select the clip on track **V2** of the timeline and then open the **Chromatic Adaptation** controls in the **Inspector** panel: **Inspector > Effects > Open FX > Chromatic Adaptation.**
2. Leave **Method** as **CAT02** in the drop-down menu. This is the method that Resolve will use to transform our image from being lit with a specific color temperature to another one of our choosing. **CAT02** is the default method and is the most suitable for most use cases, as it doesn't turn saturated blues purple like the other methods.

3. In the **Source Illuminant** section, you can select what you believe the color temperature of the original video lighting was. This can be measured in either **Standard Illuminant**, **Color Temperature**, or **CIE 1931 xy Chromaticity**. **Standard Illuminant** is the common measure used for video lights. D50 is equivalent to 5,000 K, D65 is 6,5000 K, and so on. The "D" stands for Daylight. **Color Temperature** is self-explanatory, and **CIE 1931 xy Chromaticity** is where you enter the x, y co-ordinates of the white point based on the CIE 1931 chromaticity graph. For this exercise, we will change the **Standard Illuminant** value to **D50**, which is a yellowish-white light.
4. In the **Target Illuminant** section, you can select what you want the color temperature of the video to become. Here, we will change it to **D75**, which is a bluer white light. This has the effect of removing the yellow cast of the clip by adding blue, which neutralizes the yellow.
5. Finally, repeat steps 1 to 4 for the clip on track **V1** of the timeline. In this instance, in the **Source Illuminant** section, we can change **Standard Illuminant** from **D50** to **D60** as there is less of a yellow cast in this clip.
6. In the **Target Illuminant** section, change **Standard Illuminant** to **D75** just like we did for the other clip.

Figure 10.15: Wedding scene before the Chromatic Adaptation FX

We can see the results of **Chromatic Adaptation** by comparing the footage with **Chromatic Adaptation** switched off (*Figure 10.15*) to what the clip looks like with **Chromatic Adaptation** switched on (*Figure 10.16*):

Figure 10.16: Wedding scene after the Chromatic Adaptation FX

Both clips now look less yellow; however, they still look different from each other.

Thankfully, there is another **Resolve FX Color** plugin we can use, called **Color Compressor**, to help fix this.

Using Color Compressor FX

Color Compressor is a **Resolve FX Color** plugin that allows you to compress a range of colors toward a single target color.

Applying the Color Compressor effect

Apply the **Color Compressor** FX plugin to the same clips on the timeline, just as we did with the **Chromatic Adaptation** effect. You will find the plugin in **Effects > Video > Resolve FX Color > Color Compressor**.

Even though we have applied the **Color Compressor** effect, it will do nothing until we adjust its settings.

Adjusting the Color Compressor effect

Let us look at the **Color Compressor** effect's controls in the **Inspector** panel and how we can use it to improve an image's contrast:

1. Select the clip on track **V2** of the timeline and then open the **Color Compressor** controls in the **Inspector** panel: **Inspector > Effects > Open FX > Color Compressor** (*Figure 10.17*):

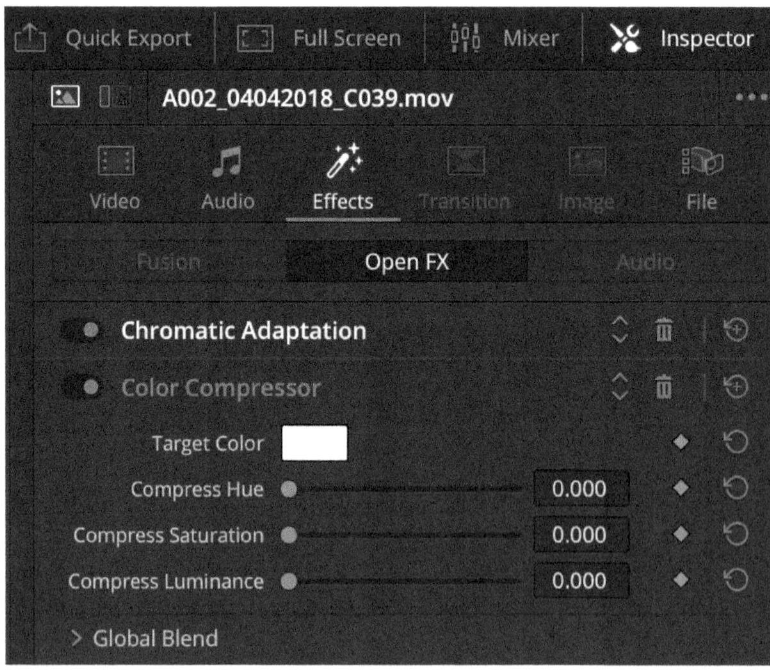

Figure 10.17: The Color Compressor settings

2. By default, the **Target Color** color swatch is set to white. We will leave this as its default setting of white, as we don't want to add a color cast to the image. However, you can equally use this effect to add a creative color cast to the video. To enable the effect, move the **Compress Hue** slider to the right-hand side to move the colors of the image towards white. We only need to move the slider a small amount (e.g., `0.248`) to make a noticeable difference. As with all the sliders, a setting of `0.000` means that no effect is applied, whereas a setting of `0.500` means that the image has been mixed so that it is halfway between **Target Color** and the original image. A value of `1.000` means that the whole image has been converted to **Target Color**.

3. By default, the **Compress Saturation** slider is set to `0.000`. For this image, changing the **Compress Saturation** setting to a value of `0.035` will make the image slightly less saturated to match the image on the right-hand side of the viewer. However, you can experiment with the slider yourself based on your personal preference. I have moved the **Compress Hue** and **Compress Saturation** sliders until they both work together to match the color and saturation of the image on video track **V1**.
4. Finally, move the **Compress Luminance** slider to the right until it matches the image on video track **V1**. In this situation, I believe the luminance is the same between the two clips, so I am going to leave this at `0.000`.
5. Now, apply **Color Compressor** to the clip on video track **V1** and make any final adjustments to match it to the clip we just adjusted on track **V2**. I only adjusted the **Compress Saturation** slider to `0.085` so they both look slightly desaturated.

For any of our adjustments, it is good practice not to change the color too much, as this can add unwanted digital artifacts in low-quality images.

Key concept – digital artifacts

A digital artifact is the unwanted changes to an image after it has been processed by a camera or software, such as applying an effects plugin.

An example of one of the most common digital artifacts is noise. Noise appears in an image as unwanted multicolored pixels (usually, stray red, green, or blue pixels) when the gain (brightness) of an image is increased beyond what the image can cope with.

Using **Compress Luminance**, we have now moved the color range of one image to imitate the color range of a second image. We have also adjusted both images so they do not look too saturated:

Figure 10.18: Before Color Compressor FX

We can see the results of **Color Compressor** by comparing the footage with **Color Compressor** switched off (*Figure 10.18*) to what the clip looks like with **Color Compressor** switched on (*Figure 10.19*):

Figure 10.19: After Color Compressor FX

I have used both the **Chromatic Adaptation** and **Color Compressor FX Color** effects to match the color of two clips to each other. As you can see, we have more creative control when using **Resolve FX Color** effects rather than just using **Auto Color**. Which tools you use is up to you, and the look you are trying to achieve.

The color-correcting plugins and tools we have covered in this chapter are just a selection of the basic free tools that are available to you in DaVinci Resolve to enhance the color of your videos, as an editor, without needing to learn about the complexity of the **Color** page.

Summary

You now have an overview of basic color theory, which can act as a good foundation for further learning and understanding how to use color in videos. You have used the **Auto Color** tool on the **Cut** page to quickly enhance the video's color and, finally, explored **DaVinci Resolve Color Management** to automatically match the camera's color space. Finally, you used the **Resolve FX Color** plugins, **Chromatic Adaptation** and **Color Compressor**, on the **Cut** page to correct for and match the different color and exposure of two different clips. We did all of this with the overall objective of enhancing the color and look of your video.

Here is what you achieved in *Chapter 10*:

- Understood basic color theory
- Learned how to use the **Auto Color** tool on the **Cut** page
- Learned how to enable and use DaVinci Resolve **Color Management**
- Learned how to use Color FX **Chromatic Adaptation** to correct the color temperature of the footage
- Learned how to use Color FX **Color Compressor** to change the color of two clips to match each other

In *Chapter 11*, we will look at how to shoot for a green screen so that we can change our backgrounds for our videos in DaVinci Resolve.

Questions

1. True or false? The human eye has cyan, magenta, and yellow light-receiving cones in the retina.
2. True or false? You can use the **Chromatic Adaptation** FX plugin to change the color temperature of the original shot.

3. True or false? The **Color Compressor** FX plugin can only change the color of the whole image and not its saturation or luminance.
4. True or false? The **Auto Color** tool is not available on the **Cut** page; you need to go to the **Color** page to use it.
5. True or false? **DaVinci Resolve Color Management** is found in **Project Settings**.

Further reading

Here are some extra web resources you can refer to regarding color theory:

- *Color science*:
    - `https://www.amnh.org/explore/ology/physics/see-the-light2/the-color-of-light`
    - `https://www.amnh.org/explore/ology/physics/play-with-color-and-lighthttps://spark.iop.org/collections/colours-two-kinds-physics-narrative`
- *Color temperature*: `https://www.studiobinder.com/blog/what-is-color-temperature-definition/`
- *Color spaces*:
    - `https://blog.frame.io/2020/02/03/color-spaces-101/`
    - `https://cie.co.at`

Get this book's PDF version and more

Scan the QR code (or go to `packtpub.com/unlock`). Search for this book by name, confirm the edition, and then follow the steps on the page.

UNLOCK NOW

Note: Keep your invoice handy. Purchases made directly from Packt don't require an invoice.

11

Adding Greenscreen Effects

Green screens have typically been used for **visual effects (VFX)** in the film industry, such as to replace a background to show a superhero flying, or on television to show a weather forecaster's map. However, there is no reason why you cannot use them to spice up your videos for social media or the web.

The need for using green screens on personal videos may arise from various motivations. For example, sometimes you may want to have the option to change the background of a video after it has been filmed, such as adding an animated graphic (for example, showing key business stats) in the background behind your presenter.

In the same vein, it is also good to use a green screen when you want to update the background of your video to suit different markets while keeping the foreground content the same.

In this chapter, we will cover how to shoot using green screen and how to work with greenscreen footage in DaVinci Resolve.

In this chapter, we are going to cover the following main topics:

- Understanding codecs
- Shooting video for green screen
- Chroma keying in DaVinci Resolve
- Creating a greenscreen effect on the Cut page using the 3D Keyer
- Creating a greenscreen effect on the Cut page using the HSL Keyer
- Removing chroma key background spill using the Despill Resolve FX plugin

Technical requirements

We will be practicing our green screen skills using footage by artist Stefania Buzatu (*StefWithAnF*), found on *Pixabay*: `https://pixabay.com/users/stefwithanf-795875/?tab=videos&pagi=8`.

To follow along with the exercises in this chapter, download the following video, which contains all the greenscreen clips needed: `Greenscreen.dra` (`https://packt.link/gbz/9781836208839`).

Or, you can use your own greenscreen footage instead. However, to get good results when using a green screen, it is necessary to know the best file type or codec to use when shooting video for green screen.

Understanding codecs

Usually, when we save our video in any editing software, including Resolve, we will be presented with a confusing array of different file formats to save our video in.

The main difference between these video file formats is the codec that they use. When exporting our video on Resolve's **Deliver** page, we are shown options for both **Format** and **Codec** (*Figure 11.1*):

Figure 11.1: Export Video settings on the Deliver page

Essentially, a video file format such as `.mov` or `.mp4` (shown by a dot followed by a three- or four-letter code at the end of a filename) is a container to store the video file in.

Each of these video files uses different ways to squeeze the video and audio information into the container. The way the video is squeezed into this file container is called a codec.

What is a codec?

A codec is a set of instructions (known as code) for the camera to help it compress a video to store it into a computer file and then uncompress it on the computer so that you can view it again. In fact, *codec* is a short way of saying *compression decompression*, or *code decode*.

To understand a codec in a practical sense, let's use the example of an inflatable mattress. To store it, you need to remove all the air from it by rolling it up and then compressing it into a bag. However, to be able to sleep on your mattress, you need to remove the mattress from the bag and reinflate it with replacement air. The process of deflating your mattress and reinflating it is what a codec does to a video file, except that instead of air, it removes video data.

Types of compression

How the codec removes data and restores it differs for each codec. Video files can be compressed in two different ways: **temporal compression** and **chroma subsampling**.

Temporal compression

Temporal is the Latin word for time. This compression treats each frame as a picture and looks for how they change over time. Not every aspect of the frame will change. This type of compression is where the codec identifies key frames that are kept and deletes the frames in between the key frames. Basically, the differences in the visual data from one key frame to another are used to recreate the missing frames in between the key frames when the video file is played back.

Temporal compression works well when there are slow changes between the frames with very little movement and with large blocks of color, such as a blue sky, as it is easier to recreate the lost visual data. Where temporal compression does not work so well is in fast-moving scenes with a lot of detail, where there are rapid changes, as this detail is not easy to recreate accurately.

Files that heavily rely on temporal compression can be difficult to play back in real time, as the computer has to recreate the missing frames as it plays the video file.

Common types of temporal compression are `H.264` and `H.265`.

Chroma subsampling

Chroma comes from the Greek word for color. This type of compression deletes color information from every other pixel of the original video file and copies (samples) the color information from the adjacent pixels when it is played back.

You would think that we would notice this loss of color; however, the human eye is less sensitive to color changes than it is to spotting changes in brightness. That is why we can remove half of the color resolution by grouping colors together and not notice any change.

Chroma subsampling takes an image and divides it into blocks of 4 x 2 pixels. Subsampling is applied to each of these 4 x 2-pixel blocks. Which pixels to keep and sample the color information from is based on the subsampling ratio. Chroma subsampling is described as a ratio of three or four numbers – that is, `4:4:4` or `4:4:4:4`.

The extra number at the end of the `4:4:4:4` ratio is based on the video having an **Alpha (transparent) channel**, which is mainly used for VFX or composite work, where it is useful to have a transparent background – this is beyond the scope of this book.

For this book, we will be looking at the three-number ratio. The first number in the ratio is based on the width of the pixel block and is always 4. The second number in the ratio is the number of samples across each row of pixels. The third number is the number of color-sample changes in the second row of pixels compared to the first row. Generally, with the third number in the ratio, the color-sample changes are either the same as the first row or zero. Here are some examples of what this might look like.

Figure 11.2 shows the original image with no subsampling applied. Eight colors are shown. This is the full-color resolution:

Figure 11.2: 4:4:4

Figure 11.3 shows subsampling applied, where all four colors are kept from the first row, and there are zero changes between rows one and two, hence the number 0 at the end of the ratio. So, only four colors are shown. This is half the original's color resolution (that is, it now only stores four colors instead of the original eight colors per sample, making the image size much smaller):

Figure 11.3: 4:4:0

Figure 11.4 shows subsampling applied with only two colors kept from the first row, and there are two changes between rows one and two. In total, four colors are shown. This is half the original's color resolution. This is the most used subsampling ratio as it is a good blend of color fidelity and compression, and is much better looking than `4:4:0` with the same amount of compression:

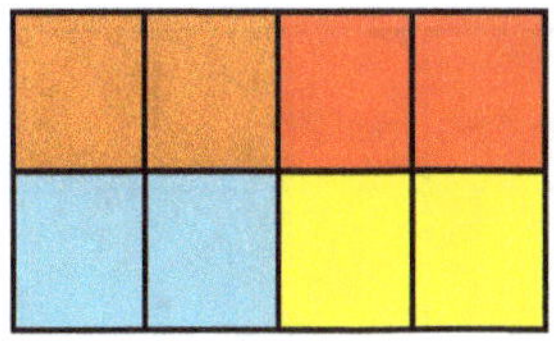

Figure 11.4: 4:2:2

Figure 11.5 shows subsampling applied with only two colors kept from the first row, and there are zero changes between rows one and two. Two colors are shown. This is a quarter of the original's color resolution. Most consumer video cameras will create video files using this ratio:

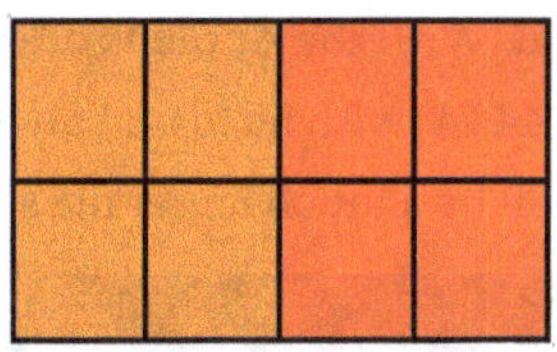

Figure 11.5: 4:2:0

Figure 11.6 shows subsampling applied with only one color kept from the first row, and there is one change between rows one and two. Two colors are shown. This is a quarter of the original's color resolution. This ratio is hardly ever used, as `4:2:0` looks much better than `4:1:1` for the same loss of color:

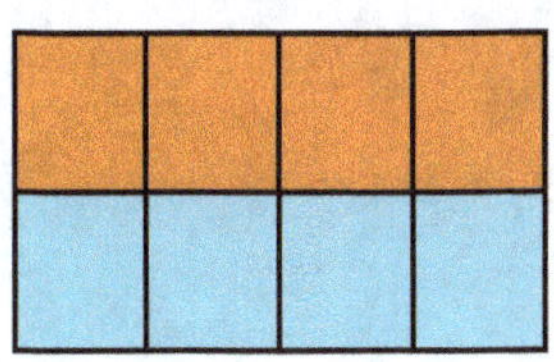

Figure 11.6: 4:1:1

Figure 11.7 shows subsampling applied with only one color kept from the first row, and there are zero changes between rows one and two. Only one color is shown. This is one-eighth of the original's color resolution. This subsampling ratio is very rarely used, as there is such a noticeable loss of quality:

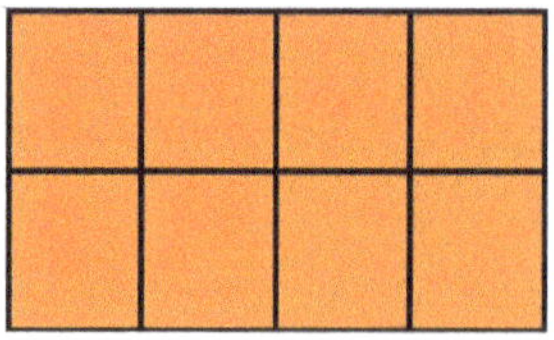

Figure 11.7: 4:1:0

As you can see, choosing the right chroma subsampling ratio can help retain the correct color information. Some file format codecs allow you to choose the chroma subsampling to apply. *Figure 11.8* shows the **Render** settings on the **Deliver** page with Apple's **QuickTime** file format with the **Apple ProRes** codec applied. With the **Apple ProRes** codec selected, you can choose a chroma subsampling ratio between **4444** (with no loss of quality) and **422** (with half of the color information). **Apple ProRes 4444** will be a much larger file size than **ProRes 422**:

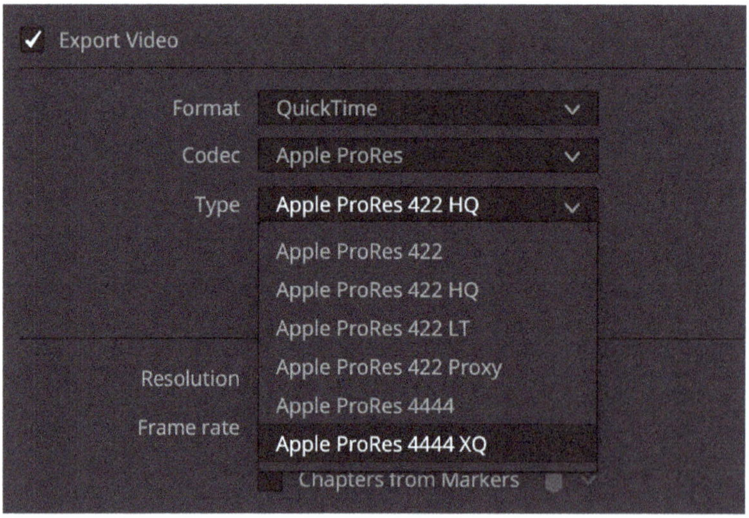

Figure 11.8: Chroma subsampling options when exporting video

Now, let us look at the different situations where we can use this knowledge of compression types to get the most out of our video images.

Types and uses of codecs

The type of codec compression used for your video file depends on how you are using the video.

Acquisition codecs

These are the codecs used by your video camera to record a video file. These are based on a balance of storage space and being quick to write to your storage medium, such as an SD card.

Some of the common consumer camera codecs are as follows:

- MPEG-4 (`.mp4`), QuickTime (`.mov`), and AVCHD (Sony and Panasonic cameras) video file formats all use `H.264` as a codec.
- Newer consumer cameras, including iPhones, give the option (HEVC file format) to use `H.265` as a codec, which is a newer, more efficient version of `H.264`. `H.265` also supports 8K video files, whereas `H.264` doesn't. However, as `H.265` is a newer format, it is not supported for playback on everyone's devices.

> **Key concept – what about RAW files?**
>
> Camera **RAW files** are neither codecs nor file formats. They are the original uncompressed raw data captured by the camera before it has been compressed into a file format. Think of RAW as being a digital negative where you can change the exposure of the video afterward.
>
> Each camera manufacturer creates professional and semi-professional cameras that record their own camera data into a RAW file – for example, BRAW is Blackmagic Design's raw camera format. To be able to see the recorded video, you need to convert it into a common video format first or use a dedicated video player app (for example, Blackmagic RAW Player) that converts the RAW video as it plays it back.

Intermediary codecs (proxy media)

Intermediary codecs are codecs that are optimized to ensure that the playback on your computer when editing a video file is quicker and smoother. Intermediary codecs are also called proxy media as they are used in proxy (replacement) for the original video camera media.

Because spatial compression codecs such as `H.264` and `H.265` have missing video frames that need to be recreated as they play back, they are not great to edit with. When editing a video, you often need to stop on a particular frame and play forward and backward quickly as you make changes. This can cause the computer to slow down as it calculates the missing video frames to show you in the video viewer as you play it back. The video in the viewer can then appear slow and out of sync with the audio, which makes editing a bit of a chore.

For this reason, video editors use what is called an intermediary codec, which is easier to edit with. The original camera format is converted into a codec that does not use as much compression and is hence easier to playback and edit.

There are two main intermediary codecs used in video editing – they are Apple's *ProRes* and Avid's *HNxHD* or *HNxHR*. HNxHR is Avid's newer intermediary codec that supports resolutions higher than HD 1080p.

To be able to create Apple's ProRes codec, you will need to own an Apple Mac, whereas Avid's HNxHD and HNxHR are supported on both Macs and PCs.

In DaVinci Resolve, intermediary codecs can be selected for use in your project in **Project Settings** > **Master Settings** > **Optimized Media and Render Cache** (*Figure 9.9*).

As a reminder from previous chapters, where we have looked at **Project Settings**, you can find it by clicking on the little gear icon at the bottom right-hand corner of the screen:

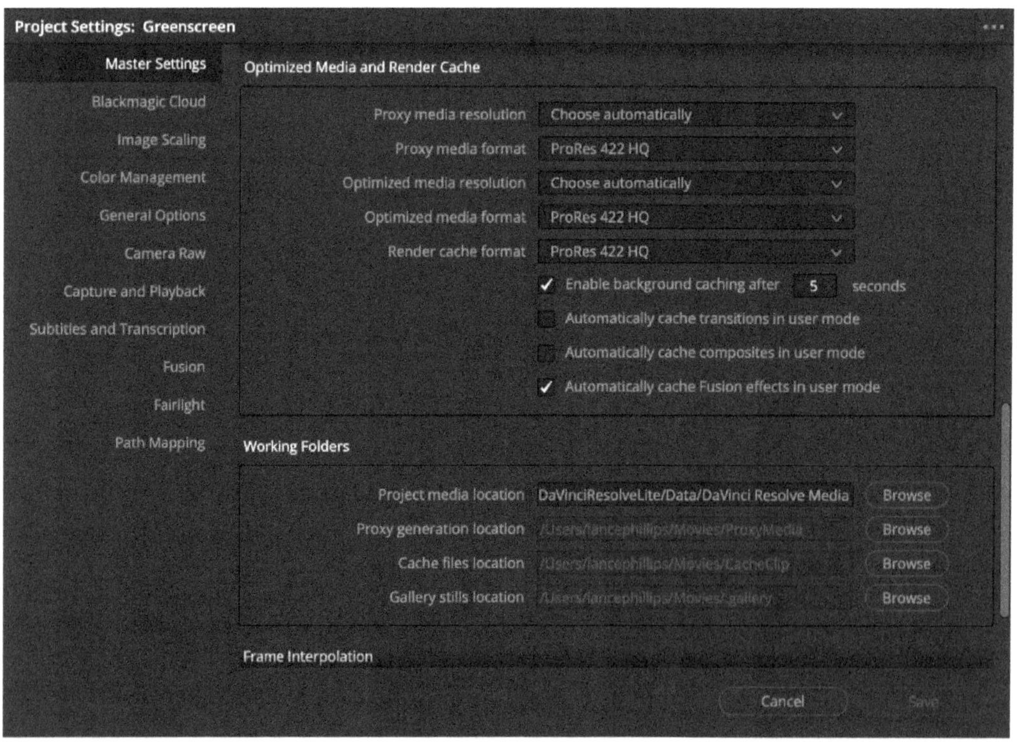

Figure 11.9: Project Settings showing proxy and optimized media

Resolve creates intermediary codecs in two ways: **Optimized Media** and **Proxy Media**.

Optimized Media is where Resolve creates the intermediary codec internally in DaVinci Resolve's media cache and does not save it as discrete media files on your computer. This is the quickest option.

To enable **Optimized Media**, follow these steps:

1. Create optimized media by right-clicking any clip or one of a group of selected clips in the **Media Pool** and selecting **Generate Optimized Media** in the pop-up menu.
2. To enable optimized media to be used: in the **Playback** menu, select **Use Optimized Media if Available.**

Proxy Media is where Resolve creates additional intermediary codec files outside of Resolve that you save to your computer's hard drive. This option is good if you want to share the proxy files with someone else so that they can work on them separately or remotely without having to spend the time to recreate intermediary codecs.

To enable **Proxy Media**, follow these steps on the **Edit** page:

1. Create proxy media by right-clicking any clip or one of a group of selected clips in the **Media Pool** and selecting **Proxy Media > Generate Proxy Media...** in the pop-up menu.
2. To enable proxy media to be used, do the following:
    - **Resolve 17**: In the **Playback** menu, select **Use Proxy Media if Available**
    - **Resolve 18 or later**: In the **Playback** menu, select **Proxy Handling > Prefer Proxies**

You can select which codec to use for either optimized or proxy media in **Project Settings** > **Master Settings** > **Optimized Media and Render Cache** (*Figure 11.10*). Here, you can choose the format, resolution, and location where the intermediary codecs will be saved:

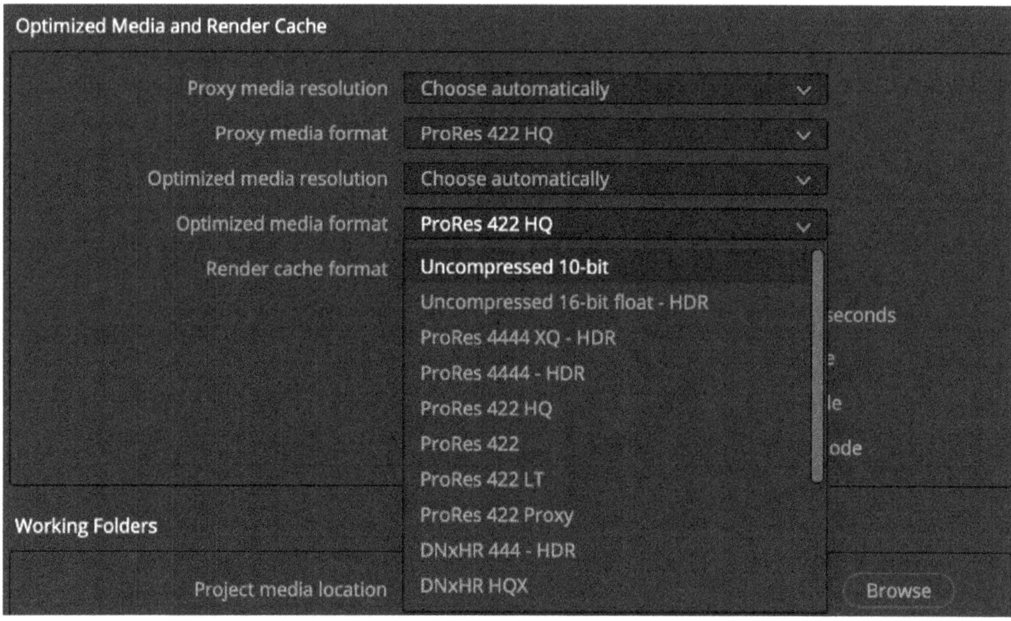

Figure 11.10: Project Settings showing the different intermediary codecs to choose from

Resolve does not limit you to choosing either **Optimized Media** or **Proxy Media**. You can use both in the same project.

Color-grading codecs

If you are color grading, you will need to have the highest quality codec for color. So, choosing a codec that supports 4:4:4:4 is important as there will be no loss of color.

You can easily select **Proxy Handling** > **Prefer Camera Originals** in the **Playback** menu, which will force Resolve to use the original camera files. You can also change the render cache media codec to suit color grading by selecting a 4:4:4:4 codec in **Project Settings** > **Master Settings** > **Optimized Media and Render Cache** (*Figure 11.10*).

Delivery codecs

These are codecs to make it easier for the final video to be watched by the audience (that is, no video lag), depending on the platform they choose to watch your video on, such as the web, a streaming service, or a TV broadcast.

Common delivery codecs for social media are QuickTime (`.mov`) and mp4 in either `H.264` or `H.265`.

There are presets in Resolve that select the best codecs for YouTube, Vimeo, and TikTok. As shown in earlier chapters, these can be found in the **Quick Export** menu.

> **Best codec for effects work**
>
> One thing to remember is that when doing any effects work, such as greenscreen or applying **Fusion** or **Color** effects, the effects will need as much of the original footage quality as possible to get the best result. In this case, use a high-quality proxy format such as `4:4:4:4` or the original source files to get the best result.

Not only is it important to know which file type to use to shoot green screen, but also how to shoot it to get the best results. This makes it easier for you to separate the background from your subject in your software editor.

Shooting video for green screen

Just to clarify, the process of removing the background of a video to replace it in post-production with a new background is commonly called **green screen**, which is not to be confused with the name of the background, which is filmed as part of this process, which is a green screen.

Let us explain how this greenscreen process works so that we can understand how to light our video specially for it.

We start by filming our central subject against a single-color background (usually a green screen). Then, in the editing software, we identify the color of the background we want to remove from the video. The software removes the specified color from the video, leaving behind a transparent layer in its place. This leads to a transparent background. We can then put another video or computer-generated graphics behind this transparent layer of our main video. The newly added video or graphics will be seen where the transparency has been created by removing the single color from our video in front.

Notice how I said a *single color*. Well, you can use any color for this process; it does not need to be green; it can be whatever the color of your background is.

DaVinci Resolve does not use the term *green screen*. Instead, it uses the term *chroma key*. Let us explain what a chroma key is.

What is a chroma key?

Originally, in the days before digital videos were a thing, a blue screen was used (instead of a green screen) as this was the easiest color to remove from film. Now, with most video being digital, we use a green screen as it is easier to remove green, as the digital video signal has twice as much information about the different tones of green as red or blue. Another benefit of using a green screen is that there are no green tones in people's skin. This makes it easier to remove the green background without also affecting the parts of our human subject.

Because any color can be used for the background screen, the technical term for the process of removing the background in videos is called **chroma keying**. *Chroma* is the Greek word for color (*khrōma*), while *key* is a Middle German word (*ki*) for splitting. So, chroma keying is splitting the video into two parts based on color. The background layer that is created is often called the *key*, and the process of chroma keying is often abbreviated to *keying*.

The most common colors used to split a video into an opaque foreground and a transparent background layer are green or blue. You can use any color if the background color is not featured in the foreground subject of the video. As a use case, when filming vegetables or plants as a subject, you would want to use blue as a background instead of green; otherwise, you would have parts of the vegetables become transparent in the video.

Here are some other top tips when filming for chroma keying.

Lighting your background

Light the background as evenly as possible so that there are minimal variations in the exposure of the background.

When lighting the background, we want to eliminate shadows in our background color, as shadows have less color in them and are harder to remove later.

To be able to do this, use diffused (not hard) lights that are directed at the background and have a wide, even spread of light.

If any parts of your background will not be seen by the camera, block them off to minimize the chance of light from the background spilling (back-spill) onto the foreground subject.

Camera settings

Do not use your camera's ISO to boost the exposure of your video, as this introduces digital noise that can affect the quality of your *key*.

Do not use any lens diffusion or smoke effects, as these can soften the image and make it harder to recognize the edges between the subject and the background. For the same reason, make sure your subject is in focus and is as sharp as possible, so use the greatest **depth of field** (**DOF**) available.

Set your camera's white balance for the light on your foreground subject.

Include a gray card at the start of your video; getting your subject to hold the card is a good idea. Use the same lighting for the gray card as you are using for your foreground subject, making sure you do not get any back-spill onto the card or your subject. This gray card can be used by Resolve to help when making automatic color corrections, as described in *Chapter 10*.

> **Key concept – gray card**
>
> A **gray card** is a middle-gray-colored card that is filmed at the start of the shot to give a reference to editing software for what middle gray should look like. This helps when trying to color balance the video later in a post (that is, make sure the image is neutral and neither too warm nor too cold in color).
>
> Middle gray is important as it is in the middle of the exposure range for our camera. It is also useful to get correct exposure for skin tones, as most skin tonal values sit on or very near to middle gray. Gray cards can also be used as a reference when manually setting your camera's white balance.

When using a zoom lens, do not use it at its widest setting, as this can create a slight vignette, which will create problems for the background key.

Use the highest resolution and least compressed video codecs possible. If it has the option, use your camera's chroma-subsampling compression of at least 4:2:2; ideally, use a non-compressed codec using 4:4:4.

Filming your subject

One of the problems of lighting a single-color background is that the color from the background can spill onto our foreground subject; this is called back-spill. This presents a problem later, as this will then remove the parts of the foreground subject where the background light has reflected onto them.

To eliminate back-spill, you need to keep the foreground subject as far away from the background as possible.

When lighting your subject, try not to create shadows from your foreground subject onto your background – that is, use a soft diffused light. This is also the case if you are using a chroma key for the floor. Using reflectors can decrease the shadows that spill on the floor.

It is best not to have your subject lying or sitting on a chroma-key floor or chair, as this will create more opportunities for back-spill, and (if your subject is a soft-edged irregular shape, such as a person) it will be difficult to separate the foreground from the background. If you need to have your subject sitting or lying down, use a section of real floor, with defined edges, which can be merged with the background later.

Make sure your subject does not have any colors that are in your background. For example, when using a blue screen, make sure your subject is not wearing blue jeans or a blue shirt.

Now that we know how to get the best-quality footage for our green screen, let us look at how we can create a greenscreen effect in DaVinci Resolve.

Preparing our chroma key in DaVinci Resolve

For the following exercise, we will remove the background of a woman reading George Orwell's *1984* and replace it with an infinite zoom video showing dystopian settings, reflecting what she is reading in the book.

First, we need to prepare our timeline so that it is ready for us to chroma key out our background. To do this, we need to find our foreground and background videos and place them in the right place on the timeline.

You can find the video clips and get the timeline ready for keying on either the **Cut** or **Edit** page. Here, we describe the **Cut** page. If you want to use the **Edit** page, you can apply the same principles. Proceed as follows:

1. Create a new timeline and name it `3D_Keyer`.

   In the **Cut** page's **Media Pool**, select **Infinite Zoom - 44658.mp4** and put it on **Video Track 1** (**V1**) of the timeline. This will be our background clip. It is important to always put out a background clip on the lowest video track, usually **V1**.

2. In the **Cut** page's **Media Pool**, select **Reading - 40098.mp4** and put it on **Video Track 2** (**V2**) of the timeline.

   This will be our foreground clip. It is important to always put out a foreground clip on the highest video track, usually **V2**.

3. Trim the end of **Infinite Zoom - 44658.mp4** on **V1** to be the same length as the **Reading - 40098.mp4** clip on **V2**.

   This is not necessary for the keying process, but it does make our timeline a bit tidier.

That's it – we are now ready to apply our keyer to the topmost clip on the timeline, after which we will remove the green, revealing the background clip underneath.

It can be confusing to decide which keyer to use in DaVinci Resolve, as there are several options. In the next two sections, we will look at the two main chroma keyers available on the **Cut** page of Resolve: the **3D Keyer** and the **HSL Keyer**.

Creating a greenscreen effect on the Cut page using 3D Keyer

The **3D Keyer** is a chroma key tool where you can quickly draw lines over the color you want to key (remove) from the background.

Every line you draw selects the corresponding colors in the 3D color space of the video. A **color space** is a 3D representation of all the colors available for your video. See *Chapter 10* for a more detailed explanation of color spaces. Hence, the tool is called **3D Keyer**, as it takes a key from the colors in this 3D color space.

You can apply the **3D Keyer** on either the **Cut** or **Edit** page (of course, you can also use the **Fusion** and **Color** pages, but that is a bit more complicated than we need it to be).

Applying the 3D Keyer

After locating the **3D Keyer** in **Effects** > **Video** > **Resolve FX Key** > **3D Keyer**, you can apply the **3D Keyer** to the selected clip in the timeline by any of the following methods, on either the **Cut** or **Edit** pages (*Figure 11.11*):

- Double-click on the **3D Keyer** in the **Effects** tab
- Drag and drop the **3D Keyer** from the **Effects** tab to the selected clip in the timeline
- **Cut** page only: Click the **Add Effect** button (located at the bottom of the **Effects** tab) as seen in the following figure:

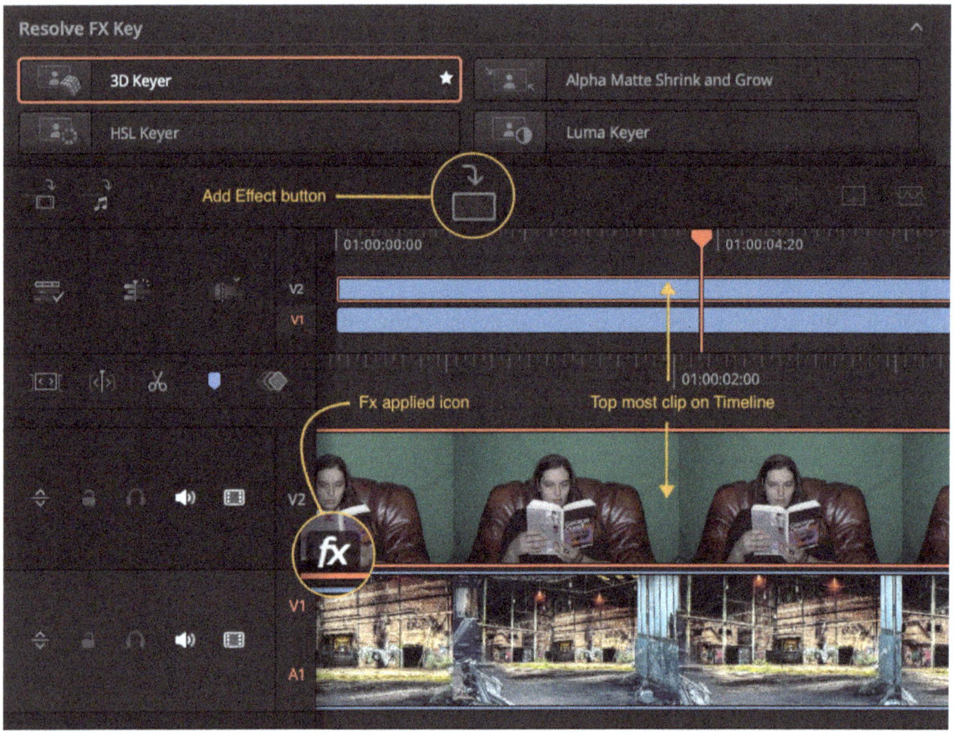

Figure 11.11: Applying the 3D Keyer on the Cut page

Make sure that you have selected the topmost video clip on the timeline before applying the keyer; otherwise, you will not see the effect, as it will be hidden under other video tracks.

You will notice that a small **fx** icon (*Figure 11.11*) has appeared at the bottom left of the clip on the timeline. This is a quick visual reminder that this clip has an effect applied to it.

Adjusting the 3D Keyer

Now that we have applied the **3D Keyer**, we need to adjust it to remove (key out) the green background to reveal our video track underneath. Proceed as follows:

1. On the **Cut** page, open up the **Inspector** to reveal the keyer's controls in the **Effects** panel (**Inspector** > **Effects** > **Open FX** > **3D Keyer**).
2. We now need to activate these controls in the viewer by selecting **Effects Overlay** > **Open FX Overlay** in the **Tools** panel below the viewer (*Figure 11.12*):

Figure 11.12: Open FX Overlay

3. Clicking in the viewer on any part of the green background will remove most of the green to reveal the video image underneath, although it is a good idea to draw a stroke on the green background close to the subject, as this is where there will be the most variance of green to be able to get a good initial selection. Wherever you first select, we will still need to tidy this up, as there are still parts of the green background showing.
4. We need to enable some options so that we can see what we are doing when selecting more parts of the green to remove:

    a. Under **Usage Options**, make sure **Show Paths** is selected (checked).

    b. Under **Output**, select **Alpha Highlight B/W**.

   You will now notice two things (*Figure 11.13*):

   - You can now see blue lines that show where you have clicked or dragged your mouse on the viewer to key out the background.
   - The image has now turned black and white (**B/W**). The white shows where the image is opaque (solid), and the black shows where the image is transparent (see-through).

Our task is to turn all of our green background black, while making sure our subject in the foreground stays white:

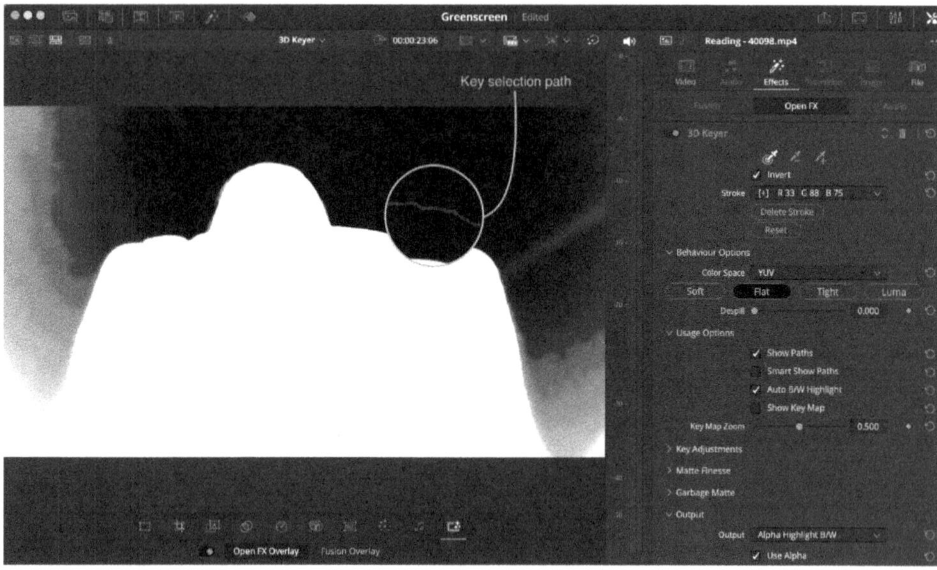

Figure 11.13: Viewer showing Alpha Highlight B/W and paths

5. Select the **Add** tool (eyedropper icon with a plus (+) symbol next to it). This tool will allow us to add to our initial selection.
6. With your mouse, click and drag on the white parts of the viewer to select them and turn them black (and hence transparent).

   If you make a mistake, you can remove the stroke you just added by selecting the **Delete Stroke** button or use the **Subtract** eyedropper tool (with a minus (-) symbol next to it) to select black parts to become white again.

7. Once you have removed most of the background, you can check your selection by changing your **Output** value to **Final Composite** to see the finished result.

   You may notice that the only green that remains is around the edges of the subject. This is tricky to select without removing the subject as well. Well, we have a tool to help with this task.

8. Select **Alpha Highlight** in the **Output** menu. This will make it easier to see the green edges as it reveals the foreground subject while showing the removed background as gray (*Figure 11.14*):

Figure 11.14: Viewer showing Alpha Highlight and a green fringe around our subject

9. To remove this green fringe, reveal the controls in the **Inspector** under **Matte Finesse**. This is where we can fine-tune the section of the background we want to remove. The area of the background we want to remove is called **Matte**. Proceed as follows:

    a. Move the **Clean Black** slider to the right to expand the amount of the background selected.

    b. You can also move the **Black Clip** slider to the right to refine the edges of the background selected.

    c. The **Clean White** and **White Clip** sliders work in the same way as the **Clean Black** and **Black Clip** sliders, but instead affect how much of the foreground is selected. In our example, we won't use these as the foreground is already pure white. However, this may not be the case if your subject was wearing green, resulting in some parts of the foreground being keyed out. In that case, you would use the **Clean White** and **White Clip** sliders to remove any black in the foreground and convert it into solid white.

   d. The **In/Out Ratio** slider will refine the selection by changing where the black and white selections meet. Move it to the left, and it shrinks the white and expands the black. Move the slider to the right, and it has the opposite effect.

   e. Finally, we can increase the **Blur Radius** slider to soften the edges of our selection between the foreground and background to make it less obvious and blend the two together.

   You may have noticed a slight green tint on the edge of the subject's hair. This is caused by some light reflected off the green screen and spilling onto our subject. This green tint looks nasty and draws our attention to the fact that this video has been green-screened. So, next, we will take care of this.

10. To remove the green lighting spill from the background, move the **Despill** slider in the **Behaviour Options** section to the right until the green spill disappears.
11. Other tools you can use to refine the key are as follows:

    - The **Pre-Filter** slider (on *page 1* of the **Matte Finesse** tools) cleans up the video image before the colors are keyed. This is a good tool to use if your original footage is low-quality and you need to tidy it up to help get a successful key.
    - You can also use **Post-Filter** (on *page 2* of the **Matte Finesse** tools) to bring back some details lost from the edges after the key (particularly the hair).

12. Now, it is just a matter of tweaking the **Matte** area by adjusting the preceding controls and using the **Final Composite Output** setting to check the result as you go.

You now have a keyed-out background that reveals the background video behind. Play back the video to check your work (*Figure 11.15*):

Figure 11.15: The end result

> **Key concept – matte**
>
> I know it sounds like the name of one of your best friends. However, **matte** is an Old French word that means both the backing of a picture and a dull, colorless surface. If you think of it, this is a good word to use to describe removing a color to reveal a background behind a picture.
>
> In early cinema, before we had computer graphics, matte artists or matte painters would paint a **background matte** onto glass to recreate a background that was impossible to film in real life (especially useful in sci-fi films such as the original *Star Wars*). The camera would then film the real foreground through the glass of this matte painting to create the illusion that the whole scene was filmed as one. The matte painting on glass and the foreground subject being filmed were carefully lined up so that you could not see the join. See the *Further reading* section of this chapter for links to a more detailed description of this process.
>
> Now, in video compositing software, we refer to the background we have selected to remove from the video as matte.

Even though the **3D Keyer** is a quick and easy way to get a successful key, there will be times it will not work because of the nature of the video. If there is an image that needs more control to get a successful key, we can use the **HSL Keyer**.

Creating a greenscreen effect on the Cut page using the HSL Keyer

The **HSL Keyer** has different options from the **3D Keyer**, as you can choose to select the key based on the **hue, saturation, or luminance** (**HSL**) of pixels in the image. This allows you to have more control over trickier keys as you can select any combination of hue, saturation, or luminance to get a successful key.

For example, there may be a background that is not a uniform green that also matches the green the subject may be wearing. However, if the background is less saturated and brighter than the subject, you can still separate the background by only selecting the saturation and luminance of the green background and not the hue.

However, unlike the **3D Keyer**, the **HSL Keyer** does not have a **Despill** option, so it is best to only use it if you cannot get a successful key using the **3D Keyer**.

Let us create a new timeline to try **HSL Keyer** on different footage. To get our greenscreen footage and create a new timeline, follow these steps on the **Cut** page:

1. In the **Media Pool**, open the bin named **HSL Keyer**.
2. Right-click the clip named `HSL_MCU.mp4` and select **Create New Timeline Using Selected Clips…**.
3. In the **Timeline Name** dialog box, name your timeline `HSL_Keyer`.
4. Click the **Create** button.

You now have a new timeline with our greenscreen footage ready for us to apply the **HSL Keyer**.

You can either add the background video track now – as we did with the **3D Keyer** – or add it later. This time, I am going to add the background after I have keyed the greenscreen clip.

Let us apply the **HSL Keyer** now.

Applying the HSL Keyer

Just as with **3D Keyer**, you can apply **HSL Keyer** on either the **Cut** or **Edit** page.

After locating **HSL Keyer** in **Effects** > **Video** > **Resolve FX Key** > **HSL Keyer**, you can apply **HSL Keyer** by any of the same methods described for **3D Keyer**.

Adjusting the HSL Keyer

Now that you have applied the **HSL Keyer**, you can change the image qualities (**Hue**, **Saturation**, **Luminance**) that Resolve selects to get a key. Trying different combinations of keying using **Hue**, **Saturation**, and/or **Luminance** can solve difficult keys, as any one of these image qualities could be creating difficulties for the key. Proceed as follows:

1. On the **Cut** page, open the **Inspector** to reveal the keyer's controls in the **Effects** panel (**Inspector** > **Effects** > **Open FX** > **HSL Keyer**).
2. Activate these controls in the viewer (just as you did for the **3D Keyer**) by selecting **Open FX Overlay** in the **Tools** panel below the viewer (*Figure 11.12*).
3. Under **Keyer Options**, you can select how Resolve chooses which part of the image to key, whether it is based on hue (color), saturation (strength of color), or luminance (how bright the image is). You can turn these options off and on individually by selecting the check box next to each option (*Figure 11.16*).

4. It is a good idea to turn each one on and off to see how it affects the key, then use the combination that works best for the clip you are keying. With this clip, I have chosen to leave all three enabled: **Use Hue**, **Use Saturation**, and **Use Luminance** (*Figure 11.16*).
5. Just as when we used the **3D Keyer**, clicking in the viewer on any part of the green background (using the **Pick** eyedropper to make the initial selection) will remove most of the green to reveal the video track underneath. However, with the **HSL Keyer**, we cannot see the selection strokes:

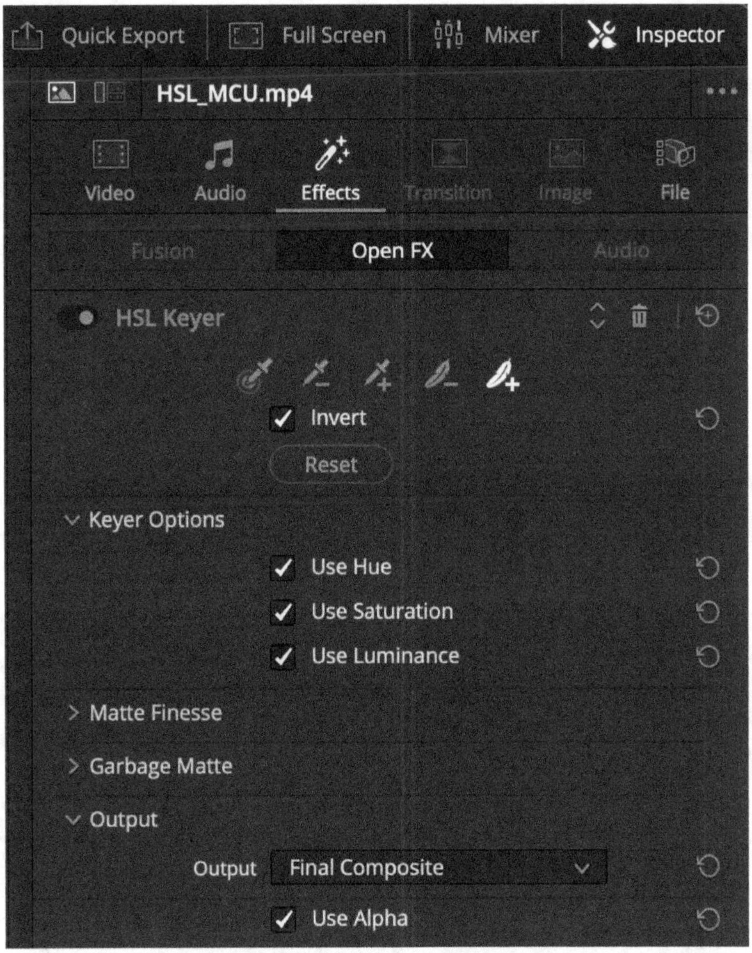

Figure 11.16: HSL Keyer controls

6. We now have our initial key. However, the remaining parts of the green screen have only been partially keyed (*Figure 11.17*), leaving dark patches of green. These patches are dark green as the green that is left is now semi-transparent, showing the black background behind (green mixed with black is dark green):

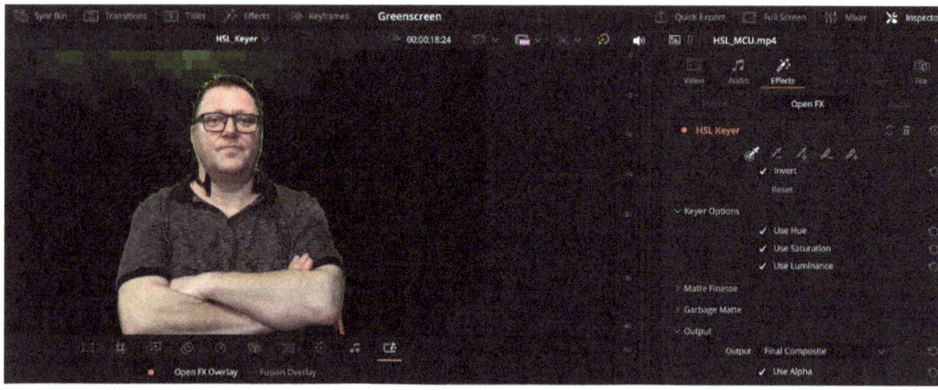

Figure 11.17: After initial selection (Pick tool)

We can use the **Add Soft** selection tool (a feather with a + sign next to it) to feather the edge of the key color that has been selected to encompass the partially keyed parts of the clip (*Figure 11.18*).

Select the **Add Soft** tool and drag on the viewer, starting over the remaining unkeyed parts of the background and finishing your mouse selection on the edge of our subject (that is, drag from the dark green at the top of the frame above their head to the edge of their hair):

Figure 11.18: After Add Soft selection

Now, we have a much better result.

7. Now that you have removed most of the background, you can check your selections by changing your **Output** value to **Alpha Highlight B/W** to see the finished result (*Figure 11.19*). Any area that is pure black is completely removed. Any area that is white is completely opaque, whereas areas that are gray are semitransparent:

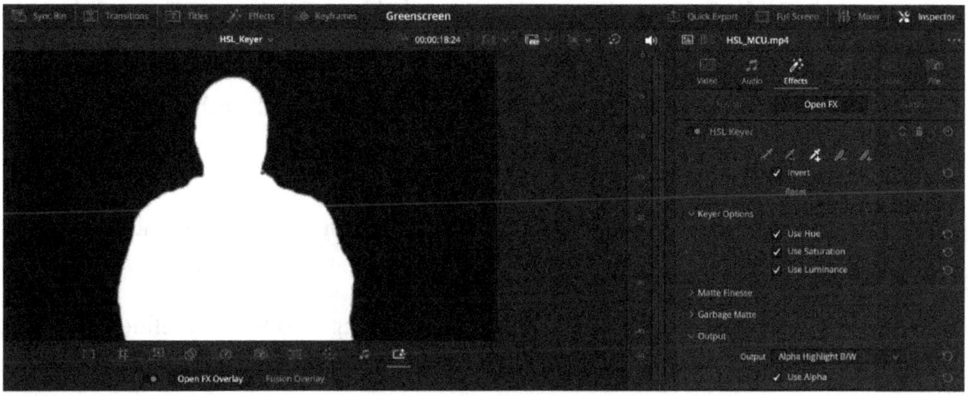

Figure 11.19: Alpha Highlight B/W

8. If you need to remove any gray areas, you can click on the **Matte Finesse** dropdown to reveal the **Matte Finesse** controls, which operate in exactly the same way as the **Matte Finesse** controls in the **3D Keyer**. Use these controls until the image is completely black and white with no gray showing.
9. Don't forget to change your **Output** value to **Final Composite** to see the finished result (*Figure 11.18*).

You may notice that the only green that remains is around the edges of the subject's clothes, face, and hair. This is tricky to select without removing the subject as well. Unlike the **3D Keyer**, the **HSL Keyer** does not have a **Despill** slider to remove this green spill.

Resolve has an extra **Resolve FX** plugin that will help with this task.

Removing chroma key background spill using the Despill Resolve FX Color plugin

The **Resolve FX Color: Despill** plugin is useful to remove despill from clips that have been chroma-keyed using chroma keyers that do not have a built-in despill function. The **Despill** plugin is also useful if you have been given a clip that has already been chroma-keyed but still has colored light spilling onto the subject from the original green screen or blue screen background that has already been removed.

For our clip, we will use the **Despill** plugin to remove the green spill that the **HSL Keyer** could not remove.

Applying the Despill plugin

Just as with the **3D Keyer**, you can apply the **Despill** plugin on either the **Cut** or **Edit** page.

After locating the **Despill** plugin in **Effects** > **Video** > **Resolve FX Color** > **Despill**, you can apply the **Despill** plugin using any of the same methods described for the other Keyers.

Adjusting the Despill plugin

Now that you have applied the **Despill** plugin, you can see an instant difference as the plugin has automatically removed the green spill from our subject's clothes and face.

Let us now see what options we have in the **Despill** plugin to help us refine how we remove background spill:

1. On the **Cut** page, open the **Inspector** to reveal the keyer's controls in the **Effects** panel (**Inspector** > **Effects** > **Open FX** > **Despill**).
2. **Despill** has only two main controls – **Key Color** and **Strength**:

    - **Key Color**: This drop-down menu allows you to select the color of the chroma key spill that you want to remove. The default setting is green, as this is the most common chroma-key screen color. However, the other options of red and blue can be useful if the chroma-key screen is one of these colors.
    - **Strength**: This slider helps reduce the strength of the **Despill** effect. This is good if you want to reintroduce some of the original color to get a better key. For most situations, this setting can be left at the default setting of `1.000`, which is full strength. Any value lower than `1.000` reduces the strength of the color removal:

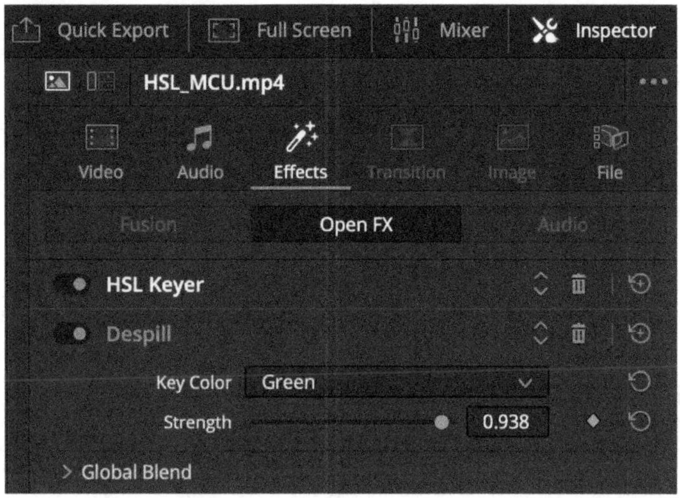

Figure 11.20: Despill controls

Now that you have removed the green background, all that remains to do is add your own background, as you did for the previous timeline.

Feel free to find your own video or photo backgrounds on websites such as *Pixabay* (`https://pixabay.com/videos/search/background/`) and try them out to find one that suits the look you want.

If you create presentations or training videos, you can export your presentation slides as videos that can be played in the background of your video presentation as you talk to your viewers about your specialist subject. An example use case is a business owner talking to the camera with slides of key products and sales figures behind them.

Summary

You now know how to set up a green screen shoot, as well as how to remove the background in Resolve using tools such as the **3D Keyer** and **HSL Keyer**. You also know how to apply the **Despill** plugin to remove background spill, as well as **Matte Finesse** controls to better refine your key.

This will help you when you want to add different artificial backgrounds to your videos, such as slide presentations, to help in presenting a video on a specific topic.

Here is what you have achieved in *Chapter 11*:

- Learned how to shoot videos for a good greenscreen effect
- Used Resolve FX keyers to create greenscreen effects on the **Cut** page using the **3D Keyer**
- Used Resolve FX keyers to create greenscreen effects on the **Cut** page using the **HSL Keyer**
- Used the **Despill Resolve FX** plugin to remove green spill

In *Chapter 12*, we will look at other AI neural engine tools that are only available in the Studio version of DaVinci Resolve, and how they can be used to speed up your editing process.

Questions

1. True or false? The lighting of our green screen does not affect our ability to get a good key.
2. True or false? The **3D Keyer** is only for keying 3D images.
3. True or false? The **HSL Keyer** does not have a **Despill** function.
4. True or false? The **Despill** plugin can only be used to remove the spill from green and blue screens.

Further reading

Here are some websites where you can delve deeper into the art of using green screen:

- The art of matte painting:

a. `https://blog.pond5.com/30867-visual-effects-matte-paintings-composited-film/`, `https://www.vanas.ca/blog/digital-matte-painting-and-its-role-in-the-film-industry`

    - `https://www.liveabout.com/matte-painting-in-film-4690782`

- Free course on the history of matte painting: `https://www.futurelearn.com/info/courses/vfx-for-filmmakers/0/steps/13286`
- Copyright-free video backgrounds: `https://pixabay.com/videos/search/background/`
- An overview of chroma subsampling:
    - `https://www.red.com/red-101/video-chroma-subsampling`
    - `https://www.videomaker.com/article/f6/15788-the-anatomy-of-chroma-subsampling/`
    - `https://www.cablematters.com/Blog/HDMI/a-comprehensive-guide-to-chroma-subsampling`

Get this book's PDF version and more

Scan the QR code (or go to `packtpub.com/unlock`). Search for this book by name, confirm the edition, and then follow the steps on the page.

UNLOCK NOW

Note: Keep your invoice handy. Purchases made directly from Packt don't require an invoice.

12

Studio-Only Techniques – Mostly AI

In *Chapter 6*, we started to look at DaVinci Resolve Studio-only tools that use the Neural Engine, such as **Resolve FX Revival**, to fix archival footage. As the Neural Engine needs a more expensive computer with a newer and faster processor, the tools that require this are usually only available in the full paid-for Studio version of Resolve and are not available in the free version.

In this chapter, we will look at the Neural Engine's **Artificial Intelligence** (**AI**) tools, only available in the Studio version of DaVinci Resolve, that can speed up your editing process. We will look at **Smart Reframe** to recompose your video for different social media formats and **Audio Transcribe** to quickly add subtitles to your clips already on the **Cut** page's timeline. We will then jump across to the **Edit** page to create **smart bins** to quickly organize video footage of people into their own individual bins. Then, finally, use **Face Detection** on the **Cut** page to search for and identify people in your footage.

In this chapter, we are going to cover the following main topics:

- Using AI Smart Reframe on the Cut page
- Using the AI Audio Transcribe tool to create subtitles
- Using AI Voice Isolation to remove background noise
- Smart bins for people on the Edit page
- Using face detection on the Cut page

If you want to stay with the free version, then you can skip this chapter, or you can read it to see whether some of these extra features make it worth your while upgrading from the free version to the Studio version of Resolve. The choice is yours!

Technical requirements

You can download the `Lance Jaggers Audition` archive file to work through the exercises in this chapter: `https://packt.link/gbz/9781836208839`. You will also need the `Chapter_4_VO` video project you created in *Chapter 4*.

Using AI Smart Reframe on the Cut page

Occasionally, when you are shooting your footage quickly, you don't always get the opportunity to frame your shot how you want. One of the advantages of shooting in 6K or even 4K is that you can zoom in on your footage to reframe your shot closer for a 1,080p film with no loss of quality. However, this is usually a manually intensive job where, on the **Cut** page, you would use the **Transform** controls under the **Tools** palette to reframe the clip.

If you need a quick turnaround for your video and you have the Studio version of Resolve, you can use the **Smart Reframe** tool, which uses Resolve's Neural Engine to recognize the subject of your video and reframe the video to create a shot centered around your subject.

This is particularly useful if you change the aspect ratio of your video from the horizontal 16:9 to the vertical 9:16 or square 1:1 aspect ratios. These ratios are often needed to display videos on social media platforms, such as *Facebook* or *Instagram*.

Let us look at how we can use **Smart Reframe** to resize our video for the social media aspect ratio of 1:1.

We are going to reframe a new project called `Lance Jaggers Audition`. This was shot on an iPhone as a 3,840 x 2,160 aspect ratio video.

I need to resize it to the square 1,080 x 1,080 aspect ratio so that I can upload it to *Instagram*. We can use **Timeline Settings** in both the free and Studio versions of Resolve to resize the aspect ratio of our video.

Changing our timeline aspect ratio

Let's begin:

1. In the **Media Pool**, duplicate the `Lance Jaggers Audition` timeline (right-click and select **Duplicate Timeline**).
2. Rename the new `Lance Jaggers Audition copy` timeline to `Lance Jaggers Audition reframed`.
3. Right-click the `Lance Jaggers Audition reframed` timeline in the **Media Pool** and select **Timeline Settings...**.
4. In the **Timeline Settings** window, deselect **Use project settings** (*Figure 12.1*); this will enable you to change the aspect ratio of your timeline and, hence, the final video.

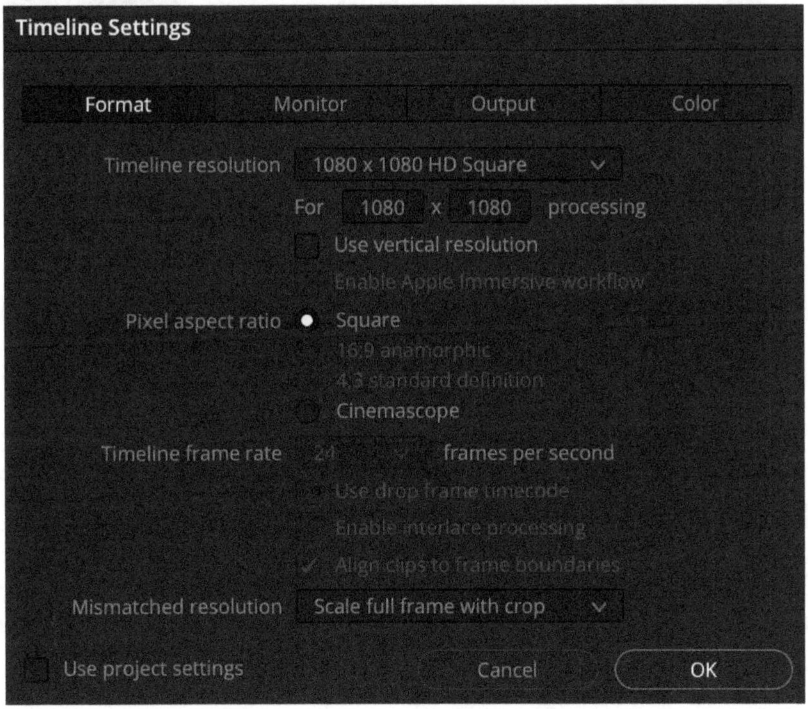

Figure 12.1: Timeline Settings

5. In the **Timeline resolution** drop-down menu, choose **1080 x 1080 HD Square** (*Figure 12.1*).
6. In the **Mismatched resolution** drop-down menu, select **Scale full frame with crop** (*Figure 12.1*).
7. Click the **OK** button to change the resolution of the entire timeline.

We have now changed our video so that the aspect ratio is no longer 3,840 x 2,160 but, instead, a more suitable square aspect ratio for *Instagram* of 1,080 x 1,080.

Figure 12.2: The video with a new square aspect ratio but with a cropped subject

Note that the timeline has cropped out the sides of the original video. However, although most of the subject remains centered within the frame, there are some parts of the video clip (*Figure 12.2*) in which the subject needs to be more centered in the frame; this is where **Smart Reframe** comes in.

Using AI Smart Reframe

Smart Reframe uses Resolve's Neural Engine to analyze the video clip for a subject and then place them in the center of the frame throughout the whole of the video clip.

Smart Reframe is not a special plugin or tool but, instead, a setting in the **Transform** panel of the clip's **Inspector**.

Let us see how we can use **Smart Reframe** to reframe our video content for social media:

1. Select the clip or clips you want to reframe on the timeline.
2. Open the **Transform** settings in the **Inspector** window (**Inspector** > **Video** > **Transform** > **AI Smart Reframe**).
3. Click on the **AI Smart Reframe** dropdown to reveal the controls (*Figure 12.3*).

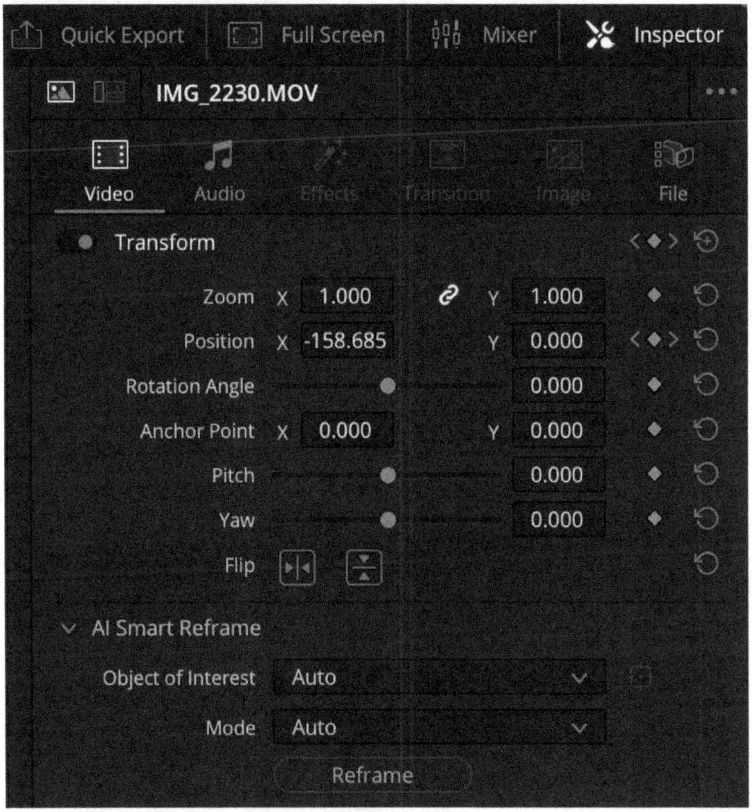

Figure 12.3: The AI Smart Reframe settings

4. The **Object of Interest** drop-down menu is set to **Auto** by default (*Figure 12.3*). We will leave this set to **Auto** and demonstrate how the **Reference Point** option works later in this chapter.
5. The **Mode** drop-down menu is set to **Auto** by default (*Figure 12.3*). The other options of **Pan Only** and **Tilt Only** will limit the reframing to vertical (**Tilt Only**) or horizontal (**Pan Only**) movement. For this exercise, we can leave this set to **Auto**.

6. Click the **Reframe** button (*Figure 12.3*). Resolve will now analyze the clip(s) (*Figure 12.4*) you have selected and change the **Transform** settings automatically to reposition your subject within the frame. A pop-up will appear to show you the progress of the analysis (*Figure 12.4*).

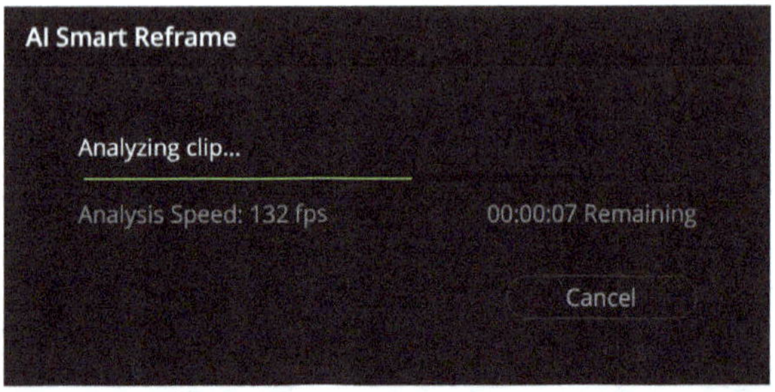

Figure 12.4: The AI Smart Reframe analyzing progress bar

You will now have a video where Resolve has analyzed the footage for any movement of the subject and automatically panned the video, keeping the subject within the frame of the new aspect ratio.

When you play back the video, it feels like a camera operator is panning the shot to match the subject's movement while keeping the subject in the center of the frame, as can be seen when comparing the clip before **Smart Reframe** (*Figure 12.2*) to after it has been applied (*Figure 12.5*).

Figure 12.5: Smart Reframe applied

If you are not happy with how Resolve has automatically reframed the subject (e.g., Resolve chose the wrong subject to re-frame around), you can manually select a **reference point** for your subject on a clip-by-clip basis.

Manually selecting a reference point

Let us explore how we can select our own subject's reference point for Resolve to reframe the aspect ratio around.

Smart Reframe automatically placed the subject into the center of the frame. However, we want to give our subject some more **looking room** and so want to place our subject more to the right of the frame as they are looking toward the left of the frame.

> **Key concept – looking/lead room**
>
> Sometimes, when framing a subject in a video, we do not always want them to be in the center of the frame.
>
> One instance of this is when our subject is looking into the frame. It is more aesthetically pleasing to have more empty space in front of the subject than behind them; this extra space in front of the subject is called *looking* or *lead* room, as it leads the audience's eyes in the direction that the subject is looking.
>
> *Looking room* can also be applied to vehicles, not just people, to give the vehicle space to be able to travel across the frame.

To do this, we will select a reference point at the front of the subject's waistcoat, which will result in moving the object slightly to the left as Resolve moves the waistcoat to the center of the frame. Let us explore how to do this:

1. Just like you did with the auto **Smart Reframe** tool, select the clip you want to reframe on the timeline and reveal the **Smart Reframe** controls in the **Inspector**.
2. Under the **Object of Interest** drop-down menu, select **Reference Point**. This will reveal a white target icon to the right of the **Object of Interest** drop-down menu. A reference point bounding box will also appear on the viewer.

   If the reference point bounding box does not show automatically, you can turn it on and off by clicking on the target icon.

3. Reposition this reference point bounding box to your new subject in the video by clicking within the box and dragging it to its new position. Let us do that to move the box so that the center covers the front of the subject's waistcoat against the white shirt sleeve (*Figure 12.6*), as this is a good high-contrast part of the image that Resolve will find easy to reframe.
4. You can also resize the bounding box by clicking and dragging on any of the corners of the box. Let us do that by resizing the bounding box to cover the waistcoat's closed buttons and part of the subject's arm (*Figure 12.6*).

Figure 12.6: Repositioned bounding box

5. Click the **Reframe** button for Resolve to reframe the aspect ratio around your selected object of interest.
6. Click on the white target icon (*Figure 12.3*) to hide the reference point bounding box in the viewer.

By placing the waistcoat in the middle of the frame, Resolve has now moved the subject more to the right (*Figure 12.7*).

Figure 12.7: The Smart Reframe result using a new object of interest

This new framing allows the subject to be framed asymmetrically, which can be more visually pleasing to the viewer.

Smart reframing reference point selection

When choosing a reference point to place the bounding box over, you will get better results if you choose a place where there is a well-defined edge or area of contrast. This enables Resolve to easily recognize the subject throughout the video clip.

In order to place the bounding box over a subject outside of the frame, you can use the **Transform** controls in the Inspector window to reposition the clip so that you can see your subject.

We have used **Smart Reframe** to be able to quickly reposition a new aspect ratio around our subject automatically. Let us now look at another Neural Engine tool that allows us to recognize people and put them automatically into their own bins, making it much easier to quickly find the footage we are looking for.

As of version 19, DaVinci Resolve Studio has some handy AI tools that assist us with speeding up the editing process, such as automatically creating subtitles using AI.

Using the AI Audio Transcribe tool to create subtitles

We have already looked at manually adding subtitles in *Chapter 4*; however, there is a new tool in the Studio version of Resolve that will automatically create subtitles for us.

Let us use this tool to add subtitles to our `Lance Jaggers Audition` project on the **Cut** page.

1. On the **Cut** page, click on the **Timeline Actions** icon (*Figure 12.8*).

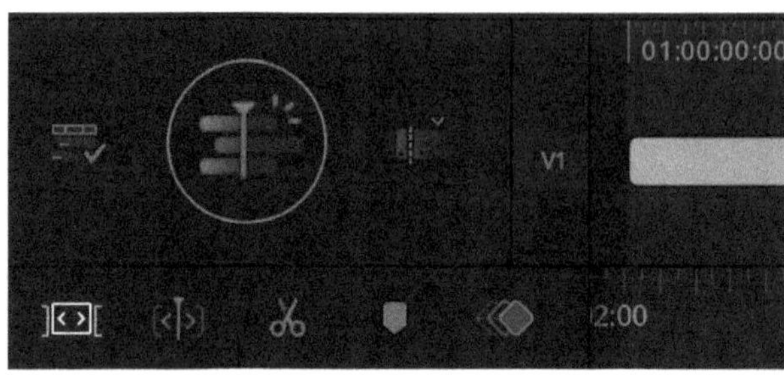

Figure 12.8: Timeline Actions icon

2. In the **Timeline Actions** pop-up menu, select **Create Subtitles from Audio** (*Figure 12.9*).

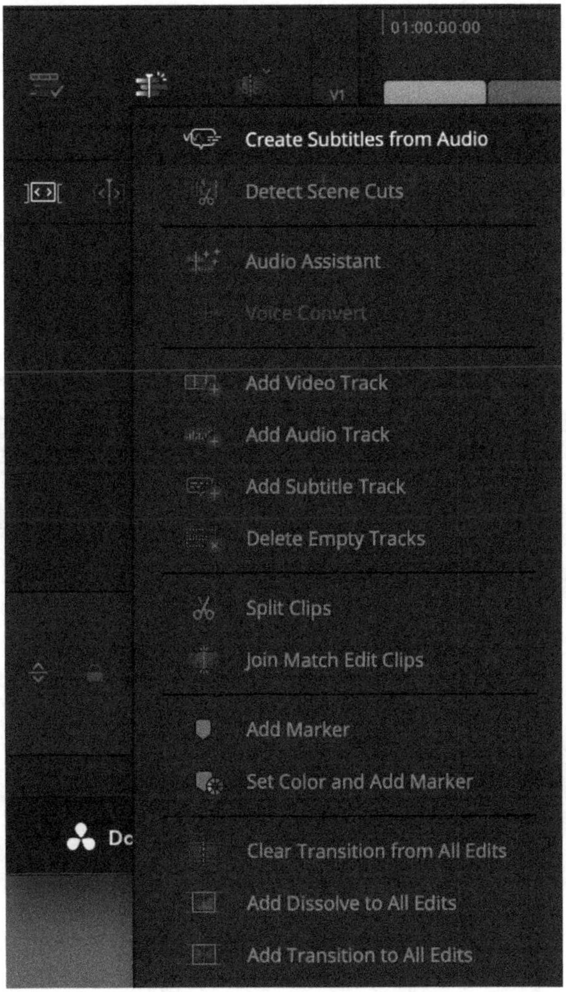

Figure 12.9: Timeline Actions menu

3. A **Create Subtitles from Audio** window will appear (*Figure 12.10*), which will give you the following options:
   - The **Language** dropdown gives you a choice of languages for the spoken audio. Choosing **Auto** gets DaVinci Resolve to choose the language automatically.
   - The **Caption Preset** dropdown will give you three options: **Subtitle Default**, **Teletext**, and **Netflix**.

- **Maximum characters per line**: Here, you can enter the numerical value for the number of characters you want to limit the subtitles to before it carries over onto a new line.
- The **Lines** dropdown will give you the option to have either **Single** or **Double** lines for your subtitles.
- **Gap Between Subtitles** allows you to enter how long a gap (measured in video frames) you want to have between each different subtitle.

You can leave these settings at their default values, or you can use the different broadcasters' standards listed in the *Further reading* section of *Chapter 4*.

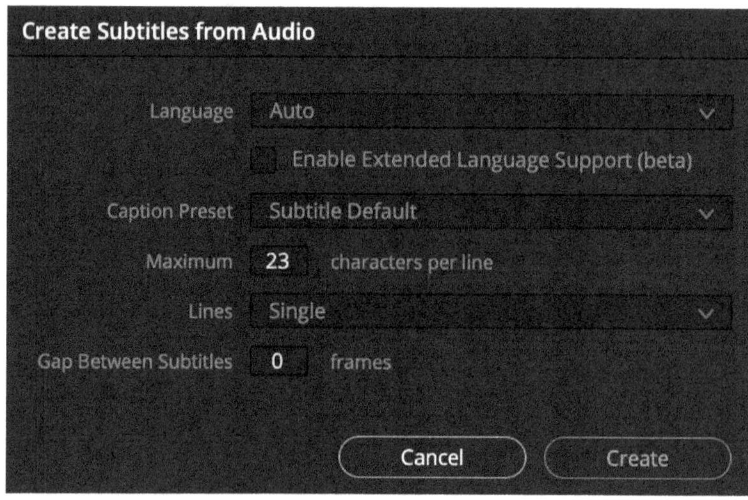

Figure 12.10: Create Subtitles from Audio window

4. Click on the **Create** button to export your subtitles.

   Resolve will show you a progress bar as it uses AI to transcribe your audio into text.

5. Once it has finished transcribing, Resolve will add your subtitles to the timeline on its own subtitle track (*Figure 12.11*).

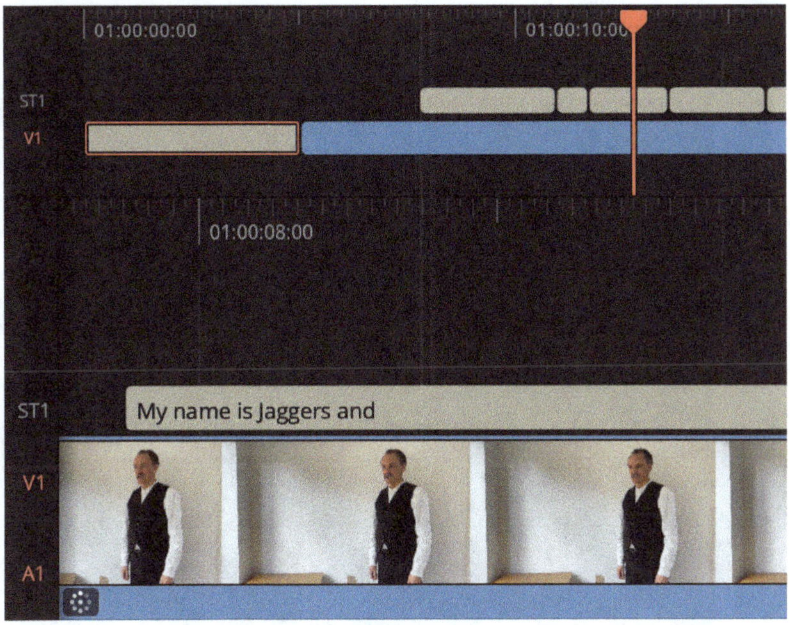

Figure 12.11: Subtitles automatically placed on the timeline

You now have subtitles on your timeline that you can then check for accuracy and edit to suit, as described in *Chapter 4*.

Using AI Voice Isolation to remove background noise

In addition to the audio fixing tools we covered in *Chapter 3*, there is an additional audio fixing AI tool that is only available in the Studio version of DaVinci Resolve. DaVinci Resolve's **AI Voice Isolation** tool is a powerful tool to remove unwanted sounds in the background while emphasizing the voice of our talent in the foreground.

Let us use **AI Voice Isolation** on our `Lance Jaggers Audition` project on the **Cut** page. We will remove some of the room echo from the background to help my voice to be heard more clearly.

1. Place the playhead over the `IMG_2230.mov` clip that is already on the timeline.

2. In the **Inspector**, reveal the **AI Voice Isolation** controls by turning on the toggle switch (*Figure 12.12*).

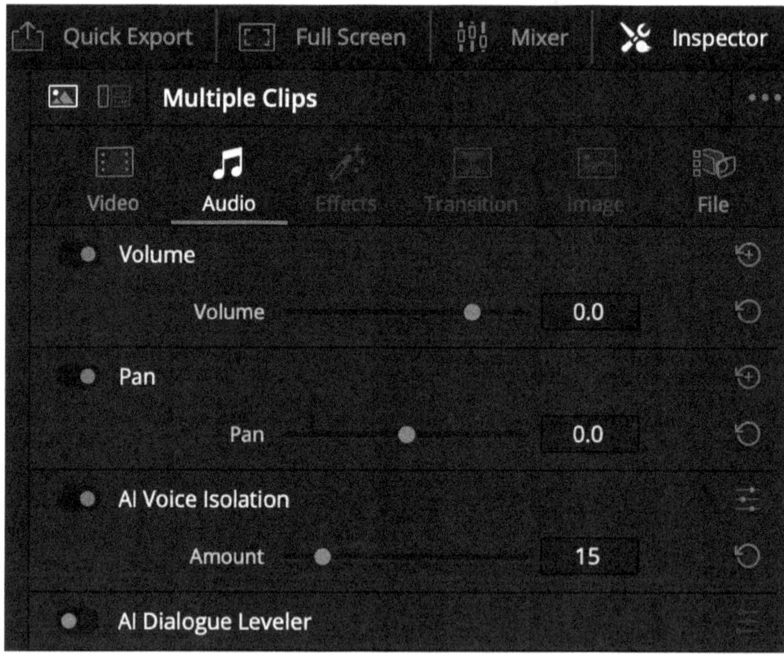

Figure 12.12: The AI Voice Isolation controls

3. Move the **Amount** slider from the default value of **100** to **15**

   The default value of 100 applies **AI Voice Isolation** to remove 100 percent of the background noise. In this case, as there is only a slight echo in the room, we are going to move the slider to **15** to apply **AI Voice Isolation** to remove only 15 percent of the background sound.

4. Play back the clip on the timeline to hear that the echo has been removed.

Being too aggressive with the use of the AI tools can make our video sound artificial. So, it is best to use them sparingly to fix problems that you cannot fix in any other way.

Smart bins for people on the Edit page

For our `Chapter_4_VO` video project, we used **Scene Detect** to chop up the `OneWeek512kb` video file into individual clips and place them in the **Media Pool**. This created over 200 video clips. To separate these clips into individual bins for each character, we would need to manually play through each video and look for clips that feature the bride and the groom, and then manually separate them into separate bins. However, we can only have one bin this way, as the bride and groom both feature in the same clips, so we can't separate them into their own bins without creating copies of each clip.

There is a better way to separate clips of different people into their own bins – with the help of smart bins.

Let us enable smart bins for our `Chapter_4_VO` video project.

Enabling smart bins

To be able to use smart bins, we first need to enable them in the **Preferences** menu:

1. Go to the **Menu** bar and navigate to **DaVinci Resolve** > **Preferences** > **User** > **Editing** > **Automatic Smart Bins** (*Figure 12.13*).
2. Enable the checkbox next to **Automatic smart bins for people metadata** (*Figure 12.13*).
3. Click the **Save** button.

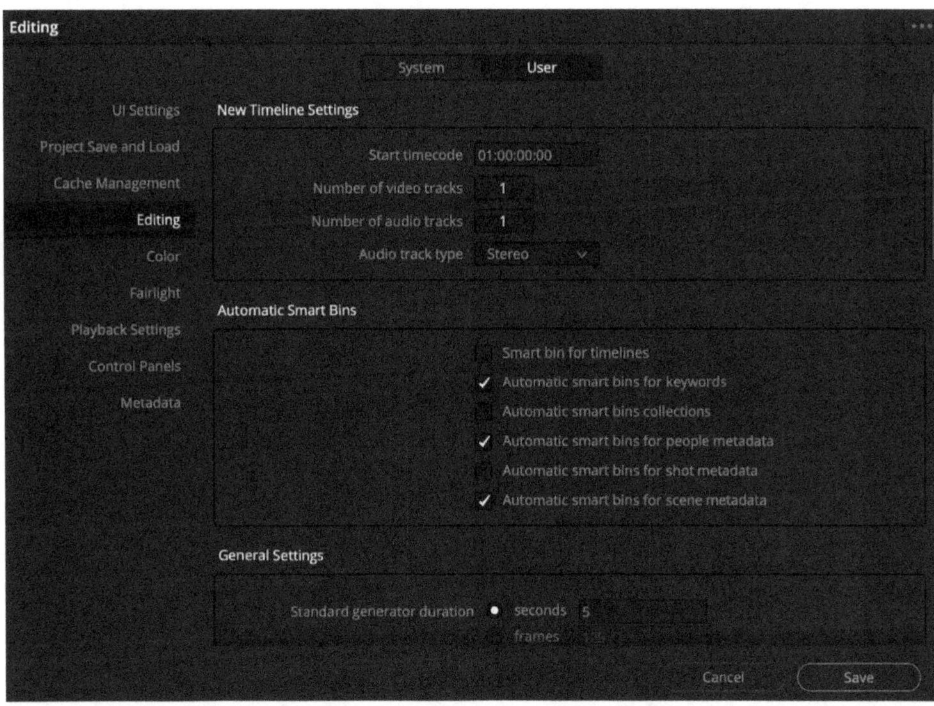

Figure 12.13: Automatic Smart Bins in Preferences

On the **Edit** page, a smart bin called **People** has now appeared at the bottom left of the **Media Pool** (*Figure 12.14*).

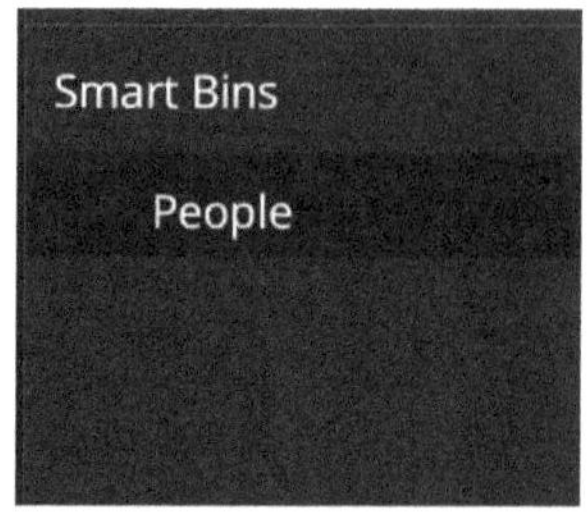

Figure 12.14: The People smart bin

Note that our **People** smart bin is empty. We now need to search for people in our footage and add their names to the metadata for each clip.

Using face detection on the Cut page

Thankfully, with the Studio version of Resolve, we don't need to add the names manually to each clip's metadata. We can use face detection to automatically recognize faces using Resolve's Neural Engine and add their names to each clip as metadata. Unlike typical metadata entries, we can do this on the **Cut** page. For this exercise, we are going to use our `Chapter_4_VO` project and select all the clips in the **Master** bin:

1. Right-click on one or several clips you have selected in the **Cut** page's **Media Pool**.
2. In the drop-down menu, select **AI Tools > Analyze Clips for People**. A progress bar will appear as Resolve analyzes your clips for people's faces (*Figure 12.15*).

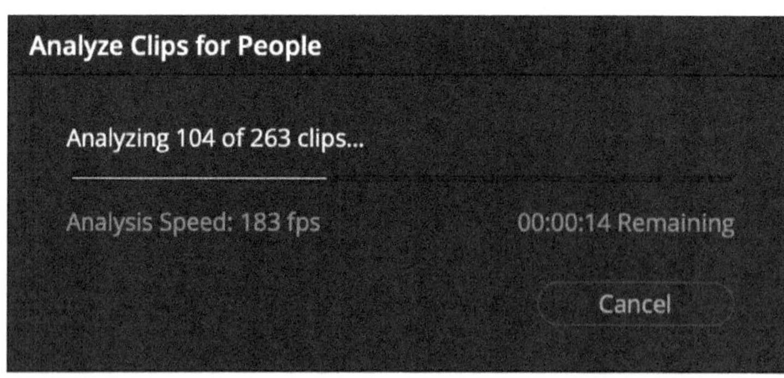

Figure 12.15: The Analyze Clips for People progress bar

After Resolve has searched for and recognized faces in your clip, it groups the faces (*Figure 12.16*) and places them into their own individual bins.

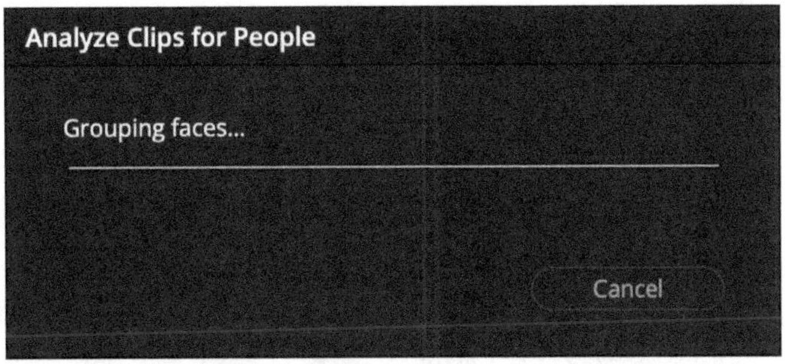

Figure 12.16: The Grouping faces… progress bar

3. Once the analysis is complete, a **People** management window appears (*Figure 12.17*):

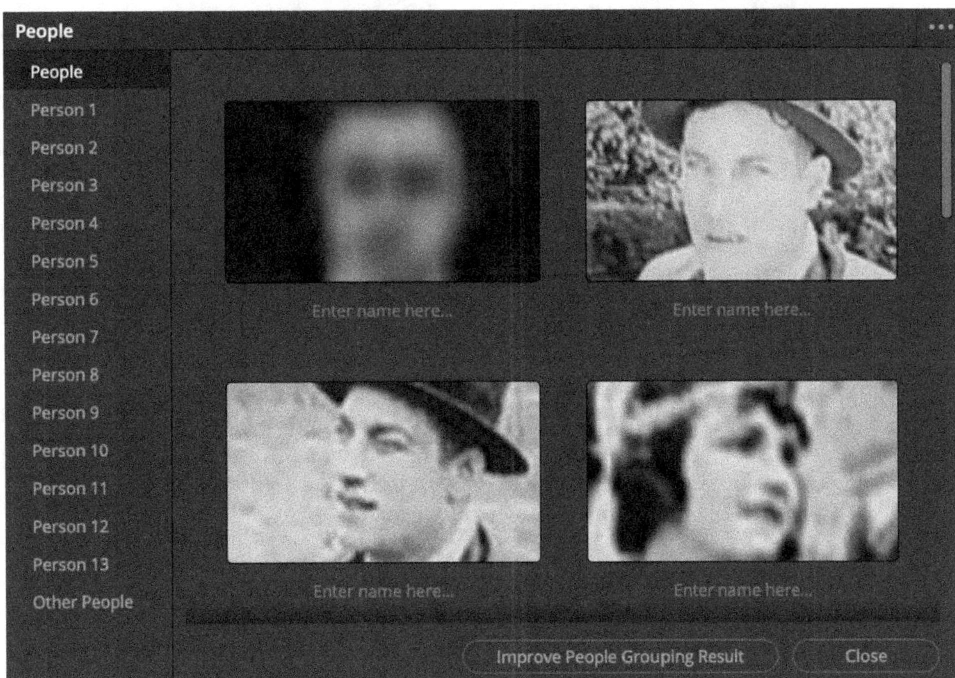

Figure 12.17: The People management window

- If an **Improve People Grouping Result** button appears, click this to help Resolve's AI identify faces that it has difficulty with. An **Improve Face Clustering** window (*Figure 12.18*) will appear, asking you to compare two images and identify whether they are of the same person or not. Click the **Yes** or **No** button, depending on whether the images are of the same person or not. If you are unsure, you can always click the **No** button and manually allocate the name at a later time.

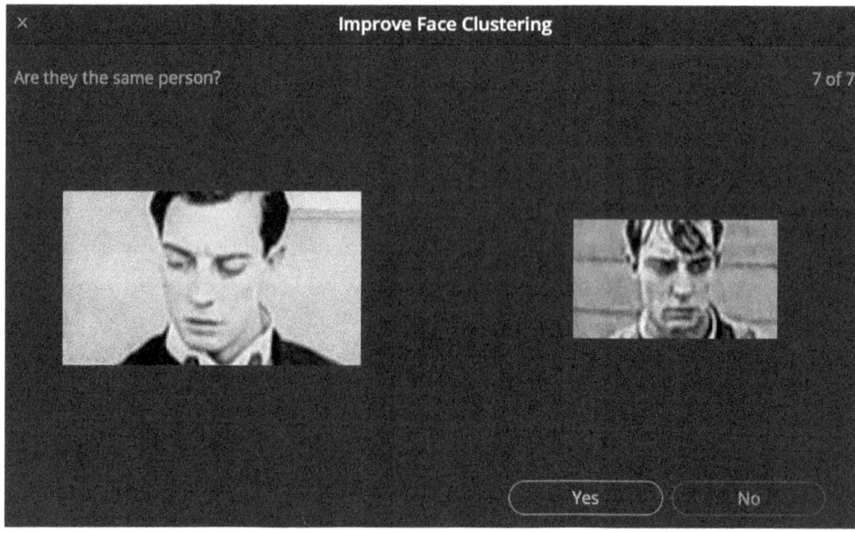

Figure 12.18: The Improve Face Clustering window

- The **People** management window (*Figure 12.17*) is split into two sections:
  - All the people Resolve has found and put into groups are listed on the left. Clicking on the **People** group will reveal thumbnails of all the people Resolve has recognized (this is the default view). The other groups listed are for each person (e.g., **Person 1**, **Person 2**, etc.) to filter only the thumbnails of clips they feature in. Finally, the **Other People** group shows the people that Resolve could not place into a distinct group.

- The main body of the window to the right has thumbnails of all the people Resolve has identified, filtered by whatever group you have selected in the list on the left.

4. Select each thumbnail and click on the **Enter name here...** text to rename each of the people that have been identified. As an example, identify the bride and groom and rename the clips as such. The name of the bin on the list will change to reflect the name changes you have made (e.g., **Person 3** has been renamed `Bride` and **Person 8** has been renamed `Groom` in *Figure 12.19*).

Figure 12.19: Renaming thumbnails

5. Open the **Other People** group by double-clicking on either the **Other People** thumbnail on the right or the **Other People** group listed on the left (*Figure 12.20*).

6. Scroll down until you see a clip where the bride has not been put into a group (*Figure 12.20*). You will see an orange box around a face, where Resolve has identified a face but does not know which person it belongs to.

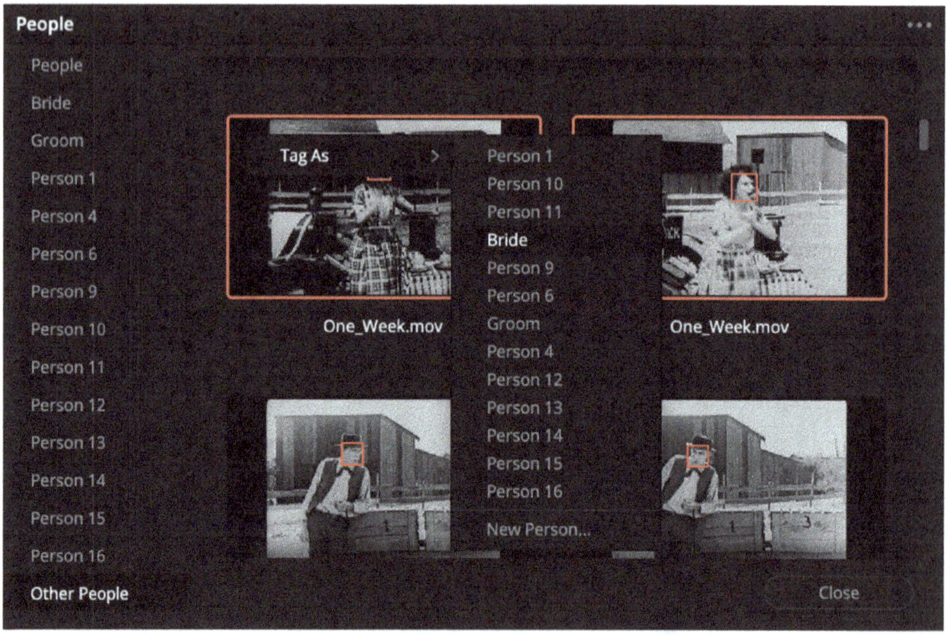

Figure 12.20: The Other People group

7. Right-click on the thumbnail of the bride and select **Tag As** > **Bride** (*Figure 12.20*). This will remove this thumbnail/s from the **Other People** group and allocate it to the **Bride** group.

   You can select more than one thumbnail to tag by *Shift*-clicking and selecting a series of thumbnails, then right-clicking on any of the thumbnails selected to tag them all. An orange border will appear around the thumbnails that are selected (*Figure 12.20*).

8. Select any of the other unnamed **Person** groups and allocate the clips in the group to the correct person's group by right-clicking on a thumbnail or series of thumbnails and selecting the correct person's name in the drop-down list (e.g., all the clips in the **Person 12** group have been reallocated to the **Bride** group in *Figure 12.21*).

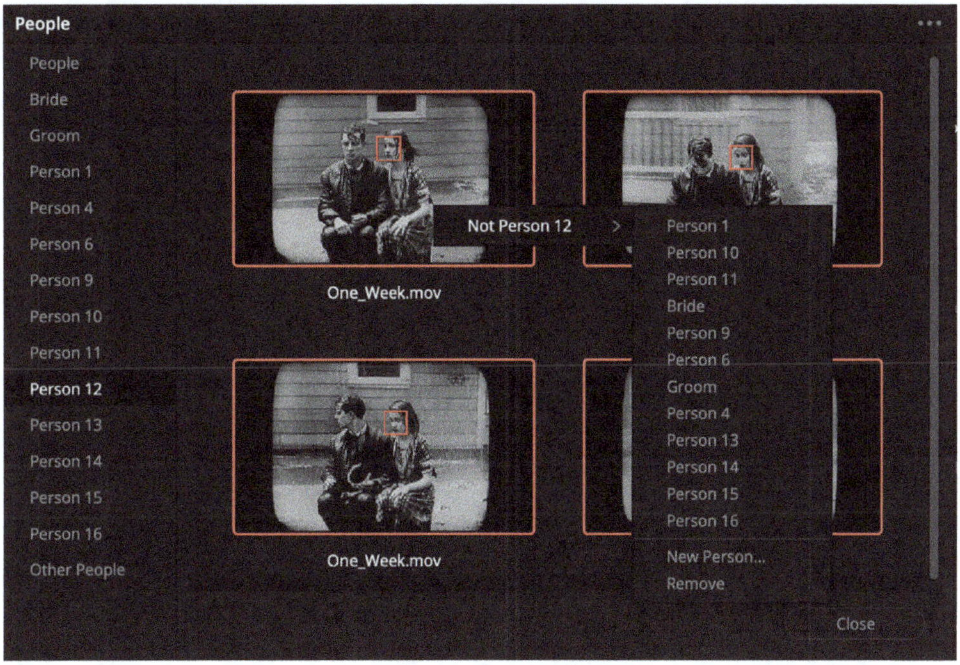

Figure 12.21: Allocating Person 12 into the Bride group

9. Once you have finished naming and allocating people to the different groups, you can click the **Close** button at the bottom right of the window.
10. Once you have closed the **People** management window, you may wonder, how do I get it back again so that I can continue to rename people if I need to? You can easily reopen the window by choosing **Workspace > People** in Resolve's menu bar.

Correcting face identification if the results are wrong

If Resolve has wrongly identified a person, you can right-click the thumbnail and select the correct person from the list if it is an existing person, or select **New Person...** to create a new group for a new person (*Figure 12.21*).

If there is an object that has been incorrectly identified as a person (e.g., a face on a t-shirt or poster), then you can right-click on the thumbnail and select **Remove** from the drop-down list (*Figure 12.21*). This will remove the "person" from the **People** management window, and no smart bin will be created for this object.

If there are too many wrong guesses and you want Resolve to start again, you can select **Reset Face Database** in the options menu (the three dots at the top right of the **People** management window in *Figure 12.21*).

Unfortunately, at the time of writing, there is no way to see smart bins on the **Cut** page. So, to see the results of our face recognition, we need to go to the **Edit** page.

In the **Smart Bins** section of the **Media Pool**, note that the **People** smart bin now has a drop-down arrow next to it. Clicking on this arrow will reveal all the **People** smart bins listed by name (including the **Bride** smart bin that we have just named – see *Figure 12.22*). Clicking on any of these smart bins will reveal only the clips that contain that person.

Figure 12.22: People Smart Bins

Also, if you look at the **Metadata > Shot & Scene** panel for each clip on the **Media**, **Edit**, **Fusion**, or **Fairlight** pages, you will see that the **People** textbox is now populated with all the names (as keywords) of the people that Resolve's facial recognition identified for that clip (*Figure 12.23*).

Figure 12.23: The Metadata panel with People keywords

The great thing about smart bins is that if we add any **People** metadata to a clip, the smart bin will be automatically updated with the new clip.

So, now you will be able to quickly organize your clips in Resolve using face detection to automatically sort clips of people into their own individual smart bins. You can also quickly change the framing of your clips to suit different aspect ratios for the various social media video platforms.

This chapter was a brief overview of some of the Neural Engine tools available in the Studio version of DaVinci Resolve that will help you create videos for social media and the web more quickly and efficiently. These tools, as well as the others covered in the rest of this book, will give you a good foundation for further exploration in using Resolve for your video editing needs.

Summary

Here is what you have achieved in *Chapter 12*:

- You learned how to use **AI Smart Reframe** to change the video framing for different social media formats
- You learned how to use the **AI Audio Transcription** tool to automatically create subtitles
- You learned how to use **AI Voice Isolation** to remove unwanted background noise
- You learned what a smart bin is and how to create bins automatically based on metadata
- You learned what face detection does and how to use it to search for and identify people in your footage

Congratulations! You have now completed the book, and you are now better equipped to continue your journey of using Resolve to edit and polish some amazing videos for your business, social media, or the web.

Good luck! I can't wait to see what you create!

Questions

1. True or false? **AI Smart Reframe** is a Resolve FX plugin found in the **Effects** panel.
2. True or false? Smart bins automatically update their content to show new clips added to the **Media Pool**.
3. True or false? **AI Voice Isolation** is a Fairlight FX plugin.

4. True or false? Face detection can recognize faces in your clips and put them into separate bins, but you still need to name each bin with the actual person's name.
5. True or false? **AI Audio Transcription** only works to transcribe subtitles for videos where the main language is English.

Further reading

Here are some articles on video composition to help you when reframing your shots:

- `https://motionarray.com/learn/filmmaking/shot-composition-framing-rules/`
- `https://en.wikipedia.org/wiki/Lead_room`
- `https://neiloseman.com/lead-room-nose-room-or-looking-space/`

Get this book's PDF version and more

Scan the QR code (or go to `packtpub.com/unlock`). Search for this book by name, confirm the edition, and then follow the steps on the page.

UNLOCK NOW

Note: Keep your invoice handy. Purchases made directly from Packt don't require an invoice.

13

Glossary

This glossary contains some of the common terms used throughout the book and in video editing with their meanings, in alphabetical order.

Artificial intelligence (AI)

A general term used to describe a computer that makes its own decisions based on data it has received.

Archive

The process and name for video and audio files that are stored when no longer used.

B-roll

Video footage that is captured in addition to the main subject or story. B-roll footage is usually of cutaways, cut-ins, or reaction shots.

Bins

Folders that are used to store video and audio clips in your video editing software.

Cache

A temporary file storage location that is hidden on your computer and allows your computer to access files very quickly.

Caching

The process of your computer writing files to your cache.

Clip

A section of video or audio.

Code

A set of written instructions that tell a computer what to do.

Color cast

Where a white, gray, or black image is not pure grayscale but has a hint of color to it.

Color grading

The process of correcting and enhancing the color of a video.

Color management

The act of managing the color of the video footage from camera to final screening, to keep the color consistent with how it was originally shot.

Color model

A theoretical model to describe how colors are mixed to create other colors.

Color space

A 3D space that contains all the color and gamma values available for a particular video standard (e.g., Rec 709).

Color temperature

The color cast of white light on a sliding scale between orange and blue.

Colorist

The person who performs color grading on a video.

Composition

The arrangement of subjects within the video frame.

Continuity editing

A style of video editing where footage that has been shot on different days and times is edited together to look like it all occurred at the same time.

Cut

The abrupt move from one video clip to another without a transition. This can also be used to describe the act of splitting a video clip into two.

Cutaway

A clip that shows other subjects away from the main action of the video (e.g., a shot of the weather).

Cut-in

A clip that shows a more detailed view of the main action (e.g., a shot of the main character's hands).

Data

Information that is stored by a computer.

Database

A place on the computer that stores data. Resolve uses a database to store all the project files.

Digital audio workstation (DAW)

A software application that allows you to edit audio, including music and other recorded sound.

Exposure

The amount of light that enters the camera to create the video's image.

An over-exposed image has too much light, making it look too bright. An under-exposed image has too little light, making the image look too dark.

Exposure controls

The settings on the camera that allow you to control how much light is recorded to create the video's image.

Frame rate/FPS

The speed at which the frames of a video image are played back to the viewer. The speed is measured by the number of frames that can be played back in one second. This is described as **frames per second** (FPS).

Frames

A video image is made up of a series of photographs that are shown back rapidly to give the illusion of movement (see the *Frame rate/FPS* section). Each of these photographs is called a frame.

Framing

The act of moving the camera in relation to the subject to change the composition of the image.

Gamma

How an image displays the contrast between the brightest and darkest parts of an image. This is based on a curve that shows the relationship between the original video level and its perceived brightness on a screen.

Graphics

A picture that is created by a computer, such as a logo or animation.

Greenscreen

A term commonly used to describe the process of shooting a video with a green background that is later removed by a computer and replaced with another still or moving image as a background.

Gray card

A card that is neutral gray with no color cast, and used to help white-balance the camera.

Hard disk drive (HDD)

Also called a hard drive. A hard drive stores data that your computer uses, such as files and applications.

ISO

Short for **International Standards Organization**, is a camera setting that increases or decreases your camera's sensitivity to light by adjusting the electrical signal to the camera sensor. The higher the ISO number, the more the camera is sensitive to light. Too high an ISO can introduce digital noise to the image due to the boost in the electrical signal.

J-cut

A video cut where the sound is heard before we see the video image.

L-cut

A video cut where the sound is heard after the video image is no longer seen.

Lead room

A video composition technique where more room is given in front of a subject to allow movement of the subject into the frame (e.g., a car driving will be framed to have more space in front of it than behind it).

Looking room

The same as lead room, but usually used to describe having more space in front of a person than behind, so that they appear to be looking into the frame rather than out of it.

Media

A general term for any files used in your video edit, including video, audio, graphics, and still pictures.

Neural Engine

Blackmagic Design's name for the AI function in DaVinci Resolve.

Neutral

An image or grayscale with no color cast to it.

Non-linear editor (NLE)

The technical name for video editing software, as opposed to old-fashioned film or tape-to-tape editing. It is named *non-linear* as you place the clips in any order on the **Timeline**. In old-fashioned linear editing, you would have to start at the beginning of the film and add each piece of footage one after another, unable to insert an edit without it overwriting the rest of the film. In an NLE, you can start at any point in the film and move all the clips around at any time.

Plugins

Small programs that add new abilities to the larger host program.

Project

The name of the file that contains all the video editing decisions of an NLE.

Reaction shot

A video of someone visually reacting to the main action of the story (e.g., an interviewer nodding in response to an interviewee's answer).

Render

The act of a computer processing data into a final viewable image.

Resolve

An abbreviation of DaVinci Resolve.

Run and gun

A style of filming often used for documentary and reality TV, where the video is captured quickly with no time to pre-plan the shoot. As the camera is handheld to help capture the scene quickly, it can lead to shaky footage.

Solid state drive (SSD)

A hard drive that has no moving parts and is more durable, lighter, and faster than regular hard drives.

Sound effects (SFX)

Short sound clips recorded to add sounds that are not in the original video to emphasize the action in the video (e.g., a door hinge squeaking).

Split edit

A cut where the sound is separated from the video, creating either a J-or L-cut.

Stills

Another word for photographs. Short for still images (compared to moving images or "movies").

Thumbnail

A small picture that represents the content of the video file or clip.

Three-point edit

An editing technique that uses an **In** and **Out** point on either the **Timeline** or the source clip and a third point marked by a playhead or either an In or Out point to determine how much of the original clip is to be used and where to place it on the **Timeline**.

Timeline

A **Timeline** is a line that visually shows events in the order that they happened. In editing software, the **Timeline** is where clips are placed and arranged in an order that represents the timing of the story being told.

Tools

Features that give you specific functionality within software by clicking an on-screen icon or button without needing to apply a plugin (e.g., the **Insert Clip** tool).

Transitions

Video effects that slowly transition from one video clip to another.

Visual effects (VFX)

Computer-generated effects that change the look of a video image.

White balance

The act of changing the color of the image to compensate for a color cast to make the white and black areas of the image neutral (e.g., adding more orange to compensate for a blue-tinted image).

Get this book's PDF version and more

Scan the QR code (or go to `packtpub.com/unlock`). Search for this book by name, confirm the edition, and then follow the steps on the page.

UNLOCK NOW

Note: Keep your invoice handy. Purchases made directly from Packt don't require an invoice.

14

Answers to Questions

Here are the answers to the questions that were at the end of the chapters in this book. Use these answers to check your understanding of each chapter.

Chapter 1, Getting Started with Resolve – Publishing Your First Cut

1. False. The Cut button removes any selected transition effects applied between clips on the timeline. This reverts the transition to a basic "cut" between clips.
2. YouTube, Vimeo, and TikTok.
3. **Smart Insert**, **Append to End**, and **Ripple Overwrite** work on **Track 1** only.
4. **Close Up**, **Place on Top**, and **Source Overwrite** all place clips on **Track 2**.
5. False. *Timecode* is the term used to describe the position of the playhead on the **Timeline**. It is displayed in hours, minutes, seconds, and frames (`HH:MM:SS:FF`).

Chapter 2, Adding Titles and Motion Graphics

1. False. A `.drp` file does not contain any media. The media will need to be imported separately and relinked to the project within Resolve.
2. False. Both **Text** and **Text+** titles offer you all the fonts available on your computer.
3. E. Cross Dissolve
4. True.

Chapter 3, Polishing the Camera Audio – Getting It in Sync

1. False. The best microphone to use is the one closest to the subject.
2. False. You can also sync separate audio to the video using timecode and by manually syncing using a visual reference in the video.
3. True. On the **Cut** page, navigate to **Effects** > **Audio** > **Fairlight FX**.
4. False. **AI Dialogue Leveler** can be found in the **Audio** section of the **Inspector**. It helps raise or lower the volume levels of different dialogue within the same clip to keep the sound more balanced.

Chapter 4, Adding Narration, Voice Dubbing, and Subtitles

1. False. You can use the Voiceover tool in the Cut page to record audio directly to the timeline.
2. False. Resolve supports `SRT` and `WebVTT` for web-based subtitles as well as the broadcast-friendly `IMSC1` or `DFXP` subtitle formats.
3. False. Pressing the *M* key in the **Cut** page will add a **Marker** on the **Timeline**.
4. False. The **Voiceover** tool on the **Cut** page will automatically recognize the microphone connected to your computer and patch it to a new VO track. You just need to click on the record button to record.

Chapter 5, Creating Additional Sound

1. True.
2. False. On the **Cut** page, navigate to **Effects** > **Audio** and choose either **AU Effects** or **VST Effects**.
3. True.
4. False. You can import SFX into any **Project Library** (database).
5. True.

Chapter 6, Working with Archive Footage

1. False. Some **Resolve FX Revival** effects, such as **Dead Pixel Fixer** and **Deband**, are available in the free version of DaVinci Resolve.
2. False. You can also change the speed of clips on the **Cut** and **Edit** pages.
3. True.
4. False. Normalizing audio can be done on both the **Fairlight** and **Edit** pages.

Chapter 7, Stabilizing Shaky Footage

1. False. Capturing stable footage is usually the better option as it saves time in post-production, and it will not lose resolution if stabilized in post-production.
2. False. You can either use the **Stabilize** tool in the clip's **Toolbar** or the **Stabilize** controls in the **Inspector**.
3. False. The stabilization controls in the **Inspector** are the same on both the **Cut** and **Edit** pages.
4. True. There are stabilization controls in the **Tracker** palette on the **Color** page, but you also have the option to use the **Classic Stabilizer**. Both allow you to select how you want your footage to be tracked and then stabilized.

Chapter 8, Hiding the Cut – Making our Edits Invisible

1. False. A Cutaway or Cut-in is a type of shot, whereas a **Split Edit** is a type of transition from one clip to another.
2. False. Continuity editing is where we edit the clips on the **Timeline** so that they appear to be continuous within the same timeframe, even though they may have been filmed in a different order on different days.
3. True.
4. False. A Cutaway is a B-roll clip used to illustrate the main action of the scene.
5. True. **Smooth Cut** can be found with all the other transitions in the **Effects** panel.
6. True.

Chapter 9, Split Screens and Picture-in-Picture

1. False. There are several ways to create a split-screen effect on the **Cut** page.
2. False. We can use **Decompose in Place** to access the clips again.
3. False. It needs to be on the topmost video layer.
4. True.

Chapter 10, Enhancing Color for Mood or Style

1. False. The human eye has light-receiving cones that are more sensitive to red, green, and blue wavelengths of light.
2. True.
3. False. You can use the **Compress Hue**, **Compress Saturation**, and **Compress Luminance** sliders to change the color, saturation, and luminance of the image.
4. False. There is an **Auto Color** tool in the **Tools** bar on the **Cut** page.
5. True.

Chapter 11, Adding Greenscreen Effects

1. False. Lighting is key to *lighting* our background evenly and with no shadows, as it is easier to remove a single color in post-production without affecting the subject.
2. False. The **3D Keyer** has nothing to do with 3D images. It can be used like any other keyer to remove a colored background, regardless of whether the video is 2D or 3D.
3. True.
4. False. There is also an option to remove the red background spill.

Chapter 12, Studio-Only Techniques – Mostly AI

1. False. AI Smart Reframe is found in the **Inspector: Inspector** > **Video** > **Transform** > AI **Smart Reframe**.
2. True. But only if the clip has metadata that matches the search terms that the **Smart Bin** is looking for.
3. True.
4. False. In the **Create Subtitles from Audio** settings, you can select which language to transcribe from in the **Language** drop-down menu.

Get this book's PDF version and more

Scan the QR code (or go to `packtpub.com/unlock`). Search for this book by name, confirm the edition, and then follow the steps on the page.

UNLOCK NOW

Note: Keep your invoice handy. Purchases made directly from Packt don't require an invoice.

15

Unlock Your Exclusive Benefits

Your copy of this book includes the following exclusive benefits:

EPUB PDF

DRM-Free PDF Version

Download DRM-free PDF and ePub copies of this book.

7-Day Packt Library Access

Get 7-day unlimited access to 8,000+ books and videos. No credit card required.

Available for first-time Packt+ trial users only.

Next-Gen Reader Access

Read this book on Packt Reader with progress sync, dark mode and note-taking.

Follow the guide below to unlock them. The process takes only a few minutes and needs to be completed once.

Unlock this book's free benefits in 3 easy steps

Step 1

Keep your purchase invoice ready for *Step 3*. If you have a physical copy, scan it using your phone and save it as a PDF, JPG, or PNG.

For more help on finding your invoice, visit `https://www.packtpub.com/en-us/unlock?step=1`.

> **Note:** If you bought this book directly from Packt, no invoice is required. After *Step 2*, you can access your exclusive content right away.

Step 2

Scan the QR code or go to `packtpub.com/unlock`.

On the page that opens (similar to *Figure 15.1* on desktop), search for this book by name and select the correct edition.

Figure 15.1: Packt unlock landing page on desktop

Step 3

After selecting your book, sign in to your Packt account or create one for free. Then upload your invoice (PDF, PNG, or JPG, up to 10 MB). Follow the on-screen instructions to finish the process.

Need Help

If you get stuck and need help, visit `https://www.packtpub.com/unlock-benefits/help` for a detailed FAQ on how to find your invoices and more. This QR code will take you to the help page.

Note: If you are still facing issues, reach out to `customercare@packt.com`.

packtpub.com

Subscribe to our online digital library for full access to over 7,000 books and videos, as well as industry leading tools to help you plan your personal development and advance your career. For more information, please visit our website.

Why subscribe?

- Spend less time learning and more time coding with practical eBooks and Videos from over 4,000 industry professionals
- Improve your learning with Skill Plans built especially for you
- Get a free eBook or video every month
- Fully searchable for easy access to vital information
- Copy and paste, print, and bookmark content

At www.packtpub.com, you can also read a collection of free technical articles, sign up for a range of free newsletters, and receive exclusive discounts and offers on Packt books and eBooks.

Other Books You May Enjoy

If you enjoyed this book, you may be interested in these other books by Packt:

Final Cut Pro Cookbook

Mike Eddy

ISBN: 978-1-83588-846-9

- Adapt the Final Cut Pro interface to streamline your workflow
- Enhance your media with color adjustments and blend modes
- Transform your storytelling skills with keyframes, masks, and visual effects
- Improve audio components through blending, effects, and additional recording
- Accelerate your editing speed with keyboard shortcuts
- Optimize team collaboration with efficient version control and sharing methods

AI for Creative Production

Iain Anderson

ISBN: 978-1-80602-581-7

- Understand modern AI foundations and ethics
- Use AI to organize, classify, and improve media
- Apply AI to images, video, and audio enhancement
- Summarize, rewrite, and translate text effectively
- Generate new text, images, video, and audio
- Automate workflows with assistants and scripts
- Evaluate AI's role in professional creative practice
- Balance efficiency, originality, and ethical concerns

Procreate for Digital Artists

Mellisa Aning

ISBN: 978-1-83508-298-0

- Build stunning backgrounds using texture, color, and composition
- Master perspective to create depth, realism, and dynamic scenes
- Control light and shadow using professional techniques tailored for Procreate
- Develop visual storytelling skills to evoke emotion through your art
- Apply color theory to improve your digital coloring skills
- Create character designs that complement your background art
- Explore digital techniques for creating engaging background concepts

Packt is searching for authors like you

If you're interested in becoming an author for Packt, please visit `authors.packt.com` and apply today. We have worked with thousands of developers and tech professionals, just like you, to help them share their insight with the global tech community. You can make a general application, apply for a specific hot topic that we are recruiting an author for, or submit your own idea.

Share your thoughts

Now you've finished *Video Editing Made Easy with DaVinci Resolve 20*, we'd love to hear your thoughts! Scan the QR code below to go straight to the Amazon review page for this book and share your feedback or leave a review on the site that you purchased it from.

`https://packt.link/r/1836208839`

Your review is important to us and the tech community and will help us make sure we're delivering excellent quality content.

Index

Symbols

A

D

E

F

G

H

I

J

K

L

M

N

O

P

T

W

Y

www.ingramcontent.com/pod-product-compliance
Lightning Source LLC
LaVergne TN
LVHW060021210926
848481LV00013B/3760
9781836208839